From Mao to Market

Rent Seeking, Local Protectionism, and Marketizati___ ___ China

In his book *From Mao to Mar*___ ___t China succeeded in moving from a Maoi___ ___conomy because the central government ___ ___local governments from forcing prices to market levels. Having partially decontrolled the economy in the early 1980s, economic reformers balked at price reform, opting instead for a hybrid system wherein commodities had two prices, one fixed and one floating. Depressed fixed prices led to "resource wars," as localities battled each other for control over undervalued commodities while inflated consumer goods prices fueled a headlong investment boom that saturated markets and led to the erection of import barriers. Although local rent seeking and protectionism appeared to carve up the economy, in reality they had not only pushed prices to market levels and cleared the way for sweeping reforms in the 1980s, they had also pushed China past the "pitfalls" of reform that entrapped other socialist economies.

Andrew H. Wedeman is currently an Associate Professor of Political Science at the University of Nebraska, Lincoln, where he specializes in the political economy of reform in contemporary China. He completed his doctorate in Political Science at the University of California, Los Angeles, in 1994 and holds masters degrees in both Political Science (UCLA, 1989) and Security Policy Studies (George Washington University, 1984). Professor Wedeman has conducted fieldwork in the People's Republic of China and Taiwan. He is the author of one book (*The East Wind Subsides: Chinese Foreign Policy and the Origins of the Cultural Revolution*) and has published articles in many scholarly journals. In addition to his fieldwork in China and Taiwan, Professor Wedeman has lived in South Korea, Thailand, Cambodia, India, and the Ivory Coast.

Cambridge Modern China Series

Edited by William Kirby, Harvard University

List of other books in the series continues after the index.

To Maggie, Kelly, Martha, and Miles

From Mao to Market

Rent Seeking, Local Protectionism, and Marketization in China

ANDREW H. WEDEMAN

University of Nebraska, Lincoln

CAMBRIDGE
UNIVERSITY PRESS

CAMBRIDGE UNIVERSITY PRESS
Cambridge, New York, Melbourne, Madrid, Cape Town, Singapore, São Paulo, Delhi

Cambridge University Press
The Edinburgh Building, Cambridge CB2 8RU, UK

Published in the United States of America by Cambridge University Press, New York

www.cambridge.org
Information on this title: www.cambridge.org/9780521809603

First published 2003
This digitally printed version 2008

A catalogue record for this publication is available from the British Library

Library of Congress Cataloguing in Publication data

Wedeman, Andrew Hall, 1958–
From Mao to market : rent seeking, local protectionism, and marketization in China /
Andrew H. Wedeman.
    p.   cm. – (Cambridge modern China series)
Includes bibliographical references and index.
ISBN 0-521-80960-6
1. China – Economic policy – 1976–2000.   2. Protectionism – China.
I. Title.   II. Series.
HC427.92 .W413   2003
330.951–dc21   2002035000

ISBN 978-0-521-80960-3 hardback
ISBN 978-0-521-10015-1 paperback

Contents

Contents

Figures and Tables

Preface

THE origins of this book lie in a bit of graduate school "bad luck." In the spring of 1991, having completed my course work at the University of California, Los Angeles, I arrived at Beijing University ostensibly to research a dissertation on coalition building within the National People's Congress (NPC). Unable to make any headway on that topic due to the tight political atmosphere at that time and the utter lack of usable data, I sought solace by reading the Chinese newspapers. As I read day after day in the cold and dark of the third-floor periodicals room of the old Beijing University Library, I became intrigued by a series of stories on "local protectionism" that appeared in *Jingji Ribao* and *Jingji Cankao*. On the surface, the stories told a tale of "economic warlords" who were slicing the Chinese economy into "dukedoms" barricaded behind networks of "bamboo walls and brick ramparts." As I explored the topic further, moving deeper and deeper into the provincial newspapers and the academic journals, it became clear that local protectionism was not only a far more interesting topic than coalition building within the NPC, but one that seemed to have profound implications for how we interpreted the reform process in post-Mao China.

At the time, many interpreted local protectionism as evidence that China was limping toward "disintegration" as the reform process "stalled out" in the early 1990s. When the Chinese economy failed to disintegrate and the reform process roared back into high gear in 1993, local protectionism was quickly relegated to the status of one of those "unintended consequences" of Deng's ad hoc approach to reform – an interesting but transitory phenomenon produced by contractions between supply and demand, as one prominent economist told me at the time. The story that emerged out of the pages of *Heilongjiang Ribao, Guizhou Ribao, Hebei Ribao*, and other provincial papers was not, however, one of some minor problem but rather a titanic struggle for control; control over a host of agricultural commodities, control over access to local markets, involving local governments, farmers, and speculators across most of China. It was also clear that local protectionism was actually a process through which rent seeking was undermining and destroying a system of fixed prices and monopolies that had been left in place when other parts of the Chinese economy had been reformed in the early 1980s. Far from an unintended consequence it was clear that local protectionism was in fact a form of "informal reform" that helped push the Chinese economy from the plan toward the market. And so I argued in my dissertation, *Bamboo Walls and Brick Ramparts*, which I completed in 1994 under the guidance of Professor Richard Baum.

It was not clear for a long time afterward, however, how significant local protectionism had been. After being "sent down" to the University of Nebraska, Lincoln, in 1994 I pondered the great "so what" question for many years as I sought to transform the dissertation into a book manuscript. But it was not until after analyzing the divergent paths taken by China, on the one hand, and the successor states to the former Soviet Union and the Eastern bloc, on the other, that it became clear that not only had local protectionism and rent seeking forced prices toward market-clearing levels and crippled the system of monopsonies through which the state sought to extract rents, it had also helped propel China across the "pitfalls of incremental reform" that had ensnared most post-Leninist economies. According to the proponents of the "big bang" approach to reform, partial reforms are likely to be hijacked by the "initial winners," degenerate into rent seeking and endemic corruption, and end up producing degenerate and dysfunctional economic systems incapable of generating long-term growth. By their logic, China's cautious reformers had done virtually everything wrong and at the time I began researching local protectionism it appeared that China was destined to remain stuck between the plan and the market.

Yet, as I argue herein, China's reforms did not bog down halfway between Mao and the market precisely because rent seeking and local protectionism continued to push the reform process forward in a chaotic and uncontrolled manner, thus setting the stage for reforms in 1993 that may have appeared radical but were in many ways actually a process of "rectifying the names." That is, reforms that brought regime policy in line with the changes wrought by rent seeking and local protectionism during the years when the top-down reform process had stalled out. China thus escaped from the pitfalls created by Deng's ad hoc, incremental approach because although it was possible for antireform forces to freeze the top-down process, they could not control the forces unleashed by Deng's attempt to juxtapose market forces and a command economy.

Over the many years, various people have contributed to the evolution of this book, often without knowing it. While I was in Beijing, Richard Garbaccio schooled me in the complexities of Chinese economic data and, most important, where to find the bookstores from whence one could get the data; Clayton Dube, who though living in a shoe factory outside Shanghai at the time, helped sharpen my thinking about local protectionism; David Holly kindly let me rummage through the voluminous clipping files of the *Los Angeles Times'* Beijing bureau; while others who must remain nameless helped provide access to various information and shared their insights. In Hong Kong, Jean Hung and Professor Kuan Hsin-chi provided a warm and stimulating intellectual environment at the Universities Service Centre where I benefited from the scholarly support and comradeship of various people, including Harold Tanner, Zhu Feng, Leslyn Hall, Pierre Landry, and Lo Chi-cheng. Back at UCLA, David Lake introduced me to political economy and the utility of trade theory to understanding the dynamics of local protectionism; Roland Stevens helped me work through some of the early modeling; while Cindy Fan supported my work throughout. At the University of Nebraska, Brian Humes endeavored to teach me the black art of game theory. Financially, this work has been supported over the years by grants from the Yenching University Alumni Association, the Graham Dissertation Fund, the Institute for Global Conflict and Cooperation, the UCLA Chancellor's Office, and the Research Council of the University of Nebraska.

I want to particularly thank Kelly Eaton and Maggie Wedeman, who have put up with my late nights in the office and long trips to Hong Kong and Beijing; Martha Wedeman, who provided invaluable editorial assistance; and Miles Wedeman who has supported my work for decades, even when it might have seemed to be going in no particular direction. Finally, I wish to thank William Kirby and Mary Child, both of whom saw the promise in my early manuscript and who linked me up with Cambridge University Press's two superb anonymous reviewers, without whom this manuscript might never have become what it is now, Alia Winters who oversaw the completion of the project, Christine Dunn who cleaned up the manuscript, and Stefan Lansburger who provided the poster used to create the book's cover.

Jingji Cankao, 3/9/91: 1
"Before the gates of Sanluan City"

1

The Pitfalls of Reform

A N examination of China's economic performance since 1970 reveals a stark divergence from those of other socialist economies. Although growth rates in China paralleled growth rates elsewhere during the 1970s, in the 1980s the Chinese economy entered a period of accelerating growth while the other economies stagnated (see Fig. 1). After 1989, the economies of the successor states to the Soviet Union and in the former Eastern bloc contracted rapidly, while the Chinese economy continued to grow rapidly. By the late 1990s, the economies of the ex-communist states had generally stabilized. In most cases, however, these economies were only marginally larger in 2000 than they had been twenty years earlier. The Chinese economy, on the other hand, was some seven times larger than it had been two decades earlier.

The great divergence of the Chinese economy from those of the Soviet Union and Eastern Europe is surprising. First, previous attempts at limited reform had generally failed. Second, and more significant, China embraced what neoclassical economists deem the "wrong" reform strategy (slow incremental reform) rather than the "right" reform strategy (rapid, comprehensive reform).[1] According to the existing literature, China's paradoxical success with incremental reform can be explained in two different ways. On the one hand, "big bang" theorists argue that China's success was neither paradoxical nor contrary to neoclassical orthodoxy but rather the result of prior conditions. Proponents of the "evolutionary" school, on the other hand, argue that China did not adopt a "wrong" reform strategy and contend that incrementalism was actually a

---

[1] It bears noting that Vietnam, which adopted a Chinese-style program of incremental reforms, has also experienced strong economic growth. See Martha de Melo and Alan Gelb, "A Comparative Analysis of Twenty-Eight Transition Economies in Europe and Asia," *Post-Soviet Geography and Economics* 37, no. 5 (May 1996): 265 and David Dollar, "Macroeconomic Management and the Transition to the Market in Vietnam," *Journal of Comparative Economics* 18, no. 3 (June 1994): 357–75.

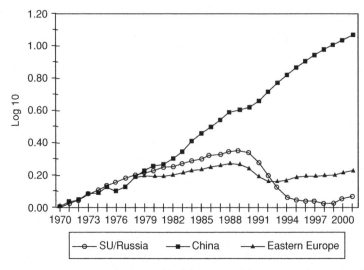

Figure 1-1. Growth in GNP.
Sources: World Bank, *World Tables 1995* and *World Development Indicators.*
Figure represents an index of growth in gross domestic product, where 1970 = 1.
Indices logged to highlight the divergent trends.

superior strategy because it allowed the Chinese economy to move from one system to another without first destroying the old system and then building an entirely new system on the rubble of the old. In this book, I will show that while both the big bang and evolutionary schools are not without considerable merit, each only partially explain why China managed to make the transition from the Maoist planned economy to an essentially market-based economy.

Neither the big bang nor the evolutionary models explain, however, why China did not become entrapped in the same "pitfalls" that ensnared the post-Soviet states. Students of the post-communist transitions in Eastern Europe and the former Soviet Union maintain that attempts to reform a socialist economy are likely to degenerate into "oligarchic capitalism" characterized by rent seeking,[2] corruption, and "crony capitalism" and stall out halfway

---

[2] As used herein, a rent is an artificially created profit that exceeds the profit obtained absent some exogenous manipulation of market conditions. Rent seeking is thus defined as activities designed to create either inflated profits or to gain control over rents previously created by artificial intervention. See Jagdish Bhagwati, "Lobbying and Welfare," *Journal of Public Economics* 14 (1980): 1069–87; Anne O. Krueger, "The Political Economy of the Rent-Seeking Society," *American Economic Review* 65 (June 1974): 291–303; James Buchanan, "Rent Seeking and Profit Seeking," in James Buchanan, Robert D. Tollison, and Gordon Tullock, eds., *Toward a Theory of the Rent-Seeking Society* (College Station, TX: Texas A & M Press, 1980): 3–15; and Robert D. Tollison, "Rent Seeking: A Survey," *Kyklos* 35, no. 4 (1982): 575–602.

between the plan and the market.[3] The pervasive shortages and price rigidities characteristic of Soviet-type economies, they argue, created a complex system of rents that are scraped off by the state or by corrupt officials in the form of bribes.[4] Where partial reforms fail to eliminate these rents quickly by decontrolling prices, the first wave of reforms are likely to trigger a wave of rent seeking and corruption as insiders seek to capture rents themselves or new "entrepreneurs" attempt to grab them. Because the gains from partial reform are likely to be highly concentrated, this relatively small class of rent seekers is less vulnerable to the collective action problem than the mass of "losers." The net result is that the initial winners are likely to gain the upper hand politically, capture the state, and use their newfound political power to block further reforms that would dissipate rents.[5] In this model, once the central planning apparatus has been weakened, a partial reform program is apt to be hijacked by a coalition of the old *nomenklatura*, "red directors," and oligarchs seeking to construct a predatory form of capitalism. Unrestrained rent seeking, however, is likely to prevent such a system from stabilizing; in the end, corrupt officials and the oligarchs are likely to drive the economy to the point of collapse.[6]

---

[3] See Kevin M. Murphy, Andrei Shleifer, and Robert W. Vishny, "The Transition to a Market Economy: Pitfalls of Partial Reform," *The Quarterly Journal of Economics* 107, no. 3 (August 1992): 889–906; Joel S. Hellman, "Winners Take All: The Politics of Partial Reform in Postcommunist Transitions," *World Politics* 50, no. 2 (January 1998): 203–34; Anders Aslund, "Why Has Russia's Economic Transformation Been So Arduous?" Paper presented at the World Bank's Annual Conference on Development Economics, Washington, DC, April 1999 (available at http://www.ceip.org); Anders Aslund and Peter Boone, "How to Stabilize: Lessons from Post-Communist Countries," *Brookings Papers on Economic Activity*, no. 1 (1996): 217–314; Oleh Havrlyshyn and John Odling-Smee, "Political Economy of Stalled Reforms," *Finance & Development* 37, no. 3 (September 2000); and de Melo and Gelb, "A Comparative Analysis of Twenty-Eight Transition Economies in Europe and Asia": 265–85.

[4] See J.M. Montias and Susan Rose-Ackerman, "Corruption in a Soviet-Type Economy: Theoretical Considerations," in Steven Rosefielde, ed., *Economic Welfare and the Economics of Soviet Socialism: Essays in Honor of Abram Bergson* (New York: Cambridge University Press, 1981): 53–83; Gary M. Anderson and Peter J. Boettke, "Soviet Venality: A Rent-Seeking Model of the Communist State," *Public Choice* 93, no. 1–2 (October 1997): 37–53; and Andrei Shleifer and Robert Vishny, "Pervasive Shortages under Socialism," *Rand Journal of Economics* 23, no. 2 (Summer 1992): 237–46. Also see Andrei Shleifer and Robert W. Vishny, *The Grabbing Hand: Government Pathologies and Their Cures* (Cambridge, MA: Harvard University Press, 1998).

[5] Joel Hellman and Mark Schankerman, "Intervention, Corruption and Capture: The Nexus between Enterprises and the State," *Economics of Transition* 8, no. 3 (November 2000): 545–76 and Thane Gustafson, *Capitalism Russian-Style* (New York: Cambridge University Press, 1999): 14.

[6] Anders Aslund and Mikhail Dmitriev, "Economic Reform versus Rent Seeking," in Anders Aslund and Martha Brill Olcott, eds., *Russia after Communism* (Washington, DC: Carnegie Endowment for International Peace, 1990).

Big bang reforms that quickly eliminate controls on prices and allow for rapid privatization, on the other hand, are likely to create economic chaos in the short term. Given an initial condition of scarcity, rapid reform will trigger inflation and windfall profits (rents) for those in control of scarce goods. Inflation and rents should, however, lead to a rapid increase in production by attracting new entrants. After a period of chaos, rents should dissipate and the economy should begin to expand rapidly. The rapidity with which the reforms and an accompanying dramatic decrease in the ability of state agencies should also prevent rent seekers from "capturing" the state and perverting the "reform" process into one that prevents the elimination of most rents.

Reforms that focus purely on transforming the economy without concurrent political reforms are also more likely to stall, according to students of the post-Soviet transitions. If the sweeping powers of the old party-state are not reduced at the same time economic reforms are introduced, cadres and state institutions will continue to be able to manipulate regulations and create rents for themselves or for private interests, as they did under the old system.[7] The resulting headlong quest for rents and loot can result in institutional implosion and, possibly, state collapse as the corrupt officials usurp the power of the state.[8] Weakening the state and reducing the ability of officials to enforce and manipulate rules and regulations arbitrarily thus reduce the threat that corrupt cadres and private rent seekers will succeed in hijacking the reform process.

In short, analyses of economic transitions in Eastern Europe and the former Soviet Union suggest that countries that adopt incremental economic reforms and remain under the control of nondemocratic regimes are more likely to evolve into degenerate economic forms. Economies that combine elements of state control with markets essentially facilitate extensive rent seeking and are more likely to bog down in this intermediate stage than those countries that marketize rapidly.

This being the case, China's reforms should have stalled somewhere between the plan and the market. Deng and his allies eschewed sweeping reforms, opting instead to move slowly, liberalizing agricultural production first and allowing new industrial sectors to grow up outside the plan. They backed away from privatizing the state sector. They also rejected price decontrols and opted instead to create a "two-track price system" that explicitly left in place rents and

---

[7] See Anders Aslund, "Lessons of the First Four Years of Systemic Change in Eastern Europe," *Journal of Comparative Economics* 19, no. 1 (August 1994): 22–38; Jan Winiecki, *The Distorted World of Soviet-Type Economies* (New York: Routledge, 1988); and M.S. Voslensky, *Nomenklatura: The Soviet Ruling Class* (Garden City, NY: Doubleday, 1984).

[8] Steven L. Solnick, *Stealing the State: Control and Collapse in Soviet Institutions* (Cambridge, MA: Harvard University Press, 1998).

assigned them to the state. Thus, they created an economy that they dubbed "socialism with Chinese characteristics." It was no longer socialist but was not yet capitalist, and instead stood awkwardly between the old Maoist command economy and the market. Moreover, China's reformers rejected political reforms. Instead, they implemented a program of decentralization that increased the power of local governments but failed to institutionalize legal structures that would prevent local officials from selectively applying economic regulations. Deng, in other words, did virtually everything wrong and China's semireformed economy should have faltered in the face of dysfunctional rent seeking. Yet the Chinese economic obviously prospered.

China managed to defy the odds against incrementalism in large part, according to the proponents of the big bang model, because its economy was so underdeveloped that extremely high rates of growth could be achieved given even marginal reform.[9] First, whereas the economies of Eastern Europe and the Soviet Union were largely industrialized by the 1980s and had essentially reached the feasible limits of growth under a planned economy, the Chinese economy remained under industrialized. In 1978, 71 percent of China's labor force was engaged in low value-added agriculture, with the result that this sector accounted for just 28 percent of gross domestic product (GDP), and yielded output value of just ¥360 per worker. Industry, on the other hand, accounted for 17 percent of employment but 49 percent of GDP and yielded output value of ¥2,504 per worker.[10] Because productivity per worker in the agricultural sector was lowered by the deployment of excessive labor, shifting surplus labor out of agriculture and into industry allowed for significant gains in productivity and hence quick gains in GDP.

Second, much of China's existing industrial capacity was underutilized prior to reform, creating considerable slack and hence room for rapid growth simply by increasing production. Third, even though China enjoyed a considerable comparative advantage in the cost of labor, trade accounted for only 10 percent of gross national product (GNP). Thus, significant gains could be obtained by expanding exports. Fourth, unlike the Soviet Union, where wage increases during the Gorbachev period had exceeded the growth in consumer goods, creating a "money overhang" and repressed inflation, China's low household

---

[9] See Hu Zuliu and Moshin S. Khan, "Why is China Growing So Fast?" *Economic Issues* 8; Jeffrey D. Sachs and Wing Thye Woo, "Understanding China's Economic Performance," Harvard Institute for International Development, Development Discussion Paper no. 575 (March 1997); Wing Thye Woo, "The Real Reasons for China's Growth," *The China Journal*, no. 41 (January 1997): 115–37; and Wing Thye Woo, "Chinese Economic Growth: Sources and Prospects," in Michel Fouquin and Françoise Lemoine, eds., *The Chinese Economy* (London: Economica, 1998).

[10] Based on data in *Zhongguo Tongji Nianjian, 1994* (Beijing: *Zhongguo Tongji Chubanshe*, 1994).

income and savings meant that inflationary pressures were low.[11] Enforced savings also meant that there was pent-up demand for consumer goods and hence a ready market for increased industrial production. The potential for growth was so strong, in fact, that even a flawed gradualist strategy would have triggered rapid gains.[12]

Several additional factors minimized the negative consequences of incrementalism, according to the believers in the big bang approach. First, although systemic reform may have unfolded in an ad hoc manner, critical reforms, such as the decollectivization of agriculture, were actually implemented in a swift, comprehensive manner and the greatest gains were realized in the areas where the most rapid and radical reforms took place.[13] Second, whereas state institutions in the former Soviet bloc either crumbled during the early days of reform or were severely weakened by reform, the center in China remained relatively strong and was able to contain rent seeking and prevent a "bank run" scramble to strip the state of all its assets.[14] Third, whereas bureaucratic interests in the former Soviet Union and Eastern bloc were deeply entrenched and had a virtual choke hold on their economies, the Chinese bureaucracy had been so battered by the twin upheavals of the Great Leap Forward and the Cultural Revolution that it was too weak to stifle reform and quickly lost its grip on the economy.[15] The big bang school thus holds that incrementalism "succeeded" in China not because it was a wise strategy but rather because the repressed economic forces were so strong that even the "wrong" strategy was likely to produce "good results."[16] China, in other words, achieved rapid growth despite Deng's incremental reforms.

---

[11] de Melo and Gelb, "A Comparative Analysis of Twenty-Eight Transition Economies in Europe and Asia."

[12] Sachs and Woo, "Understanding China's Economic Performance": 2–4.

[13] Jeffrey Sachs and Wing Thye Woo, "Structural Factors in the Economic Reforms of China, Eastern Europe, and the Former Soviet Union," *Economic Policy* 9, no. 18 (April 1994): 101–45 and Wing Thye Woo, "The Art of Reforming Centrally Planned Economies: Comparing China, Poland, and Russia," *Journal of Comparative Economics* 18, no. 3 (June 1994): 276–308.

[14] Murphy, Schleifer, and Vishney, "The Transition to a Market Economy": 906 and Steven L. Solnick, "The Breakdown of Hierarchies in the Soviet Union and China: A Neoinstitutional Perspective," *World Politics* 48, no. 2 (January 1996): 209–38.

[15] Woo, "The Art of Reforming Centrally Planned Economies."

[16] It is difficult to understate the big bang school's contempt for gradualism. Woo, for example, writes:

> Gradualism is not like a person putting his pants on one leg at a time and big bang with the person jumping into his pants. The more accurate picture of gradualism is a person putting one leg into the pants and then stopping for a meditative smoke because he is insecure about whether he would not be better off with a fig leaf or a loincloth instead.

Woo, "The Art of Reforming Centrally Planned Economies,": 276–308.

The mainstream "evolutionary" school in the China field itself, however, maintains that gradualism was the key to successful reform in China. Whereas reformers in Eastern Europe and the former Soviet Union sought to shift quickly from a command-based economy to a market-based economy by eliminating existing economic institutions, China's reformers sought to modify existing institutions and thereby increase overall efficiency. China's reformers, therefore, sought to stimulate growth and introduced limited market mechanisms in an instrumental and incremental fashion. Reform was designed to release underutilized resources and reallocate them to more efficient use.[17] During the early stages, this was done in a bold manner that was not necessarily different from the big-bang approach. But the scope of change was much more limited. Whereas reformers using a shock-therapy approach mounted a frontal assault on the entire economic system, reformers in China targeted specific inefficiencies with the aim of accelerating growth in selected sectors where the greatest gains in efficiency were likely to be realized: agriculture and foreign trade.[18] Policy makers approached reform with fundamentally different assumptions:

> Policy makers in Russia and Eastern Europe have behaved as if they believed that successful transition would result in sustained growth. The Chinese have reversed the direction of causality: sustained growth permits a successful transition, while falling output and incomes greatly hamper it.[19]

Because the goal of reform was growth rather than systemic change, China's reformers left intact the main elements of the old command economy and allowed them to continue to function, thus preventing a sudden drop in output. New market-driven sectors were then established alongside the command sector, not by reallocating resources from the plan sector, as would be done in a shock-therapy reform, but rather by mobilizing new resources in formerly suppressed sectors.[20] As a result, China's gradualist approach avoided the "J-curve"

---

[17] Richard Pomfret, "Growth and Transition: Why has China's Performance Been So Different?" *Journal of Comparative Economics* 25, no. 3 (December 1997): 422–40.

[18] Kang Chen, Gary H. Jefferson, and Inderjit Singh, "Lessons from China's Economic Reforms," *Journal of Comparative Economies* 16, no. 2 (June 1992): 201–25.

[19] Keith Griffin and Azizur Rahman Khan, "The Chinese Transition to a Market-Guided Economy: The Contrast with Russia and Eastern Europe," *Contention* 3, no. 2 (Winter 1994): 104.

[20] Justin Yifu Lin and Cai Fang, "The Lessons of China's Transition to a Market Economy," *CATO Journal* 16, no. 2 (Fall 1996); Louis Putterman, "The Role of Ownership and Property Rights in China's Economic Transition," in Andrew G. Walder, ed., *China's Transitional Economy* (New York: Oxford University Press, 1996): 85–102; and Louis Putterman, "Dualism and Reform in China," *Economic Development and Cultural Change* 40, no. 3 (April 1992): 467–93.

phenomenon (a short-term drop in output as resources shift, followed by a rise once they have been redeployed).[21] Moreover, because the marketized sector grew more rapidly than the planned sector, the balance between the sectors shifted over time. As a result, the Chinese economy gradually "grew out of the plan" and it was only after the marketized sector had become firmly entrenched that China's reformers began to try to marketize the planned sector.[22] The process was bold in its inception, but not cataclysmic, as it was in Eastern Europe and Russia, with the result that China's reformers were able to proceed "by trial and error, with frequent mid-course corrections and reversals" and muddle through rather than risking the entire process on a single roll of the dice.[23]

The evolutionary school also maintains that as this evolutionary process began to unfold, existing economic actors responded positively to changing incentive structures that linked local government revenues to expenditures, enterprise revenues to profits, and local government revenues to local enterprise profits. By linking local governments' interests to the performance of the local economy, these reforms gave raise to a series of "hybrid" economic institutions suited to the "contradictions" created by the continued coexistence of the plan and the market.[24] Local governments in some areas thus adopted a strategy of "local state corporatism" based on a developmental alliance between local governments and the emerging nonstate sector, "government officials themselves have become market-oriented actors," and "cadre entrepreneurs" forged "corporatist alliances" with the managers of local collectively owned enterprises and private businessmen to overcome weak market structures.[25] In other areas reform gave rise to "state entrepreneurialism" and an "entrepreneurial state" that largely

---

[21] Justin Yifu Lin, Fang Cai, and Zhou Li, *The China Miracle: Development Strategy and Economic Reform* (Hong Kong: Chinese University Press, 1996). Also see Justin Yifu Lin, Fang Cai, and Zhou Li, "Why Has China's Economic Reform Been Successful?" unpublished manuscript, available at http://www.fraserinstitute .ca/montelerin/papers/china_success/.

[22] Barry Naughton, *Growing Out of the Plan: Chinese Economic Reform, 1978–1993* (New York: Cambridge University Press, 1995) and Barry Naughton, "What is Distinctive about China's Transition? State Enterprise Reform and Overall System Transformation," *Journal of Comparative Economics* 18, no. 3 (June 1994): 470–90.

[23] John McMillan and Barry Naughton, "How to Reform a Planned Economy: Lessons From China," *Oxford Review of Economic Policy* 8, no. 1 (Spring 1992): 130–43.

[24] For a critical review of several of the key works in this literature, see Shu-yun Ma, "Understanding China's Reforms: Looking Beyond Neoclassical Explanations," *World Politics* 52, no. 4 (July 2000): 586–603.

[25] Jean C. Oi, *Rural China Takes Off: Institutional Foundations of Economic Reform* (Berkeley, CA: University of California Press, 1999); Andrew G. Walder, "Local Governments as Industrial Firms: An Organizational Analysis of China's Transitional Economy," *American Journal of Sociology* 101, no. 2 (September 1995): 263–301; and Victor Nee, "Organizational Dynamics of Market Transition: Hybrid Forms, Property Rights, and Mixed Economy in China," *Administrative Science Quarterly* 37, no. 1 (1992): 1–27.

eschewed rent seeking in favor of cooperation with local enterprises or set up its own market-oriented businesses.[26]

As state institutions became market-oriented actors individual cadres also became "bureaucratic entrepreneurs." Yet, because state institutions and cadres remained politically and socially embedded they tended to pursue economic, political, and social goals that provided public goods for their communities and private goods for themselves and their units simultaneously. Thus rather than give rise to a degenerate form of oligarchic rent seeking, partial reform in China spawned a new form of market-based "developmental communism."[27] The combination of a reformist leadership in Beijing and developmentalist governments at the provincial level created a "dual developmental state" in which both center and locality had a common interest in promoting rapid growth.[28] State monopolies thus became "arbitrage-seeking commercial traders" and "quasi-commercial" agencies while the People's Liberation Army became an "entrepreneur" and many of its officers evolved into market-oriented "soldiers of fortune."[29]

The rise of bureaucratic entrepreneurialism was, of course, accompanied by a rise in rent seeking as many nouveaux bureaucratic entrepreneurs sought to parlay their public authority into windfall profits and rents. The ability of individual agencies and localities to engage in extensive rent seeking was, however, limited by the emergence of a "semifederalist" system in which capital became

---

[26] Jane Duckett, "Bureaucrats in Business, Chinese Style: The Lessons of Market Reform and State Entrepreneurialism in the People's Republic of China," *World Development* 29, no. 1 (January 2001): 23–37; Jane Duckett, "The Emergence of the Entrepreneurial State in Contemporary China," *The Pacific Review* 9, no. 2 (1996): 180–98; Jane Duckett, *The Entrepreneurial State in China: Real Estate and Commerce Departments in Tianjin* (New York: Routledge, 1998); Marc Blecher, "Development State, Entrepreneurial State: The Political Economy of Socialist Reform in Xinju Municipality and Guanghan County," in Gordon White, ed., *The Chinese State in the Era of Economic Reform: The Road to Crisis* (Armonk, NY: M. E. Sharpe, 1991): 265–91; and Marc Blecher and Vivienne Shue, *Tethered Deer: Government and Economy in a Chinese County* (Stanford, CA: Stanford University Press, 1996).

[27] Lance L.P. Gore, *Market Communism: The Institutional Foundation of China's Post-Mao Hyper-Growth* (New York: Oxford University Press, 1998): ch. 3.

[28] Ming Xia, *The Dual Developmental State: Development Strategy and Institutional Arrangements for China's Transition* (Brookfield, VT: Ashgate, 2000): chs. 2 and 8.

[29] Scott Rozelle, Albert Park, Jikun Huang, and Hehui Jin, "Bureaucrat to Entrepreneur: The Changing Role of the State in China's Grain Economy," *Economic Development and Cultural Change* 48, no. 2 (January 2000): 227–52; Albert Park and Scott Rozelle, "Reforming State-Market Relations in Rural China," *Economics of Transition* 6, no. 2 (November 1998): 461–80; Thomas J. Bickford, "The Chinese Military and its Business Operations: The PLA as Entrepreneur," *Asian Survey* 34, no. 5 (May 1994): 460–74; James Mulvenon, *Soldiers of Fortune: The Rise and Fall of the Chinese Military-Business Complex, 1978–1998* (Armonk, NY: M.E. Sharpe, 2000); and James Mulvenon, "Military Corruption in China," *Problems of Post-Communism* 45, no. 2 (March–April 1998): 12–22.

increasingly mobile. If a locality engaged in excessive rent seeking, capital would migrate to other localities while "competitive liberalization" forced local governments to progressively improve market conditions or face an outflow of capital.[30] Local governments thus found themselves forced to rely more on promoting market-oriented growth than predatory rent seeking.[31]

The configuration of forces was such that once the reformers opened a crack in the central planning "monolith," a dynamic process was unleashed that "[pried] the crack open ever more widely" and created "a process of change that became irreversible."[32] This was clearly the case in the agricultural sector, according to Kelliher, Yang, and Zhou, where "spontaneous reform" occurred at the local level as "Mao's serfs" replaced collective agriculture with a new system of household farming, even before the center embraced decollectivization. In fact, spontaneous, bottom-up "reforms" frequently outpaced "top-down" reforms emanating from Beijing and in many cases "reforms" announced by Beijing simply ratified and legitimated spontaneous grassroots reforms.[33] Moreover, limited success early on legitimated progressively more radical reforms and ensured that the reform process did not falter during its infancy.[34] This meant that reform was actually a "phase transition," an:

> evolving, co-evolving, chaotic, self-organizing, path dependent, and mutually catalytic process of change that is driven not by sequencing, as argued

---

[30] Gabriella Montinola, Yingyi Qian, and Barry Weingast, "Federalism, Chinese Style: The Political Basis for Economic Success," *World Politics* 41, no. 1 (October 1996): 50–81; Wang Yijiang and Chang Chun, "Economic Transition under a Semifederalist Government: The Experience of China," *China Economic Review* 9, no. 1 (Spring 1998); and Dali L. Yang, *Beyond Beijing: Liberalization and the Regions in China* (New York: Routledge, 1997).

[31] Yingyi Qian and Hehui Jin, "Public vs. Private Ownership of Firms: Evidence from Rural China," *Quarterly Journal of Economics* 113, no. 3 (August 1998): 773–808; Yingyi Qian and Jiahua Che, "Insecure Property Rights and Government Ownership of Firms," *Quarterly Journal of Economics* 113, no. 2 (May 1998): 467–96; and Jiahua Che and Yingyi Qian, "Institutional Environment, Community Government, and Corporate Governance: Understanding China's Township-Village Enterprises," *Journal of Law, Economics, and Organization* 14, no. 1 (April 1998): 1–23.

[32] McMillan and Naughton, "How to Reform a Planned Economy": 131.

[33] See Daniel Kelliher, *Peasant Power in China: The Era of Rural Reform 1979–1989* (New Haven, CT: Yale University Press, 1992); Yang, *Beyond Beijing*; Dali L. Yang, *Calamity and Reform in China: State, Rural Society, and Institutional Change since the Great Leap Forward* (Stanford, CA: Stanford University Press, 1996); and Kate Xiao Zhou, *How the Farmers Changed China: Power of the People* (Boulder, CO: Westview, 1996). Also see David Zweig, *Freeing China's Farmers: Rural Restructuring in the Reform Era* (Armonk, NY: M.E. Sharpe, 1997).

[34] Yingyi Qian, "The Institutional Foundation of China's Market Transition," in Boris Pleskovic and Joseph Stiglitz, eds., *Annual World Bank Conference on Development Economics 1999* (Washington, DC: World Bank, 2000): 289–310.

in the gradualist model, or extensiveness, as argued in the shock therapy model, but rather the structures within which the transition occurs and the dynamic feedback effects generated by the transition process.[35]

And because the transition occurred at the margin between chaos and order, existing institutions could not contain these dynamic forces, yet were still strong enough to prevent the process from degenerating into anarchy. The result was a "balanced" and "continuous" destruction of old structures and construction of new structures, with reforms in one sector driving systemic change without triggering systemic collapse.

While these new hybrids were evolving, resistance from entrenched bureaucratic interests was reduced, according to the second part of the gradualist argument, by adopting a graduated shift from the system of administratively fixed prices and mandatory quotas to a system of floating prices and market allocation.[36] Under the prereform price system, fixed prices had allowed various state institutions to scrap off rents. Price reform thus threatened the interests of strategically placed institutions. By adopting a "two-track" approach to price reform, one that retained fixed prices for "state" consumers but raised prices for other consumers, China's "risk-averse" reformers were thus able to "mitigate the resistance from powerful bureaucrats" by "grandfathering" their rights to preexisting rents.[37] By raising and relaxing controls over out-of-plan prices, however, the two-track system also allowed for partial marketization and hence opened up space for new entrants. As a result, whereas previous reforms in socialist economies had generated antireform coalitions, reforms in China succeeded because there were no losers.[38]

---

[35] Jin Dengjian and Kingsley E. Haynes, "Economic Transition at the Edge of Order and Chaos: China's Dualist and Leading Sectoral Approach," *Journal of Economic Issues* 31, no. 1 (March 1997): 79–108.

[36] William Byrd, "The Plan and the Market in the Chinese Economy: A Simple Equilibrium Model," *Journal of Comparative Economics* 13 (1989): 177–204; and Zhang Xiaoguang, "Modeling Economic Transition: A Two-Tier Price Computable General Equilibrium Model of the Chinese Economy," *Journal of Policy Modeling* 20, no. 4 (August 1998): 483–511.

[37] Anthony Y.C. Koo and Norman P. Obst, "Dual-Track and Mandatory Quota in China's Price Reform," *Comparative Economic Studies* 37, no. 1 (Spring 1995): 1–17; Lawrence J. Lau, Qian Yingyi, and Gérard Roland, "Reform without Losers: An Interpretation of China's Dual-Track Approach to Transition," *Journal of Political Economy* 108 (February 2000): 120–42; Leong Liew, *The Chinese Economy in Transition* (Brookfield, VT: Edward Elgar, 1997): ch. 7; Leong H. Liew, "Rent-Seeking and the Two-Track Price System in China," *Public Choice* 77, no. 2 (October 1993): 359–75; and Leong H. Liew, "Gradualism in China's Economic Reform and the Role for a Strong State," *Journal of Economic Issues* 29, no. 3 (September 1995): 883–96.

[38] Lau, Qian, and Roland, "Reform without Losers."

Finally, according to Perkins, China's reformers were simply lucky.[39] While hybrid economic forms, compensation of the losers, administrative decentralization, and so forth may have played critical roles in China's transition from the plan to the market, Deng and his allies never had a blueprint for reform. Instead, they crossed the gap between the plan and the market by "feeling for the stepping stones," groping and innovating as they went along.[40] They managed through sheer luck to stumble upon a set of policy changes that the gradualist school points to as the key to China avoiding the pitfalls of partial reform.

Despite their strong disagreement over the efficacy of shock therapy versus gradualism, advocates of both the "evolutionary" and "big bang" schools accept that China's rapid growth was largely a function of favorable structural circumstances. Reform freed the Chinese economy from a series of politically created constraints that had depressed growth during the prereform period. These theorists also agree that reform faced only limited initial opposition because of a combination of prior political developments that had weakened entrenched bureaucratic interests and other potential opponents of reform. The two schools diverge, however, over the question of why the initial winners failed to stall the reform process halfway between the plan and the market, as was the case in Russia. Proponents of the big bang school imply that although the initial winners might have wanted to stall reforms, a strong center was able to prevent extensive rent seeking and could continue to push the reform process forward. Proponents of the evolutionary school, by contrast, tend to see the initial winners as rapidly adapting to the emerging market economy and, because they had to operate outside the plan, developing a vested interest in the deepening of reform. Like big bang theorists, proponents of the evolutionary school also tend to believe that although rent seeking did occur, the fact that power was highly fragmented and constrained meant that local governments and individual state bureaus could engage in rent seeking at the margins but could not force a freezing of the reform process. Both the big bang and evolutionary schools, therefore, conclude that China escaped the worst ravages of incremental and (hence) incomplete reform because, even though rent seeking and corruption increased, the reform process was never halted and China did not fall into the same pit of "predatory," "robber-baron," "vampire," or "mafiya" capitalism that Russia sank into after the collapse of the Soviet Union.[41]

---

[39] Dwight Perkins, "Completing China's Move to the Market," *The Journal of Economic Perspectives* 8, no. 2 (Spring 1994): 23–46.

[40] Richard Baum, *Burying Mao: Chinese Politics in the Age of Deng Xiaoping* (Princeton, NJ: Princeton University Press, 1994): 17.

[41] See Chrystia Freeland, *Sale of the Century: Russia's Wild Ride from Communism to Capitalism* (New York: Crown Business, 2000): Paul Klebnikov, *Godfather of the Kremlin: Boris*

AN ALTERNATIVE EXPLANATION

Looking back from a vantage point in the late 1990s or early 2000s, one might accept such a conclusion. In the early 1990s, before Deng Xiaoping's "Southern Tour," it was much less clear that China had, in fact, avoided the pitfalls. Between 1988 and 1991, it appeared that reform had stalled and the Chinese economy was beginning to degenerate into chaos as rent seeking "economic warlords" fought repeated "resource wars" and threw up dense networks of "bamboo walls and brick ramparts" around local markets. Corruption seemed to be rising at an explosive rate. Bureaucrats were opening "briefcase companies" (*pibao gongsi*) that arbitraged between the plan and market prices. Managers of state-owned enterprises were engaging in "spontaneous privatization" or "pocket switching," stripping off state assets to create new private firms or "joint ventures" using Hong Kong–based shell companies to disguise the theft of state funds. The sons and daughters of senior cadres, known as the princelings, were going into business, trading their knowledge of the political terrain and access for sizable "consulting fees." An aborted attempt at price reform and excessive investment finally triggered double-digit inflation and panic buying during the summer of 1988.

As corruption, chaos, and anxiety increased, the Chinese Communist Party (CCP) appeared to be increasingly paralyzed. General Secretary Hu Yaobang had been sacked in 1987 largely because of his support of bold reform. His successor, Zhao Ziyang, had been forced to accept the blame for the 1988 inflationary crisis and had been forced to turn over responsibility for economic policy to Premier Li Peng. Li, with the support of conservative patriarch Chen Yun, promptly slammed on the economic brakes with a policy of retrenchment and recentralization that froze the reform process in place. The following spring, after antigovernment demonstrations erupted in Beijing and other major cities, Zhao was ousted as general secretary and replaced by the relatively unknown and putatively weak Jiang Zemin. Following violent suppression of the demonstrations in Beijing, the political atmosphere grew increasingly cold as the party cracked down on antiregime groups and suppressed calls for accelerated reform.

Berezovsky and the Looting of Russia (New York: Harcourt, 2000); Stefan Hedlund, *Russia's "Market" Economy: A Bad Case of Predatory Capitalism* (London: UCL Press, 1999); Stephen Handelman, *Comrade Criminal: Russia's New Mafiya* (New Haven, CT: Yale University Press, 1995); Gustafson, *Capitalism Russian-Style*; Peter Reddaway and Dmitri Glinski, *The Tragedy of Russia's Reforms: Market Bolshevism against Democracy* (Washington, DC: United States Institute of Peace Press, 2001); Grigory Yavlinksy, "Russia's Phony Capitalism," *Foreign Affairs* 77, no. 3 (May–June 1997): 67–80; and Serguey Braguinsky and Grigory Yavlinsky, *Incentives and Institutions: The Transition to a Market Economy in Russia* (Princeton, NJ: Princeton University Press, 2000).

Their ranks decimated by the post-Tiananmen purges and in political disarray, the "liberal" camp was ill positioned to press for a new round of reforms. Li and the "conservatives," however, seemed incapable of rolling back the changes that had been implemented during Hu's and Zhao's tenures.

To some it thus appeared that the transition process had, as White put it, "deadlocked" halfway between the plan and the market in a system plagued by the "worst" features of both systems.[42] Shirk also concluded that, by the late 1980s, reform had "stalled halfway."[43] Stall was, in fact, to be expected, according to proponents of the "fragmented authoritarian" model. Despite an appearance of a centralized, top-down power structure, power was actually diffused across a wide range of centers, each of which held a degree of veto power over decisions affecting its bureaucratic interest. Decisions generally had to be made on the basis of consensus.[44] Those institutions that had enjoyed access to rents before reform and whose rents had been protected during the first two rounds of reform had common cause with other institutions that had gained access to rents and rent-seeking opportunities during the first stages of reform by opposing a further deepening of reform. In particular, both the old entrenched interests and the initial winners had a common interest in blocking price reforms that would have replaced the two-track price system with a system of floating market prices. The two-track system not only bestowed rents on those operating within the plan in the form of depressed input prices, it also created an array of opportunities for various institutions to obtain new rents by arbitraging between price tracks, buying at the fixed price and selling at the market price. The entrenched interests and initial winners also shared a common interest in preserving monopsony and monopoly structures that facilitated rent scraping and limited access to rents. The political system, therefore, seemed to create a situation in which the deck was not only stacked against the deepening of reform, but also was stacked against any effort by Li Peng and the conservatives

---

[42] Gordon White, *Riding the Tiger: The Politics of Reform in Post-Mao China* (Stanford, CA: Stanford University Press, 1993): 145. Also see Jan S. Prybyla, "Economic Reform of Socialism: The Dengist Course in China," *Annals of the American Academy of Political and Social Science* 507 (January 1990): 113–23.

[43] Susan L. Shirk, *The Political Logic of Economic Reform in China* (Berkeley: University of California Press, 1993). Shirk, however, also argued that even though rent seeking may have blocked reform of the price system and state enterprises, growth of the nonstate sector was likely to push the transition from plan to market forward.

[44] See Kenneth G. Lieberthal, "Introduction: The 'Fragmented Authoritarianism' Model and Its Limitations," in Kenneth G. Lieberthal and David M. Lampton, eds., *Bureaucracy, Policy, and Decision Making in Post-Mao China* (Berkeley: University of California Press, 1992): 1–30; David M. Lampton, "A Plum for a Peach: Bargaining, Interest, and Bureaucratic Politics in China," *ibid.*: 33–58; and Kenneth Lieberthal and Michel Oksenberg, *Policy Making in China: Leaders, Structures, and Processes* (Princeton, NJ: Princeton University Press, 1988).

to roll back reforms and recentralize economic control.[45] Looking at China in 1990–1, it would have appeared that the big bang argument was correct in claiming that incremental reform was doomed to fail because the beneficiaries of partial reform would still have the political power to throttle the process and keep in place a degenerate system that enabled them to engage in extensive predatory rent seeking.

Although reform seemed to stall out in 1988–9, it did not die. On the contrary, the reform process not only restarted in 1992, it clearly accelerated. By 1993, the Chinese economy seemed well on its way to "growing out of the plan."[46]

The rapid revival of reform in 1992–3 raises two important questions. First, why was China able to escape from the trap of dysfunctional partial reform, given the existence of a political equilibrium that effectively paralyzed the policy-making process? Second, why was there so little opposition in 1992–3 given the depth of opposition to comprehensive reform in 1987–8?

The common answer to the first question is that by 1992 it had become clear that retrenchment was an economic failure and that the failure of retrenchment had become a political liability. Gilley, for example, writes that "Li Peng was eventually swept off the tracks by his own economic policies" and Jiang, with the support of the provinces, attacked and pushed aside Li Peng's attempt to retrench, resocialize, and recentralize the economy.[47] Baum similarly argues that by late 1991, Deng had become "convinced that failure to push ahead boldly with reform would invite the type of disaster that had befallen other communist regimes." He thus left Beijing in early 1992 to rally support in the provinces for an attack on Chen Yun's conservative faction in the capital. As support for Deng's reform initiative mounted outside Beijing, members of the conservative bloc jumped onto the bandwagon one by one, leading to a rapid political realignment that cleared the way for a new round of reform.[48] Huang also points to fear of political unrest as tipping the balance in favor of renewed reform. He argues that Li Peng's retrenchment "overshot" its objective of reining in excessive investment. Instead of cooling off the economy, retrenchment triggered a recession and a surge in unemployment. Moreover, retrenchment failed to cut inflation, leading to a politically dangerous combination of high unemployment

---

[45] Joseph Fewsmith, *Dilemmas of Reform in China: Political Conflict and Economic Debate* (Armonk, NY: M. E. Sharpe, 1994): 248; Ruan Ming, *Deng Xiaoping: Chronicle of an Empire* (Boulder, CO: Westview, 1992): 327–28.

[46] Naughton, *Growing Out of the Plan*: 273 and 289–390.

[47] Bruce Gilley, *Tiger on the Brink: Jiang Zemin and China's New Elite* (Berkeley: University of California Press, 1998): 173.

[48] Baum, *Burying Mao*: 340–1 and 345–8.

and declining real income. The regime thus began to ease restrictions on credit in 1991 and abandoned its austerity program in March 1992.[49]

Ruan Ming contends that: "Along with the collapse of the coup in the Soviet Union, the policies of 'administrative ratification and readjustment' and 'opposing peaceful evolution' of the Jiang-Li [faction] failed miserably." At this juncture, faced with a solid conservative bloc at the center that threatened his position as supreme political arbiter, Deng turned to the provincial leadership, whose refusal to implement retrenchment had effectively stymied Li Peng's attempt to recentralize the economy, and began building a new countervailing coalition. Aided by Jiang's defection from the conservative camp, Deng broke the conservative coalition's grip on the party center. Once the conservative roadblock had been removed, the reform process took up where it had left off in 1988 even though Deng remained ambivalent about radical reform. "The market economy smashed the 'ideological forbidden zone' that once upon a time had prohibited inquiry into whether an initiative was 'in the nature of capitalism or socialism'" and thus cleared the way for the resurrection of the reform faction within the party leadership.[50]

In contrast to the view that retrenchment failed and that its failure set the stage for the political demise of Chen Yun's conservative coalition, Naughton asserts that retrenchment had stabilized China's economy by the end of 1991. This made possible renewed economic reform without the concurrent threat of inflation and economic instability that had necessitated retreat in 1988. He writes:

> This transition was remarkably smooth, even for the most sensitive commodities. Supplies of most goods were fairly abundant, so there were few extreme surges in price after decontrol. But even more important was the fact that a functioning market had already been created around the remaining plan sectors. . . . The plan had already become the island surrounded by an ocean of market price transactions so the final liquidation of the plan was not difficult.[51]

In this book, I offer a different answer. In line with the evolutionary school, I too see the shift in 1992 as relatively easy – once Deng's Southern Tour and the subsequent crumbling of Chen Yun's antireform coalition had removed the political obstacles to reform. Unlike Naughton, I see the ease of the transition

---

[49] Yasheng Huang, *Inflation and Investment Controls in China: The Political Economy of Central-Local Relations during the Reform Era* (New York: Cambridge University Press, 1996): 173–4.

[50] Ruan, *Deng Xiaoping*: 242–5.

[51] Naughton, *Growing out of the Plan*: 287–9.

to a "socialist market economy" not as a direct function of the success of retrenchment, but rather as a result of uncontrolled and unanticipated changes that had taken place during the retrenchment. Specifically, I contend that a period of chaotic rent seeking, manifest in what is popularly known as "local protectionism" (*difang baohu zhuyi*),[52] crippled the system of state price controls and the monopoly structures that had blocked marketization prior to 1988. As a result, China's economy was considerably closer to de facto marketization in 1992, when political conditions shifted in a direction more favorable to renewed reform than they had been in 1988, when Li Peng sought to block further reform with his policy of retrenchment. I further contend that a process of informal reform transformed the Chinese economy during the retrenchment and that this transformation was possible only because the political stalemate that stalled reform created conditions in which the center could not prevent local actors from unintentionally destroying the foundations of the old command economy. In other words, the Chinese economy evolved out of the plan because political stalemate made it impossible to freeze the transformation halfway between the plan and the market.

Stalled reform may have been a stable political equilibrium – or perhaps more simply a political stalemate – but it was not a stable systemic equilibrium. On the contrary, bureaucratic rent seeking in a context of fragmented authority, wherein the center could not control or prevent unbridled rent seeking, was an inherently unstable systemic equilibrium. The "system" that the opponents of comprehensive reform froze in place when they blocked price and tax reforms in 1988 was inherently unstable because it rested on a series of macroeconomic distortions that only could be maintained by a strong central authority that was capable of preventing opportunistic rent seeking by elements of the state apparatus. Without such an authority and centralized control, competitive rent seeking inexorably leads to the rapid dissipation of rents because competition will quickly push prices upward from the levels fixed by administrative fiat and toward market-clearing levels. Uncontrolled competitive rent seeking will act as a form of de facto price reform.

---

[52] The Chinese term "local protectionism" (*difang baohu zhuyi*) is a catchall term applied to a wide range of noncompliant local behaviors. Its major use has been in reference to inter local economic conflicts. The term has, however, also been used to refer to local biases in the courts (i.e., a tendency to rule in favor of locals regardless of the merits of a case), the tendency of local cadres to protect each other from outside scrutiny and to cover up each others' misdeeds, and to place the interests of the locality above those of the nation. Many of these practices are also lumped together under the rubric of "localism" (*difang zhuyi*) and refer to the usurpation of power by local governments. As used herein, local protectionism refers to the illicit and irregular use of administrative controls by local governments to interfere with the flow of commodities between localities.

The same structures and veto gates that caused political paralysis in the area of policy making and allowed the proponents of partial reform to block both further progress and retrogression also made it nearly impossible for any bureaucratic institution, including the central leadership, to exercise effective control over the state apparatus. The center was thus unable to prevent individual institutions from engaging in egoistic and opportunistic behavior. In this environment, individual institutions were free to pursue rents recklessly and relentlessly, without regard for the effects of their actions on the sustainability of the structures that created rents and in whose defense they had banded together to block comprehensive price and fiscal reforms. Paralysis on a political level thus created a situation that might be termed "institutional anarchy." Institutional anarchy in an environment of extensive rent seeking, in turn, rapidly and decisively undermined the system of "bureaucratic control"[53] that was putatively frozen in place in 1988.

Specifically, institutional anarchy and bureaucratic rent seeking, manifested in the form of local protectionism, crippled many of the monopoly and monopsony structures left in place during the first two stages of reform. At the same time, it drove prices upward in what amounted to an unplanned process of price decontrols. Local protectionism is something of a catchall term used by both Chinese and Western scholars to denote a range of illegal localist behaviors whose primary objective was the capture and monetization of rents legally "owned" by the center. Local governments, mostly at the subprovincial level, usurped the monopsony and monopoly authority granted them as agents of the center and which were supposed to control the setting of prices and allocation of rent-producing commodities and used their power to "steal" the center's rents. A variety of administrative measures, including bans on exports of undervalued raw materials and imports of overvalued finished products, the construction of local industries through which undervalued raw materials could be transformed into overvalued finished products, were used to block the transfer of rents to other jurisdictions. Similar measures were also used to divert undervalued raw materials onto black markets where they could be sold at prices above the level fixed by state monopsonies.

Ostensibly, local protectionism resulted in the fragmentation of China's internal economy, and worked at direct cross-purposes to central efforts to create unified national markets. By the late 1980s, in fact, local protectionism appeared to have progressed to the point that Chinese and Western observers began to

---

[53] Janos Kornai, "The Affinity between Ownership Forms and Coordination Mechanisms: The Common Experience of Reform in Socialist Countries," *Journal of Economic Perspectives* 4, no. 3 (Summer 1990): 131–47.

see it as a fundamental threat to the survival of the Chinese state.[54] China, they argued, was rapidly sliding into chaos as "economic warlords" battled for control over rents and split the economy into hostile "economic dukedoms" and fought a series of protracted interregional commodity wars. As the 1989–90 recession deepened, local governments began to build "bamboo walls and brick ramparts" around their jurisdictions. Regional blockades and illegal customs posts as dense as "trees in a forest" blocked the movement of goods and capital between localities. With the center apparently unable to halt the mounting economic chaos, it appeared that China's economy was being dragged ever farther away from marketization. Central paralysis and headlong local rent seeking seemed to be pushing the economy toward economic feudalism as local protectionism undermined even the limited market structures put in place during the first two rounds of reform.

When China's economy failed to collapse into chaos and after the center succeeded in restoring order in fall 1990, most Sinologists relegated local protectionism to the status of another negative consequence of Deng Xiaoping's ad hoc approach to reform. Goodman, for example, wrote that "provincial merchantilism" may have appeared to show that "economic and, by extension, political power has passed, or is passing, from the centre to the provinces." He argued that, when shorn of broad and simplistic historical analogies, crude economic determinism, and the unsustainable assumption that central-provincial relations are inherently antagonistic, the evidence suggested that local protectionism and interregional economic conflicts were manifestations of changes in the "shape" of the current Chinese state, not its collapse.[55]

Fitzgerald warned that the significance of anecdotal evidence of interregional conflicts, including reports of armed patrols to prevent the export of goods

---

[54] See *Far Eastern Economic Review (FEER)*, October 13, 1988; *Washington Post (WP)*, December 11, 1988; and *WP*, December 12, 1988; Maria Hsia Chang, "China's Future: Regionalism, Federation, or Disintegration," *Studies in Comparative Communism* 25, no. 3 (September 1992): 211–27; Chien-min Chao, "*T'iao-t'iao* vs. *K'uai-k'uai*: A Perennial Dispute Between the Central and Local Governments in Mainland China," *Issues and Studies* 27, no. 8 (August 1991): 31–46; and Wang Shaoguang, "Central-Local Fiscal Politics in China," in Jia Hao and Lin Zhimin, eds., *Central-Local Relations in China: Reform and State Capacity* (Boulder, CO: Westview, 1994): 106–8.

[55] David S. G. Goodman, "The Politics of Regionalism: Economic Development, Conflict, and Negotiation," in David S.G. Goodman and Gerald Segal, eds., *China Deconstructs: Politics, Trade and Regionalism* (New York: Routledge, 1994): 1–20 and David S.G. Goodman, "Provinces Confronting the State?" in Kuan Hsin-chi and Maurice Brosseau, eds., *China Review 1992* (Hong Kong: Chinese University Press, 1992): 3.2–3.19. On the dubious utility of analogies to the warlord era see also Brantly Womack, "Warlordism and Regionalism in China," in Richard H. Yang, Jason C. Hu, Peter K. H. Yu, and Andrew N.D. Yang, eds., *Chinese Regionalism: The Security Dimension* (Boulder, CO: Westview, 1994): 21–41.

from one region to another, were not only "easily overstated," but that proponents of the fragmentation thesis also ignored signs of increasing interregional cooperation.[56] Chung also pointed out that even if reform had weakened the center and may have unleashed certain centripetal forces, these tendencies toward regional fragmentation were offset by an expansion in voluntary integration in the form of expanded horizontal economic cooperation, a conclusion echoed by Jia and Wang.[57] On the other hand, Yang and Wei saw local protectionism and interregional conflict not as evidence of political fragmentation but rather as a manifestation of the growth of competitive forces unleashed by marketization and the willingness of local governments to take advantage of opportunities to bend policy to their advantage.[58]

Economists came to similar conclusions, viewing local protectionism as a transitory phenomenon born of the economic irrationalities associated with partial reform. Naughton, for example, suggested that even though local governments might erect a variety of trade barriers to protect "their" enterprises, such barriers were apt to have only a limited impact because individual local governments control only a tiny part of the economy. Thus, efforts to impose monopolistic controls were likely to fail in the face of outside competition.[59] Other economists, including those who have devoted the greatest attention to the problem of local protectionism, also minimized its long-term significance, portraying it primarily as a function of price distortions and shortages. It was, they say, a barrier to the growth of integrated markets, but a problem that will ultimately dissipate or be solved through a deepening of price reform.[60]

---

[56] John Fitzgerald, "Reports of My Death Have Been Greatly Exaggerated: The History of the Death of China," in Goodman and Segal, eds., *China Deconstructs*: 21–58.

[57] Jae Ho Chung, "Central-Provincial Relations," in Lo Chi Kin, Suzanne Pepper, and Tsui Kai-Yuen, eds., *China Review, 1995* (Hong Kong: Chinese University Press, 1995): 3.1–3.45; Jae Ho Chung, "Studies of Central-Provincial Relations in the People's Republic of China: A Mid-Term Appraisal," *China Quarterly*, no. 142 (June 1995): 487–508; and Jia Hao and Wang Mingxia, "Market and State: Changing Central-Local Relations in China," in Jia and Lin, eds., *Changing Central-Local Relations in China*: 35–65.

[58] Dali L. Yang and Houkai Wei, "Rising Sectionalism in China?" *Journal of International Affairs* 49, no. 2 (Winter 1996): 456–76 and Dali L. Yang, "Reforms, Resources, and Regional Cleavages: The Political Economy of Coast-Interior Relations in Mainland China," *Issues and Studies* 27, no. 9 (September 1991): 43–69.

[59] Naughton, *Growing Out of the Plan*: 232.

[60] See Andrew Watson and Christopher Findlay, "The 'Wool War' in China," in Christopher Findlay, ed., *Challenges of Economic Reform and Industrial Growth: China's Wool War* (Sydney, Australia: Allen and Unwin, 1992): 163–80; Keith Forster, "China's Tea War," Chinese Economic Research Unit, University of Adelaide, Working Paper no. 91/3; Zhang Xiaohe, Lu Weiguo, Sun Keliang, Christopher Findlay, and Andrew Watson, "The 'Wool War' and the Cotton Chaos: Fibre Marketing in China," Chinese Economic Research Unit, University of Adelaide, Working Paper no. 91/14; Andrew Watson, Christopher Findlay, and Du Yintang, "Who Won the 'Wool

In this book, I recast the significance of rent seeking and local protectionism. Rather than viewing them as by-products or unintended consequences of partial reform, I consider them critically important forces of change. Rent seeking and local protectionism were, of course, consequences of partial reform and specifically the failure to decontrol prices combined with administrative and fiscal decentralization. The failure to decontrol prices left rents in place. Rents could be monetized by arbitraging between the plan and the emerging market and could also be obtained by moving into the production of scarce consumer goods. Decentralization increased local governments' autonomy and gave them new opportunities to capture rents. Fiscal decentralization linked local spending to local revenues and hence gave local governments motives to seek rents. Partial reform thus triggered a scramble for rents similar to the scramble that erupted in Russia during the early 1990s.

In contrast to those who see China as skipping over the pitfalls of partial reform, I assert that China fell into the pitfalls. As predicted by Hellman, Schliefer, Aslund, and others, partial reform in China unleashed a wave of rent seeking. The dynamics and politics of rent seeking were fundamentally different in China. In Russia, the benefits of incomplete shock therapy were relatively concentrated, giving rise to a new class of powerful oligarchs who were then able to parlay their newfound wealth into the political power needed to bend state policy to their rent-seeking interests. Incremental reform in China, on the other hand, freed local governments to engage in rent seeking. More numerous and less well positioned, the initial winners in China were unable to capture the policy-making process. Instead, they found themselves locked in a fratricidal struggle over rents that ultimately dissipated most of the rents they sought to capture. Moreover, local rent seeking encroached on central rent seeking and effectively robbed the state sector, and the bureaucratic interests that stood behind it, of rents. Local protectionism also deprived in-plan producers of needed inputs and access to markets. Mounting local rent seeking and intensified local protectionism thus split the antireform camp into antagonistic camps.

The lure of rents and the resulting battle for control over rent-producing commodities in China, therefore, triggered a process of change that drove the economy steadily closer to the market. Specifically, rent seeking and local protectionism performed three crucial functions that formal reforms failed to fulfill.

War'? A Case Study of Rural Product Marketing in China," *China Quarterly*, no. 118 (June 1989): 213–41; Anjali Kumar, "China's Reform, Internal Trade and Marketing," *Pacific Affairs* 7, no. 3: 323–39; and Anjali Kumar, "Economic Reform and the Internal Division of Labour in China: Production, Trade and Marketing," in Goodman and Segal, eds., *China Deconstructs*: 99–130.

First, they shattered the monopsony structures through which the state forced down prices for key agricultural commodities and blocked access to these commodities by nonstate consumers. Second, they crippled the state's ability to fix agricultural commodity prices arbitrarily. Third, they moved the economy from chronic shortages to glut. By forcing de facto price reform and undermining the institutional foundations of the planned economy, rent seeking and local protectionism thus produced conditions that made it possible for Deng and the reformers to initiate a third round of reforms in 1992–3. These new reforms were much bolder than those blocked by the conservatives between 1984 and 1988, largely because rent seeking and local protectionism had dissipated the rents that vested bureaucratic interests had sought to defend. Rent seeking and local protectionism, in short, drove China's economy beyond the pitfalls of reform and made possible the rapid growth and marketization that set the experience so dramatically apart from that of other former socialist economies.

OVERVIEW OF THE BOOK

I begin my analysis in Chapter 2 with an examination of the evolution of state policy toward commerce and domestic trade during the early 1980s. China's reformers approached marketization in an ad hoc and often contradictory manner. On the one hand, they recognized the importance of invigorating internal trade and reducing the administrative barriers that had split the Chinese economy into a series of local cells separated from each other by semipermeable barriers. To facilitate market activity, they "commercialized" parts of the economy, scaled back the extent of the planned economy, and allowed greater movement of goods across administrative boundaries. But, the reformers did not simply throw the internal market open. Unwilling to allow complete decontrol and unwilling to cede control over a series of monopsonies that allowed state-owned enterprises access to cheap raw materials and, hence, rents, the reformers attempted to create a semimarketized system wherein monopsonies and monopolies coexisted alongside markets.

This hybrid system was, as I show in Chapter 3, inherently unstable. Herein I argue that by distorting prices, a typical Leninist economy not only creates rents, it also creates a complex series of macroeconomic distortions, including a combination of artificially induced shortages and inflated demand, that can only be sustained through the application of tight, centralized control. Absent tight control, such a system will begin to move back toward equilibrium as diverse actors, including officials and state institutions, seek to capture the rents created by distorted prices. My analysis thus suggests that if reformers decide to concurrently relax controls over economic activity at the same time they decentralize the fiscal system, this will reduce central controls sufficiently to unleash a scramble for rents in which prices will be forced back to market-clearing levels, thus eliminating rents, and supply and demand will be brought back into rough equilibrium.

In Chapter 4, I examine a number of these price wars. Between 1984 and 1991, the Chinese media reported more than sixty "commodity wars," with the most intense periods being 1988 and 1989. During these wars, local governments frequently resorted to what I shall term "export protectionism," by which I mean a reliance on export barriers to prevent the outflow of undervalued commodities. Some involved major commodities, such as cotton, tobacco, silk, wool, ramie, sugarcane, and tea. Most involved relatively minor commodities, including anise, bluish dogbane, melon seeds, castor oil, and licorice root. Many of these minor wars involved commodities not subject to tight state controls after 1984; in many instances, the wars involved little more than a headlong scramble for control over local supplies, followed by a sudden increase in prices. In many cases, prices were ultimately pushed so high that speculative pressures and a surge in supply culminated in the collapse of local markets. Most of these minor wars were also fought over products whose prices the center had already decontrolled. As a result, these wars caused little tangible structural change.

The major wars, on the other hand, involved conflict over institutional structures, specifically between officials who controlled the old state monopsonies and others actors who sought to capture a share of these monopsony rents. When we see the cotton market, the tobacco market, the silk market, and the wool market erupting into a commodity war, we are therefore looking at conflicts that are rooted in the reformers' decision to deregulate and decontrol commodity markets only partially. At the same time, these wars resulted in structural change, not only because they resulted in attacks on the old monopsony system, but also because they drove up prices. By raising prices, they caused supply to expand. Ultimately, rising prices and increasing supply pushed many of these commodity markets to the point at which prices were no longer set by administrative fiat but rather by competitive bidding among rival buyers. Once such conditions existed, effective marketization had taken place and whatever was left of the old monopsony was rendered obsolete. To the extent that monopsony institutions survived the commodity wars, they did so either because local actors had incentives to perpetuate them, albeit as de facto local monopsonies rather than as agents of the central monopsonies, or as institutional artifacts.

As conflicts over agricultural commodities engulfed the rural sector, local protectionism spread into the urban commercial sector. In Chapter 5, I shift from export protectionism to import protectionism. Like export protectionism, import protectionism had its roots in price distortions left in place by the reformers' failure to decontrol prices. Under the old pricing system, the prices of raw materials were generally artificially depressed and those for finished products, particularly consumer goods, were artificially inflated. When industrial reforms undertaken in the mid-1980s reduced barriers to entry, local governments gravitated toward those commodities that commanded high prices and, hence, generated high profits. The result was an expansion in the production of these goods.[61] Excessive investment, however, ultimately led to excess supply. When Li Peng's 1988 retrenchment triggered recession in the winter of 1989–90, local governments moved to seal off local markets and protect local manufacturers from outside competition, seeking to prevent losses of rents and simultaneously avert the possibility of bankruptcies and layoffs. The result was a dramatic increase in the level of import protectionism.

Just as local protectionism appeared to be spiraling out of control, the center stepped in with a couple of proclamations ordering an end to local protectionism. On the surface, the notion that a few of slips of paper could bring a halt to local protectionism must strike some as implausible. But, as I show in Chapter 6, by the time the center stepped in, import protectionism had largely run its course. Whereas export protectionism can be associated with inflationary periods, during which the gap between fixed prices and market-clearing prices will increase, import protectionism is apt to occur during recessions when demand drops below supply, thus forcing producers to compete in tight buyers' markets. Thus, once the economy began to revive in the fall of 1990 and demand began to expand once more, the utility of import protection was already rapidly declining because buyers' markets were already giving way to sellers' markets. Moreover, despite their apparent fixation on monopolizing local markets, rapid expansion of production during the boom years prior to 1989 had made many localities dependent on exports to other markets. The center's demand that local governments dismantle import barriers thus came at an opportune time because it simply reduced the danger of "unrequited cooperation" that otherwise might have deterred local governments from dismantling their import barriers. As I discuss in the latter part of Chapter 6, neither export nor import protectionism disappeared after the end of the 1989–90 recession but after the "high tide" of 1989–90 local protectionism gradually waned as marketization deepened.

In the final chapter, I assess the cumulative effects of rent seeking and local protectionism and describe how they pushed the economy toward the market. Fearful that price decontrols in a condition of shortage would trigger inflation, that inflation would trigger social unrest, and that social unrest would strengthen

---

[61] See Barry Naughton, "Implications of the State Monopoly over Industry and Its Relaxation," *Modern China* 18, no. 1 (January 1992): 14–41.

the hand of the conservatives, Deng shied away from price reform in 1984. When an overheated economy pushed inflation to double-digit levels in 1988 and rumors of price reform triggered panic buying, Deng backed away from the reform camp and threw his support behind Chen Yun and the conservatives. Three years later, when he faced renewed political pressures to reinvigorate the economy in 1991, Deng had much less to fear from a bold program of reform. Rent seeking had pushed the economy from a condition of shortage to one of glut and had pushed prices progressively upward toward market-clearing levels. The plan and market tracks of the two-track price system had thus converged and many of the rents that had existed in 1984 had disappeared. Many of the monopoly and monopsony structures from which state agencies had extracted rents had also ceased to function effectively. Thus, even before Deng's Southern Tour, conditions had evolved in a manner that was favorable to renewed top-down reform because "dramatic" reform entailed little more than a "rectification of names" that would bring regime policy back into line with economic reality. Thus I conclude that by 1992–3 the chaos associated with China's descent into the pitfalls of incremental reform had, in reality, already produced many of the systemic changes necessary for marketization during the mid-1990s.

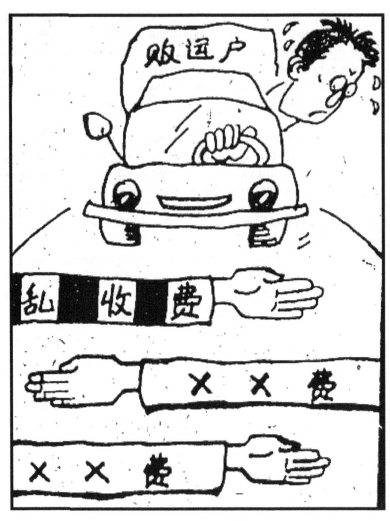

Xi'nan Jingji Bao, 9/5/88
"Fee Collectors"

2

Policy and Institutional Change

THE structures that gave rise to local protectionism grew out of three changes and one nonchange in the policy environment. First, in the early 1980s, Deng's reform coalition abandoned Mao's stress on local self-sufficiency and replaced it with a strategy that stressed the expansion of interregional trade and interdependence. Second, they partially demonopolized China's internal commerce and opened up new space for interregional markets. Third, they adopted fiscal reforms that, in conjunction with administrative devolution, altered the property-rights relationship between local governments and the local economy in ways that transformed local governments from purely administrative entities into administrative-cum-economic actors. Finally, they opted not to decontrol prices. Instead, they introduced some market prices and set up a parallel price system. Rents were thus not only left in place, but could now be monetized more easily by arbitraging between the market and the plan. This combination created new space for local governments to pursue a greater share of the rents left in place by the reformers' decision not to decontrol prices. In conjunction with the decollectivization of agriculture, it also gave the real producers of those rents – China's farmers – a chance to try to grab back part of the monies that the state stripped out of their pockets by skewing prices in its favor. Reform, therefore, inadvertently triggered a battle over rents, in which trade barriers were key weapons in the struggle to localize the monetization of rents.

OPENING CHINA'S INNER DOORS

China's reform leadership came to power vowing to "open to the outside and invigorate the domestic economy."[1] China must, they believed, forsake autarkic

---

[1] Wan Fang, Song Fucheng, and Yu Chunguang, "*Zhongshi liutong guocheng, ba jingji gaohuo*" (Attach importance to circulation and invigorating the economy), *Hongqi*, no. 10 (1980): 22–5;

economic development and incorporate itself into the international economy. China must also, they continued, throw open its inner doors. Although overshadowed by the opening of the outer door, the opening of China's "inner doors" was an integral part of China's post-1978 economic reform strategy. Speaking in 1984, Deng Xiaoping declared: "Invigoration of the domestic economy also means opening the domestic economy. There are, in fact, two open policies: open to the outside and open to the inside."[2] Seven years later, Minister of Commerce Hu Ping reiterated that the external and internal openings were actually two aspects of one policy.[3]

The policy of opening up to the inside grew directly out of the reformers' critique of the Maoist economic model. China's reformers believed that Maoist economic policies had created a system marred by serious inefficiencies, thereby retarding China's economic development.[4] Among these inefficiencies, they believed, was the rigidity of the system of vertical and horizontal administrative barriers that fragmented the economy into ministerial and territorial segments. Because resources, labor, and capital could not easily move across administrative boundaries, cooperation across vertical and horizontal lines was difficult and unreliable. As a result, localities and ministries internalized crucial production functions, ultimately becoming largely self-contained or even autarkic. In conjunction with other structural inefficiencies, inter alia, excessive investment in heavy industry, underinvestment in agriculture, price policies that discouraged growth in agriculture, autarky promoted backwardness, wasted resources, and hindered growth, according to the reformers.[5] Overcoming these problems required the "smashing of barriers and

---

"Zhengdang yao cujin dui wai kaifang, dui nei gaohuo jingji" (Party rectification must promote the opening to the outside and invigoration of the domestic economy), *Hongqi*, no. 11 (1984): 45–6 and *Renmin Ribao* (2/26/84): 2 and (3/4/82): 1.

[2] Quoted in Hong Qing, *"Weishenme shuo dui nei gaohuo yejiu shi dui nei kaifang"* (Why do we say that invigorating the domestic economy is also opening the domestic economy?), *Hongqi*, no. 9 (1985): 47–8.

[3] *Nongmin Ribao* (5/13/91): 1.

[4] *"Guanyu jingji guanli tizhi gaige zongti shexiang de chubu yijian"* (Preliminary opinion on systemic reform of the economic management system), December 3, 1979, in *Zhongyao Jingji Tizhi Gaige Guihua Ji (1979 nian – 1987 nian)* (Collection of materials on China's economic system reform) (Beijing: *Zhonggong Zhongyang Dangxiao Chubanshe*, 1988): 1–22 and Zeng Bijun and Lin Muxi, *Xin Zhongguo Jingji Shi* (Economic history of new China) (Beijing: *Jingji Ribao Chubanshe*, 1990): 299–303.

[5] Liu Guoguang and Wang Ruisun, "Restructuring the Economy," in Yu Guangyuan, ed., *China's Socialist Modernization* (Beijing: Foreign Languages Press, 1984): 91–5 and Qiao Xiangwu and Huo Yunchan, *"Weishenme bixu fandui diqu jingji fengsuo?"* (Why is it necessary to oppose regional barriers?), *Hongqi*, no. 9 (1982): 41–2.

opening of doors" between regions.[6] As argued in the Sixth Five-Year Plan (FYP):

Developing economic and technical cooperation between regions is of great significance in giving full play to local advantages, achieving a nationwide overall balance, invigorating the economy, promoting the development of production and progress in technology and improving social economic results.[7]

Increasing domestic economic integration was also seen as critical to rapid development. Rapid development and modernization, the reformers believed, required large-scale imports of technology and capital that were to be financed by a major expansion in exports.[8] Seeking to minimize the time needed to expand exports, the reformers directed existing industries along the coast to shift over to export production. Seeking to maximize export earnings, the reformers proposed that "cheap" Chinese raw materials be combined with "cheap" Chinese labor. Thus, they directed raw material–producing regions in China's interior to expand production and feed inputs into export industries along the coast.[9] The reformers also called for a policy of import-substitution industrialization (ISI) so that imports could be limited to capital goods that China could not produce itself.[10]

The success of concurrent export-led development (ELD) and ISI depended heavily on opening China's domestic economy. For ELD to work, the coast had

---

[6] *Guomin Jingji he Shehui Fazhan Di Qige Wunian Jihua, 1986–1990* (Seventh five-year plan for social and economic development) (Beijing: Renmin Chubanshe, 1986): 104.

[7] *The Sixth Five-Year Plan of the People's Republic of China for Economic and Social Development (1981–1985)* (Beijing: Foreign Languages Press, 1984): 179.

[8] *Guomin Jingji he Shehui Fazhan Di Qige Wunian Jihua, 1986–1990*: 91–2. Also see K. C. Tan, "Editor's Introduction: China's New Spatial Approach to Economic Development," *Chinese Geography and Environment* 2, no. 4 (Winter 1989–90): 3–21; G. L. R. Linge and D. K. Forbes, "The Space Economy of China," in G. L. R. Linge and D. K. Forbes, eds., *China's Spatial Economy* (Hong Kong: Oxford University Press, 1990): 10–34; and Ma Hong, *New Strategy for China's Economy* (Beijing: New World Press, 1984): 117–50.

[9] Originally, the Sixth FYP defined two macroregions, the coast and the interior. The Seventh FYP split the interior into central and western regions and called for the center to expand heavy industrial, raw material, and agricultural production while the less developed west concentrated on infrastructure development. The Eighth FYP and Ten-Year Economic and Social Development Program adopted in 1991 left this tripartite division of labor intact. *Guanyu Guomin Jingji he Shehui Fazhan Shi Nian Guihua he Di Bage Wu Nian Jihua Gangyao de Baogao* (Report on the outline of the Ten-Year Economic and Social Development Program and the Eighth FYP) (Beijing: Renmin Chubanshe, 1991): 31–2.

[10] Robert Kleinberg, *China's "Opening" to the Outside World: The Experiment with Foreign Capitalism* (Boulder, CO: Westview, 1990): 14.

to have access to the interior's raw materials. For ISI to work, domestic manufacturers had to have access to China's large domestic markets.[11] Moreover, the reformers realized that modernization required a shift from labor-intensive to capital-intensive production. They envisioned a process whereby the coast would use export earnings to finance technical upgrading. Labor-intensive production would gradually shift to the interior, where costs would remain low. By gradually redeploying low-tech industry westward, China would continue to profit from its abundant labor while also moving into higher valued-added capital-intensive production. Finally, as coastal industries shifted out of domestic production and over to export production, interior-based producers would take over responsibility for fulfilling domestic demand.[12] Ultimately, interregional economic cooperation would lead to the development of unified national markets and facilitate the flow of capital, labor, and resources among regions.[13] Trade, particularly in materials not subject to central allocation, would also increase demand for raw materials and, thus, less developed regions' welfare.[14]

Initiatives to open up China's domestic markets began soon after the advent of reform. In 1978, the reformers began to dismantle some of the trade monopolies established by the state during the socialization of commerce in the 1950s.[15] They reduced the number of commodities allocated by the State Planning Commission (SPC), central ministries, and provincial planning bureaus.[16] In the rural sector, they revived rural markets as early as January 1978 and granted farmers the right to sell above-quota output in reopened urban "free markets"

---

[11] *"Shenme shi duo qudao shangpin liudao, weishenme yao shixing duo qudao shangpin liudao"* (What are multiple commercial circulation channels and why should we implement a policy of increasing the number of channels?), *Hongqi*, no. 5 (1982): 29–30.

[12] *Renmin Ribao* (1/4/84): 5 and (4/13/84): 5.

[13] Chen Jiaze, *"Tidu tuiyi he fazhanji - zengzhangdian lilun yanjiu"* (Study of the movement by echelon, development pole, and growth point theories), *Jingji Yanjiu*, no. 3 (1987): 33–9 and Li Rengui, *"Quyu jingji fazhan zhong de zengzhangji lilun yu zhengce yanjiu"* (The growth pole theory in China's regional development and the study of policies), *Jingji Yanjiu*, no. 9 (1988): 63–70.

[14] Tong Dalin and Song Yanming, "Horizontal Economic Integration Is a Beachhead to Launch Urban Reforms," *Chinese Economic Studies* 20, no. 2 (Winter 1986–7): 26–35.

[15] See Andrew Watson, "The Reform of Agricultural Marketing in China Since 1978," *China Quarterly*, no. 113 (March 1988): 1–28.

[16] Dorothy J. Solinger, *Chinese Business Under Socialism* (Berkeley: University of California Press, 1984): 115–23. Prior to 1980, central planners allocated 256 types of commodities, ministerial authorities 581, and local governments 7,560. In 1981, the number of commodities under unified control was reduced to seventeen. By 1987, the number had been cut to eight. Audrey Donnithorne, *China's Economic System* (New York: Frederick A. Praeger, 1967): 272–317 and *Zhongguo Baike Nianjian* (Encyclopedic yearbook of China), 1980–8 (Beijing: Zhongguo Dabaike Quanshu Chubanshe, 1980–8): 1980: 310; 1981: 224–5; 1982: 297; 1983: 436; 1984: 401; 1986: 294; and 1988: 324.

in early 1979.[17] Over the next several years, additional reforms increased the number of agricultural products farmers could sell outside of state-controlled commercial channels.[18]

The reformers also sought to expand interregional trade and economic cooperation. In 1980, the State Council encouraged localities to establish "horizontal links" (*hengxiang guanxi*) and abandon policies of local autarky.[19] In April 1982, the State Council rebuked local governments for improperly limiting interregional trade by raising blockades. Regional blockades (*diqu fengsuo*), the State Council declared, were a backward practice that harmed the nation, weakened socialist planning, carved up the unified socialist market, and must be eliminated.[20] In June, a second State Council document called for smashing regional blockades separating urban and rural areas.[21] The communiqué of the Third Plenum of the Twelfth Party Congress in October 1984 declared that there was an "urgent need to unclog the channels of circulation," "smash blockades," and "open doors . . . between economically more developed and less developed areas."[22]

During 1983 and early 1984, the State Council lifted many of the restrictions on long-distance trade by farmers.[23] In 1986, the central government adopted

---

[17] G. William Skinner, "Rural Marketing in China: Repression and Revival," *China Quarterly*, no. 103 (September 1985): 407.

[18] "*Nong fuchanpin yigou yixiao jiage zanxing guanli banfa*" (Provisional management regulations on the negotiated purchase and sale prices for agricultural sideline products), July 30, 1981, in *Zhongyao Jingji Fagui Ziliao Xuanbian* (Compilation of selected important economic laws and regulations) (Beijing: Zhongguo Tongji Chubanshe, 1987): 1246–9; "*Guowuyuan guanyu shutong chengxiang shangpin liutong qudao kuoda gongyepin xia xiang de guiding*" (State Council regulations on the expansion of the transportation and sale of township industrial products in villages), June 17, 1982, in *ibid.*: 1063–4; "*Shangye Bu guanyu wancheng liangyou tonggou renwu he shixing duo qudao jingying ruoyu wenti de shixing guiding*" (Ministry of Commerce trial regulations on the marketing of edible oils after fulfillment of unified purchase quotas), January 22, 1983, *ibid.*: 1064–6.

[19] "*Guowuyuan guanyu tuidong jingji lianhe de zanxing guiding*" (Provisional State Council regulations for promoting economic alliances), July 1, 1980, in *Zhongyao Jingji Fagui Ziliao Xuanbian*: 62–3.

[20] "*Guowuyuan guanyu zai gongpin gouxiao zhong jinzhi fengsuo tongzhi*" (State Council notice prohibiting blockades of industrial products), in *Zhongyao Jingji Fagui Ziliao Xuanbian*: 1062–3.

[21] "*Guowuyuan guanyu shutong cheng xiang shangpin liutong qudao kuoda gongye pin xia xiang de guiding*" (State Council regulations on dredging commodity circulation channels between towns and villages and expanding the volume of industrial products getting to the villages), in *Zhongyao Jingji Fagui Ziliao Xuanbian*: 1063–4.

[22] "Communiqué of the Third Plenary Session of the Twelfth Central Committee," October 20, 1984, as cited in Harold Hinton, ed., *The People's Republic of China: A Documentary Survey* (Wilmington, DE: Scholarly Resources, 1986): 636 and 628.

[23] *Xinhua Domestic Service* (4/10/83), in *Foreign Broadcast Information Service, Daily Report: China* (henceforth *FBIS-China*), (4/13/83): K1–13; "Circular of the Central Committee of

a new set of policies designed to promote "horizontal economic alliances" (*hengxiang jingji lianhe*). According to the Horizontal Economic Alliances (HEA) policy, advanced areas would invest in the development of resource production, transportation infrastructure, and basic industry in less advanced areas.[24] This investment would allow backward areas to expand production of the raw materials required by industries in the developed areas, facilitate their movement from one region to the other, and, by stimulating industrialization in less developed regions, help close regional economic gaps.[25]

Eliminating internal trade barriers was not synonymous with adopting a policy of "free trade." On the contrary, the reformers envisioned a process that would eliminate obsolete state trading monopolies and replace them with a system of market allocation while retaining other state monopolies. In his annual work report to the NPC in the spring of 1984, for example, Premier Zhao Ziyang stated:

> [We] should . . . transform the existing commodity circulation system, which consists of unified purchase and supply of goods according to administrative divisions and levels, into an open, multi-channel system with fewer intermediate links, so that a . . . network extending to all parts of the country will be formed to ensure the smooth flow of goods . . . exchange of goods between different regions and the expansion of a single socialist market.[26]

To establish direct links between producers and consumers and between different regions, Zhao continued:

> It is necessary to reduce in a planned way the variety and quantity of farm and sideline products subject to unified or fixed state purchase and to expand the scope of free purchase and markets.[27]

---

the Chinese Communist Party on Rural Work During 1984," translated in *China Quarterly*, no. 101 (March 1985): 132–42; and "*Guowuyuan guanyu hezuo shangye zuzhi he geren fanyuan nong fuchanpin ruogan wenti de guiding*" (State Council regulations on several questions regarding the transport for sale of agricultural sideline products by commercial cooperatives and private individuals), February 25, 1984, *Guowuyuan Gongbao*, no. 24 (1984): 124–6.

[24] "*Guowuyuan guanyu jinyibu tuidong hengxiang jingji lianhe ruogan wenti de guiding*" (State Council regulations regarding several problems involving the promotion of horizontal economic ties), March 23, 1986, *Guowuyuan Gongbao*, no. 8 (April 10, 1986): 221–2.

[25] Zhang Wanqing, ed., *Quyu Hezuo yu Jingji Wangluo* (Regional cooperation and economic networks) (Beijing: Jingji Kexue Chubanshe, 1989): 27.

[26] *Xinhua* (5/31/84), in *FBIS-China* (6/1/84): K8.

[27] *Ibid.*: K8.

Ultimately, Zhao envisioned the establishment of an internal trade system in which:

> Apart from certain kinds of essential means of production and badly needed consumer goods, which will remain under the control of the state and be supplied according to plan, all goods produced over and above the plan or not covered by it can be traded freely.[28]

Similarly, Minister of Commerce Liu Yi told a reporter from *China Daily* that his ministry would gradually reduce its monopoly on the distribution of goods and would support efforts to enhance the autonomy of locally owned supply and marketing cooperatives. Liu made it clear, however, that the state would continue to play an active and authoritative role in regulating commodity allocation.[29]

According to an editorial in *Renmin Ribao* that appeared soon after Zhao's 1984 Work Report, "state monopoly purchasing and marketing . . . [run] counter to economic law and must be replaced by 'free purchase and marketing,' namely reducing in a planned way the variety and quantity of the commodities of which the purchase is monopolized and assigned by the state . . . ."[30] A second editorial some weeks later declared:

> The state monopoly for purchasing and marketing was a correct and necessary measure in the previous historical period. However, the rigid adherence to "state monopoly" under the present economic condition cannot be said to be correct and necessary. We should not think that a planned economy is nothing other than a "state monopoly" and that market regulation is nothing but capitalism.[31]

Like Zhao, *Renmin Ribao* did not advocate total decontrol of domestic trade. On the contrary:

> To make policies less restrictive by no means implies that the planned economy will be weakened. In the future, the state will continue to assign,

---

[28] *Ibid.*: K9.

[29] *Renmin Ribao* (7/14/84), in *FBIS-China* (7/16/84): K12. Support for commercial reform survived Zhao's downfall in 1988. After he took over control of the economy from Zhao and implemented a program of recentralization, conservative Premier Li Peng voiced continued support for reductions in the scope of state trade monopolies. In his 1989 report to the National People's Congress, for instance, Li stated: "All essential means of production, except those under special control, should go on the market in open trading according to relevant regulations." *Xinhua* (3/20/89), in *FBIS-China* (3/20/89): 36.

[30] *Renmin Ribao* (6/4/84), in *FBIS-China* (6/11/84): K20–1.

[31] *Renmin Ribao* (7/30/84), in *FBIS-China* (8/1/84): K17.

in a unified manner, plans for the purchasing and marketing of major agricultural and sideline products.[32]

In explaining the objectives of commercial reforms, *Ban Yue Tan* declared:

> The [CCP] Central Committee and the State Council have decided that starting this year [1985], with the exception of individual types of products, no state monopoly for the purchase of farm products will be practiced. In its place will be purchase by contract and through the market .... That is to say, the system of state monopoly for the purchase of farm products, which has been practiced for the last 30-odd years, will be gradually abolished.[33]

The state would, the article stated, continue to purchase agricultural commodities and regulate markets to ensure the stability of prices and supplies, but would rely on a combination of purchase by contract and a countercyclical purchasing policy designed to prevent rapid decreases and increases.[34] On a macro level, therefore, commercial reform provided for the development of a new system of interregional trade based on markets, supplemented by state allocation of scarce commodities.

In addition to gradually reducing the scope of administrative transfers conducted through state-controlled channels, the reformers' new commercial strategy called for the expansion of voluntary interregional cooperation. In its endorsement of interregional economic cooperation, the Third Plenum of the Twelfth Central Committee urged localities to enter into cooperative ventures on the basis of "mutual benefit and reciprocity."[35] State Council regulations implementing the HEA policy in 1986 specifically stipulated that:

> On the basis of voluntary participation, and guided by the principles of "diversity, reciprocity, common growth, and making the best use of the advantages and bypassing the disadvantages," lateral economic ties between enterprises should not be restricted by regional, departmental, and professional differences or by differences in ownership.[36]

In his 1987 report to the NPC, Zhao Ziyang, one of the chief advocates of the HEA policy, stated: "We should adhere to the principle of voluntary participation and mutual benefit."[37] That same year, *Hongqi* argued that interregional

---

[32] *Ibid.*: K18.
[33] *Ban Yue Tan* (2/10/85), in *FBIS-China* (3/6/85): K3.
[34] *Ibid.*: K5.
[35] Liu Zhenya and Zhang Zhenxi, eds., *Zhongguo Quyu Jingji Yanjiu* (Studies on China's regional economy) (Beijing: Zhongguo Jingji Chubanshe, 1991): 57.
[36] *Xinhua* (3/23/86), in *FBIS-China* (4/1/86): K1.
[37] *Xinhua* (4/11/87), in *FBIS-China*, (4/14/87): K12.

economic cooperation should allow for the "free circulation of commodities according to objective economic laws . . . and the removal of barriers between regions and departments."[38]

Gradualism and combining "a new circulation system characterized by openness,"[39] with continued state monopolies was a necessity, rather than a contradiction, according to the authors of China's commercial reforms. State monopolies grew out of an economy of shortages in which state controls were necessary to ensure deliveries of critical raw materials to industrial producers and food for urban residents.[40] After shortages eased, state monopolies outlived their purpose and eventually became barriers to development by blocking further increases in production and hampering the flow of commodities. Thus, commercial reform focused on the elimination of obsolete monopolies. Monopolies that remained necessary, because of continuing shortages or insufficiently developed markets, would be retained until increases in production made it possible to shift over to market regulation.[41] Monopolies that supplied low-cost inputs to state-owned enterprises also continued to operate, thus helping ensure their profitability.

In early 1988, however, Zhao began to back away from a policy of interregional integration after running into opposition from interior provinces that felt that integration favored established industrial centers along the coast. An open domestic market, they complained, exploited the interior by forcing it to export cheap raw materials to coastal industrial centers and hampered the establishment of local manufacturers by exposing local "infant industries" to unfair competition with established coastal manufacturers.[42] In early 1988, Zhao unveiled the Coastal Development Strategy (CDS). Ostensibly, the CDS called for simultaneous export-led and import-substitution development.[43] The more developed coast would shift over to export processing,

---

[38] Wan Dianwu, "Some Questions Concerning Reform of the Commodity Circulation System," *Hongqi*, no. 17 (September 1987), in *FBIS-China* (9/25/87): 24.

[39] Ding Shengjun, "Why is it Necessary to Expand the Scope of Regulation by the Market Mechanism in the Rural Areas?" *Hongqi*, no. 22 (November 16, 1985), in *FBIS-China* (12/11/85): K14.

[40] *Ibid.* and *Renmin Ribao* (6/22/82) in *FBIS-China* (6/30/82): K9–10.

[41] *Renmin Ribao* (1/28/83), in *FBIS-China* (2/2/83): K17. Also see *Heilongjiang Provincial Service* (1/7/84), in *FBIS-China* (1/9/84): S1; *Heilongjiang Ribao* (11/17/86), in *FBIS-China* (12/4/86): S1–4; and *Heilongjiang Provincial Service* (10/15/86), in *FBIS-China* (10/21/86): S1.

[42] Andrew Wedeman, "West Against East: China's Coastal Development Policy as a Source of Inter-regional Conflict," paper presented at the Centre for Asian Studies, Chinese University of Hong Kong, "Conference on Policy Implementation in China," Hong Kong, September 1991.

[43] See Dali L. Yang, "Patterns of China's Regional Development Strategy," *China Quarterly*, no. 122 (June 1990): 230–57; Dali L. Yang, "China Adjusts to the World Economy: The Political Economy of China's Coastal Development Strategy," *Pacific Affairs* 64, no. 1 (Spring 1991):

importing raw materials, semifinished products, capital, and technology for use in manufacturing exportable finished products. The interior, meanwhile, would engage in import-substitution industrialization, thus minimizing imports and thereby increasing China's net trade surplus.[44] On the surface, the CDS simply sought to capitalize on China's comparative advantage in labor, create a new regional division of labor, and thereby accelerate economic development.

The CDS, however, contained a second agenda: reducing "east-west" inter-regional economic conflicts.[45] According to the authors of the CDS, developed regions along the coast bore most of the blame for the mounting interregional economic conflicts and the eruption of a series of major resources wars. In introducing the strategy, for example, Zhao Ziyang stated:

What with the demand for raw materials from the coastal processing in-dustries and the economic development of the inland areas, the old method of relying solely on the inland areas for all raw materials will not do, for it will inevitably aggravate competition for raw materials between the coastal and inland areas.[46]

Thus:

It is necessary to ask the coastal areas, as they work on reform and on expediting their opening up, to avoid unnecessary conflicts and friction with the country's economy as a whole.... While seeking economic de-velopment, the coastal areas should avoid scrambling for raw materials and [domestic markets].[47]

42–64; and Fuh-wen Tzeng, "The Political Economy of China's Coastal Development Strategy," *Asian Survey* 31, no. 3 (March 1991): 270–84.

[44] Li Peng, "Report on the Work of the Government" (delivered at the First Session of the Seventh National People's Congress on March 25, 1988), *Beijing Review* (4/25/88): 36.

[45] Lardy suggests the existence of perhaps even a third agenda. He notes that increased imports of raw materials would provide relief for traditional industrial centers (e.g., Tianjin, Shanghai, and Liaoning), which found themselves deprived of inputs by the emergence of new industrial centers not only in traditional raw material–producing regions but also in places such as Guangdong, Fujian, Jiangsu, and Zhejiang. This suggests that the CDS not only sought to reduce "east-west" tension (i.e., tensions between manufacturing and raw material–producing regions) but also "north-south" tensions (i.e., tensions been old and new industrial centers). See Nicholas Lardy, *Foreign Trade and Economic Reform in China, 1978–1990* (New York: Cambridge University Press, 1992): 132–3.

[46] "Zhao on Coastal Areas' Development Strategy," *Beijing Review* (2/8/88): 19.

[47] *Ibid.*: 23. Coastal manufacturing centers had been criticized as early as 1986 for concentrating on domestic manufacturing and failing to move out of low-technology, energy-intensive indus-tries. See Chinese Academy for Social Sciences (CASS), Group for Studying the Experiences of the Sixth Five-Year-Plan Period, "Economic Construction and Reform During the Sixth Five-Year-Plan," *Social Sciences in China*, no. 7 (1986): 23–58.

Zhao also accused coastal areas of consuming too much of China's scarce capital resources and of fueling inflation.[48] Demand for capital along the coast, he said, left the center with insufficient resources to promote development in the interior while excessive capital construction along the coast caused inflation, which was then "exported" to the rest of the country.[49]

To remedy the situation, the CDS called for the coast to concentrate on export processing. Large-scale imports of raw materials and capital would allow the coast to decrease its demand for domestic raw materials and capital. Large-scale exports of finished products, meanwhile, would decrease the coast's reliance on domestic markets, thus allowing infant industries in the interior to expand their market share and accelerate their development. Increased reliance on global markets would, in effect, decrease, if not end, competition between coast and interior. Under the general heading of export promotion, therefore, the CDS would have segregated the interior and the coast, leaving the interior free to pursue import-substitution industrialization. Regional segregation would have, at least indirectly, legitimized internal trade barriers blocking the flow of resources out of raw material–producing regions.[50]

The reforms proposed during the early and mid-1980s did not, therefore, call for the marketization of China's internal trade system. On the contrary, they envisioned a system in which state monopolies coexisted alongside markets and in which prices remained subject to state controls. As such, the partial reforms articulated in the open to the inside strategy would have left China "between the monopoly and the market."

---

[48] Concern over the inflationary impact of price decontrols along the coast was clearly evident in the leadership's presentation of the CDS. Vice Premier Tian Jiyun, for example, warned coastal areas "they must be careful to avoid possible friction with the overall economic stability of the country when they take measures for further reforms and opening. When coming to the question of price, they should be prudent and have corresponding measures so as to reduce as much as possible the impact of inland regions." "Speech by Vice Premier Tian Jiyun at the Working Conference on the Opening of Coastal Areas (Excerpts)," in *Almanac of China's Foreign Economic Relations and Trade, 1989* (Hong Kong: China Resources Advertising Company, 1989): 22.

[49] "Zhao on Coastal Areas' Development Strategy": 23.

[50] Supporters of the CDS tended to equivocate on the issue of regional segregation. After calling on coastal manufacturers to shift over to imported raw materials, they sought to silence those who might brand the policy as biased in favor of the coast by arguing that increased exports would stimulate demand for domestic raw materials. In conjunction with increased capital imports, this would allow development along the coast to "trickle sideways" or "trickle down" into the interior, allowing it to benefit from the CDS as well. "Zhao on Coastal Areas' Development Strategy": 23; Li, "Report on the Work of the Government": 36; David Chen, "Zhao Forced to Retrace Steps to Coastal Regions," *South China Morning Post* (6/30/88); "Coastal Strategy to Benefit All," *Beijing Review* (7/11/88): 10; and *Renmin Ribao* (3/18/87): 2.

COMMERCIAL REFORM

Pursuant to their goal of opening up domestic markets through partial de-monopolization, the reformers modified the existing system of administrative allocation and replaced it with a commercial system that combined elements of plan and market. During the Maoist period, state monopolies controlled most commerce. The CCP began to replace markets with state trading monopolies soon after it seized power in 1949. Major wholesalers were initially placed under the supervision of the Ministry of Trade and then transformed into state trading companies.[51] During 1952–3, the state banned most rural trade as part of its campaign against "hoarding" and "speculation."[52] After it assumed control over wholesaling and rural trade, the state proceeded to impose administrative controls on both the purchase and sale of commodities. Key commodities, including industrial inputs, were subject to "planned purchase and planned supply" by state commercial bureaus, central ministries, and state trading monopolies.[53] Important agricultural commodities were subject to "unified purchase" (*tongyi shougou*) by local supply and marketing cooperatives and were then marketed by these quasi-state organizations.[54] Sales of other commodities remained technically free from administrative controls and were theoretically subject to only normal commercial controls. Local markets, however, were tightly regulated and prices were either fixed or tightly controlled.[55]

Other regulations limited the physical movement of goods. Farmers could generally travel only to local markets because anything they wished to transport

---

[51] Donnithorne, *China's Economic System*: 273–7.

[52] Edward Friedman, Paul G. Pickowicz, and Mark Selden, *Chinese Village, Socialist State* (New Haven, CT: Yale University Press, 1991): 173 and 280–1.

[53] Key commodities, known as "Category I," came under the administrative control of the State Planning Commission in the early 1950s. By the late 1950s, the list of Category I goods had increased to thirty-eight, including grain, edible oils, raw cotton, cotton yarn, and cotton cloth. Commodities subject to unified purchase during this period included cured tobacco, kenafe, ramie, hemp, sugarcane, silk cocoon, tea, hogs, wool, cashmere, leather and hides, native paper, native sugar, tung oil, bamboo products, lacquer, walnuts, almonds, melon seeds, chestnuts, medicinal herbs, apples, oranges, and aquatic products. For a full list of Category I and II goods during the 1950s, see Donnithorne, *China's Economic System*: 284 and Udo Weiss, "China's Rural Marketing Structure," *World Development* 6 (May 1978): 660.

[54] Although theoretically established by rural inhabitants, the supply and marketing cooperatives came under the administrative control of the All China Federation of Supply and Marketing Cooperatives which, in turn, came under the supervision of the Ministry of Commerce. Donnithorne, *China's Economic System*: 284; Weiss, "China's Rural Marketing Structure": 661; Skinner, "Rural Marketing in China": 339; and Audrey Donnithorne, "The Organization of Rural Trade in China since 1958," *China Quarterly*, no. 8 (October 1961): 78.

[55] Donnithorne, China's Economic System: 88 and 284.

had to be carried on their backs, in wheelbarrows, or on bicycles. Farmers also were not allowed to transport local specialty crops[56] across county boundaries. In some areas, farmers could attend markets only on officially designated "rest days" and were thus limited to markets within a few hours' walk of their homes.[57] Access to more distant markets was further limited because farmers needed passes to travel outside their brigades.[58] Peddlers had to obtain licenses from the counties in which they wished to trade and had to carry travel permits.[59] Except for those living within the same county-level jurisdiction, farmers could not enter towns and cities or sell produce in urban "free markets."[60] Even collective units had to get letters of authorization from county, prefectural, or provincial authorities before transporting goods to other areas for sale.[61] Fluctuations in the macropolitical environment further constrained markets and trade.[62]

The urban-industrial sector witnessed a similar bureaucratization of commerce. Industrial and consumer goods were classified into different categories and subject to varying degrees of state control.[63] Key commodities came under the direct control of the Ministry of Commerce or were removed entirely from

---

[56] The term "local specialty crop" included virtually all major nongrain and nonindustrial crops subject to state purchasing.

[57] Skinner, "Rural Marketing in China": 401; Weiss, "China's Rural Marketing Structure": 656; and Anita Chan and Jonathan Unger, "Grey and Black: The Hidden Economy of Rural China," *Pacific Affairs* 55, no. 3 (Fall 1983): 457. Even in the absence of formal state monopsonies, the ban on cross-jurisdictional commerce forced farmers to sell all above-quota produce to the state. By partitioning the market into segments dominated by state-controlled supply and marketing cooperatives, the ban thus resulted in de facto monopsonies. Friedman, Pickowicz, and Seldon, *Chinese Village, Socialist State*: 174.

[58] Sulamith Heins Potter and Jack M. Potter, *China's Peasants: The Anthropology of a Revolution* (New York: Cambridge University Press, 1990): 303–4.

[59] Donnithorne, "Organization of Rural Trade Since 1958": 87.

[60] Skinner, "Rural Marketing in China": 401.

[61] Chan and Unger, "Grey and Black": 464.

[62] During "liberal" periods, above-quota Category II goods and Category III goods could be sold on rural markets. Even Category I goods beyond those required by the state might be offered for sale during such periods. During "radical" periods, Category II commodities might be reclassified as Category I, sales of above-quota goods restricted, and rural markets shut down. Skinner, "Rural Marketing in China": 399; Weiss, "China's Rural Marketing Structure": 653; and Chan and Unger, "Grey and Black": 452–71. Also see David Zweig, *Agrarian Radicalism in China, 1968–1981* (Cambridge, MA: Harvard University Press, 1989).

[63] Industrial goods were divided into categories: "Category I" goods allocated by the State Planning Commission; "Category II" goods allocated by the various industrial ministries; and "Category III" goods regulated by local governments. Both Category I and Category II goods came under "unified purchase and distribution" by state monopolies. Category III goods could be sold on wholesale markets. In practice, because cross-jurisdictional trade by private traders was effectively prohibited, this meant either direct contract sales to consuming units or sales via state commercial channels. Donnithorne, *China's Economic System*: 254, 285, and 290–1.

commercial channels and placed under the control of various central ministries and planning departments. Other industrial products, including most consumer goods, were less tightly regulated. Individual economic ministries and, to a lesser extent, localities, however, retained control over distribution of products produced by factories under their control.[64] State agencies also took over an increasing share of urban retail trade, absorbing most private retail outlets in 1956.[65]

By the late 1950s, therefore, interregional movements of industrial goods effectively ceased to function on a market basis and became a matter of planned allocation. Movements of producer goods, including raw materials and other inputs, came under the supervision of the SPC, operating through a hierarchy of ministerial, provincial, and subprovincial planning bureaus.[66] Consumer goods, although subject to state planning, were not formally subject to state allocation. Nevertheless, chronic shortages led to the adoption of a system of rationing and allocation by state commercial channels, with the net result that the allocation of consumer goods became a de facto state monopoly.[67]

Once the state bureaucracy had largely absorbed commerce, regime policy tended to discourage interregional trade. As a general rule, bureaucratization encouraged different organizations and localities to internalize production.[68] Regime policy also periodically attacked what commercial activity remained outside administrative controls and limited horizontal interactions among localities. In December 1958, for example, the Central Committee and State Council formally banned horizontal exchanges between rural units, mandating

---

[64] Also see Carl Riskin, "China's Rural Industries: Self-Reliant Systems or Independent Kingdoms?" *China Quarterly*, no. 73 (March 1978): 93. Urban markets for handicrafts and other goods produced by "small" enterprises functioned up until the Cultural Revolution but then fell victim to radical attacks on the vestiges of capitalism. As a result, by the 1970s state commercial bureaus and rural supply and marketing cooperatives largely monopolized the distribution and sale of consumer goods. Solinger, *Chinese Business Under Socialism*: 200–1 and Lynn T. White III, "Low Power: Small Enterprises in Shanghai, 1949–1967," *China Quarterly*, no. 73 (March 1978): 45–76.

[65] Solinger, *Chinese Business Under Socialism*: 316–18.

[66] Thomas Lyons, "Planning and Interprovincial Co-ordination in Maoist China," *China Quarterly*, no. 121 (March 1990): 36–60; and Donnithorne, *China's Economic System*: 271.

[67] Dwight H. Perkins, *Market Control and Planning in Communist China* (Cambridge, MA: Harvard University Press, 1966): 177–97 and Dennis L. Chin, "Basic Commodity Distribution in the People's Republic of China," *China Quarterly*, no. 84 (December 1980): 744–54.

[68] Donnithorne, *China's Economic System*: 271 and 287 and Lyons, "Planning and Interprovincial Co-ordination in Maoist China." Solinger's study of "relational contracting" testifies to the strength of the "pull" of the institutional structure, even after the decontrol of exchange. Dorothy J. Solinger, "Urban Reform and Relational Contracting in Post-Mao China: An Interpretation of the Transition from Plan to Market," in Richard Baum, ed., *Reform and Reaction in Post-Mao China: The Road to Tiananmen* (New York: Routledge, 1991): 104–23.

that henceforth all sales and purchases pass upward, vertically, through state commercial channels.[69] Although the ban was subsequently lifted, regime policy encouraged self-sufficiency and even autarky.[70]

By the late 1970s, some of the barriers created by the bureaucratization of commerce had begun to break down as a result of the proliferation of "underground" markets. Farmers circumvented official restrictions on the movement of goods and the range of goods they could sell, resorting to "smuggling" and other subterfuges.[71] Recognizing that they could not stop the growth of "gray" and "black" markets, local officials in many areas simply turned a blind eye to these practices.[72] Communes and production teams, meanwhile, began to sign contracts directly with factories, bypassing state commercial channels and establishing new horizontal linkages, albeit ones that remained essentially non-market in character.[73] Within the planned industrial sector, a similar system of "direct supply" also emerged.[74]

In 1979, the reformers began to disentangle markets from the administrative system. In the countryside, the first years of the reform period witnessed a series of minor reforms, including renewed support for rural markets. Under the new household responsibility system, compulsory sales to the state were cut back, allowing farmers to retain a greater share of the harvest for household consumption or sale.[75] Early reform policies, however, legalized local markets but continued to restrict severely the development of commercial exchanges

---

[69] Weiss, "China's Rural Marketing Structure": 652.

[70] After the Great Leap, for example, the State Council overturned its 1958 ban on horizontal exchanges by rural units and authorized local commercial units to engage in bilateral exchanges. In 1963, the central government granted communes permission to trade across administrative boundaries. *Ibid.*: 652–3; William Hinton, *Shenfan: The Continuing Revolution in a Chinese Village* (New York: Random House, 1983): 287–9; and Donnithorne, "Organization of Rural Trade since 1958": 82.

[71] Chan and Unger, "Grey and Black": 458; Kelliher, *Peasant Power in China*: ch. 5; and Anita Chan, Richard Madsen, and Jonathan Unger, *Chen Village: The Recent History of a Peasant Community in Mao's China* (Berkeley: University of California Press, 1984): 135.

[72] Chan and Unger, "Grey and Black": 460.

[73] Weiss, "China's Rural Marketing Structure": 656.

[74] Christine Wong, "Material Allocation and Decentralization," in Elizabeth Perry and Christine Wong, eds., *The Political Economy of Post-Mao China* (Cambridge, MA: Council on East Asian Studies, Harvard University, 1985): 257.

[75] Jean C. Oi, *State and Peasant in Contemporary China: The Political Economy of Village Government* (Berkeley: University of California Press, 1989): 156–9. Regulations issued by the Shandong provincial government in 1981, for example, stated:

> Using nonmotorized means, commune members are allowed to transport for sale agricultural and sideline products which belong to the third category, which are not marketed, or basically are not marketed, by state commercial departments and which are too abundant to be marketing out in localities [sic]. Meanwhile, by motor-driven means, commune

between markets. Farmers still could not use motor vehicles or boats to transport produce to distant markets. As was the case during the Maoist era, they had to transport produce to markets under their own power or consign their produce to local commercial departments for sale in distant markets.[76] Local authorities, meanwhile, were enjoined from raising local purchase prices above those prevailing in surrounding areas so as to avoid interregional price competition.[77] Central Committee Document No. 1, issued in early 1982, thus equivocated, calling for establishment of new commercial channels but stipulating that state commercial bureaus and supply and marketing cooperatives would retain primary responsibility for rural marketing.[78]

Official regulations notwithstanding, farmers in various localities began to acquire walking tractors, boats, and trucks from the disintegrating communes and use them to engage in long-distance transport. As these informal trade networks sprang up, the state progressively adopted a more liberal attitude toward rural trade. In 1982, two separate State Council notices warned that "regional blockades" hampered the development of urban-rural trade.[79] The following year, Central Committee Document No. 1 tentatively endorsed private long-distance trade, with the caveats that local authorities must carefully regulate commerce and traders must register with local authorities, pay all required taxes, sell only goods not designated for unified purchase, and sell only after state purchasing agents had fulfilled planned targets.[80] Provisional regulations issued by the State Council shortly afterward specified that collective enterprises and individuals could transport farm produce across both county and provincial boundaries and that farmers could bring produce into cities and towns

members are allowed to transport such products for sale in accordance with certificates issued by the county-level industrial and commercial bureaus.

Shandong Provincial Service (10/17/81), in *FBIS-China* (10/21/81): O9.

[76] "Instruction of the State Council to Strengthen Market Administration and Crack Down on Speculation, Profiteering and Smuggling" (January 7, 1981), in Victor F.S. Sit, ed., *Commercial Laws & Business Regulations of the People's Republic of China, 1949–1983* (vol I: National) (Hong Kong: Taidao Publishing, 1983): 260–1.

[77] "*Guojia Jiage Zongju guanyu guanche zhixing Guowuyuan 'guanyu yange kongzhi wujia, zhengdun yijia de tongzhi' de tongzhi*" (Price Bureau notice on implementing the State Council's notice on strictly controlling prices and rectifying negotiated prices) (December 9, 1980), in *Zhongyao Jingji Fagui Ziliao Xuanbian*: 1237–8.

[78] Watson, "The Reform of Agricultural Marketing in China since 1978": 12–13.

[79] "State Council Circular on Prohibiting Blockages in the Purchasing and Marketing of Industrial Goods," April 10, 1982, in *Commercial Laws & Business Regulations of the People's Republic of China* (vol. II) (Hong Kong: Taidao Publishing, 1984): 200–1 and "State Council Decision on Unblocking Commodity Circulation Channels between Urban and Rural Areas and Increasing the Supply of Industrial Goods in the Countryside," *Ibid.*: 202–3.

[80] *Xinhua* (4/10/83), in *FBIS-China* (4/13/83): K7–8.

for sale.[81] According to the director of the State Industrial and Commercial Administration, Ren Zhonglin, the new policy allowed farmers to transport goods to other areas if most of what was offered for sale was produced by the farmer and he obtained a "self-marketing certificate."[82] The ban on private motor vehicles, however, remained in place.[83]

It was not until 1983–4 that the reformers finally legitimated long-distance trade. In September 1983, the Ministry of Commerce reduced the number of agricultural products subject to planned and unified purchase.[84] The ministry decontrolled trade only in specified agricultural commodities. Most heavy industrial goods, including, inter alia, coal, steel, and petroleum, remained under state control and were thus excluded from trade. Many consumer goods, meanwhile, remained subject to rationing. These caveats notwithstanding, the September 1983 policy freed up a wider range of commodities for trade.

The big push came in January 1984 with the issuance of Central Committee Document No. 1. The document declared:

Circulation is an indispensable link in the process of commodity production: therefore, in order to grasp production, we must grasp circulation.

[81] *"Guojia Jingji Tizhi Gaige Weiyuanhui, Shangye Bu guanyu gaige nongcun shangpin liutong tizhi ruogan wenti de shixing guiding"* (System Reform Commission and the Ministry of Commerce: Preliminary regulations on reform of the rural commodities circulation system), February 21, 1983, in *Zhongyao Jingji Fagui Ziliao Xuanbian*: 92; *"Shangye Bu guanyu wancheng liangyou tonggou renwu hou shixing duo qudao jingying ruogan wenti de shixing guiding"* (Trial regulations of the Ministry of Commerce regarding implementation of the policy of allowing additional channels for sale of edible oils after completion of unified purchase by the state), January 22, 1983, in *Guowuyuan Gongbao*, no. 397 (3/13/83): 74–5; and *"Chengxiang jishi maoyi guanli banfa"* ([State Council] Measures for managing urban and rural markets), February 5, 1983, in *Zhongguo Nongcun Fagui (1983)* (Chinese Rural Laws) (Beijing: Nongye Chubanshe, 1985): 366–73.

[82] *Xinhua* (1/30/83), in *FBIS-China* (2/8/83): K16–18.

[83] Provincial regulations deviated in some cases from those enacted by the State Council. Heilongjiang, for instance, did not extend permission to engage in long-distance trade to individual households, restricting it instead to state and collective commercial enterprises. *"Guanyu fangkuan nongfupin gouyun zhengce de ji xiang guiding"* (Heilongjiang People's Government regulations reducing restrictions on purchase and transport of sideline products), March 25, 1983, *Zhongguo Nongcun Fagui*: 391–5. Guangdong, on the other hand, went beyond central regulations, authorizing farmers to trade in unregulated goods and above-quota grain, cotton, edible oil, and timber, products that remained subject to state monopsonies according to central regulations. *"Guangdong sheng cheng xiang jishi maoyi guanli shishi xize"* (Guangdong province detailed regulations on implementation of urban and rural market controls), November 30, 1983, *ibid.*: 406–11.

[84] *"Shangye Bu guanyu tiaozheng nong fuchanpin gouxiao zhengce zuzhi duo qudao jingying de baogao"* (Ministry of Commerce, report on revised regulations on purchasing and sale of agricultural sideline products and increasing commercial channels), September 28, 1983, *Guowuyuan Gongbao*, no. 418 (12/25/84): 1053–6.

At present, what has become more and more noticeable is the failure of circulation to match the development of commodity production . . . . Commercial operations should be simplified as much as possible and direct flow of commodities between the producing and marketing areas should be organized.[85]

To this end, it directed that supply and marketing cooperatives should be commercialized (i.e., made responsible for their own profits and losses), state commercial bureaus should reduce direct purchasing, and agricultural products not covered by planned purchase and above-quota supplies of goods not covered by unified purchase should be allowed to flow among localities. In February 1984, the State Council granted farmers formal permission to trade across county and provincial lines, traffic in selected commodities still covered by state purchasing regulations (but only after state quotas had been met), use motor vehicles in trade, and purchase motor transport.[86] Regulations issued by provincial governments during the following months affirmed these rights.[87] Local and national newspapers followed up with numerous articles announcing the dismantling of local restrictions on the movement of goods, including customs posts (*guanqia*),[88] attacking "leftist" opposition to opening up China's domestic markets, and heralding the advent of a new era in rural commerce.[89] Additional regulations announced in early 1985 did away with mandatory

---

[85] "Circular of the Central Committee of the Chinese Communist Party on Rural Work During 1984" (January 1, 1984), in *China Quarterly*, no. 101 (March 1985): 137.

[86] In many ways, authorizing farmers to use motor vehicles and motorized vessels for trade was of at least equal importance with other regulations reducing the number of commodities subject to state purchase quotas. Without motor transport, farmers simply could not get to distant markets. As a result, this reform gave farmer traders the physical ability to engage in trade. "*Guowuyuan guanyu hezuo shangye zuzhi he geren fanyuan nong fuchanpin ruogan wenti de guiding*" (State Council regulations on the coordination of commercial organization and private traffic in agricultural sideline products) (February 25, 1984), in *Zhongyao Jingji Fagui Ziliao Xuanbian*: 1071–2; "*Guowuyuan guanyu nongcun geti gongshangye de ruogan guiding*" (State Council regulations on rural individual commercial and industrial enterprises) (February 27, 1984), in *ibid.*: 1073–4; and "*Guowuyuan guanyu nongmin geren huo lianhu gouzhi jidong che ban he tuolaji jingying yunshuye de ruogan guiding*" (State Council regulations on the purchase of motor vehicles and tractors by individual farmers and teams for the purpose of commercial cartage) (February 27, 1984), in *ibid.*: 484–5.

[87] See the various provincial regulations reproduced in *Zhongguo Nongcun Fagui (1984)* (Chinese Rural Laws) (Beijing: *Nongye Chubanshe*, 1986): 540–603.

[88] These customs posts were primarily police and public security checkpoints set up by local governments to control the movement of people and goods in accordance with state policy.

[89] See *Hunan Ribao* (5/24/84): 1 and (3/14/84): 1; *Jiangxi Ribao* (4/23/84): 1; and *Henan Ribao* (6/23/84): 2.

---

purchase quotas for additional agricultural commodities, including cotton and wool.[90]

Industrial reforms enacted by the Third Plenum of the Twelfth CCP Party Congress in October 1984 liberalized exchanges within the industrial sector.[91] While retaining planned allocation, the state commercial apparatus, and a two-tiered price system, new regulations allowed enterprises greater leeway in marketing their products.[92] In addition to cutting back on the number of products covered by planned allocation and reducing planned purchase quotas, these reforms also indirectly decontrolled the urban-industrial sector by encouraging rapid expansion of the collective sector, sales of whose products fell largely outside the central planning system.[93]

The reforms of 1984 by no means entirely deregulated internal trade. Farmers could not just jump on their walking tractors and chug off to distant markets at will. Traders had to obtain business licenses, carry proof of tax payments, obtain passes and vehicle permits, and so forth. A complex set of bureaucratic agencies, many of which dated to the 1950s, continued to play a direct role in the purchase and allocation of agricultural commodities. Many industrial goods also remained under tight administrative control.[94] Nevertheless, by loosening administrative controls and, perhaps equally important, granting individuals the right to engage in commercial activity across administrative boundaries, these reforms loosened the state's grip on allocation. Yet the state remained unwilling to deregulate fully and continued to claim monopsony rights over a range of critical goods, including those from which state-owned industries extracted rents (e.g., tobacco, cotton, silk) or whose price the state wished to suppress for political reasons (grain).

Commercial reform also loosened the center's grip on the purchase and distribution of commodities still subject to state purchase. Although central agencies

---

[90] Terry Sicular, "China's Agricultural Policy during the Reform Period," in Joint Economic Committee, Congress of the United States, *China's Economic Dilemmas in the 1990s: The Problems of Reforms, Modernization, and Interdependence* (Armonk, NY: M. E. Sharpe, 1991): 347–53.

[91] Solinger, "Urban Reform and Relational Contracting in Post-Mao China": 110.

[92] "*Zhonggong Zhongyang guanyu jingji tizhi gaige de jueding*" (Decision of the CCP Central Committee on reform of the economic system), October 20, 1984 in *Zhongyao Jingji Fagui Ziliao Xuanbian*: 128.

[93] Dorothy J. Solinger, "Commercial Reform and State Control: Structural Changes in Chinese Trade, 1981–1983," in Dorothy J. Solinger, *China's Transition from Socialism: Statist Legacies and Market Reforms 1980–1990* (Armonk, NY: M. E. Sharpe, 1993): 65–81.

[94] William A. Byrd, *The Market Mechanism and Economic Reforms in China* (Armonk, NY: M. E. Sharpe, 1991): 44–68 and Akira Fujimoto, "Market Disorder and Reform in the Distribution System," *JETRO China Newsletter*, no. 86 (May–June 1990): 7–11.

headed up the various purchasing systems, monolithic central trade bureaucracies did not extend down to the local level. Each purchasing system consisted of a hierarchy of central, provincial, prefectural, and county-level trading corporations, each under the dual supervision of the central government and local governments at the corresponding level. The tobacco monopsony, for example, was headed by the State Tobacco Monopoly Bureau, which supervised the China Tobacco Corporation.[95] The Tobacco Corporation, in turn, supervised provincial tobacco companies, which oversaw prefectural and municipal tobacco companies, which oversaw county tobacco companies. At the bottom of this bureaucratic pyramid, local supply and marketing cooperatives were responsible for the actual purchase of cured tobacco from growers and retail sales of cigarettes.

The state purchasing system, in fact, rested on a foundation composed of the local supply and marketing cooperatives, which had responsibility for purchasing a wide range of agricultural commodities. According to regulations promulgated in 1981, the cooperatives were responsible for purchasing Category I[96] and Category II[97] products on behalf of the central ministries.[98] As a result, the cooperatives acted as purchasing agents for the Ministry of Commerce, the Ministry of Foreign Trade, the Ministry of Textiles, and the Ministry of Light Industries, as well as the Tobacco Monopoly Bureau. The cooperatives were also responsible for purchases of above-quota Category II products, which they bought at negotiated prices set by provincial authorities, and for regulating prices for Category III products. In addition, the supply and marketing cooperatives acted as retail outlets for the sale of both consumer goods and producer goods used by the agricultural sector,[99] for which state commercial bureaus acted as wholesale distributors.

Although they acted as agents of central trading corporations, by the mid-1980s the state no longer had direct and exclusive property rights over cooperatives. Originally set up as farmer-owned enterprises the cooperatives came under the de facto control of the Ministry of Commerce during the Great Leap

---

[95] Guowuyuan Yanjiu Ketizu, *Nongchanpin Liutong Tizhi Gaige yu Zhengce Baozhang* (Policy safeguards for the reform of the circulation of agricultural products) (Beijing: Honggi Chubanshe, 1992): 57.

[96] Before 1985, Category I commodities included quota purchases of grain, edible oil, and cotton. After 1985, these products were no longer subject to quota delivery but were purchased by contract.

[97] After 1985, Category II goods included tobacco, wool, silk cocoons, tea, catalpa oil, tung oil, wood oil, citronella oil, peppermint oil, sugar beets, and sugarcane.

[98] "*Gongxiao she maoyi huozhan guanli shixing banfa*" (Trial measure for the management of supply and marketing cooperative warehouses), *Zhongyao Jingji Fagui Ziliao Xuanbian*: 1046–9.

[99] *Ibid.*

Forward. State control increased during the Cultural Revolution. Ultimately, the state assumed de jure ownership in 1977, when the cooperatives were formally transferred from the collective to the state sector.[100] Farmers began to regain formal ownership of the cooperatives in 1982, when the Ministry of Commerce issued trial regulations allowing farmer shareholders to participate in the selection of cooperative managers and to receive profit dividends.[101] By 1984, 95 percent of the cooperatives had reverted to collective status, making them autonomous local actors, at least on paper.[102]

Although official state policy encouraged the supply and marketing cooperatives to act as autonomous local agencies, the cooperatives remained subject to considerable state control.[103] The cooperatives did double duty: "on the one hand they shoulder the task of procuring and marketing products under the state plan, while on the other hand they sell products for farmers. . . ."[104] The cooperatives also remained under the thumb of local governments, which continued to exert de facto control over them, even though they no longer had formal control. Paradoxically, therefore, the "re-collectivization" of the cooperatives had the effect of weakening the influence of their vertical principals (i.e., the ministries) and strengthening the influence of their horizontal principals (i.e., local governments). To the extent that the collective gained a new degree of autonomy, it was not from local governments, but rather from external bureaucratic control.[105]

Other policy changes reinforced the autonomy of local agents within the state trading system. In 1984, State Council regulations reducing the number of commodities subject to state purchase monopolies gave provincial governments leeway in implementing these reforms.[106] Provincial governments were also given the power to determine whether or not above-quota Category I and II commodities could be sold on free markets after fulfillment of state purchase targets. Other State Council regulations designated the county as the basic unit in commodity circulation and ordered that wholesale operations come under the control of county authorities.[107] Specifically, the State Council called for

[100] *Xinhua* (1/2/84), in *FBIS-China* (1/9/84): K23–4.
[101] *Xinhua* (11/7/82), in *FBIS-China* (11/16/82): K13–14; *Xinhua* (3/8/83), in *FBIS-China* (3/10/83): K12–13; and *Xinhua* (3/15/83), in *FBIS-China* (3/21/83): K7–8.
[102] *Xinhua* (1/2/84), in *FBIS-China* (1/9/84): K23–4.
[103] *China Daily* (2/23/84), in *FBIS-China* (2/23/84): K6–7; *Xinhua* (5/31/84), in *FBIS-China* (6/1/84): K9; *China Daily* (7/14/84), in *FBIS-China* (7/16/84): K12; and *Hongqi*, no. 17 (September 1, 1987), in *FBIS-China* (9/25/87): 25.
[104] *Xinhua* (2/26/83), in *FBIS-China* (3/10/83): K16.
[105] *Renmin Ribao* (3/24/86), in *FBIS-China* (4/1/86): K24.
[106] *Xinhua* (3/8/84), in *FBIS-China* (3/13/84): K14–15.
[107] *Xinhua* (7/24/84), in *FBIS-China* (7/27/84): K6 and *Xinhua* (2/26/83), in *FBIS-China* (3/10/83): K16.

the establishment of unified county cooperatives to direct wholesale and distribution operations at the local level. Provincial and prefectural governments were ordered to interfere as little as possible with the operations at the county level. After 1984, the supply and marketing cooperatives also had the option of bypassing state wholesalers and purchasing consumer goods directly from manufacturers. Prices for consumer goods were negotiable based on cost and availability. Prices for agricultural producer goods, including chemical fertilizer, chemicals, and diesel oil, however, remained subject to state control.

Organizationally, therefore, the opening of China's inner door and commercial reform created a complex and contradictory system of internal trade. On the one hand, the central government continued to claim monopoly rights on the purchase and allocation of selected commodities. State-controlled commercial bureaus also continued to act as wholesalers, thus leaving them in control of interregional transfers of many goods. On the other hand, the system of state monopolies depended on quasi-autonomous local purchasing agents to buy commodities and forward supplies to state-controlled wholesale channels. Retail sales also passed through the hands of these same quasi-autonomous local agencies. Thus, even though reform left in place a system of state monopolies, these monopolies were no longer monolithic but had become increasingly fragmented.

RENTS AND PROPERTY RIGHTS

At the same time that commercial reform fragmented and undermined the old state monopolies, the absence of price reform left in place a series of rents, rents that were supposed to continue to flow into state coffers. The early reform period witnessed a series of price increases. Prices, however, continued to be regulated, particularly the prices of key raw materials.[108] This meant that price distortions introduced by the quasi-Stalinist economic system put in place during the 1950s continued to exist. At that time, the new communist regime first stabilized and then froze prices.[109] After freezing prices, the new regime did not

---

[108] Li Zuoyan, "*Dui jiandaocha wenti de yanjiu*" (Research on the price scissors), *Nongye Jingji Wenti*, no. 2 (1992): 14–21 and Zhao Ping, "'*Jiandaocha' yu nongye de gongxian*" (The price scissors and agriculture's contribution), *Nongye Jingji Wenti*, no. 2 (1992): 20–6.

[109] See Zeng Bijun and Lin Muxi, eds., *Xin Zhongguo Jingji Shi*: 18–26; Hsin Ying, *The Price Problems of Communist China* (Hong Kong: Union Research Institute, Communist China Problem Research Series, 1954); Carl Riskin, *China's Political Economy: The Quest for Development since 1949* (New York: Oxford University Press, 1987): ch. 3; and Tong-eng Wang, *Economic Policies and Price Stability in China* (Berkeley: University of California, Institute of East Asian Studies, China Research Monograph, no. 16, 1980).

open a formal Preobrazhensky-type price scissors.[110] It nevertheless allowed a form of price scissors to open by allowing raw material prices, including agricultural prices, to increase more slowly than consumer prices. Relative prices thus diverged in a manner that made inputs artificially cheap compared to finished products. This allowed the state to siphon money out of the agricultural sector and concentrate it in the industrial sector, within which wages were kept low, thus inflating gross profits.[111] Depressed prices for heavy industrial products, including capital goods, created a secondary siphon that pumped money out of

---

[110] In the 1920s, Soviet economist Evgeny Preobrazhensky proposed that the state create a series of rents by depressing input prices and inflating consumer prices. The resulting price scissors (so named because prices would diverge in a manner like that of an open pair of scissors) would inflate industrial profits and concentrate in profits the final stages of production from whence the state could siphon them off and reallocate them to heavy industrial development. See E. Preobrazhensky, *The New Economics*, Brian Pearce, trans. (Oxford: Clarendon Press, 1965): 110–12. Mao, however, rejected Preobrazhensky's idea of using the price scissors to squeeze agriculture and instead called for an improvement in agriculture's terms of trade. In 1956, he argued:

> The Soviet Union has adopted measures which squeeze the peasants very hard. It takes away too much from the peasants at too low a price through its system of so-called obligatory sales and other measures. This method of capital accumulation has seriously dampened the peasants' enthusiasm for production. You want the hen to lay more eggs yet you don't feed it, you want the horse to run fast but yet you don't let it graze. Our policies towards the peasants differ from those of the Soviet Union. . . . In the exchange of industrial and agricultural products we follow a policy of narrowing the price scissors, a policy of exchanging equal or roughly equal values. The state buys agricultural products at standard prices while the peasant suffers no loss, and, what is more, our purchase prices are gradually being raised.

Mao Zedong, "On the Ten Major Relationships," April 25, 1956, in *Selected Works of Mao Tsetung*, vol. 5 (Beijing: Foreign Languages Press, 1977): 291. Mao's objections to the use of prices to exploit the peasantry notwithstanding, the fact that prices were frozen at 1952 parities left in place a scissors gap that had opened in the 1930s. For discussions of the width of the scissors gap in 1952 and price trends during the pre-war period see Ren Bo, "*Guanyu gongnongye shangpin bijiao de chubu yanjiu*" (A tentative analysis of comparative prices of agricultural and industrial products), in Zhang Wenmin, Zhang Zhuoyuan, and Wu Jinglian, eds., "*Jianguo yilai shehui zhuyi shangpin shengchan he jiazhi guilu lunwen xuan*" (A compilation of selected articles on socialist commodity production and the law of value since the establishment of the PRC) (Shanghai: Shanghai Renmin Chubanshe, 1979): 942–61; Thomas G. Rawski, *Economic Growth in Prewar China* (Berkeley: University of California Press, 1989): 175–6; and Lloyd E. Eastman, *The Abortive Revolution: China Under Nationalist Rule, 1927–1937* (Cambridge, MA: Harvard University Press, 1990): 184.

[111] See Shigeru Ishikawa, "Resource Flow between Agriculture and Industry – The Chinese Experience," *The Developing Economies* 5, no. 1 (March 1967): 3–49; Shigeru Ishikawa, "Patterns and Processes of Intersectoral Resource Flows: Comparison of Cases in Asia," in Gustav Ranis and T. Paul Schultz, eds., *The State of Development Economics* (New York: Basil Blackwell, 1988): 283–331; Nicholas R. Lardy, *Agriculture in China's Modern Economic Development* (New York: Cambridge University Press, 1983): ch. 3; Katsuji Nakagone,

that sector and into the light industrial sector, which reaped inflated profits from the sale of finished products. Finally, the state collected inflated industrial profits and allocated the lion's share to capital construction. In theory, the result was "forced draft industrialization" whereby the relatively limited capital stocks of the economy were concentrated in investment while consumption was kept to a minimum.

The price scissors policy had spatial consequences. Because industry tended to be concentrated first in urban areas and more generally in coastal areas, the price scissors transferred capital out of rural areas and into urban areas and out of the largely agricultural hinterland and into former treaty ports, such as Shanghai and Tianjin, and the Japanese-built industrial complex in Northeast China. These industrial centers thus acted as "price basins" into which flowed undervalued raw materials and out of which flowed overpriced finished products.[112] Because the central government laid claim to the resulting profits, rents were then transferred from these profit basins into central coffers, from whence they were either allocated for the support of the center, used to finance capital investments, or reallocated back to the localities in the form of budgetary subsidies and transfers.[113]

Price and fiscal reforms threw this system into disequilibrium by, on the one hand, retaining rents while at the same time hampering the redistribution of rents and opening up new competition for rents. The early stages of reform involved a series of fairly substantial price increases, particularly in the rural sector where the terms of trade for key commodities had been allowed to deteriorate during the Maoist era. Prices were not decontrolled. Initially, the reformers apparently hoped that they could adjust prices administratively. When it became clear that it was simply impossible to regulate prices effectively, this effort foundered and was abandoned. Fearing that deregulation would trigger inflation because of ongoing shortages – shortages that were, in many cases, a function of

"Intersectoral Resource Flows in China Revisited: Who Provided Industrialization Funds?" *The Developing Economies* 27, no. 2 (June 1989); Sheng Yuming, *Who Provided Industrialization Funds in China?* (Adelaide, Australia: Chinese Economy Research Unit, University of Adelaide, 1991); and Bruce Stone, "Relative Prices in the People's Republic of China: Rural Taxation through Public Monopsony," in John W. Mellor and Raisuddin Ahmed, eds., *Agricultural Price Policy for Developing Countries* (Baltimore: The Johns Hopkins University Press, 1988): 124–54.

[112] Zeng Bijun and Lin Muxi, eds., *Xin Zhongguo Jingji Lishi* and Lynn T. White III, *Shanghai Shanghaied?* (Hong Kong: Centre of Asian Studies, University of Hong Kong, 1989): 9.

[113] Xu Changming, "*Guanyu 'qingxieshi quyu' jingji zhengce de sikao*" (Some thoughts on "regionally biased" economic policies), *Jingji Wenti Tansuo*, no. 1 (1989): 21–5.

irrational prices – and social instability, the reformers rejected that option at the Moganshan Conference in September 1984.[114] Instead, they adopted a system of mixed prices known as the dual-track price system.[115] Under this system, goods were priced according to the consumer. Consumers operating within the plan paid artificially low prices. Consumers operating outside the plan had to pay higher "negotiated prices." In theory, those consumers who paid the lower price were then obligated to sell their output to the state at below-market prices, which would have deprived them of the benefits of rents and allowed the state to capture them instead. In actual practice, the dual-price system was greatly complicated because there was never a strict division between in-plan and out-of-plan consumers. The same enterprise, for example, might receive inputs at both the depressed fixed price and the higher market price and sell the same output at both prices.[116] Adoption of the dual-price system, thus, did not entirely eliminate rents.

It did, however, impose limits on access to rents. In this regard, enterprises in the nonstate sector (collective and township and village-owned enterprises, as well as state-owned enterprises operating outside the plan) were specifically discriminated against because they lacked access to rent-generating raw materials and had to purchase supplies on regular markets at higher prices. Yet, if these enterprises obtained access to under-priced raw materials, they stood to reap substantial benefits.

More directly, the absence of effective price reform left in place terms of trade that discriminated against the agricultural sector. Price increases in the late 1970s narrowed the scissors gap but did not close it entirely. According to Zhao Ping, price increases authorized in 1978 and 1979 closed the scissors gap from its maximum width of 58.87 percent in 1978 to 23.89 percent in 1984.[117] As a

---

[114] Chen Yizi, *Zhongguo: Shi Nian Gaige yu Ba Jiu Minyun – Beijing Liu Si Tusha de Beihou* (Ten years of reform in China and the 1989 democracy movement – background to the June 4th massacre in Beijing) (Taipei: Lianjing Chuban, 1990): 65–7.

[115] Fewsmith, *Dilemmas of Reform in China*: 137.

[116] Naughton, *Growing Out of the Plan*: 220–6.

[117] Zhao Ping, "*'Jiandaocha' yu nongye de gongxian*" (The 'price scissors' and agriculture's contribution), *Nongye Jingji Wenti*, no. 2 (1992): 20–1. Also see Li Fengmin, "*Dui 'jiandaocha' yu nongye de gongxian" ji ge wenti de shangque*" (A comment on several problems with "The 'price scissors' and agriculture's contribution"), *Nongye Jingji Wenti*, no. 7 (1992): 51– 2; Li Zuoyan, "*Dui jiandaocha wenti de yanjiu*" (Research on the price scissors problem), *Nongye Jingji Wenti*, no. 2 (1992): 14–16; Liu Fuyuan, "*Pocu jiandaocha de miwu*" (The illusory elimination of the price scissors), *Zhongguo Nongcun Jingji*, no. 2 (1992); and Li Yuzhu, "*Gongnongye chanpin jiandaocha zhi wo jian – yu Liu Fuyuan tongzi shangque*" (The agricultural-industrial price scissors – a comment on Liu Fuyuan's conception), *Nongye Jingji Wenti*, no. 7 (1992): 46–50.

result, the price scissors continued to extract a substantial "hidden contribution" from the agricultural sector, the value of which Zhao, et al. estimated at ¥25.86 billion in 1984.[118] The spatial distribution of raw material production and manufacturing, meanwhile, remained such that these rents would also have continued to flow out of the agricultural hinterland and into the old profit basins. In contrast to Mao, who had favored the deconcentration of industry and extensive industrialization in the hinterland, the reformers embraced development strategies that were "tilted" in favor of the still more developed coastal provinces.[119] Their strategy called for "industry in the east, agriculture in the west, light industry in the east, heavy industry in the west."[120] Seeking to maximize growth in exports, the reformers hoped to concentrate high-profit light industries along the coast, where they would not only have better access to international markets, but would also be able to take advantage of the coast's better developed infrastructure. As a result, coastal areas were given preferential access to foreign technology and capital; more export licenses; and higher foreign exchange retention rates.[121] Although these preferential policies did not create new rents, they nevertheless helped perpetuate the coast's advantage in terms of industrial concentration.

Moreover, in the context of a partially marketized and commercialized economy, preferential policies gave established industrial centers advantages over less developed regions. Not only did these established centers have advantages in terms of access to the export market and, hence, the ability to generate new foreign investment and export earnings, they also had better developed infrastructure. Because these regions derived an investment advantage from relatively high-profit industries, when the center decentralized administrative control over industry, this afforded established industrial centers greater

---

[118] Zhou Shulian, Chen Dongsheng, and Pei Shuping, eds., *Zhongguo Diqu Chanye Zhengce Yanjiu* (Research on China's regional industrial policy) (Beijing: Zhongguo Jingji Chubanshe, 1990); Xiu Dingben, *Zhongguo Jingji Dili* (Economic geography of China) (Beijing: Zhongguo Caizheng Jingji Chubanshe, 1991); and Zhang Wengui, Tao Guangliang, Dai Juanping, and Ke Xiaodan, eds., *Zhongguo Shangye Dili* (Commercial geography of China) (Beijing: Zhongguo Caizheng Jingji Chubanshe, 1988).

[119] Barry Naughton, "The Third Front: Defense Industrialization in the Chinese Interior," *China Quarterly*, no. 115 (September 1988): 351–86.

[120] Li Zhengyi, "*Dui difang fengsuo wenti de shencheng sikao*" (In-depth examination of the problem of local blockades), *Caijing Yanjiu*, no. 11 (1991): 3–8.

[121] Xu Changming, "*Guanyu 'qingxieshi quyu' jingji zhengce de sikao*" (Some thoughts on "regionally biased" economic policies), *Jingji Wenti Tansuo*, no. 1 (1989): 21–5 and Lardy, *Foreign Trade and Economic Reform in China*: 55–6.

access to investment capital. That coastal areas were also granted permission early on to experiment with new management systems gave them yet another "initial advantage" over the hinterland, which helped to perpetuate the uneven distribution of industry. Finally, privileged access to export markets enabled coastal areas to capture rents by arbitrage, that is, by buying exportable commodities at low Chinese prices and reselling them at higher international prices.[122]

The net result was a system of price distortions that continued to pump capital out of the agricultural sector and into the industrial sector through an agricultural-industrial price scissors, out of heavy industry and into light industry through a secondary price intra-industrial scissors, and out of the hinterland and into the coast through what might be termed an west-east price scissors.[123] Given the spatial distribution of industrial activity, these price scissors combined to discriminate against less developed regions, particularly those producing raw materials and in favor of those where industry, and particularly light industry, was concentrated. Raw material–producing regions often received a double whammy because they not only exported undervalued raw materials, they then imported overpriced consumer goods.[124]

Whereas the prereform fiscal system at least attempted to ensure some sort of equitable reallocation of rents, the fiscal system that evolved in the early 1980s made it increasingly difficult for the center to transfer a share of rents back to raw material–producing areas.[125] By dividing fiscal resources between center and locality, by making local governments more directly dependent on their ability to generate local revenues, and by granting them greater leeway in how local revenues would be spent, the reforms transformed local governments from largely administrative entities into political-cum-economic actors. This transformation was reinforced by reforms that reassigned property

[122] Ma Daqiang, "*Zouchu 'shoufang xunhuan' de sikao*" (Some thoughts on the 'cycle of tight and loose'), *Jingji Gongzuozhe Xuexi Ziliao*, no. 35 (1990): 14–22.

[123] Li Zuoyan, "*Dui jiandaocha wenti de yanjiu*" (Research on the price scissors), *Nongye Jingji Wenti*, no. 2 (1992): 14–21 and Zhao Ping, "*'Jiandaocha' yu nongye de gongxian*" (The price scissors and agriculture's contribution), *Nongye Jingji Wenti*, no. 2 (1992): 20–6.

[124] Li Zhengyi, "*Dui difang fengsuo wenti de shencheng sikao*" (In-depth examination of the problem of local blockades), *Caijing Yanjiu*, no. 11 (1991): 3–8.

[125] Nicholas R. Lardy, "Economic Planning in the People's Republic of China: Central-Provincial Fiscal Relations," in Joint Economic Committee, Congress of the United States, *China: A Reassessment of the Economy* (Washington, DC: Government Printing Office, 1975): 94–115; Nicholas R. Lardy, "Centralization and Decentralization in China's Fiscal Management," *China Quarterly*, no. 61 (March 1975): 25–60; Nicholas Lardy, *Economic Growth and Distribution in China* (New York: Cambridge University Press, 1978); and Wang Shaoguang and Hu Angang, *The Political Economy of Uneven Development: The Case of China* (Armonk, NY: M. E. Sharpe, 1999).

rights over local industries to local governments.[126] The net result was the creation of a system in which the fiscal interests of local governments – and the material interests of cadres whose salaries and bonuses were dependent on the size of the local budget – were tied to the profitability of local industry.

The concurrent division of public revenues into budgetary, extrabudgetary, and self-raised funds tightened this link. Whereas budgetary funds were generally subject to sharing between the center and the locality, thus making it possible for the center to use the unitary budget to transfer funds from one locality to another, neither extrabudgetary funds nor self-raised funds were liable to the same sorts of reallocation, particularly during the early reform period.[127]

---

[126] See Huang, *Inflation and Investment Controls in China*: ch. 2; Huang Yasheng, "Web of Interests and Patterns of Behavior of Chinese Local Economic Bureaucracies and Enterprises during Reforms," *China Quarterly*, no. 123 (September 1990): 431–58; David Zweig, "The Domestic Politics of Export-Led Development: The Case of Zhangjiagang, Jiangsu Province," paper presented at the 45th Annual Meeting of the Association for Asian Studies, Los Angeles, March 25–8, 1993; Y. Y. Kueh, "Economic Reform in China at the *Xian* Level," *China Quarterly*, no. 96 (December 1983): 665–88; Andrew G. Walder, "China's Trajectory of Economic and Political Change: Some Contrary Facts and Their Theoretical Implications," paper presented at the mini-conference on "Chinese and Eastern European Transition: On Divergent Roads?" Center for Social Theory and Comparative History and Center for Chinese Studies, University of California, Los Angeles, June 7, 1993; Andrew G. Walder, "Evolving Property Rights and their Political Consequences," in David S. G. Goodman and Beverly Hooper, eds., *China Quiet Revolution: New Interactions between State and Society* (New York: Longman Cheshire, 1994): 3–18; Jean Oi, "Fiscal Reform and the Economic Foundation of Local State Corporatism in China," *World Politics* 45, no. 1 (October 1992): 99–126; Jean Oi, "Local Government Response to the Fiscal Austerity Program, 1988–1990," paper presented at University of California, Los Angeles, March 23, 1991; Jean C. Oi, "The Role of the Local State in China's Transitional Economy," in Andrew G. Walder, ed., *China's Transitional Economy* (New York: Oxford University Press, 1996): 170–87; Victor Nee, "Organizational Dynamics of Market Transition: Hybrid Forms, Property Rights, and Mixed Economy in China," *Administrative Science Quarterly* 37 (1992): 1–27; Victor Nee and Sijin Su, "Local Corporatism and Informal Privatization in China's Market Transition," paper presented at the mini-conference on "Chinese and Eastern European Transition: On Divergent Roads?" Center for Social Theory and Comparative History and Center for Chinese Studies, University of California, Los Angeles, June 7, 1993; and Louis Putterman, "The Role of Ownership and Property Rights in China's Economic Transformation," in Walder, ed., *China's Transitional Economy*: 85–102.

[127] Self-raised funds came from the profits of township and village enterprises. Extrabudgetary funds came from the profits of state-owned and collective enterprises, as well as various fees, local surtaxes, and income from fines. See Andrew Wedeman, "Budgets, Extra-budgets, and Small Treasuries: The Utility of Illegal Monies," *Journal of Contemporary China* 9, no. 25 (November 2000): 489–511.

Instead, these funds remained the property of the units that collected them and were subject only to local reallocation.[128] By partitioning public funds in this manner, the new fiscal system shielded a portion of local industrial profits – including those obtained from price-induced rents – from redistributive taxation through the unitary budget.

Because the profitability of local industry was in part a function of rents, this new fiscal arrangement, which is known in Chinese as "eating in separate kitchens," divided local governments between those whose economies were on the "right side" of the price scissors and those whose economies were on the "wrong side" of the price scissors.[129] Economies on the wrong side of the scissors were those that concentrated on the production of raw materials and agricultural commodities, which were exported to industrial centers, trans- formed into finished products, and sold at inflated prices. These economies thus exported rents to local economies located on the right side of the price scissors. Local governments in these areas were able to reap the fiscal benefits of rents by siphoning off a share of the profits of local industries. Fiscal partitioning, meanwhile, reduced the backward redistribution of rents from economies on the right side of the scissors to those on the wrong side. As a result, policy changes in the early 1980s created a situation in which local governments on the right side of the scissors continued to "enjoy happiness" at the expense of those on the wrong side of the scissors, who were left to "eat bitterness."

Although the decision to leave rents in place was clearly one of the most im- portant factors, the existence of rents was hardly sufficient. As Wu Jiangi points out, it was the combination of fiscal reform in a system of distorted prices that led to interregional and intergovernmental conflicts over the apportionment of rents.[130] For serious interregional conflict and local protectionism to develop, a whole series of other factors had to exist. Local governments had to have a

---

[128] The bulk of extrabudgetary funds nominally belonged to state-owned enterprises while local governments actually controlled only a relatively small percentage of these funds. Local govern- ments, however, frequently dictated how enterprise funds were spent or illegally expropriated their funds.

[129] Li Youpeng, "*Diqu fengsuo de xianzhuang ji queding wenti de jianyi*" (The current status of regional blockades and recommendations for their resolution), *Jingji Gongzuozhe Xuexi Ziliao*, no. 56 (1990): 14–23 and Shen Liren and Dai Yuanchen, "*Woguo 'zhuhou jingji' de xingcheng ji qi biduan he genyuan*" (The origins and negative consequences of China's 'feudal economies'), *Jingji Yanjiu*, no. 3 (1990): 12–19 and 67.

[130] Wu Jianqi, "*Lun 'tiao-tiao kuai-kuai': chansheng, houguo, zhili*" (A discussion of the emer- gence, consequences, and control of vertical and horizontal divisions), *Caijing Lilun Yu Shijian*, no. 2 (1991): 1–6. A selection of Chinese analyses on the origins of local protectionism have been translated and are available in Andrew H. Wedeman, ed., "Regional Protectionism," *Chinese Economic Studies* 26, no. 5 (Fall 1993).

vested interest in ensuring that rents were not exported and this interest had to be sufficiently strong to motivate them to adopt policies that placed them in direct violation of central regulations that mandated that rents belong to the center. Local governments had to have sufficient economic autonomy not only to ban exports of undervalued raw materials but also to invest in forward-processing and import-substitution industries. Established and potential consumers of undervalued raw materials had to have incentives to seek rent-producing raw materials aggressively, even when local governments in raw material–producing regions sought to block their export. And, perhaps most important, the center had to lack the ability to command obedience from all localities. If the center had been omnipotent, its power would have prevented local rent seeking and held fixed prices in place. But the center was not omnipotent and it could not prevent local rent seeking. And because it could not prevent local rent seeking, as I argue in Chapter 3, it could not prevent rent seeking from forcing a shift from fixed prices back toward market-clearing levels.

CONCLUSION

In this chapter, I have proposed that rather than view local protectionism primarily as a sign that the Chinese state may be lurching toward fragmentation and collapse, we ought to view it as an intense and open conflict between the central government, local governments, and various nonstate actors for control of rents created by state manipulation of prices. I have argued that the conflict grew directly out of a series of policy changes that loosened the controls on interregional economic interaction that allowed for the creation of new markets, that linked the interests of local governments more tightly to the local tax base, and that bestowed greater economic autonomy on these same local governments. I have also argued that the reformers' decision not to decontrol prices over key commodities left a series of rents in place. The result was a multifaceted conflict as local governments and others fought for control of these rents.

To a large extent, the basic argument that I advance is not necessarily controversial. Economists such as Watson, Findlay, Forster, Kumar, and so forth, also argue that local protectionism evolved out of the failure to rationalize prices and was characterized by intense and open rent seeking.[131] I, however, assert

---

[131] Watson and Findlay, "The 'Wool War' in China"; Forster, "China's Tea War"; Zhang, Lu, Sun, Findlay, and Watson, "The 'Wool War' and the 'Cotton Chaos': Fibre Marketing in China"; Watson, Findlay, and Du, "Who Won the 'Wool War'?"; Kumar, "China's Reform, Internal Trade and Marketing"; and Kumar, "Economic Reform and the Internal Division of Labour in China."

that because the center could neither deter nor prevent other actors, including its own local agents, from competing for rents, local protectionism and rent seeking will drive prices up toward market-clearing levels. As prices rise, supply will increase while demand will decrease. Over time, the ultimate result of this process will be a market-based equilibrium and the elimination of skewed prices and the rents created by skewed prices. Local protectionism and rent seeking thus act as a form of price deregulation and reform, albeit a form that is characterized by a high degree of chaos and intense interregional conflict.

Unknown
"So many tolls"

3

Rent Seeking and Local Protectionism

IN Chapter 2, I asserted that given a non-omnipotent center, local rent seeking will drive prices to market-clearing levels, thus causing supply and demand to equilibrate, thereby setting the stage for a formal shift from a plan-based economy to a market-based economy. In making this claim, I do not assume that the center must be enfeebled. It need not and central government in China was not feeble. Fiscal and administrative decentralization notwithstanding, Beijing retained a relatively tight grip on the provinces.[1] Below the provincial level, however, a complex, multilayered hierarchy of dyadic principal-agent relationships and information asymmetries made it hard for the center to effectively monitor and control lower levels of the state structure. Even under the best of circumstances, therefore, Beijing's grip on the grassroots level is inherently uncertain.[2] This meant that a breakdown in central control was not a necessary precondition to unleash rent seeking.

The price system left in place by the decision to defer price reform in 1984 was vulnerable to rent seeking because it was not a stable, self-sustaining equilibrium. By inflating one set of prices while depressing other prices, the Chinese price system disequilibriated supply and demand, created gaps between fixed prices and market-clearing prices, and spawned a network of rents. In theory, "the state" creams off these rents and uses them to fund "forced draft industrialization." To capture these rents and to maintain prices at disequilibrium

---

[1] See Huang, *Inflation and Investment Controls in China*; Linda Li, *Centre and Province – China 1978–1993: Power as a Non-Zero-Sum* (New York: Oxford University Press, 1998); and Andrew Wedeman, "Agency and Fiscal Dependence in Central-Provincial Relations in China," *Journal of Contemporary China* 8, no. 20 (March 1999): 103–22.

[2] See Andrew Wedeman, "Incompetence, Noise, and Fear in Central-Local Relations in China," *Studies in Comparative International Development* 34 (2001): 59–83.

levels, however, "the state" must have a monopoly on rent seeking and must prevent rent seeking by other actors, including elements of the state institutions it creates to capture and monetize rents. If the "state" – or more precisely the "center" – cannot effectively control these institutions and its monopoly on rent seeking is broken, competitive rent seeking, manifest most visibly in the form of "local protectionism," will push prices toward a market equilibrium. A command economy based on distorted prices is thus inherently vulnerable to rent seeking and even seemingly minor reductions in central controls can lead to collapse – if effective central control is not quickly restored.

The vulnerability of a command economy to rent seeking can be illustrated by first examining the microeconomic consequences of the opening of a stylized "price scissors" and the structures needed to maintain prices at disequilibrium. By then analyzing the consequence of a removal of controls it is possible to delineate how rent seeking will drive a command economy toward market equilibrium. Once we have delineated the overall process by which the market will displace the plan, it is possible to further disaggregate the model and specify how localities located on the "wrong" side of the price scissors ought to respond to a loosening of control and how their actions will trigger the bidding wars that will drive prices to market-clearing levels. The resulting stylized model suggests that although local protectionism may have appeared chaotic there is actually a very clear inner "logic" governing the manner in which the anarchic local rent system moves a command economy toward the market.

SCISSORS AND RENTS

Despite their reputed ability to resist reform, simple economic analysis suggests that plan-based economies such as existed in China prior to reform are inherently unstable and can only be maintained under conditions of relatively tight central control. The structural instability of a command economy can be best illustrated by examining the consequences of opening a price scissors such as that advocated by Preobrazhensky in the 1920s. According to Preobrazhensky, by forcing agricultural prices down and forcing consumer prices up, the state could compensate for a lack of indigenous capital by inducing "forced savings" or "primitive socialist accumulation." Specifically, he argued that by depressing farm prices and inflating consumer prices the state could "buy cheap and sell dear" thereby "squeezing" surplus value out of agriculture and urban consumers. The state could then pump the bulk of surplus value into the heavy industrial

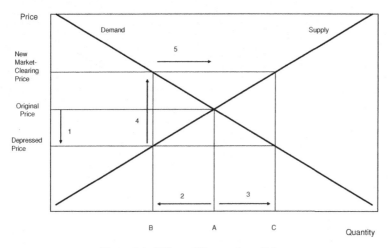

Figure 3-1. Effect of Depressing a Price.

sector and use it to fuel "forced draft industrialization."[3] Low agricultural prices, moreover, would reduce the cost of living for industrial workers, allowing the state to suppress urban wages, lower industrial costs, increase industrial profits, and thus further increase capital accumulation and create more capital for forced draft industrialization.

Although Prebrazhensky's price scissors might have allowed a regime to force down consumption and force up accumulation, distorting prices in such a manner was inherently problematic because it created a series of macroeconomic disequilibria. If producers were free to respond to price changes, opening up such a price scissors would cause supplies for undervalued commodities to contract while increasing demand for these commodities and supplies of over-valued commodities to expand while reducing demand for these commodities. As shown in Figure 3-1, forcing prices down (1) will cause a contraction (2) of supplies of undervalued commodities (from A to B) and an expansion (3) of demand (from A to C), thus creating a contrived shortage (equal to C-B). The contrived shortage will, in turn, drive up the market-clearing price (4), thus creating a gap between the market-clearing price and the "scissors price." Because a rent can be obtained by arbitraging between the scissors price and the new market-clearing price, opening a price scissors will thus encourage the formation of black markets. The existence of black markets and higher black-market

---

[3] Preobrazhensky, *The New Economics*: 110–12. Also see Alexander Erlich, *The Soviet Industrialization Debate, 1924–1928* (Cambridge, MA: Harvard University Press, 1967): 177–8; and Alec Nove, *An Economic History of the U.S.S.R.* (New York: Penguin Books, 1969): ch. 6.

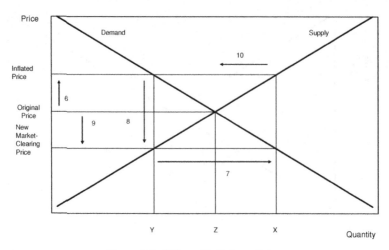

Figure 3-2. Effect of Inflating a Price.

prices will create incentives for producers to expand production (5) beyond the level set by the scissors price. The higher black-market price, however, also causes demand to contract. Falling demand and increasing supply will, of course, drive prices down and eventually prices, supply, and demand should converge back at the initial market equilibrium (A). In the process, the scissors price will become irrelevant as all goods will flow toward the black market and will be sold at black-market prices, not the prices fixed by the state.

As shown in Figure 3-2, in the case of prices that have been artificially inflated by the opening of a price scissors, if producers and consumers are free to respond to price changes, raising the fixed price above the initial market price (6) will increase (7) supply (from Z to X) but decrease (8) demand (from Z to Y), thereby creating a contrived glut. Oversupply will, in turn, drive the market-clearing price downward (9). Falling market-clearing prices will then cause demand to increase, while pulling supply down (10). Once again, the result will be a return to the original equilibrium and the state-inflated price will become obsolete (Z).

A stylized Preobrazhensky-type economy prevents a reversion to the initial market equilibrium by forcing up the production of undervalued commodities, limiting production of overvalued commodities, decoupling the financial interests of producers from prices, and eliminating markets. Forcing up production of undervalued commodities can be achieved by the imposition of delivery quotas. Limiting production of overvalued commodities can be achieved by barring the entry of new producers, imposing production quotas, and underinvesting in productive capacity. Financial interests can be decoupled from prices by taxing away enterprise revenues and substituting budgetary subsidies as the sole source of enterprise income. Markets can be eliminated by imposing planned allocation and distribution of commodities. The survival of a Preobrazhensky-type economy, in other words, requires a "command economy" because a price scissors creates a series of macroeconomic disequilibria that can only be sustained by tight controls over economic activity. Leninist regimes' emphasis on heavy industry further exacerbates the inherent disequilibrium of a Preobrazhensky-type economy by severely limited investment in overpriced consumer goods, thus adding a contrived shortage in this area to price-induced gaps between the supply and demand for undervalued raw materials. The typical communist economy is, therefore, characterized by a combination of administratively induced shortages that create numerous opportunities for rent seeking.

Absent tight control, a Preobrazhensky-type system will break down. If production quotas and controls are eliminated or relaxed, producers will curtail production of underpriced commodities while increasing production of overpriced commodities. If barriers to entry are lowered, the number of firms engaged in the production of overpriced commodities will increase. If investment is allocated on the basis of expected profitability, firms will cut the production of underpriced commodities and increase productive capacity in overpriced, undersupplied sectors. If their income is linked to profits, producers will cut back on production of underpriced commodities and shift over to the production of overpriced commodities. Falling supplies of underpriced commodities will, however, push up the price that consumers will pay to obtain scarce supplies and create a black market for these commodities. Higher black-market prices will create incentives for producers to reexpand production and to divert supplies on the black markets. Similarly, as production of overpriced commodities increases and high prices drive down demand, producers will have incentives to sell their goods on black markets at prices below the price set by the state and to cut back on production. Black-market prices will thus pull the system back toward its original equilibrium. A Preobrazhensky-type system will only survive, therefore, so long as its authors rigorously suppress black markets and force producers to produce at levels other than those specified by the laws of supply and demand. Absent such control, rent seeking will shift goods onto black markets where they will be traded at market-clearing prices, not prices set by the state. As the scope of black markets increases, "good prices," to paraphrase

Gresham's Law, will chase out "bad prices" and eventually render state-fixed prices irrelevant.

A sudden or total breakdown of control is not needed to trigger significant movement away from a plan-imposed disequilibrium. Even a partial relaxation or increased uncertainty about the center's ability and willingness to maintain control can initiate a shift away from the disequilibrium created by the price scissors and toward a market-based equilibrium, if we assume that the economy is populated by actors who prefer more to less. Such "rational" actors will presumably seek rents whenever the expected value of rent seeking (i.e., the gains from rent seeking times the probability of not getting caught) is greater than (a) the penalties inflicted on those caught engaged in illegal rent seeking and black marketeering and (b) the payoff for remaining a "loyal" agent.[4] Where rents are high and the gains from rent seeking significant, even a small change in the risk of getting punished may be sufficient to trigger rent seeking. Moreover, because the probability that any one violator getting caught and punished decreases as the number of violators increases, even a slight decrease in the odds of getting punished has the potential to cascade into a full-scale breakdown. Exactly where the "tipping points" below which the probability of getting punished must fall before limited rent seeking begins and beyond which wholesale rent seeking ensues will be a function of a variety of situational factors (magnitude of rents and punishments, the risk propensity of individual actors, etc.). But, given significant rents, we would expect some degree of rent seeking and black marketeering even under tightly controlled conditions and would further expect to see exponential increases in black marketeering as controls become looser.

Once controls have weakened sufficiently to induce rent seeking, the only way to prevent movement toward a market-based equilibrium is to reimpose tight control because the existence of parallel black markets will almost inexorably push prices back toward market-clearing levels. A limited retightening can slow down the decay or limit the size of black markets, but only a full restoration of control and the elimination of black markets can keep the system at a Preobrazhensky-type disequilibrium. Restoring control is likely to prove difficult, however, because the actors who have the most to gain from a breakdown in control are the "control institutions" themselves. In a

---

[4] For example, if rent seeking yields a payoff of $100 and the probability of getting caught is one in ten, the expected value of rent seeking will be $100 * 0.90 = $90. If those who get caught are fined $200, then the expected cost of rent seeking will be $200 * 0.10 = $20. Because the expected value of rent seeking is greater than the expected cost, an actor seeking to maximize her income would engage in rent seeking, assuming that the payoff for loyalty is less than $90.

stylized command economy, the "state" extracts rents from producers and consumers by controlling purchasing, production, and distribution. Rents, however, are only monetized when a finished product is sold to a consumer. Prior to that, rents derived from both the underpricing of inputs and overpricing of outputs exist only in theoretical terms. If the "state" relies on a series of separate institutions to procure, process, and distribute commodities, this means that its procurement and manufacturing "agents" actually pass along a "shadow rent" to its distribution agent, who monetizes the rent and then deposits the cash rent in the "state's" coffers controlled by some central authority or "principal."

As institutions of the state, each of these agents may ultimately obtain a share of the rents they generate and monetize. But each can obtain a greater share by hijacking the rents rather than passing them along. The distribution agent can hijack the monetized rents he collects by simply embezzling them. The manufacturing agent can hijack the rent either by selling directly to consumers and pocketing the rent or, in the case of undersupplied goods, by increasing production and selling on the black market. The procurement agent, meanwhile, can divert undervalued commodities to the black market, sell them at the market-clearing prices, and pocket the difference between the deflated procurement price and the shortage-inflated black-market price.

Even if an agent eschews rent seeking and remains loyal, he may find himself robbed of whatever share of the rent the center may have rebated to him in the past because other agents steal the rents they have passed along. Thus, for instance, if the procurement agent loyally forwards supplies of undervalued inputs to the manufacturing agent, she may end up with nothing because the manufacturing agent sells output on the black market and pockets the monetized rent or because the distribution agent embezzles the rent after he sells finished goods passed on to him by the manufacturing agent. Loyal agents may also find themselves blamed for thefts by other agents. A dishonest manufacturing agent who has diverted goods to the black market may accuse the procurement agent of providing him with insufficient supplies of necessary inputs or accuse the distribution agent of falsely underreporting deliveries. Under such uncertain conditions, agents may conclude that egoistic rent seeking is preferable to being left with the "sucker's payoff." A diminution of control can, in other words, trigger an implosive collapse as individual state institutions abandon their roles as agents of the state's rent-seeking system and become egoistic rent seekers.

In theory, all these "initial winners" have a vested interest in keeping prices at their Preobrazhensky disequilibrium and to maintain the system of rents spawned by the opening of the price scissors. Individually, however, each prefers to arrogate as much of the rent to his own coffers, even if this means engaging in black marketeering and hence undermining the viability of the system of fixed prices. Each also has an egoistic interest in tailoring production according to the dictates of black-market prices that are subject to the law of supply and demand rather than administrative fiat. Each thus prefers a restoration of controls that prevents rent seeking by others but allows for him to free ride. Thus, for instance, the distribution agent would like to seek the principal bringing the procurement and manufacturing agents to heel but does not want to see a restoration of controls that would prevent him from embezzling all or part of the rents he monetizes "on behalf" of the principal. And none of the agents would like to see the principal eliminate black markets because that would deprive them of illicit means to monetize the rents that pass through their hands. Rather than aid and abet the principal's efforts to restore control and prevent black marketeering from closing the price scissors, therefore, the principal's agents are more likely to do what they can to frustrate such efforts and prevent a restoration of control. Because the ability of agents to resist the reimposition of tight controls will be a function of "local autonomy," it follows that the more authority has been defused through the state hierarchy the more intense resistance will be and, in the extreme case where decentralization has produced institutional gridlock, attempts to "turn the clock back" are likely to fail.

While supply and demand disequilibria render a Preobrazhensky-type economy vulnerable to implosion, the emphasis on heavy industrial development common in Leninist systems implies that the implosion will begin with a battle for control over undervalued commodities and then evolve into a fight for control of markets for overvalued outputs. Sectors characterized by depressed prices suffer from the greatest contradictions because depressed prices create downward pressure on supply while concurrently inflating demand. This combination necessitates the imposition of production quotas to push up supply and rationing to allocated insufficient supplies. Given a relaxation of controls over production without concurrent price decontrols, production of these commodities is likely to fall, thus exacerbating shortages. As supply contracts and demand outstrips supply, a fierce struggle for control over existing supplies is likely to erupt as consumers scramble to meet their needs and middlemen scramble to cash in on the rents that can be obtained from controlling increasingly scarce supplies. Shortages and a scramble for control over declining supplies will increase the market-clearing price, and hence the price consumers are willing to pay on the black market to obtain the scarce good. As the market-clearing prices diverge farther from the state-fixed prices, the rents that can be obtained from arbitraging between the fixed and black-market price will increase and thus the gains from rent seeking will increase. So long as controls remain loose, rising black-market prices should cause supply to re-expand while also reducing demand and eventually supply and demand should come into equilibrium. Once rents have dissipated, excessive competition for these commodities should tamper off and "normal" markets should emerge and the fixed price, even assuming the state continues to set prices, will be rendered irrelevant.

Underinvestment in consumer goods production, meanwhile, will create a lag between a relaxation of controls and eruption of competitive rent seeking. If controls have been reduced, existing producers will presumably expand output as quickly as possible and begin investing in new productive capacity. Rents will also lure in new entrants. Because it takes time to build new productive capacity, however, output will increase incrementally. In addition, underin-vestment in these sectors prior to reform means that overpriced commodities are generally undersupplied in a command economy, with the result that their market-clearing price will actually be greater than the "inflated" fixed price. At the outset, therefore, producers will face vast unmet demand and doubly inflated prices. Such conditions are likely to trigger an investment fever and excessive construction of new productive capacity. So long as supply lags behind demand and sellers' markets prevail, however, expanding production by one supplier will not infringe on the interests of other suppliers. On the contrary, the emergence of black markets for these goods will benefit existing producers because this will allow them to sell products at the doubly inflated black-market price and capture additional rents. Eventually, however, a rent-driven investment boom will cause productive capacity to outstrip demand and markets will become saturated. The resulting shift from sellers' markets to buyers' markets will put downward pressure on market-clearing prices, cause inventories to pile up, cut rents, and trigger increasingly fierce rivalry for market control. *Under such conditions*, "begger-thy-neighbor" import protectionism becomes more likely as rival producers seek to monopolize segments of the market. Although rent seeking will tend to drive markets toward saturation, import protectionism is likely to occur anytime demand falls below supply and hence may be expected during economic downturns.

To summarize, an economy based on skewed prices is inherently unstable and can be maintained only if some central authority imposes a system of tight control and eliminates alternative markets, including the black market. Absent controls, the rents created by the forced divergence between fixed prices and market-clearing prices will interact with price scissors–induced gaps between supply and demand to push prices, supply, and demand back toward their original market equilibrium. Because the very institutions created by the central authority to monetize rents are immediate beneficiaries of a loosening of controls that create new space for them to divert rents away from central coffers and into their own, a relaxation of control will likely trigger implosive rent seeking by state institutions. Such rent seeking will manifest itself first in the imposition of export controls over undervalued and undersupplied commodities and in the rapid expansion of productive capacity of overpriced commodities, many of which are likely to have been undersupplied due to regime policies stressing investment in heavy industry at the expense of overpriced consumer goods. The first phase of the breakdown of a system based on skewed prices is, therefore, likely to be most dominated by "export protectionism." Rising production of overpriced commodities will, however, ultimately saturate markets and when sellers' markets give way to buyers' markets "import protectionism" will likely increase rapidly as local governments try to shield local producers from outside competition. Although both export and import protectionism may appear to be "anti-market forces," in actuality both are manifestations of rent-seeking behavior that is not only responsive to market forces, albeit black-market forces, but also operates to dissipate rents and reequilibrate supply and demand. Rent seeking and local protectionism, in other words, serve to break down a weakened Preobrazhensky-type economy.

RENTS AND WARS

Although deductive analysis suggests that rent seeking by state institutions will undermine and eventually close an administratively induced price scissors if central control falters, the process by which rent seeking closes the price scissors is likely to be characterized by intense and chaotic conflicts among state institutions. In the Chinese case, once administrative and fiscal decentralization loosened controls, rival rent seekers quickly found themselves locked into a series of "resource wars" as local governments fought each other for control of undervalued raw materials. On the surface, these wars appeared as confusing, anarchic battles between petty "economic warlords." Analysis of the environment created by partial reform, however, reveals a logic to both the structure of these "wars" and their evolution. In particular, it becomes evident that these resource wars were in fact complex bidding wars involving a combination of local industrialization and black marketeering.

In a stylized command economy, the center generally relies on a series of agents to capture and monetize rents. In the case of agricultural commodities, for example, one agent is charged with procuring inputs at deflated prices from farmers. The procurement agent forwards supplies to a second agent, who converts them into finished products and then forwards them on to wholesalers and retailers who sell the finished goods to consumers at inflated prices. Profits and rents are remitted to the central treasury and then redistributed by the central authority, with a share siphoned off for investment and central administrative costs, and other shares possibly remitted back to the center's various agents in the form of budget subsidies. If the center exercises tight control and redistributes shares of its rents "equitably," rent seeking by its agents should be limited to petty theft and pilferage, in part because tight controls deter rent seeking by the agents and in part because the agents receive a share of the rents they procure and monetize on behalf of the center. In a perfect command economy, therefore, the center's agents are presumably indifferent to whether they are tasked with procuring, processing, or marketing because it does not matter whether they are on the "wrong side" of the prices scissors (the side characterized by depressed prices) or the "right side" of the price scissors (the side characterized by inflated prices).

Fiscal decentralization will, however, radically alter this situation by dividing localities into two distinct groups. Although the center may continue to redistribute rents among its agents, localities on the wrong side of the price scissors will find themselves "exporting" rents to localities on the right side of the price scissors because the income from the monetized rents will accrue to enterprises engaged in the processing and sale of overvalued outputs. Local governments in manufacturing regions will thus draw their revenues from a tax base whose profits have been inflated by the price scissors while those in raw material–producing regions must draw their revenues from a tax base that has been deflated by the price scissors. Moreover, raw material–producing localities are not only denied direct access to inflated profits, they "export" a share of the monetized rent when they import finished products from manufacturing regions.

Assuming that local governments seek to maximize their revenues, local governments in raw material–producing regions should seek to reduce the outflow of rents. Rather than continue to "fertilize others' fields" with rents, these governments could localize the monetization for rents by building forward-processing industries (FPI) that transform locally produced raw materials into finished, and hence rent-producing, products.[5] Supporting these "infant

---

[5] Feng Lianggeng, "*Dui nong fuchanpin shougou 'dazhan' de sikao*" (Reflections on agricultural sideline products purchasing wars), *Shangye Jingji Luntan*, no. 2 (1989): 18–20; Sun Ziduo, "*Nongchan maoyi dazhan xingcheng de yuanyin, weihai he queding tujing*" (The emergence of

industries," however, means that local governments have to block the export of undervalued raw materials and divert them into local processors.[6] Gaps between the depressed procurement price and the market-clearing price, however, create a second avenue: black marketeering. Rather then passively shipping undervalued raw materials to consumers in other localities, local government in raw material–producing regions could divert supplies away from the state allocation system and sell them instead to buyers willing to pay the market-clearing price, which will be inflated above the fixed price by both price-inflated demand and by shortages induced by price deflation. Black-market prices will be further inflated by rising demand by consumers ineligible for "in-plan allocations" of input.

Prior to reform, local governments in raw material–producing regions had limited opportunities to monetize rents locally because the bulk of investment funds were centrally controlled and they had only limited authority to set up local enterprises. Administrative decentralization and the expansion of the collective sector, however, gave them greater leeway and hence the opportunity to begin setting up local processing and "in-plan" manufacturing plants. These localities were, of course, supposed to continue to supply existing manufacturers with undervalued raw materials. In practice, however, weaknesses in the central supervisory system made it possible to divert supplies to local plants or onto black markets without incurring excessive risks.

Such opportunities exist because, as noted previously, the structure of the Chinese state militates against effective central control. In theory, the Chinese state is a unitary structure in which the center is the "principal" and local governments serve as its "agents." Like any principal, the center faces monitoring problems and hence its ability to control and police its agents is inherently imperfect. The Chinese state is not, however, a simple, two-level principal-agent system, but rather consists of a hierarchy of governments that stretches down from the center to the province, then through prefectures, municipalities, and counties to the township and village levels, below which are the actual procurement agencies, manufacturing enterprises, and wholesalers engaged in the monetization of rents.[7] In other words, if we think of the center as the

---

agricultural trade wars, their negative consequences, and means of solution), *Zhongguo Nongcun Jingji*, no. 11 (1988): 26–30; and Li Wenyi "*Lun woguo shichang fazhan de difang baohu zhuyi wenti*" (A discussion of the problem of local protectionism in the development of domestic markets), *Nanfang Jingji*, no. 2, pt. 1 (1990): 38–40 and no. 3, pt. 2 (1990): 5.

[6] Li Shihua, "*Difang baohu zhuyi pouxi*" (An analysis of local protectionism), *Jingji Lilun yu Jingji Guanli*, no. 3 (1991): 67–9.

[7] See Wedeman, "Incompetence, Noise, and Fear in Central-Local Relations in China": 59–83.

principal, the province becomes a first-order agent, the prefecture-municipality a second-order agent, the county-urban district a third-order agent, and the township a fourth-order agent. Grassroots organizations such as the village committee, neighborhood committee, and the economic enterprise are thus fifth-order agents of the center.[8] Rather than a single principal-agent information asymmetry, the Chinese state structures contain multiple asymmetries, with the result that the quality of information reaching the center can deteriorate quickly even given relatively low levels of "noise."[9] As the quality of information about the behavior of her agents deteriorates, it naturally becomes increasingly hard for the principal to discern whether her agents are correctly performing the task assigned them and to determine why "mistakes" were made when things appear to have gone wrong. Mistakes and misdeeds may, therefore, go undetected, mistakes may be incorrectly ascribed to misdeeds, and misdeeds may be erroneously ascribed to mistakes simply because the principal receives inaccurate information.

Information asymmetries are not, however, the only barrier to effective central control of grassroots agents. The principal also faces a multilayered adverse selection problem. Under the terms of the "one level down" *nomenklatura* system in operation during the 1980s, the center had oversight over a relatively small number of senior appointments at the provincial level.[10] Below the provincial

---

[8] Although grassroots organizations such as the village and neighborhood committee function as agents of the unitary state, they are legally nonstate mass organizations, not state institutions, and are not, therefore, staffed with state cadres.

[9] A multilevel principal-agent structure with information asymmetries degrades information in a manner similar to the way that messages become distorted as they are whispered from child to child in the game of "telephone." Thus, in a five-level principal-agent hierarchy with one principal and five agents, for example, even if the information passed from each agent to the next level is 95 percent accurate, the probability that the information received by the principal is accurate will be only 77 percent. If the quality of information falls to 87 percent at each level, the odds that the center receives accurate information falls to just over fifty-fifty.

[10] According to the system adopted in 1984, Central Committee approval was required for appointments to the positions of provincial party committee secretary, deputy secretary, and members of the committee's standing committee; the head and deputy heads of provincial advisory committees; the secretary and deputy secretaries of provincial discipline inspection commissions; provincial governor and deputy governors; the mayors and deputy mayors of Beijing, Tianjin, and Shanghai; the chairman and deputy chairmen of autonomous regions; advisers to these senior officials; the chairmen and deputy chairmen of the provincial people's congresses and the provincial political consultative conferences; the presidents of provincial high courts; and the heads of the provincial procuratorates. John P Burns, "China's *Nomenklatura* System," *Problems of Communism* 36, no. 5 (September–October 1987): 45.

level, the province approved senior appointments at the prefectural and municipal levels, which approved appointments at the county level, which in turn made appointments at the township and village levels. Rather than pick its grassroots agents, the center thus actually only picked its first-order agents (senior provincial cadres). The first-order agents then selected the center's second-order agents (senior prefectural and municipal cadres), who in turn selected its third-order agents (senior county-level cadres), who then selected the center's fourth-order agents (senior township and village cadres), who ultimately selected fifth-order agents (senior enterprise managers, village and neighborhood cadres). Because hidden information prevents a principal, in the case of the Chinese state an "agent-cum-principal," from being sure that the agent she selects is reliable and competent, the problem of adverse selection is thus replicated each time an agent picks a subagent. Thus, just as even low levels of noise can significantly degrade the quality of information reaching the principal from a fifth-order agent, even low incidences of adverse selection can multiply into a serious problem in a complex, multilayered hierarchy, with the result that the principal cannot be sure whether the agents selected by her agent's agents, and so forth, are in fact competent and reliable.

The problem of adverse selection is exacerbated by the "cadre responsibility system." In theory, even though the center does not pick its subprovincial agents, each agent is held responsible for the actions of his subagents and thus a chain of transitive responsibility links the grassroots to the center. The cadre responsibility system, however, tends to transform the transitive chain of responsibility into an intransitive series of dyadic relationships. Under the terms of this system, cadres' compensation and career prospects are contractually linked to the fulfillment of performance targets set by their direct superiors.[11] This tends to make cadres "hyper-responsive" to the demands of their direct superiors, but indifferent to demands from higher levels when the demands of higher levels conflict with those of their direct superiors. Agents, in other words, owe loyalty to their direct superiors but not necessarily to their superior's superiors. At the same time, however, the transitive chain of responsibility makes cadres liable for the misdeeds and mistakes of their subordinates. Thus, rather than relay information on the mistakes and misdeeds of their subordinates, cadres have incentives to cover up shortcomings and provide as little information as possible to their superiors about the activities of their subordinates and to "contaminate" what information they do pass upward with "dirt" and "noise."

---

[11] Li Lianjiang and Kevin J. O'Brien, "Selective Policy Implementation in Rural China," *Comparative Politics* 31, no. 2 (January 1999): 167–86.

The "natural decay" of information quality created by the existence of multiple information asymmetries, the multilayered adverse selection problem, and the incentives for subordinates to render loyalty only to their direct superiors and for superiors to cover up for their subordinates thus create complex monitoring and control problems for the center. To a certain extent, the presence of multiple parallel monitoring systems within the Chinese state compensates for these problems by allowing the center to use one set of agents to monitor another.[12] Each monitoring system is, however, subject to the same principal-agent problems and hence while dense monitoring may increase the reliability of information reaching the center, even under optimal conditions the center will never have certain control over the grassroots level.

Underlying problems of supervisory slack that create opportunities for agents to engage in "strategic disobedience" are further complicated by the contradictory incentives facing cadres, particularly those in underdeveloped regions. Although cadre contracts frequently specify a variety of performance targets, local leaders are frequently judged primarily on their success in increasing local industrialization and tax collection. This creates cross-pressures on cadres in raw material–producing regions. On the one hand, they are supposed to act as agents of central monopsonies. In this role, they are supposed to procure local commodities at depressed prices and forward them to other localities, along with the rents embedded in them. On the other hand, they are also supposed to promote local industry and expand the local tax base, which they can do by promoting local processing and manufacturing based on undervalued local raw materials and monetizing rents locally. A cadre who opts to "loyally" fulfil his role as a procurement agent may thus find himself criticized or even penalized for not fulfilling his responsibility to increase local industry and tax collections. The choice of which path to follow is complicated by the uncertainties of weather, pests, and the possibility that local farmers will sell their produce to other buyers or withhold stocks in hope that prices will rise. A "loyal" procurement agent may thus discover that he simply cannot meet the delivery quota. Given these conflicting demands, a career and income maximizing (but risk averse) cadre might quite rationally choose to build new local industries and channel locally produced inputs into these factories rather than fulfilling his obligations to the central monopsony even absent a desire to illicitly pursue rents.

---

[12] Systems operating parallel with the state apparatus include the party committee system, the party discipline inspection system, the state supervisory system, the judicial procuratoral system, and the ministerial bureau system.

Supervisory slack, uncertainty, and contradictory incentives thus combined to make local rent seeking a viable alternative, particularly for those local governments left fiscally disadvantaged by the decision to eschew price reform. As noted previously, one option open to these local governments was to set up new processing industries and to monetize rents locally rather than allow other localities to do so. Local governments in raw material–producing regions can, however, also capture rents by diverting commodities onto the black market. Black marketeering has several advantages over local industrialization. First, the short-term profits from black marketeering are likely to be greater than those from local industrialization due to the investment costs and lags associated with building up new local industries. Second, whereas local industrialization will tend to increase local governments' revenues, some percentage of which may end up in cadres' pockets in the form of bonuses, the bulk of monies earned from black marketeering will presumably likely flow directly into cadres' pockets.[13] Black marketeering is, however, also a more risky strategy than local industrialization. Local industrialization provides a degree of "cover" because local governments can first claim that local factories consume "surplus" commodities and then claim, once the factories have been built, that local factories should have priority over those in other localities. Black marketeering, on the other hand, is essentially a crime and is thus likely to be rather more difficult for cadres to "explain away" if they get caught, which is a possibility, but not a certainty, given the structurally induced supervisory slack characteristic of the Chinese state apparatus.

Whether cadres in a particular raw material–producing locality opt for local industrialization or black marketing as means to capture rents will depend on (a) the availability of local investment capital, (b) their time horizons, and (c) their propensity for risk. Which strategy cadres in a particular raw material–producing locality opt for is less important for the purposes of our analysis than the underlying fact that the levels of supervisory slack within the Chinese state apparatus are sufficiently high so that we can expect that a loosening of controls will encourage local governments located on the wrong side of the price scissors to abrogate their roles as agents, usurp the authority given them as agents of central procurement monopsonies in an effort to prevent the outflow of rents, and try to monetize these rents either by setting up

---

[13] For a discussion of the variable utility of different types of licit and illicit income see Wedeman, "Budgets, Extra-budgets, and Small Treasuries."

local processing plants or by selling undervalued commodities on the black market.[14]

Increased rent seeking by local governments located on the wrong side of the price scissors will have a direct and immediate impact on the fiscal interests not only of the center whose rents they encroach on, but also on localities situated on the right side of the price scissors. Regardless of whether they seek to capture rents through local industrialization or black marketeering, local governments in raw material–producing regions are likely to either embargo all exports of undervalued raw materials or severely restrict planned deliveries to factories in other localities. Declining deliveries will deprive factories in "manufacturing" regions of needed inputs, forcing them to either cut back or cease production. Falling production will cut profits, reduce local tax revenues, and thus hurt local governments. Moreover, an end to deliveries of undervalued inputs will rob these localities of the rents that they had previously imported from raw material–producing areas and hence the opportunity to engage in illicit rent seeking themselves.

Local governments in manufacturing regions have several options when faced with such a loss of inputs. They can passively acquiesce, in which case the loss of needed inputs will cause a drop in local revenues. They can turn to the black market and buy needed inputs from their erstwhile suppliers at higher prices. Paying more for inputs will, of course, cut profits but will prevent local factories from "starving to death" for want of inputs. Or they can counterattack. Herein it is critical to remember that local governments in raw material–producing regions are not the actual producers of most commodities. On the contrary, they

---

[14] It can be demonstrated using formal modeling, however, that a "mix" of local industrialization and black marketeering is the "optimal strategy." A mix of local industrialization and black marketeering has several advantages. First, local industrialization provides "cover" for the diversion of undervalued commodities onto the black market because cadres can claim that stocks sold on the black market were consumed by local factories. Second, profits from black marketeering can be used to fund local industrialization. Third, a mix minimizes the risks associated with speculative black marketeering by providing a means of disposing of stocks if they cannot be sold on the black market. Fourth, whereas the gains from black marketeering will disappear after bidding wars have dissipated rents, local industries are likely to continue to earn ordinary profits and generate tax revenues even after prices have been forced to market-clearing levels. Although "optimal" according to mathematical calculation, there is no certainty that all localities will pursue such a strategy. Some may lack the capital needed to set up new local industries, some may care only about maximizing short-term income and opt for black marketeering alone, some may reject black marketeering and concentrate on building up local industries alone, and some may eschew rent seeking altogether and remain loyal servants of the center. What the formal model suggests, however, is that the probability that many will pursue rents using a mixed strategy of local industrialization and black marketeering is high.

act as local monopsonists, buying commodities from, in most cases, farmers at depressed prices. Rents from underpricing, in other words, are extracted not from the locality in which the commodities are produced but rather from the farmers whom the state forces to accept depressed prices. Because rent-seeking local governments can maximize rents either by maximizing the spread between what they pay local farmers and the black-market price or between costs and output prices, these governments have strong incentives to ruthlessly suppress prices even after they abrogate their roles as central agents. In fact, they have incentives to push prices down below those fixed by the center because they now stand to capture the entire rent rather than exporting it and sharing in only a fraction of the total. Given a spread between the "farm gate" price offered by local monopsonies and the black-market price, consumers denied supplies or asked to pay higher prices can attempt to bypass local export barriers and buy directly from the farmers, offering them prices higher than the local monopsony price but lower than the prevailing black-market price. Private middlemen and speculators can also attempt to cash in by arbitraging between differences between local monopsony prices and black-market prices.

Assuming that the local export barriers are not leakproof and that farmers opt to sell their produce to the highest bidder, attempts by local governments in raw material–producing areas to embargo exports are thus likely to trigger bidding wars between local monopsonies and outside buyers.[15] The lure of profits from arbitraging between depressed monopsony prices and black-market prices is also likely to trigger competition between purchasing units in different raw material–producing regions for control of rent-producing commodities. Export protectionism is thus likely to degenerate into complex, multisided resource wars.

As a resource war intensifies, even localities that may have eschewed rent seeking will find themselves forced to throw up export barriers because the lure of higher prices in other areas will drain off local supplies, making it difficult for "loyal" localities to meet their procurement and delivery quotas or forcing them to raise prices above those set by the center. As export barriers proliferate, it will become increasingly difficult for the center to differentiate between "legitimate barriers" meant to halt the flow of commodities onto the black market and "illegitimate barriers" set up by rent-seeking local governments. As it

---

[15] Selling to the highest bidder entails risks for the farmer because state regulations stipulate that certain commodities must be sold to the state monopsony. There is, however, a considerable body of evidence showing that farmers are willing to run risks to obtain higher prices for their produce. See Oi, *State and Peasant in Contemporary China*; Zhao, *How the Farmers Changed China*; and Kelliher, *Peasant Power in China*.

becomes more difficult for the center to differentiate between legitimate and illegitimate export barriers and hence between loyal and disloyal agents, not only will the probability that disloyalty will be detected and disloyal agents punished diminish, the probability that loyal agents may find themselves accused of disobedience will increase. Under such circumstances, rent seeking and local protectionism are likely to proliferate. Disintegration may, therefore, begin when a few local governments usurp their authority and then quickly cascade into more widespread rent seeking as bidding wars engulf entire regions where particular undervalued commodities are produced.

Because these resource wars will be linked to the harvest, they are likely to erupt rapidly and quickly spread across regions. Thousands of purchase stations spread across large areas, potentially millions of farmers, and "armies" of buyers are thus likely to become involved, creating a level of confusion that will make it extremely difficult for the center to sort out who is ultimately responsible. Monitoring systems are apt to become overwhelmed by contradictory signals as those involved point fingers at each other, at "unknown" and often "long gone" outsiders, issue false or misleading claims about local conditions and production, and destroy, hide, and falsify evidence of their own culpability. The center thus may not figure out what is going on until after the conflict has subsided. Moreover, the center is likely to confront conflicts over multiple commodities and thus be faced with a constantly shifting battlefield as one conflict ebbs and another explodes. Under these sorts of conditions, imperfect controls are apt to crumble and, as they break down, the level of conflict is likely to increase further as the disincentives for illicit rent seeking fall.

In a frictionless economic world, competition between rival bidders would quickly push prices to market-clearing levels and hence render fixed prices irrelevant. In the real world, movement toward market-clearing prices is apt to be uneven. To begin with, the continued existence of local monopsonies and barriers to the free flow of commodities will impede price movements and tend to keep local prices at below market-clearing levels. Moreover, the nature of agricultural production ensures that the process will not occur quickly because cropping decisions necessarily lag behind price changes. Given the initial condition of shortage and demand that has been inflated both by the artificially low price assigned to a commodity and rent seeking–induced expansion of industries based on it, the preliminary rounds of a bidding war will push prices rapidly upward. As prices appear to skyrocket, farmers will have incentives to significantly increase production in the following cropping cycle. A rapid increase in prices will, however, push demand down, with the result that supply may exceed demand in the next round of the bidding war, leading to falling prices. Falling prices will, in turn, signal farmers that they should cut back production in the next cropping cycle while at the same time stimulating demand. The lag between planting and harvest, combined with the natural uncertainties created by weather and pests, are also conducive to rampant speculation as producers and buyers bet on future market conditions. Market conditions are thus likely to be very unstable as the old system of fixed prices gives way to a market-based system of prices.

To summarize, a weakening of central controls over a commodity whose price has been artificially depressed is likely to first produce export protectionism as local governments in raw material–producing areas seek to capture rents by either diverting stocks into newly constructed local processing plants or on the black markets. Export protectionism is, however, likely to trigger bidding wars as outside buyers, including both established "in-plan" consumers, new "out-of-plan" consumers, and private profiteers seek to evade export restrictions and purchase stocks directly from producers. Given the inability of supply to respond instantaneously to changes in demand, prices are likely to bid up amid high levels of speculation. Rapidly rising prices should, in turn, trigger a surge in production while also pushing demand downward. As the intensity and complexity of conflict increases, central controls are apt to break down, giving rise to ever-greater levels of rent seeking. Assuming that no single actor gains monopoly control over the emerging market, over time rising production and weakening demand should move the market toward a stable equilibrium at which point rents will have dissipated.

The caveat "assuming that no actor gains monopoly control" is critical because if any actor or coalition of actors can halt competitive rent seeking, they can once again force prices downward and restore the old monopsony system. Individually, all of the contenders in the battle for rents have a vested interest in preventing purchase prices from rising and suffer when competition bids black-market prices higher because rising purchase prices cut rents. All would thus be better off if monopsony prices could be maintained. The "initial winners" from a weakening of central authority have incentives to try to maintain the structures that allow the state to extract rents even as they steal rents from the center. Yet, so long as demand is greater than supply and the black-market price diverges from the fixed price, competition for scarce supplies and rent seeking will push purchase prices upward. The only way for the initial winners to prevent competition from pushing up purchase prices is to eliminate black markets and tightly control access to scarce commodities. The initial winners, in other words, face the same problem that the center faces and yet they lack the nominal authority to ban rent seeking by others and the power to enforce such a ban. Efforts to reach cooperative agreements to halt internecine rent seeking are thus likely to fall victim to free riding and cheating. Efforts to restore central authority, on the other hand, are likely to run up against considerable resistance as the initial winners seek to prevent the center from reclaiming rents they have usurped. As a result, even though rent-seeking local governments would prefer that purchase prices remain at the level fixed by the state, they lack the ability to stifle the competition that drives them upward and dissipates the rents they seek.

CONCLUSION

As I have argued in this chapter, maintaining prices at a disequilibrium that allows a state to extract rents from producers and consumers requires the imposition of a system of tight controls and the elimination of markets, including black markets. For such a system, even "partial decontrol" can prove fatal because if the institutions created to control prices and monetize rents on behalf of the state are free to pursue rents themselves, the result will be uncontrolled battles for undervalued commodities in which rival rent seekers will find themselves bidding prices up to market-clearing levels and thereby dissipating rents. Given the undersupply of overpriced commodities, a loosening of controls will induce a rapid expansion of productive capacity and ultimately the saturation of markets and the forcing downward of prices to market-clearing levels.

In light of the theoretic vulnerability of a system of distorted prices to partial decontrol, the attempt by Deng and his reformist allies to partially reform the Chinese economy can be interpreted as setting the stage for an unintended implosion. They loosened control over agriculture; sanctioned the reformation of markets; weakened restrictions on movement; authorized the expansion of a largely uncontrolled, locally owned collective industrial sector; and linked the financial interests of local governments to the profitability of the local economy. Yet, at the same time, they also tried to maintain a system of fixed prices that stripped rents out of raw material–producing regions, thus depriving local governments in these areas of potential revenues. The center, in effect, loosened its grip on both the producers from whence rents were extracted and also the agents whom it charged with extracting rents on its behalf. The center, in other words, expected producers and its agents to continue to loyally abide by the terms of a system that extracted rents from the former and allowed them to slip through the hands of the latter, even though its ability to control both was lessened. Moreover, partial reform created a situation in which rendering loyal service hurt local governments in raw material–producing areas financially and had potentially negative consequences for individual cadres whose compensation and career prospects were linked by contract to their ability to increase local industry and raise local revenues. Partial reform, in other words, not only gave these local governments new opportunities to engage in illicit rent seeking, it also gave them motives to usurp the power granted to them as agents of the center's rent exaction system.

In so doing, the center struck at the system's weakest link. The extraction and monetization of rents required the contribution of three sets of agents acting on the center's behalf. Local procurement agencies were tasked with buying commodities from producers at prices that created "shadow rents." Commodities were then handed over to manufacturing agents, who were expected to convert them into finished products and then hand these goods over to wholesale agencies and retailers, who would then sell them at inflated prices to consumers, thereby monetizing the shadow rent, and then deposit the cash rent into central coffers. Rents thus passed through the hands of a series of agents, none of whom had a formal right to the rent. The system is, of course, vulnerable to theft as each agent has incentives to steal all or part of the rents that pass through their hands. Theft by the distribution agent, however, would be simple embezzlement and hence would have little effect on prices. Attempts to monetize the rent by the manufacturing agent by selling finished products on the black market might force a change in prices if he increased production beyond the level set by the state and sought to take advantage of shortage-inflated black-market prices, thus eventually forcing changes in output prices without necessarily forcing changes in input prices.

Rent seeking by the procurement agent, on the other hand, had immediate and profound effects on input prices. To monetize the rent, the procurement agent had to either set up local factories and convert the undervalued commodity into a sellable finished product or divert stocks of the commodity onto the black market where it could be sold at black-market prices, thus allowing the procurement agent to pocket the difference between the depressed fixed procurement price and the inflated black-market price. Either way, rent seeking by the procurement agents not only deprived the center of its rents, it also deprived the manufacturing agent of necessary inputs and the distribution agent of products to sell, thereby throwing the entire production system out of kilter. Moreover, rent seeking by the procurement agent robbed both the manufacturing and distribution agent of the opportunity to engage in opportunistic rent seeking. Rather than sit by and allow the procurement agent to reap all the benefits created by distorted prices, these agents had incentives to counterattack by sending buyers into raw material–producing areas to buy commodities directly from producers at prices above those offered by the local monopsony. Competition for scarce commodities is thus likely to trigger bidding wars in which prices will ultimately reach market-clearing levels unless "order" is restored and rent seeking eliminated.

Thus, even though Deng and his allies shied away from price reform, they nevertheless triggered a process of implosive rent seeking wherein state institutions forced prices back toward market-clearing levels because the system they sought to maintain was not at equilibrium and its survival depended on the willingness of the local governments most disadvantaged by the system to continue to allow rents to slide through their hands without "plucking" any of these "golden eggs." As will be shown in the following chapters, it did not take long for the "logic" of opportunistic rent seeking to overcome whatever innate loyalty local governments in raw material–producing regions might have felt to their role as agents of the state rent-generating system.

Shaanxi Ribao, 3/23/85: 2
"Why the wild goose can't fly"

4

Export Protectionism

L OCAL protectionism first became a highly visible issue during the later 1980s when a series of what the Chinese referred to as "resource wars" erupted. During the early 1980s, as predicted in Chapter 3, local governments, particularly those in less developed areas, expanded local industry. To support local infant industries, local preference policies were embraced by a number of provincial governments. Yunnan's 1981 economic plan, for example, stated "purchasers should not look to producers outside the province to purchase products" and in 1982 the provincial governor said that local cash crops should be fed into local industries rather than exported to other provinces.[1] That same year, the governor of Gansu remarked: "As a matter of principle we do not want to buy things from other provinces."[2] The chairman of the Ningxia-Hui Autonomous Region, on the other hand, stated that:

> It is not right to passively protect... enterprises by means of administrative measures because... economic blockades between one area and another have been lifted. We must [however] give aid to up-to-standard products.... If our products are up to the required quality, and up to state standards, and if the prices are reasonable, then the commercial and materials departments, as well as industrial enterprises, must give priority to [local] products.... We should not seek far and wide for what lies close at hand.[3]

Many localities went beyond promoting local purchasing and erected a variety of administrative barriers that hampered imports of a variety of goods; in 1983, the central government complained that various local governments had diverted

---

[1] *Joint Publications Research Service (JPRS)*, nos. 78452 (7/6/81): 23 and 80749 (5/6/82): 14.
[2] *JPRS*, no. 80334 (4/16/82): 30–1.
[3] *JPRS*, no. 81581 (8/19/82): 15.

stocks of cement, rolled steel, iron, coal, motor vehicles, and lumber that had been earmarked for delivery to state-owned local industries.[4]

Officially, the center opposed local protectionism. In 1980, regulations issued by the State Council forbade local governments and bureaus from restricting imports of goods from other regions or exports of resources as mandated by the state plan.[5] But it was not entirely averse to policies that protected infant industries. As a commentary by the official New China News Agency explained:

> Restrictions have been placed on the flow of products from other places into the local market. In some localities, rules have been set up stipulating that no commercial department should purchase from other places any commodity that can be produced locally. Certainly, local products should be protected and developed, but the key question here is how to protect and develop them. If the local products are of poor quality and are uncompetitive, using the blockade method to protect them can only make the enterprises manufacturing these products content with the existing state of affairs and refuse to advance. As a result, they would be unable to change their backwardness, even after a long period of time.[6]

Protecting struggling infant industries, in other words, was acceptable but protecting aging dinosaurs was not.

Local protectionism in the form of administrative restrictions on trade remained a persistent problem throughout the early 1980s. It was not until the reform progress moved from the first stage of decollectivization to the second stage of commercial and industrial reform in 1984–5 that local protectionism became a major issue.

As noted in Chapter 1, local protectionism is something of a catchall term for local governments' tendency to place local interests above those of the center and to use their authority to illicitly protect local interests. As used in discussions of interregional economic conflict, local protectionism has this broad meaning but also refers more narrowly to the erection of illicit local trade barriers and the use of discriminatory regulations to protect the local economy and local economic interests from outside competition. We can, however, distinguish two forms of local protectionism: export protectionism and import protectionism.

---

[4] *Xinhua* (7/20/83).

[5] "*Guowuyuan guanyu kaizhan he baohu shehui zhuyi jingzheng zanxing guiding*" (Provisional State Council regulations on developing and preserving socialist competition), in *Zhongyao Jingji Fagui Ziliao Xuanbian*: 64.

[6] "*Guowuyuan guanyu zai gongpin gouxiao zhong jinzhi fengsuo tongzhi*" (State Council notice prohibiting blockades of industrial products), in *Zhongyao Jingji Fagui Ziliao Xuanbian*: 1062 and *Xinhua* (7/18/84), in *FBIS-China* (7/23/84): K9–10.

Export protectionism involved the use of barriers to restrict the outflow of commodities. Import protectionism involved the use of barriers to restrict the inflow of commodities. The distinction between export and import protectionism lies not only in their directional orientation but also in their relationship to prices and rents. Moreover, as argued in Chapter 3, given initial conditions such as existed in China in the mid-1980s, export and import protectionism are distinct in their sequencing, with export protectionism occurring almost immediately after the relaxation of controls on undervalued commodities and import protectionism developing only as output markets began to reach saturation. Thus from approximately 1985 to 1989, export protectionism predominated. During the second phase, which occurred in winter of 1989–90, import protectionism predominated.

Export protectionism grew out of contradictions between the supply for industrial crops, such as cotton, silk, tobacco, and wool, which remained depressed because the state continued to seek rents by fixing prices at below-market levels, and demand, which was rising as the number of out-of-plan consumers increased. As a result, partial decontrol of rural markets in 1983–4 triggered a scramble for rents and supplies as local governments in raw material–producing areas sought to either localize the monetization of rents and feed them into local coffers or to extract a share of the rents from consumers in other regions by diverting local supplies onto emerging black markets, where out-of-plan consumers were willing to pay market prices. Diversion of supplies either onto the black market or into local industries, however, meant that in-plan consumers found themselves unable to obtain needed inputs, with the result that the erection of export barriers by local governments in raw material–producing areas triggered "counterattacks" by manufacturing regions, often with the backing of the center whose own industries were one of the major consumers of "cheap" raw materials. The result was a series of prolonged, and in some cases large-scale, "resource wars."

This same dynamic did not occur in sectors such as steel, coal, and petroleum. Although these commodities also remained subject to state pricing policies that left them seriously undervalued (the price of coal was in fact so low that the cost of production was often higher than its wholesale price). Unlike agricultural commodities, however, these sectors remained more vertically integrated and under the control of the central ministries. Vertical integration tended to reduce opportunistic rent seeking for several reasons. First, rents created by depressed input prices tended to be passed along within the same institutions as they moved through the productive cycle and were thus often monetized by the same institution responsible for procurement. Thus, in contrast to agricultural commodities where rents were passed between institutions with the result that those responsible for procurement were likely to find themselves eating bitterness while those responsible for monetization feasted on a rich diet of rents, there were fewer institutional contradictions between those engaged in procurement and those engaged in monetization. Second, vertical integration made it easier to monitor the behavior of subordinate agencies and to control opportunistic rent seeking. Third, although incentives for rent seeking were present, the center was more likely to directly compensate institutions that suffered losses because they passed rents on to other state-owned institutions. Many of these sectors were, in fact, heavily subsidized. Local governments, by contrast, were less likely to receive direct compensation for exported rents because of the decentralized nature of the fiscal system. Fourth, the procurement and production process in these sectors tended to remain under the direct control of local bureaus of the central ministries rather than being shared between central departments and local governments. Local governments, therefore, had only indirect access to rent-bearing commodities and hence fewer opportunities to usurp control. Thus, even though local governments in a coal-producing region may have wished to halt the outflow of rents in the form of undervalued coal and to divert supplies onto the black market where coal sold at several times the state price, their opportunities were much more constrained. As a result, the "reform dynamic" that we see in the case of agricultural commodities did not occur in all sectors, but only in those sectors in which local governments had a degree of autonomy from the center and hence could get away with infringing on the center's monopsony claims.[7]

Whereas we can trace the rise of export protectionism to depressed raw-material prices, we can trace the rise of import protectionism to inflated consumer prices. During the Maoist era, the state kept consumer prices high relative to agricultural commodity prices. At the same time, however, it also allocated the bulk of investment capital to the construction of heavy industry, with the result that even though consumer goods tended to be overpriced, they also remained in short supply. Given these conditions, when the second round of economic reforms gave local governments greater flexibility over investment,

---

[7] This does not mean, however, that rent seeking did not occur in these more tightly controlled sectors. On the contrary, rent seeking was widespread but tended to take the form of corruption rather than local protectionism. In these sectors, individual officials and institutions involved in the allocation of undervalued commodities frequently engaged in "official profiteering" by diverting supplies onto the black market, where they could obtain quick profits by arbitraging between depressed in-plan prices and the much higher market prices. There were also cases of localities attempting to block exports or to tax exports. Localities in Shanxi province, China's leading producer of coal, for example, frequently interfered with coal exports. Even so, a "coal war" did not erupt, as was true in the case of agricultural commodities, because these localities were never in a position to block large-scale exports by agencies of the central government.

they invested heavily in light industry, where capital costs were relatively low, demand was strong, and profits were high. Because local governments across China tended to invest in the same sectors, the result was a pattern of rapid and reduplicative industrial expansion. Nevertheless, demand continued to exceed supply in most cases, a condition that not only fueled additional investment but also sustained black markets for scarce goods. Rising inflation and the advent of retrenchment in 1988, however, caused demand to contract at a time when investment had pushed productive capacity to saturation levels, causing a sudden piling up of unsold inventory when sellers' markets suddenly became buyers' markets. As the 1989–90 recession set in and local industries faced the prospect of having to curtail production, local governments threw up import barriers to secure local markets for local producers and to guard against dumping by other localities.

GENESIS

Export protectionism increased rapidly after 1984–5 as competition for valuable commodities intensified and then erupted into open conflict between buyers and among sellers, with 1988 and 1989 being the worst years. Between 1984 and 1990, the Chinese press carried reports of some 100 different wars involving 50 different commodities. In some cases, the commodities involved were key industrial raw materials, such as cotton, sugarcane, soybeans, and wool, or valuable export goods, such as tea, ramie, and silk. Some, such as tobacco, could be easily transformed into highly profitable goods. Others were much less visible commodities, such as anise, pine rosin, lichees, camphor oil, jujubes, castor oil, jasmine, peppermint oil, licorice root, and cassia. Still others were outright obscure, including bluish dogbane, jellyfish, "devil taro," and a variety of medicinal plants. Conflicts over key food crops, including grain, hogs, eggs, seafood, garlic, rapeseed, and apples, also erupted.

Most of these commodities were officially classified as Category III goods and hence were not subject to formal state monopsonies, although their prices were subject to regulation by local governments. Conflicts over these goods, therefore, tended to push prices upward toward market levels, if they had been fixed below that level, but did not necessarily result in institutional change. Conflicts over Category II goods, which included grain, edible oil, cotton, tobacco, wool, silk cocoons, tea, Chinese catalpa oil, tung oil, wood oil, citronella oil, peppermint oil, sugar beets, and sugarcane, as well as a long list of medicinal herbs and plants, on the other hand, not only served to push up prices, but also involved direct attacks on the state's right to control the allocation of all or a major portion of these commodities.[8] From the point of view of systemic transformation, therefore, conflicts over Category II goods were of greater significance than those over Category III goods.

Moreover, from the perspective of central-local relations, whereas conflicts over Category III goods could be construed as purely local in nature (i.e., conflicts between localities), conflicts over Category II goods, particularly cotton, tobacco, and silk, were central-local in nature because conflicts over these commodities involved local attacks on central prerogatives. A significant share of these crops was earmarked for delivery to state-owned enterprises. Thus, attempts to divert these commodities were tantamount to an attempt to hijack rents belonging to the center. Conflicts over Category II goods, in other words, involved direct attacks on the monopsony structures that the center had sought to retain after decontrolling the rural economy.

On the eve of these resource wars, the state retained considerable control over prices. A third of all agricultural commodities purchased by the state in 1984 were sold at set prices (*paijia*), another third at higher "over quota prices" (*chaogou jiajia*), and 14.4 percent at negotiated prices (*yi jia*). Less than 20 percent were sold at floating market prices (*shi jia*). The state also accounted for three-quarters of total purchases, and sales directly to industry accounted for only 14 percent.[9] Thus, even though decollectization had shifted responsibility for production to individual households, the supply and marketing cooperatives maintained a strong grip on the purchase and distribution of key cash crops and, hence, leverage over their prices.

In 1985, the state relaxed the old system, shifting a number of goods, including cotton and wool, from Category I to Category II and replacing the old system of mandatory sales with one based on contracts. Adoption of the new contract system did not mean that the state relinquished its claim on Category II commodities. In point of fact, the state's intention in changing the system was self-serving. As Oi and Kelliher point out, the system of quota delivery was predicated on conditions of persistent shortage and allowed the state to procure commodities at below their market-clearing prices.[10] Procurement price increases and the devolution of cropping decisions to individual households in the early 1980s had led to major increases in production of many crops, including both grain and key cash crops such as cotton, tobacco, jute, and ramie, as well as substantial increases in silk cocoon and wool production. In 1984, a

---

[8] After 1985, only timber remained a Category I commodity and hence subject to unified purchase. At that time, edible oil, grain, and cotton that had been subject to unified purchase were reclassified as being subject to quota purchases based on contracts.

[9] *Zhongguo Tongji Nianjian, 1985*: 479.

[10] Oi, *State and Peasant in Contemporary China*: 171–2 and Kelliher, *Peasant Power in China*: 113.

combination of increased sown acreage and favorable weather yielded bumper crops and created glut conditions in a sector only recently characterized by persistent shortages. As production rose, the state's procurement costs increased and by 1984 it found itself saddled with surplus commodities as farmers sold stocks to the state at premium prices higher than prevailing market prices.[11] In 1985, when the glut drove market prices below those fixed by the state, the center sought to minimize its costs by replacing the unified delivery system with a new system of delivery contracts.[12] Under this new system, the state would no longer automatically buy commodities from farmers but would instead only guarantee to purchase a set amount and at a set price. The state would therefore no longer pay premium prices and would not act as a "buyer of last resort" for stocks that farmers could not dispose of on the free markets.

Thus, the new system continued to stipulate that the state had first claim on Category II goods and that it would continue to set procurement prices. The center, in other words, sought to shift from being a pure monopsonist to being a "discriminating monopsonist," that is, a monopsonist that elects to purchase only as much of a good as it wishes but that continues to fix prices in a manner that allows it to create monopsony rents. So long as glut conditions prevailed, it was relatively easy for the state to act as a discriminating monopsonist. But when gluts gave way to dearth and shortages grew, as they did in many cases after 1985, a variety of actors, including not the least local agents of the state monopsony and out-of-plan consumers, attacked the prerequisites of the state monopsony and the state-owned industries that depended on it for cheap inputs in a effort to capture rents created by fixed prices. As attacks on its monopsony rights intensified, the center responded by ordering a resumption of unified purchase and hence a tightening of its monopsony controls. Almost without exception, however, conflicts continued to intensify, leading to a series of large-scale interregional resource wars that, in most cases, continued for several years as the center fought with its own agents for control over Category II commodities.

In the pages that follow I examine four major resource wars in detail: the cotton war, the tobacco war, the wool war, and the silk cocoon war. There

---

[11] Farmers were able to force up the average price for commodities sold to the state by increasing production and hence the amount they sold to the state at the higher premium price. According to regulations, the state was essentially obligated to buy whatever the farmers wanted to sell. The farmers, however, had the option to sell excess stocks (that is, in excess of their basic quota and supplemental quota) on the free market. Not surprisingly, when market prices fell below the above-quota premium price and the negotiated price (which was often the same as the premium price but could fall below it), they expected the state to buy their crops at above-market prices. Kelliher, *Peasant Power in China*: 126–7.

[12] Terry Sicular, "Plan and Market in China's Agricultural Commerce," *Journal of Political Economy* 96, no. 2 (April 1988): 289–90.

Fujian Ribao, 3/30/84: 2
"Hey what's this?"

were other major wars over economically important Category II commodities, including a long series of conflicts over grain and hogs, as well as the tea war. The four wars I have selected to study in detail, however, were the most intense and geographically extensive conflicts. They were also arguably the most critical conflicts because they involved commodities over which the state had long claimed monopsony rights and from which the state had traditionally extracted considerable rents. Moreover, even though others are worthy of in-depth study (particularly the grain, hog, and egg wars), the selection is such that we obtain a reasonably clear-cut picture of the actual dynamics of the resource wars that erupted during the later 1980s and, hence, the conflicts generated by the partial marketization of China's rural economy.

THE COTTON WAR

In 1954, the state monopolized the purchase and allocation of raw cotton, designating it as a "planned purchase" commodity under the exclusive control of the State Company for Cotton, Yarn, and Cloth, with the supply and marketing cooperatives as its designated purchasing agent.[13] Prices were fixed at approximately 30 percent above prewar levels and households (later brigades) were assigned procurement quotas, for which the state paid them the fixed price, minus taxes, and were allowed to retain only a small fraction of the harvest for individual use. With the exception of a short period during 1956 when the state allowed the revival of rural free markets, cotton prices remained tightly regulated throughout the Maoist period.[14] Between 1953 and 1977, the state procurement price rose from ¥90 per *dan* (approximately 50 kilograms) in 1953, to ¥102 in 1965, and then ¥104 in 1977, for a net increase of 15.5 percent in twenty-five years.[15] As a result, cotton prices lagged well behind other agricultural prices, which rose 72 percent during the same period.[16] Despite declining terms of trade, cotton production increased during the 1950s from approximately 1 million tons in 1952 to 2.3 million tons in 1966 before declining slightly to an average of about 2.1 million tons in the mid-1970s, of which 98 percent went to the state as of 1979.[17]

Fearing that farmers would take advantage of the new household responsibility system to cut back on production, the state raised the procurement price to ¥114 in 1978 and then boosted it again to ¥134 in 1979 and ¥159 in 1980. At that time, the state split the households' procurement quota into a mandatory base quota, for which the state paid the low fixed or list price, and a secondary quota, for which they received a "premium" price 30 percent higher than the quota price. In theory, farmers could sell any surplus cotton at a still higher "negotiated price."[18] In many areas, however, the negotiated price was the same as the premium price. Moreover, the state continued to take almost the entire crop. Production nevertheless increased dramatically during the early 1980s, rising from an average of 2 million tons in the mid-1970s to 3 million tons in 1981, 3.5 million tons in 1982, 4.6 million tons in 1983, and peaking at 6.2 million tons in 1984.[19]

---

[13] Donnithorne, *China's Economic System*: 284, 349 and Philip C. C. Huang, *The Peasant Family and Rural Development in the Yangzi Delta, 1350–1988* (Stanford, CA: Stanford University Press, 1990): 174.

[14] Lardy, *Agriculture in China's Modern Development*: 39.

[15] W. Hunter Colby, Frederick W. Crook, and Shwu-Eng H. Webb, *Agricultural Statistics of the People's Republic of China* (Washington, DC: United States Department of Agriculture, 1992): 264.

[16] *Zhongguo Wujia Tongji Nianjian, 1989* (China Price Statistics Yearbook) (Beijing: Zhongguo Tongji Chubanshe, 1990): 68.

[17] Kelliher, *Peasant Power in China*: 121; Colby, et. al., *Agricultural Statistics of the People's Republic of China*: 83; and Lardy, *Agriculture in China's Modern Development*: 123.

[18] Kelliher, *Peasant Power in China*: 126–7.

[19] Colby, et. al., *Agricultural Statistics of the People's Republic of China*: 83.

Even though the state increased cotton prices only modestly between 1980 and 1984, raising them 7.5 percent from ¥159 in 1980 to ¥172 in 1983–4,[20] increasing cotton production threatened to become a major financial burden as procurement costs jumped from approximately ¥860 million in 1980 to approximately ¥2 billion in 1984. Moreover, as production surged, market prices fell below the state's fixed price. In Anhui, for example, the local market price for low-grade cotton dropped to a mere ¥20 per *dan*.[21] Faced with a glut, the State Council authorized farmers to sell above-quota cotton directly to textile mills, including those operating outside the plan, and directed that the state should begin cutting back on above-quota purchases by implementing a system of purchase contrasts that limited the amount of above-quota cotton the state would buy.[22]

Cotton-purchasing stations, meanwhile, started to illicitly cut prices by paying the low-grade price for high-grade cotton. In parts of Shandong, cadres forced prices down as much as 50 percent in this manner, which allowed them to siphon off the difference between what they paid farmers and the official procurement price.[23] Elsewhere, procurement stations refused to purchase cotton from farmers unless they kicked back part of the purchase price or simply withheld part of the purchase price.[24]

The State Council's decision to liberalize the cotton sector quickly proved a disaster. Faced with the same glut that led the state to cut back on purchases and made it difficult to sell surplus cotton, farmers cut back on production, decreasing the area sown with cotton from 103.9 million *mu* in 1984 to 77.1 million *mu* in 1985.[25] In a single year, cotton production dropped 29 percent from over 6 million tons to 4.5 million tons. In 1986, shortages of fertilizer and low prices led to additional cutbacks in sown area and production, with the result that output fell to 3.5 million tons, a 44 percent drop compared to 1984. Demand, however, continued to rise as total investment in the cotton textile sector increased 268 percent between 1980 and 1985.[26]

---

[20] *Ibid.*: 264.

[21] *Nongmin Ribao* (7/23/84): 2.

[22] "*Zhonggong Zhongyang Guowuyuan jinyibu huoyue nongcun jingji de shi xiang zhengce*" (Notice of the Central Committee and the State Council on ten policies designed to invigorate the rural economy), *Zhongyao Jingji Fagui Ziliao Xuanbian*: 222 and *Xinhua* (3/4/84), in *FBIS-China* (3/6/85): K7.

[23] *Nongmin Ribao* (7/21/86): 1.

[24] *Zhongguo Shangye Bao* (8/16/86): 1.

[25] *Zhongguo Tongji Nianjian, 1991*: 340 and 347.

[26] *Zhongguo Fangzhi Gongye Nianjian, 1991* (Beijing: Fangzhi Gongye Chubanshe, 1992): 318–30 and *Zhongguo Tongji Nianjian, 1991*: 624.

As gaps opened between supply and demand during the summer of 1985, out-of-plan cotton mills rushed to sign purchase agreements with farm households, bypassing authorized purchasing agents and snapping up stocks designated for purchase by the state.[27] During the summer of 1986, prefectures fought prefectures and counties fought counties in Hebei as legal cotton markets collapsed. Local governments and factory agents "vied for purchases" and engaged in "panic buying."[28]

In some areas, purchasers began to "raise grades and raise prices," offering farmers the price for high-grade cotton for low-grade cotton.[29] Some offered farmers fertilizer at cut prices. Other localities adopted coercive tactics, forcing farmers to sell above-quota cotton to the supply and marketing cooperatives at the quota price instead of allowing them to sell it directly to textile mills. In Xinghua County (Jiangsu) farmers reneged on their purchase contracts, selling their cotton instead to purchasers in neighboring localities who were willing to pay more than the local supply and marketing cooperative. Cadres responsible for purchasing on behalf of the state, meanwhile, began buying cotton on their own accounts and reselling it to buyers representing out-of-plan textile mills or engaged in speculation and official profiteering. As the 1987 purchasing season approached, purchasing bureaus in Hubei "foddered the horses and sharpened the weapons" in anticipation of open warfare, while Binzhou, Huimin, Yangxin, and Zhanhua counties in Shandong began fighting over cotton supplies as soon as the harvest came in.

Seeking to defuse the cotton war, the central government first ordered farmers to arrange sales of above-quota cotton through local supply and marketing cooperatives, which were responsible for ensuring that state quotas were filled before any market sales took place, and ordered that market prices remained within limits set by the state.[30] In August 1985, the State Planning Commission directed local purchasing agencies to ensure that state procurement targets and provincial requirements were fulfilled before farmers were allowed to market above-quota cotton. The commission also ordered that interprovincial transfers occur only if local supplies were inadequate. All interprovincial purchases were

---

[27] *Jingji Ribao* (11/15/85): 2.

[28] *Hebei Ribao* (8/27/88): 1.

[29] *Zhongguo Shangye Bao* (10/16/86): 1 and (8/16/89): 1; *Nongmin Ribao* (7/21/86): 1; *Xinhua Ribao* (12/22/86): 1 and (10/10/88): 1; *Hubei Ribao* (8/18/87): 1; and *Dazhong Ribao* (10/18/88): 1.

[30] "*Shangye Bu, Guojia Wujia Ju guanyu hetong dinggou yiwai mianhua shougou jiage de tongzhi*" (Ministry of Commerce and State Price Bureau notice on prices for above-contract quota cotton purchases) (11/26/85) in *Zhongguo Nongye Fagui (1985)* (Chinese Rural Laws) (Beijing: Nongye Chubanshe, 1987): 339–40.

to be channeled through the cotton and fiber corporations in cotton-growing localities and direct purchases from farmers were forbidden.[31]

After limited controls failed to prevent a cotton war in 1986, the State Council ordered rural cotton markets closed and reintroduced unified purchasing and management in 1987 and local governments were ordered to "harmonize" purchase policies and prices.[32] The following year, the central government banned unauthorized foreign exports of cotton, prohibited purchases by unauthorized units and individuals, imposed a ban on construction of new cotton mills, and forbade interregional purchases of cotton by mills located outside cotton-producing regions.[33] Cross-border purchasing by local purchasing agencies was banned and setting up purchasing stations along borders prohibited.[34] Seeking to decrease demand, the Ministry of Commerce called for a moratorium on the construction of new cotton mills, including small mills in cotton-growing regions.[35] At a cotton summit held in August 1988, Vice Premier Tian Jiyun told provincial officials that they must strictly adhere to state purchasing policy and must not create local "two-track price systems."[36] Tian also reiterated the State Council's directives ordering unauthorized out-of-plan cotton mills to cease production.[37]

New controls over cotton purchasing did not, however, end the cotton war. In July 1988, in fact, conditions deteriorated to the point that a Vice Minister of Commerce warned that cotton-growing regions were on the verge of "civil war."[38] Conflicts multiplied rapidly as the cotton-purchasing season progressed.

---

[31] *Xinhua* (8/13/85), in *FBIS-China* (8/15/85): K1.

[32] "*Guojia Wujiaju guanyu jiao bianxiang tigao mianhua shougou jiage de tongzhi*" (State Price Bureau notice on correcting disguised price increases for cotton purchases) (9/16/87) (Notice No. 117), in *Wujia Wenjian Xuanbian (1987–1988)* (Selected price documents) (Beijing: Zhongguo Wujia Chubanshe, 1989): 161; *Jingji Ribao* (8/10/87): 1; *Renmin Ribao* (7/28/88): 1; *Hebei Ribao* (8/27/88): 1; and *Hubei Ribao* (8/18/87): 1.

[33] "*Guowuyuan guanyu zuohao yi jiu ba ba nian du mianhua shougou gongzuo he jiaqiang mianhua shichang guanli de tongzhi*" (State Council notice regarding 1988 cotton purchasing work and strengthening the management of cotton markets), in *Wujia Wenjian Xuanbian (1987–1988)*: 188–9 and "*Shang Bumen, Guojia Ji Wei, Guojia Jing Wei guanyu jiaqiang mianhua, mian duanrong jihua guanli de tongzhi*" (Ministry of Commerce, State Planning Commission, and State Economic Commission notice on strengthening cotton and cotton wadding planning and management) (1/20/88), *Guowuyuan Gongbao*, no. 4/557 (3/1/88): 125–6.

[34] *Jingji Ribao* (8/10/87): 1; *Henan Ribao* (8/18/88): 1; and *Hebei Ribao* (8/27/88): 1.

[35] *Xinhua* (7/26/88), in *FBIS-China* (8/3/88): 55–6.

[36] The two-track price system referred to here should not be confused with the formal two-track price system. In the context mentioned previously, two-track price system refers to the practice of offering to purchase cotton at prices above those authorized by the state.

[37] *Jingji Ribao* (8/28/89): 1; *Jingji Cankao* (8/28/89): 1; *Jingji Ribao* (8/8/90): 1; *Jingji Cankao* (8/8/90): 1; and *Zhongguo Shang Bao* (8/14/90): 1.

[38] *Renmin Ribao* (7/28/88): 1.

Farmers in Langfang City (Hebei) rushed to ship cotton across the border into Beijing after purchase stations in Tong County (Beijing) illegally raised local purchase prices.[39] Many localities resorted to illegal price increases by paying top-grade prices for low-grade cotton or creating "two-track price" systems whereby local purchase prices exceeded those fixed by the central government. In Hebei, local governments adopted policies of "self-production, self-marketing, self-use," allowed "cotton black markets" to operate more or less openly, commissioned purchasers to buy directly from farmers in violation of regulations limiting purchasing to units approved by commercial authorities, and lied about local production and purchases to cover up illegal purchasing and local use. Local governments around Shijiazhuang (Hebei) established a system of illegal price subsides to circumvent official prices. Within a matter of weeks, the unified purchase system in Jiangxi had collapsed and the Shandong-Henan-Jiangsu, Jiangsu-Shanghai-Zhejiang, and Henan-Hubei borders were engulfed by war. As competition among local purchasing agencies drove prices upward, farmers began to withhold cotton in anticipation of further price increases, thereby further exacerbating supply-demand contradictions.

In a renewed effort to prevent a cotton war in the summer of 1989, the center once again ordered local supply and marketing cooperatives to assume unified control over cotton purchasing and banned direct purchases by cotton mills.[40] It also ordered cotton-importing provinces to compensate cotton-growing provinces for their share of price subsidies (half the total of ¥10 per *dan*, with the center paying the other half).[41] To assure local compliance, the center and provincial governments dispatched "cotton purchase inspection groups" to patrol "hot spots" along provincial borders.[42] Purchase policies based on "local production, local use" were outlawed. A new system of interregional transfers

---

[39] Paul Leung, "China: Short of Everything," *Textile Asia* (May 1989): 71–2; *Hebei Ribao* (11/4/88): 2 and (8/25/89): 1; *Renmin Ribao* (1/5/89): 1; *Nongmin Ribao* (9/5/88): 1; and *Nongmin Ribao* (10/17/88), in *FBIS-China* (10/26/88): 43–4.

[40] "*Guowuyuan guanyu jiaqiang 1989 nian du mianhua shougou gongzuo de tongzhi*" (State Council notice on strengthening cotton purchasing work for the 1989 season) (August 16, 1989), *Guowuyuan Gongbao*, no. 15/596 (September 12, 1989): 583–5 and "*Guojia Wujia Ju, Shangye Bu, Caizheng Bu guanyu yi jiu ba jiu nian du mianhua shougou jiage ji youguan wenti de tongzhi*" (Notice by the State Price Bureau, the Ministry of Commerce, and Ministry of Finance regarding prices for the 1989 cotton purchasing season and related problems) (July 19, 1989), in *Wujia Wenjian Xuanbian (1989)* (Beijing: Zhongguo Wujia Chubanshe, 1990): 112–14.

[41] "*Guowuyuan guanyu tiaozheng mianhua shougou zhengce de tongzhi*" (Notice by the Sate Council regarding rectification of cotton purchasing policy) (January 8, 1989), in *Wujia Wenjian Xuanbian (1989)*: 105–6.

[42] *Jingji Ribao* (7/24/89): 1; *Renmin Ribao* (7/24/89): 1; *Jiangxi Ribao* (9/14/89): 1 and (9/9/90): 1; *Jingji Cankao* (1/13/92): 2; *Hubei Ribao* (8/25/89): 1; *Beijing Domestic Service* (2/25/89), in *FBIS-China* (2/28/89): 61; and *Xinhua* (8/26/89), in *FBIS-China* (9/1/89): 41.

based on contracts was also implemented in 1989. According to these new regulations, supply and marketing cooperatives in cotton-growing areas:

[Must put] local users and users in other localities on an equal footing. Provinces and autonomous regions must ensure the supply of textile cotton... according to the state plan. They must not supply less or refuse to supply cotton. Nor should they divert cotton supply for other uses.[43]

The central government also encouraged local governments to sign "treaties" agreeing not to engage in cross-border purchasing. Local governments were quick to respond to this policy. As conflicts intensified in 1988, for example, the governments of Beijing, Tianjin, and Hebei signed agreements banning cross-border purchasing, restricting price increases, and limiting bank loans for cotton purchasing to authorized units.[44] In Jiangsu, the provincial cotton and fiber corporation brokered talks among border localities that resulted in the signing of an agreement banning the erection of purchase stations along county borders. According to the agreement, units caught buying cotton from other localities would be fined and those involved disciplined. The governments of Shanghai and Zhejiang adopted similar measures, banning cross-border purchasing. Counties along the Zhejiang-Jiangsu border agreed that henceforth whoever signed purchase contracts in advance would have exclusive rights to supplies, that other units would not attempt to outbid previously agreed upon prices, and that nobody would use cash advances or fertilizer to attract cotton sellers. In Shandong, the government of Huimin Prefecture ordered local officials to shut down illegal purchasing stations along county borders, stop buying cotton from outside their own counties, and strictly adhere to state-set prices. Localities caught buying out-of-county cotton would be fined ¥300. In October, Hebei, Shandong, Henan, Jiangsu, and Anhui signed a five-province agreement prohibiting price competition and the erection of purchasing stations along their borders. Xingtai Prefecture (Hebei) organized leadership small groups to inspect and regulate purchasing and set up "joint patrols" with neighboring Linxi and Qinghe counties to prevent cross-border purchasing. Nanguan and Wei counties (Hebei) appointed "cotton czars" to stabilize markets.

Local governments continued to look to treaties as a means to prevent renewed conflict in 1989. In April, counties in Suxian Prefecture (Anhui) signed a series of agreements banning illegal cross-border purchasing.[45] Before the opening

---

[43] *Xinhua* (9/9/89), in *FBIS-China* (9/19/89): 36–7.

[44] *Zhongguo Shangye Bao* (9/24/88): 1; *Jingji Ribao* (10/8/88): 1 and (11/11/88): 2; *Xinhua Ribao* (10/10/88): 1; *Dazhong Ribao* (10/18/88): 1 and (10/28/88): 1; and *Renmin Ribao* (11/7/88): 2.

[45] *Jingji Cankao* (4/16/89): 2 and (12/5/89): 2; *Hubei Ribao* (8/25/89): 1; *Jiangxi Ribao* (9/14/89): 1; and *Henan Ribao* (11/23/89): 1.

of the cotton purchasing season, the Hubei provincial government convened a meeting of cadres from cotton-growing counties at which all agreed to abide by the central government's unified purchase policy. In Jiangxi, the provincial government deployed "cotton-purchase inspection groups" along the borders of major cotton-growing counties to prevent illegal cross-border purchasing. The government of Henan held a telephone conference among cotton-growing counties in November to avert further escalation of intercounty conflicts. An agreement between Jiangsu and Shandong provinces shut down large unregulated cotton markets in Xiajin County (Shandong) and Pei County (Jiangsu) that had been a source of serious conflicts in earlier years.

In 1990, Beijing, Tianjin, Hebei, Jiangsu, Anhui, Henan, Shandong, Hubei, and Hunan signed a nine-province mutual nonaggression pact in which local supply and marketing cooperatives promised not to initiate cross-border price competition.[46] Zhejiang deployed inspection teams from the provincial supply and marketing cooperative and commercial bureau to pacify cotton-growing counties in Jinhua, Quzhou, Taizhou, and Shaoxing Prefectures. Hebei ordered local governments in cotton-growing regions to set up formal mechanisms to ensure interregional coordination and told local purchasing agents not to set up unauthorized stations along county borders.

Despite the imposition of unified purchase and the signing of a host of interregional nonaggression pacts, the cotton war resumed as soon as the new cotton crop came onto the market in 1989. In Shandong, farmers bypassed official purchase stations, illegally selling "night cotton" directly to local factories.[47] Local officials in that province also improperly allowed township and village cotton mills to fraudulently purchase cotton directly from farm households. In Jiangsu, officials in Xiangshui County saw local cotton flow out of the county day and night after purchase stations in neighboring counties illegally raised prices and provoked a seven-county cotton war. In Hubei, units from neighboring counties set up illegal purchasing stations in Tianmen City, causing a massive outflow of cotton. By the fall, a major cotton war had engulfed most cotton-producing regions.

Unified purchase and interregional treaties enjoyed some successes. In 1989, cadres in Dangshan County (Anhui) stabilized markets badly disrupted by the cotton war the previous year by negotiating a complex series of agreements with counties in neighboring Henan, Jiangsu, and Shandong provinces, as well

[46] *Zhongguo Shangye Bao* (8/18/90): 1; *Zhejiang Ribao* (10/24/90): 1; *Hebei Ribao* (9/14/90): 1; and *Jingji Cankao* (10/5/90): 2.

[47] *Dazhong Ribao* (9/9/89): 1; *Jingji Cankao* (9/27/89): 1; *Jingji Ribao* (11/3/89): 1; *Nongmin Ribao* (11/3/89): 2; and *Renmin Ribao* (11/16/89): 2.

as other counties in Anhui.[48] The following year, counties along the Tang River in Henan and Hubei ended years of conflict by agreeing that they would not purchase a single *jin* of cotton from farmers in other counties, establishing a system of uniform prices, dismantling purchase stations located along their borders, and setting up joint inspection teams.

Even as the center tried to hold the unified purchase system together, prices climbed dramatically, with the average price per *dan* increasing from approximately ¥175 in 1987, to ¥250 in 1989, and then ¥310 in 1990, for a net increase of 77 percent in four years, well in excess of the 42 percent increase in overall prices during this same period. In the major cotton-growing province of Henan, prices rose nearly 70 percent in three years, rising from ¥175 to ¥295. In neighboring Shandong, also a major cotton grower, prices increased 80 plus percent from ¥170 to ¥305, while prices in Hunan nearly quadrupled from ¥105 in 1987 to ¥415 in 1990.[49]

The narrative of the cotton war thus far can be summarized as one of a commodity sector thrown into chaos by the center's decision to partially deregulate at a time when supply had begun to fall precipitously but demand continued to rise steadily. A shift from procurement by compulsory quotas to one based on contractual delivery might have been relatively easy under glut conditions because surplus production could have flowed into the out-of-plan textile sector without threatening the state-owned textile mills' access to raw cotton. The steep decline in raw cotton production, however, meant that it was simply impossible to meet the combined demand of state-owned textile mills and out-of-plan mills. Seeking to ensure supplies for state-owned mills, the center responded by imposing unified purchase and thus attempting to severely limit the amount of raw cotton available for sale to out-of-plan mills. Unified purchase was, however, inherently flawed because its success depended on the willingness of local governments in cotton-growing areas to feed supplies to state-owned mills, on whose profits they had few property-rights claims, while letting locally owned mills, on whose profits they had property-rights claims, starve. Moreover, it depended on the willingness of local governments and cadres to resist the temptation to reap windfall profits that could be earned by selling local cotton to out-of-plan mills.

Considerable pressure to divert supplies away from the state monopsony came from the fact that the rapid increase in the cotton textile sector noted previously came largely as a result of expansion of textile production in cotton-growing

---

[48] *Jingji Cankao* (12/5/89): 2 and *Nongmin Ribao* (1/15/90): 2.

[49] Based on data in *Zhongguo Wujia Tongji Nianjian, 1989* and *Zhongguo Guonei Shichang Tongji Nianjian, 1990–1991* (Beijing: Zhongguo Tongji Chubanshe, 1990 and 1991).

regions and the collective and township and village sectors more generally. At the outset of the reform period, the cotton textile sector was characterized by relatively high profits. In fact, among state-owned firms, textiles had the third highest rate of profit.[50] Moreover, cotton spinning and weaving were relatively low-tech industries, with relatively modest start-up costs and rapid returns on investment.[51] Local governments throughout China invested heavily in cotton textiles leading to a doubling in total installed manufacturing capacity, as measured in cotton spindles, between 1980 and 1989.[52] A considerable share of this new capacity was in the out-of-plan collective sector. In 1987, 22 percent of the gross output value of the textile sector came from township and village enterprises (TVEs). Two years later, TVEs accounted for 27 percent of gross output value, with the bulk (90 percent) coming from mills located in ten coastal provinces, with Jiangsu and Zhejiang alone accounting for 64 percent of total TVE production.

The textile sector in the major cotton-growing provinces of Shandong, Jiangsu, Hubei, and Henan, which accounted for approximately two-thirds of total raw cotton production in 1981, also expanded rapidly, with cloth production increasing 62 percent in Shandong, 32 percent in Jiangsu, 37 percent in Hubei, and 17 percent in Henan between 1981 and 1989.[53] Other areas also expanded cloth production aggressively. In Fujian, Ningxia, Guangxi, Yunnan, Guangdong, Heilongjiang, and Jilin (which combined produced less than a half percent of China's total raw cotton) cotton cloth production grew an average of 29 percent between 1981 and 1989.

Even though textile production rose in cotton-growing regions, the cotton textile sector remained "maldistributed" in that textile production continued to be concentrated outside the major cotton-growing provinces. In 1987, for example, provinces that produced no raw cotton accounted for 11 percent of installed spinning capacity, while those whose share of total cotton production was less than their share of total spinning capacity accounted for nearly half (49.33 percent) of installed capacity but just over a tenth of total cotton production (see Table 4-1). Conversely, the major cotton-growing provinces (Anhui, Xinjiang, Hubei, Jiangsu, Henan, Hebei, and Shandong), which produced 89.27 percent of total cotton output, accounted for just 50.57 percent

[50] Naughton, "Implications of the State Monopoly Over Industry and Its Relaxation": 26–7.

[51] Historically, textiles have been an entrée industry for economies during the early stages of industrialization.

[52] *Zhongguo Fangzhi Gongye Nianjian, 1991* (Beijing: Fangzhi Gongye Chubanshe, 1992): 318–31 and *Zhongguo Tongji Nianjian, 1986*: 260.

[53] Based on data in *Zhongguo Tongji Nianjian, 1981*: 236 and *Zhongguo Tongji Nianjian, 1990*: 463.

Table 4-1. *Spatial Distribution of Cotton Textile Sector, 1987*

Province	Installed Spindles (10,000)	Percentage Total Installed	Cumulative Percent Capacity	Cotton Production (10,000 tons)	Percentage Total Cotton	Cumulative Percent Cotton	Locational Coefficient
Xizang	0.0	0.00	0.00	0.0	0.00	0.00	
Ningxia	2.9	0.11	0.11	0.0	0.00	0.00	
Qinghai	3.3	0.13	0.24	0.0	0.00	0.00	
Neimenggu	13.8	0.53	0.77	0.0	0.00	0.00	
Fujian	35.0	1.34	2.11	0.0	0.00	0.00	
Jilin	35.2	1.35	3.47	0.0	0.00	0.00	
Guangxi	37.3	1.43	4.90	0.0	0.00	0.00	
Heilongjiang	64.3	2.47	7.37	0.0	0.00	0.00	
Guangdong	68.0	2.61	9.98	0.0	0.00	0.00	
Yunnan	26.9	1.03	11.01	0.0	0.01	0.01	
Guizhou	18.3	0.70	11.72	0.1	0.01	0.02	59.68
Beijing	46.5	1.79	13.50	0.3	0.06	0.08	29.16
Liaoning	121.7	4.68	18.18	0.3	0.07	0.15	66.14
Gansu	10.3	0.40	18.57	0.5	0.12	0.27	3.36
Tianjin	78.7	3.02	21.60	1.3	0.30	0.57	10.02
Shanghai	226.2	8.69	30.29	1.5	0.36	0.93	24.26
Hunan	85.0	3.27	33.55	5.6	1.31	2.24	2.50
Shaanxi	105.3	4.05	37.60	5.6	1.32	3.56	3.05
Jiangxi	49.5	1.90	39.50	5.9	1.39	4.96	1.36
Zhejiang	93.0	3.57	43.07	6.5	1.54	6.50	2.32
Shanxi	58.6	2.25	45.32	7.8	1.84	8.33	1.23
Sichuan	104.3	4.01	49.33	10.2	2.39	10.73	1.67
Anhui	92.9	3.57	52.90	18.6	4.39	15.12	0.81
Xinjiang	38.0	1.46	54.36	28.0	6.59	21.71	0.22
Hubei	222.4	8.54	62.90	43.9	10.34	32.05	0.83
Jiangsu	378.8	14.55	77.45	44.4	10.46	42.51	1.39
Henan	166.7	6.40	83.86	57.0	13.43	55.94	0.48
Hebei	165.7	6.37	90.22	62.6	14.75	70.69	0.43
Shandong	254.5	9.78	100.00	124.4	29.31	100.00	0.33
TOTAL	2,603.1			424.43			

Sources: Based on data in *Zhongguo Fangzhi Tongji Nianjian, 1988* and *Zhongguo Tongji Nianjian, 1988.*

of installed spinning capacity. Among the major cotton-producing provinces, only in Jiangsu did the local share of spinning capacity exceed that of local cotton production. Thus, although the bulk (78.81 percent) of China's cotton crop was grown in the six provinces of Anhui, Xinjiang, Hubei, Henan, Hebei, and Shandong, two-thirds (36.02 percent) of the cotton-spinning sector was located in other provinces. This created a situation in which underpriced cotton grown in the six major growing provinces was likely to be fed into mills elsewhere and hence the "valued added" from artificially depressed cotton prices was apt to occur outside cotton-growing regions.

Moreover, the maldistribution of textile production actually increased between 1981 and 1989. Whereas in 1981 fourteen provinces (which when combined produced just 1 percent of China's raw cotton) accounted for 19 percent of cloth production, in 1989 seventeen provinces (which when combined produced slightly less than 1 percent of China's raw cotton) accounted for 26 percent of cloth production. The "big four" (Hubei, Henan, Jiangsu, and Shandong), which produced 66 percent of China's raw cotton in 1981 and 68 percent in 1989, meanwhile, saw their share of cotton cloth production increase from 36 percent in 1981 to 40 percent in 1989, at which point mills in these provinces accounted for 42 percent of installed spinning capacity.[54]

A simple comparison of percentages of raw cotton produced and textile production suggests that the spatial distribution ought not to have been an issue. After all, the big four's share of raw cotton production exceeded their share of textile production. However, mills in both the major cotton-growing provinces and textile centers elsewhere faced chronic shortages in the late 1980s. Cotton mills in cotton-growing provinces were operating below capacity by 1989. In 1989, mills in Shandong, Hubei, Henan, Anhui, and Xinjiang complained that they could not obtain sufficient supplies.[55] Mills in Jiangsu could only obtain enough raw cotton to operate at 75 percent of capacity. Cotton mills in Henan, China's second largest cotton producer, found themselves facing shortfalls of over a million *dan*.

Mills outside China's major cotton-growing provinces also faced severe shortages of raw cotton. In 1989, two years after the implementation of unified purchase, cotton mills in Beijing, Tianjin, and Shanghai reported that they received only 55 percent of allocated inputs.[56] The following year, deliveries from cotton-growing regions to state-owned mills in Shanghai fell a third short of those called for by the state allocation plan. As a result, Shanghai's mills, which were capable of processing 6 million *dan* of raw cotton a year and which were to receive 4.4 million *dan* from the state allocation system, received only 2.8 million *dan*, forcing one in six mills to shut down. State-owned mills in Tianjin that had the capacity to process 2.1 million *dan* and were allocated 1.4 million *dan* by the state, received only 780,000 *dan*. By the end of 1990, most mills in the city were operating at two-thirds capacity. Mills in Neimenggu, Heilongjiang, Fujian, Guangdong, and Yunnan received a little more than one-third of the amount of cotton promised them by the state plan. Cotton mills in

---

[54] *Zhongguo Fangzhi Tongji Nianjian, 1990*: 347.

[55] *Jingji Cankao* (8/4/89): 1; *Jingji Ribao* (7/23/90): 1; *Jiefang Ribao* (12/13/90): 3; and *Jiefang Ribao* (12/17/90): 3.

[56] *Xinhua* (8/22/89): 1; *Jingji Ribao* (7/23/90): 1; and *Jiefang Ribao* (12/13/90): 3 and (12/17/90): 3.

Beijing were also forced to close down for two months as a result of a lack of raw cotton.

Shortages gave local governments in cotton-growing regions incentives to block exports. Although hard data are not available, rough estimates of supply and demand by province yield a general sense of the magnitude of these incentives. According to *Jingji Ribao*, total demand for raw cotton was 5 million tons in 1988.[57] Given domestic production of 4.14 million tons, total demand of 5 million tons would imply a gross shortage of approximately 860,000 tons. Foreign imports of 34,000 tons[58] would have reduced the gross gap between demand and supply to 826,000 tons for a net shortfall in supply of about 17 percent. The spatial distribution of demand can be estimated by assuming that the spatial distribution of demand corresponds to the spatial distribution of installed capacity (as measured by installed spindles). Supply can then be estimated by assuming that output is supply constrained and that this constraint will be reflected in changes in the utilization rate of installed capacity. I thus calculate each province's share of total capacity and multiply that figure by 5 million to estimate demand, compare output per spindle in 1988 to the average for 1980–3, and then multiply estimated demand by the utilization rate to estimate supply.[59] Subtracting estimated supply from estimated demand yields an estimate of shortfalls, while subtracting local production from estimated supply then yields an estimate of imports or exports.

These admittedly rough calculations show that the major cotton-exporting provinces of Hebei, Shandong, and Henan likely experienced shortages that could have been eliminated by reducing exports to other provinces (see Table 4-2).[60] Shortfalls for these three provinces totaled 473,800 tons versus total domestic exports of 1.47 million tons. Textile mills in these provinces, whose average output of cloth per installed spindle was 65 percent of what it had been prior to 1984, were thus presumably forced to operate at below capacity because of a shortage of ginned cotton created by exports to mills in other provinces. If these provinces had reduced exports to ensure supplies for local mills, however, total domestic exports would have fallen from 1.78 million

---

[57] *Jingji Ribao* (3/24/89): 2.

[58] *Zhongguo Tongji Nianjian, 1990*: 650.

[59] $\text{Demand}_{prov} = \dfrac{\text{Spindles}_{prov}}{\text{Spindles}_{total}} \times \text{Demand}_{total}$

$\text{Supply}_{prov} = \text{Demand}_{prov} \times \dfrac{\text{Cloth per spindle}_{1988}}{\text{Cloth per spindle}_{1980-3}}$

[60] Hebei, Shandong, and Henan accounted for 83 percent of estimated domestic exports. Because foreign imports accounted for less than half a percent of total supply, I have not factored these stocks into my calculations of estimated supply.

Table 4-2. *Estimated Supply and Demand for Raw Cotton, 1988*
(10,000 metric tons)

Province	Utilization Rate (Percent)	Estimated Demand	Estimated Supply	Estimate Shortfall	Local Production	Estimated Domestic Imports	Estimated Domestic Exports
Beijing	92.57	7.35	6.80	0.55	0.27	6.53	
Tianjin	80.64	13.37	10.79	2.59	1.01	9.78	
Hebei	66.42	38.39	25.50	12.89	57.68		32.18
Shanxi	109.88	9.77	10.73	−0.97	8.68	2.05	
Neimenggu	105.46	2.20	2.33	−0.12	0.00	2.33	
Liaoning	85.83	20.69	17.76	2.93	0.60	17.16	
Jilin	88.64	5.84	5.18	0.66	0.00	5.18	
Heilongjiang	90.81	11.10	10.08	1.02	0.00	10.08	
Shanghai	96.69	36.51	35.30	1.21	1.33	33.97	
Jiangsu	76.23	72.14	54.99	17.15	56.22		1.23
Zhejiang	79.99	27.20	21.76	5.44	4.37	17.39	
Anhui	87.36	17.05	14.89	2.15	20.63		5.74
Fujian	83.84	6.18	5.18	1.00	0.00	5.18	
Jiangxi	83.01	8.63	7.16	1.47	3.25	3.91	
Shandong	63.54	61.22	38.90	22.32	113.70		74.80
Henan	65.78	35.56	23.39	12.17	63.71		40.32
Hubei	85.25	40.58	34.60	5.99	36.19		1.59
Hunan	79.68	14.34	11.43	2.91	4.39	7.04	
Guangdong	72.46	11.70	8.48	3.22	0.00	8.48	
Guangxi	78.57	6.27	4.93	1.34	0.00	4.93	
Sichuan	88.92	18.13	16.12	2.01	8.78	7.34	
Guizhou	85.84	2.88	2.48	0.41	0.11	2.37	
Yunnan	81.94	4.36	3.57	0.79	0.04	3.53	
Xizang							
Shaanxi	82.30	19.39	15.95	3.43	5.53	10.42	
Gansu	89.27	1.90	1.70	0.20	0.51	1.19	
Qinghai	94.36	0.59	0.55	0.03	0.00	0.55	
Ningxia	100.33	0.47	0.47	−0.00	0.00	0.47	
Xinjiang	92.55	6.18	5.72	0.46	27.81		22.09
TOTAL	80.27	500.00	396.74	103.26	414.81	159.88	177.95

Sources: Cotton Spindles from *Zhongguo Fangzhi Gongye Nianjian, 1990*: 344–7. Cotton production from *Zhongguo Tongji Nianjian*, various years.

tons to 1.31 million tons, which would have increased total shortfalls in the remaining provinces over 50 percent from 558,800 tons to 851,900 tons.

Exports not only deprived local mills in these provinces of needed inputs, but their exporting ginned cotton rather than converting it into cloth deprived these provinces of real income. Given a national wholesale price for raw cotton of ¥4,170 per ton in 1988, an average procurement cost of ¥4,002 per ton, and central subsidies of ¥100 per ton, it would have cost purchasing agencies in Hebei, Shandong, and Henan ¥5.75 billion to buy 1.47 million tons of ginned cotton, which would have had a total value of ¥6.14 billion on the wholesale market.[61] The net profit from exports would have been ¥395 million. If, however, these provinces had rechanneled stocks from exports to cover local shortfalls totaling 473,800 tons, local mills could have produced additional cotton cloth with a retail value of ¥4.70 billion.[62] Based on the industry-wide profit and tax rate of 6.67 percent, this additional output would have yielded a total ¥315 million in profits and taxes. Exports of "surplus" cotton would have then yielded net profits of ¥268 million. Shifting cotton from exports to provincial consumption, therefore, would have increased net provincial earnings from ¥395 million to ¥583 million, a gain of 48 percent.[63] Put another way, exporting stocks that could have been used by local mills cost these provinces ¥188 million, according to my analysis.

These estimates of net gains from reduced exports are admittedly rough, and the figures should not be considered hard and fast. Nevertheless, they delineate clear profit-based motives for banning cotton exports. Moreover, the estimates also show that even in the absence of true rents, raw material–producing regions had a clear rationale for reducing exports, given nationwide shortages of raw cotton and underutilized local processing capacity.

Faced with persistent shortages that gave major cotton-growing provinces incentives to suspend or curtail exports, the center was obviously fighting an uphill battle against export barriers. As repeated bidding wars forced prices up, however, supply was beginning to expand. In 1990, production increased from 3.79 million tons in 1989 to 4.51 million tons, a 19 percent increase. The following year, production hit 5.68 million tons, just 10 percent below the level reached during the bumper year of 1984.[64] Rising supply combined with weakening demand, a result of the 1989–90 recession, and decreases

---

[61] The central government and local governments each paid a ¥5 per *dan* subsidy. Because subsidies paid by the exporting province come out of its coffers and are then recouped by the province when exports are sold on the wholesale market, I have omitted the provincial subsidy from my calculations. It should be noted that in 1989, the State Council required that the importing province repay the exporting province for its share of price subsidy costs.

[62] Estimated based on meters of cloth per ton of ginned cotton times an average retail price for cotton cloth of ¥2 per meter.

[63] Evidence from Dezhou Prefecture (Jiangsu) suggests that this calculation may significantly underestimate the losses incurred by exporting raw cotton rather than spinning it into cloth. In Dezhou, raw cotton costing ¥1 yielded ¥4.55 in income for textile mills and profits and taxes worth ¥0.98 – a nearly 100 percent profit for the manufacturing locality compared with the 13 percent return in taxes and profits estimated previously. *Nongchanpin Liutong Tizhi Gaige yu Zhengce Baozhang*: 101.

[64] *Zhongguo Tongji Nianjian, 1992*: 359; *Jingji Ribao* (2/11/90): 1; *Jingji Cankao* (7/26/90): 2; and *Hebei Ribao* (11/13/90): 4.

consumption, thus eased the pressure and for the first time in many years cotton-growing regions enjoyed a modicum of stability. Shanxi, Anhui, Hunan, Gansu, and Xinjiang all succeeded in fulfilling or overfulfilling their quotas without triggering a new cotton war. Perennially volatile areas of Zhejiang, Hunan, and Sichuan and along the Henan-Hubei border also enjoyed peace. Problems nevertheless continued to crop up in 1990. Despite repeated attempts at mediation, local governments in cotton-growing regions continued to restrict access to local supplies while other regions scrambled for short supplies. Hebei, for example, witnessed a series of conflicts. Trouble erupted in Li County after purchasing stations in neighboring Raoyang County illegally raised prices, causing a sudden rush of cotton out from Li County. After prices in Handan City rose above those in Cheng'an County, farmers used bicycles and carts to ship supplies out of low-priced Cheng'an. Amid signs of mounting conflict, the center again banned the opening of rural cotton markets and ordered local purchasing units to adhere strictly to state prices.[65] The Hebei cotton war notwithstanding, by the fall of 1990 the center was prepared to claim that its policy of unified purchase, interregional nonaggression pacts, and deploying central ceasefire monitors had brought the cotton war to an end.

Nevertheless, the center continued to require that the demand of state-owned mills be met before other units were allowed to begin buying raw cotton.[66] Subsequent regulations ordered local governments not to engage in arbitrary price increases, not to export cotton to other provinces before state quotas had been met, not to substitute low-grade cotton for high-grade cotton required by the quota, and threatened fines if localities exported cotton before the state quota had been met.[67]

Provincial governments also retained tight controls over cotton purchasing into 1991. Many required that all purchasers obtain licenses and imposed a system of export "permits" to prevent smuggling. In Hebei, the provincial government admonished local cadres not to allow farmers to smuggle cotton across county borders, banned direct purchasing by cotton mills, and demanded that local purchasing stations strictly abide by official state prices. Jiangsu, Shandong, Henan, and Anhui renewed previous agreements banning cross-border purchasing.

[65] "*Guowuyuan guanyu zuohao yi jiu jiu ling nian du mianhua shougou he diaobo gongzuo de tongzhi*" (State Council notice on the purchase and allocation of cotton for the 1990 season) (9/1/90), *Guowuyuan Gongbao*, no. 19/638 (11/7/90): 712–13.
[66] Zhang, Lu, Sun, Findlay, and Watson, "The 'Wool War' and the 'Cotton Chaos'": 12.
[67] *Jingji Ribao* (8/12/91): 1 and (9/18/91): 1; *Renmin Ribao* (9/30/91): 1; and *Nongmin Ribao* (9/24/91): 1 and (9/26/91): 1.

Despite continued efforts to control cotton purchasing and increases in the production of raw cotton, the cotton war rekindled in 1991 as renewed economic growth increased the demand for raw cotton. Although the central government claimed that the presence of central inspection teams had stabilized the situation in forty-five major cotton-growing regions, the State Council admitted that localities along the Hebei-Shandong-Henan, Jiangsu-Shandong, Anhui-Henan, and Beijing-Tianjin-Hebei borders continued to engage in illegal cross-border purchasing.[68] Wuji County, Jin County, and Gancheng City (Hebei) witnessed a renewed scramble for cotton supplies after unauthorized units offered prices higher than those offered by authorized purchasing stations. Elsewhere, Shandong failed to extinguish the flames of war, and local purchasing agents continued to manipulate the grading of cotton and covertly increase prices. Local officials in Liaocheng, Heze, Huimin, and Dezhou prefectures diverted stocks of high-quality cotton away from state channels, shipping low-grade cotton to mills in Beijing, Tianjin, and Shanghai instead. Fifty thousand *dan* of cotton flowed out of Yantai County (Shandong) after a price war erupted along the Shandong-Jiangsu border.

Trouble also erupted along the Anhui-Henan border. Unhappy with prices in their home province, farmers in Shangqiu Prefecture (Henan) shipped their cotton across the border into Anhui. When local authorities in Henan attempted to block illegal exports, farmers circumvented their barriers. As one farmer explained: "They block by day so we go in the dark of night. They block the big roads so we go by the small roads. They set up roadblocks so we detour around them." Farmers smuggled cotton in small quantities, thus limiting their losses if they got caught and their cotton was confiscated. When told by local cadres that shipping cotton across the border was illegal, even when it was sold to supply and marketing cooperatives in other counties, one farmer replied derisively: "It's all the same patriotic cotton (*aiguo mian*), why can't we sell it to Anhui. Selling it to Anhui isn't selling it to foreign country is it?"[69]

Determined to halt the flow of cotton across the border into Anhui, officials in Henan started fining farmers ¥2 for each kilogram they fell short of their quotas.[70] Police; cadres from the commercial, tax, and price bureaus; representatives of the local supply and marketing cooperatives; and village cadres intensified patrols along roads and at exit points in an effort to stop smuggling. Fines and blockades, however, could not stop farmers from crossing into Anhui.

---

[68] *Jingji Ribao* (10/20/91): 1; *Renmin Ribao* (10/20/91): 1 and (11/19/91): 1; *Nongmin Ribao* (9/26/91): 1; *Fazhi Ribao* (10/15/91): 1; and *Jingji Cankao* (3/8/91): 2.
[69] *Nongmin Ribao* (10/18/91): 1.
[70] *Nongmin Ribao* (10/18/91): 1 and *Renmin Ribao* (11/19/91): 1.

As a result, between September 21 and October 6, more than 6,000 tons of Henan cotton were sold to purchasing stations in Anhui. Problems were not limited to the Anhui-Henan border. On the outskirts of Beijing, local purchasing stations fought each other for supplies and engaged in cross-border competition with counties in Tianjin. In Henan, out-of-plan cotton mills set up illegal purchasing stations in Taiqian County, bid up prices, and fought with official stations for farmers' crops.

The center responded to signs of trouble immediately, dispatching cadres to monitor 300 purchasing stations along the Hebei-Shandong-Henan-Jiangsu border.[71] The presence of central inspectors – and the largest cotton crop since 1984 – seemed to work. By mid-October, according to the Ministry of Commerce, conflicts had been brought under control and, for the first time since 1985, the state's purchasing quotas were overfulfilled. Markets remained relatively stable in 1992. The following year, however, brought renewed problems after overcast and rainy weather reduced the cotton crop.

The ebb and flow of the cotton war between 1985 and 1992 reflects the complexity of the conflict and the rent-seeking interests that drove it. Once triggered by a combination of increasing demand and stagnant or declining supply, the cotton war evolved into a highly complex, multilayered conflict. On a regional level, the cotton war pitted cotton-growing regions against manufacturing regions as the former embargoed exports and starved mills in the latter, prompting buyers from manufacturing regions to "attack" cotton-growing regions in search of supplies. On a second level, it pitted domestic manufacturers against foreign trade bureaus, each seeking to buy "cheap" Chinese cotton, the former for processing into exportable cotton textiles, the latter for direct export.[72] On a third level, it pitted state-owned textile mills operating within the plan and entitled to in-plan allocations of raw cotton against collectively owned mills operating outside the plan and dependent on markets for supplies.[73] On a fourth level, it pitted collective mills in one locality against collective mills in others. On a fifth level, it pitted mills against speculators.[74] Finally, it pitted farmers against the state cotton monopsony, with the farmers seeking to sell to the higher bidder and

---

[71] *Fazhi Ribao* (12/12/91): 1; *Renmin Ribao* (12/2/91): 1 and (2/28/92); and *Jingji Cankao* (11/15/93): 1.

[72] Despite mounting shortfalls in domestic supplies and increasing imports of raw cotton, China exported raw cotton throughout the later 1980s. Zhang, Lu, Sun, Findlay, and Watson, "The 'Wool War' and the 'Cotton Chaos'": 11.

[73] *Jiefang Ribao* described this aspect of the cotton war as a "war between big and small" (*da xiao dazhan*). *Jiefang Ribao* (12/13/90): 3.

[74] *Zhongguo Shangye Bao* (7/28/88): 1.

the monopsony seeking to force the farmers to sell to it at the depressed fixed price.

These layers all intersected in local governments. As the owners of collective mills, local governments in cotton-growing regions had incentives to block exports of scarce cotton to other regions, the state sector, and collective mills owned by other local governments. Even if they did not rechannel local supplies into local mills, local governments in cotton-growing regions had incentives to engage in illegal speculation and seek rents by reselling local supplies on black markets.

Although local governments in cotton-growing regions were clearly implicated in the cotton war, local governments in manufacturing regions were not visibly involved. Instead, the main "aggressors" were nongovernmental actors: factory buyers and speculators. Using prices as their primary weapon, these nongovernmental actors "invaded" cotton-growing regions by either crossing into them and buying directly from growers or by setting up illegal purchasing points outside cotton-growing regions and encouraging growers to smuggle their cotton out of cotton-growing localities. Even though buyers and speculators may have come from manufacturing regions, there is little evidence that local governments in those regions orchestrated attacks on cotton-growing regions.

The cotton war nevertheless involved conflict between the rent-seeking interests of local governments in cotton-growing and manufacturing regions because, when factory buyers and speculators invaded cotton-growing areas, they were essentially acting as proxies for local governments in manufacturing regions. Buyers and speculators, after all, were seeking to obtain supplies that could be sold to collectively owned mills in manufacturing regions, mills in which local governments had vested financial interests and from which they obtained monetized rents. Thus, even though the role of local governments in cotton-growing regions was more prominent (because they actually raised export barriers), local governments in manufacturing regions were party, albeit indirectly, to the war because they benefited from attacks conducted by nongovernmental buyers and speculators.

The central government's initial response to the cotton war was an effort to end it by administrative fiat. As conflicts erupted, it issued what amounted to cease and desist orders in the summer of 1986. When this effort failed to ensure fulfillment of state purchasing quotas, the central government reintroduced unified purchase. According to the regulations issued in 1987 and reiterated thereafter, unified purchase imposed a central monopsony on raw cotton and forbade all trafficking in cotton except by agents of the central Cotton and Fiber Corporation. Local supply and marketing cooperatives, acting under the joint supervision of the Cotton and Fiber Corporation and its provincial, prefectural, and county-level companies, were to purchase cotton and forward it to the state, which would control its allocation and distribution. On paper, therefore, unified purchase recentralized the cotton sector and outlawed vertical export barriers.[75] In reality, unified purchase did not eliminate vertical export barriers; cotton-growing areas continued to embargo deliveries to the state, even though the central government issued progressively harsher restrictions on illegal export protectionism.

Central intervention proved largely ineffectual because, to paraphrase a commentary in *Nongmin Ribao*, the "wind and rain of central policy failed to move the solid mountains" of local rent seeking.[76] As *Jingji Ribao* noted, even though members of the central leadership, the ministries, and various provincial governments "held numerous meetings, rushing about and entreating all quarters" to stop fighting, attempts to end the cotton war proved of little avail. After local governments in cotton-growing regions agreed to implement central purchasing policies and remove illegal export barriers, provincial governors and city mayors from cotton-short areas still had to "conspire" and "barter" with cotton-growing regions to secure supplies, "treading over a thousand mountains and crossing ten thousand seas, suffering a thousand hardships and ten thousand bitternesses."[77]

Nor did unified purchase transform local supply and marketing cooperatives into agents of a tightly organized central monopsony. On the contrary, supply and marketing cooperatives frequently behaved like competitive independent local monopsonies. From 1987 onward, in fact, it is only partially accurate to characterize the cotton war as a war between cotton-growing regions and textile-manufacturing regions. Instead, it is better characterized as a "civil war" among cotton-growing regions dominated by raids and counterraids launched by local supply and marketing cooperatives in one cotton-growing area against neighboring cotton districts.

Although intended to eliminate export barriers, unified purchase actually became a facade behind which local governments continued to engage in export protectionism. In the name of implementing unified purchase, they banned exports, monopolized the purchasing of cotton, and used local police and militia

---

[75] *"Guojia Wujia Ju guanyu jiao bianxiang tigao mianhua shougou jiage de tongzhi"* (State Price Bureau notice on correcting disguised price increases for cotton purchases) (September 16, 1987) Notice No. 117, in *Wujia Wenjian Xuanbian (1987–1988)*: 161; *Jingji Ribao* (8/10/87): 1; and *Renmin Ribao* (7/28/88): 1.

[76] *Nongmin Ribao* (2/14/90): 2.

[77] *Jingji Ribao* (7/23/90): 1.

forces to prevent "smuggling."[78] In addition, unified purchase gave local governments the right to strictly control local purchase prices and deny farmers access to alternative markets. Unified purchase put local governments in cotton-growing regions in a position to legally embargo exports to collective mills located in manufacturing regions. Embargoes of deliveries to state-owned mills were, of course, illegal. Nevertheless, cotton-growing regions continued to block these exports as well.

Subsequent central attempts to control cross-border conflicts among cotton-growing regions by brokering interlocal nonaggression pacts not only did little to prevent cotton-growing regions from embargoing deliveries to the state, they actually tended to reinforce the power of local monopsonies. The system of fragmented local monopsonies spawned by the subversion of unified purchase to local rent-seeking interests was highly vulnerable to self-destructive competition among local monopsonies. The system was, in fact, inherently unstable. As suggested in Chapter 3, so long as cotton can be smuggled across local boundaries and excess demand created gaps between fixed and market-clearing prices, competition for supplies and speculation will drive prices upward to the point at which rents disappear. Collusion among local monopsonists in the form of agreements not to infringe on each other's rents can, on the other hand, eliminate the potential for self-destructive competition and can thereby preserve rents.

A system of nonaggression pacts thus enabled local monopsonists to collude among themselves in defense of rents. In theory, pacts are not actually necessary because tit-for-tat retaliation will teach local rent seekers the futility of competition. Assuming rentiers learn to cooperate before rents disappear, cooperation among cotton-growing regions should have emerged, even in the absence of nonaggression pacts. In the case of the cotton war, central sponsorship of nonaggression pacts actually helped hasten the process by bringing rentiers in cotton-growing regions together. Moreover, central sponsorship facilitated the process by providing external guarantees against opportunistic defection. Yet despite all of these factors, war continued as local governments fought each other for control over lucrative stocks of raw cotton.

The center's attempt to end the cotton war by mandating unified purchase and prodding local governments to enter into nonaggression pacts, to sum up, failed. Instead of forcing local governments to tear down export barriers, central policies created a facade behind which cotton-growing areas were not only able to block exports to manufacturing regions, but also continue to embargo deliveries to the state. Subsequent intervention eased fratricidal conflicts among cotton-growing regions, but did not result in a general dismantling of export

---

[78] *Jingji Ribao* (6/14/90): 1.

barriers. In fact, it was not until after war-induced price increases led to a 25.66 percent increase in cultivated areas and favorable weather led to an 18.37 percent increase in output per hectare that a 49.22 percent increase in cotton production between 1989 and 1991 led to a real lull in the cotton war.[79] Even then, because peace resulted from a temporary balancing of supply and demand, rather than real structural change, the "cotton peace" lasted only as long as supplies remained abundant.

Collusion among cotton-growing regions and the easing of supply-demand contradictions did not succeed in entirely stabilizing cotton markets. Attempts to tighten controls suffered from a combination of poor financing and official profiteering. In many areas, official procurement stations lacked enough cash to pay for purchases at prices farmers were willing to accept. They found themselves in a bind. If they abided by state price policies, farmers would sell their cotton elsewhere. If they raised prices, they could obtain cotton, but at a cost that exceeded the amount of cash allocated to them by the Agricultural Bank of China. During 1988, for example, localities in Jiangsu, Hubei, Shandong, Henan, and Hebei discovered that the only way they could secure supplies for local mills was to match prices offered by other localities and speculators. Having received only enough cash from the Agricultural Bank of China to pay for state-quota purchases at official prices, they had to cover the difference by issuing illegal IOUs (*baitiaozi*).[80] In theory, farmers received higher prices. In reality, the prices they received were largely on paper.

Not only did local governments resort to IOUs, they also defaulted on promises to provide farmers with fertilizer, fuel, and grain if they fulfilled their cotton quotas.[81] In many areas, cadres simply stole supplies of fertilizer and diesel fuel allocated by the state and sold them on black markets.[82] In other areas, they refused to sell supplies at official prices and demanded higher prices

---

[79] *Zhongguo Tongji Nianjian, 1992*: 352 and 365.

[80] *Nongmin Ribao* (10/17/88): 1.

[81] In 1986, the State Council implemented a policy of compensating farmers for selling grain to the state at low prices by granting them 6 kilograms of fertilizer and 6 kilograms of diesel fuel for each 100 kilograms of grain handed over to the state. Policies similar to the "three links" (*san guagou*) were used to ensure that farmers sold their cotton to the state. Farmers frequently received partial payment in kind rather than in cash. Localities in Anhui, for example, offered to sell Henan farmers 15 kilograms of fertilizer and 50 kilograms of grain for every 100 kilograms of cotton sold at a total cost of ¥15 less than localities in Henan. "*Shangye Bu, Nongmuyuye Bu, Zhongguo siyou huagong gongsi guan yu shiliang hetong dinggou yu gongying huafei, chaiyou guaguo shitou banfa*" (Ministry of Commerce, Ministry of Agricultural, Livestock, and Fisheries Industries, and China Petroleum and Chemical Corporation notice on implementation of linkages between contract quotas and supplies of fertilizer and diesel fuel) (2/14/87), in *Guowuyuan Gongbao*, no. 6/529 (3/21/87): 226–30 and *Nongmin Ribao* (10/18/91): 1.

[82] "A Mystery: Where is the Money Going?" *China News Analysis*, no. 1366a (8/15/88): 2–3.

or kickbacks.[83] Cadres also abused local monopsonies by cheating farmers out of prices legally due them for the cotton they sold to the state.[84]

The resulting combination of IOUs, failure to provide promised inputs, and abuses encouraged farmers to seek out purchasers in other localities, including representatives of factories operating outside the plan and thus unable to obtain supplies either through state supply channels or from the local governments' irregular supply system willing to pay hard cash.[85] In northeastern Henan, for example, farmers smuggled their cotton across the border to Cao County (Shandong) arguing that they had no choice because local prices were too low to cover the cost of fertilizer and other inputs. Similarly, in Li County (Hebei) farmers illegally sold their cotton to speculators rather than "hand over cotton and eat losses" after local cadres stole supplies of fertilizer and diesel fuel.

By 1993–4, farmers had learned to play sophisticated games, withholding their cotton until black-market prices forced the state to raise legal prices, or taking advantage of black markets themselves. Ironically, farmers actually came to welcome export protectionism and efforts to restrict free markets because, as one farmer in Jiangsu explained: "The more strictly [local supply and marketing cooperatives] enforce the regulations, the higher the [black-market] price goes. They give us more opportunity to make money."[86] Farmers had also learned to fight back. In Hubei, six farmers beat a state buyer to death after he refused to pay illegal prices for their cotton[87] and attacked others who sought to prevent smuggling.

The pattern of interregional economic conflict observed in the cotton war can be summarized as follows. First, high rates of profits induced local governments to invest in expanding textile manufacturing. Second, a combination of rapid expansion in manufacturing and slower growth in cotton production created shortages.[88] Third, the spatial distribution of raw cotton production and cotton cloth manufacturing capacity was such that, in a situation of shortage, exports of cotton "starved" the local cotton mills, forcing them to operate below capacity and giving their owners – local governments – incentives to block exports. Mills in manufacturing regions also faced shortages and thus they, and indirectly their

---

[83] *Hebei Ribao* (11/13/90): 4 and *Jingji Ribao* (11/1/89): 3.

[84] For example, purchasing agents reportedly "split hairs" in grading cotton, grading it as low as possible, and forcing farmers to accept payment based on the price for lower grade cotton. *Hebei Ribao* (11/13/90): 4.

[85] *Renmin Ribao* (11/16/89): 2; *Jingji Cankao* (11/17/88): 2; and *Hebei Ribao* (11/19/88): 1.

[86] *Wall Street Journal* (11/15/94).

[87] *Reuters* (11/1/94) and (11/8/94).

[88] Slow growth in the production of inputs can be explained, of course, as a direct function of Preobrazhensky's Dilemma: artificially low raw-cotton prices reduced farmers' incentives to grow cotton.

local government owners, had incentives to "invade" cotton-growing areas in search of supplies. Cotton mills owned by the central government, meanwhile, found themselves deprived of supplies when local governments diverted supplies to the collective sector. As shortages became more acute, black marketing and smuggling increased, thereby diverting additional cotton supplies away from state channels.

Fourth, as contradictions between raw material–producing and manufacturing regions and between the state and collective sectors intensified, the central government attempted to solve purchasing problems by abandoning marketization and reverting to administrative allocation and unified purchase.[89] Although putatively designed to strengthen central control over rent-producing commodities, unified purchase actually increased the local governments' ability to block exports and interfere in interregional trade by granting locally controlled supply and marketing cooperatives monopsony control over raw cotton. Fifth, when competition erupted between these local monopsonies, the central government sought to disengage the warring parties by negotiating "cease-fire" agreements or "truces" among cotton-growing localities. Yet, by 1989–90 the center was trying to prop up an institutional structure that no longer served the interests of those entrusted with its defense and who were, in actuality, actively subverting the center's erstwhile monopsony to their own rent-seeking interests using the pretext of implementing unified purchase to tighten local monopsony control over cotton markets. Localization of the cotton monopsony, however, was itself failing as market forces continued to push up prices as competition for control over raw-cotton supplies led to repeated bidding wars between – ironically – these newly established local monopsonies.

THE TOBACCO WAR

In many ways, the tobacco war replicated the cotton war. Cured tobacco production and cigarette manufacturing were spatially maldistributed. Over half of all cigarettes produced in 1987, for instance, were produced in provinces that when combined accounted for less than 20 percent of cured tobacco production,

---

[89] Unified purchase remained in force through 1993. In August 1992, the State Council accepted a proposal to allow the provisional reopening of cotton markets in Shandong and Henan in 1993 and in other provinces in 1994. A new cotton war in 1994, however, derailed these reforms and unified purchase was not abolished as planned. *"Guowuyuan pi zhuan Guojia Tigaige Wei guanyu gaige mianhua liutong tizhi yijian de tongzhi"* (State Council notice of transmittal to the State System Reform Commission of proposed reforms of the cotton circulation system) (8/22/92), in *Guowuyuan Gongbao*, no. 30/715 (1/15/93): 1270; *"Guanyu gaige mianhua liutong tizhi de yijian"* (Proposals for the reform of the cotton circulation system), *ibid.*: 1270–3; and *Xinhua* (10/21/94), in *BBC Summary of World Broadcasts* (hereafter *BBCSWB, Far East*) (10/27/94).

Tianjin Ribao, 11/25/90: 6
"We'll let you off cheap this time"

with a tenth of total cigarette production occurring in provinces that produced no cured tobacco (see Table 4-3). Guizhou, Heilongjiang, Henan, and Yunnan, that when combined produced 65 percent of all cured tobacco, accounted for only 29 percent of the cigarettes produced in 1987.

Cigarette manufacturing was also highly profitable. In fact, cigarette manufacturing had the highest sectoral rate of profit and taxes (¥63.59 per ¥100 of retail sales in 1980 and ¥54.96 per ¥100 in 1989). Cigarette production yielded an astronomically high rate of return on investment (¥723.98 in gross profits and taxes annually per ¥100 of fixed investment). Profits and taxes from cigarette manufacturing were a major source of public revenues (taxes and profits from the cigarette manufacturing sector accounted for 4.82 percent of total profits and taxes in 1980 and 11.07 percent in 1989). The tobacco sector, in short, was prime territory for rent seeking and it is not surprising that it experienced significant growth during the 1980s. Between 1980 and 1989, investment in fixed assets more than doubled from ¥708.59 million to ¥1,825.44 million.[90]

---

[90] *Zhongguo Gongye Jingji Tongji Nianjian, 1990* (Beijing: Zhongguo Tongji Chubanshe, 1991): 212 and *Zhonghua Renmin Gongheguo 1985 Nian Gongye Pucha Ziliao*, vol. 4 (Beijing: Zhongguo Tongji Chubanshe, 1988): 262.

Table 4-3. Spatial Distribution of Tobacco Sector, 1987

Province	Cigarette Production (10,000 Cases)	Percentage of Total Cigarette Production	Cumulative Percentage of Cigarette Production	Cured Tobacco (10,000 Tons)	Percentage of Cured Tobacco Production	Cumulative Percentage of Tobacco Production	Locational Coefficient
Xizang	0.00	0.00	0.00	0.00	0.00	0.00	NA
Zhejiang	1.86	0.06	0.06	0.00	0.00	0.00	
Qinghai	2.52	0.09	0.15	0.00	0.00	0.00	
Shanghai	9.01	0.31	0.46	0.00	0.00	0.00	
Tianjin	50.04	1.74	2.20	0.00	0.00	0.00	
Beijing	87.83	3.05	5.25	0.00	0.00	0.00	
Xinjiang	92.36	3.21	8.46	0.00	0.00	0.00	
Neimenggu	8.32	0.29	8.74	0.00	0.00	0.00	
Jiangxi	22.99	0.80	9.54	0.10	0.06	0.06	12.71
Ningxia	16.43	0.57	10.11	0.20	0.13	0.19	4.54
Hebei	89.06	3.09	13.20	0.30	0.19	0.38	16.41
Jiangsu	101.10	3.51	16.71	0.40	0.25	0.63	13.97
Shanxi	32.89	1.14	17.85	0.40	0.25	0.88	4.54
Guangdong	20.89	0.73	18.58	0.40	0.25	1.13	2.89
Guangxi	93.71	3.25	21.83	1.30	0.82	1.95	3.98
Hunan	47.90	1.66	23.49	1.50	0.94	2.89	1.76
Anhui	49.12	1.70	25.20	1.57	0.99	3.87	1.73
Gansu	106.94	3.71	28.91	2.10	1.32	5.19	2.81
Jilin	55.68	1.93	30.84	2.60	1.63	6.83	1.18
Hubei	229.58	7.97	38.81	4.40	2.76	9.59	2.88
Shaanxi	90.41	3.14	41.95	5.00	3.14	12.73	1.00
Sichuan	206.45	7.17	49.11	5.30	3.33	16.06	2.15
Liaoning	153.05	5.31	54.43	5.30	3.33	19.39	1.60
Guizhou	59.33	2.06	56.49	8.70	5.46	24.85	0.38
Fujian	238.60	8.28	64.77	9.70	6.09	30.94	1.36
Shandong	242.20	8.41	73.17	15.26	9.58	40.53	0.88
Heilongjiang	146.38	5.08	78.25	21.20	13.31	53.84	0.38
Henan	300.24	10.42	88.67	33.60	21.10	74.94	0.49
Yunnan	326.34	11.33	100.00	39.90	25.06	100.00	0.45
TOTAL	2,881.23			159.23			

Source: Zhongguo Tongji Nianjian, 1988: 251 and 354.

115

For tobacco-producing regions, in particular, manufacturing of cigarettes locally was preferable to exporting cured tobacco to other regions. As a local official in Bijie Prefecture, Guizhou, where taxes on tobacco accounted for 60 percent of local income, explained: "Taxes on the sale of cured tobacco are 36 percent, taxes on cigarettes are 60 percent, who doesn't want to set up a tobacco factory?"[91] Even where local governments did not set up new cigarette factories, control over supply was fiscally important. As a local official in the Henan-Hubei border area, where taxes on tobacco accounted for 40 percent of local revenues, observed, "Whoever purchases more, profits more."[92] As was true in the case of the cotton war, therefore, rent seeking encouraged local governments in these regions to engage in extensive export protectionism.

The tobacco war was not, however, simply a mirror image of the cotton war. Whereas the cotton war was essentially a battle for control over the cotton harvest, the tobacco war involved two distinct subconflicts. On one level, competition for cured tobacco pitted tobacco-growing regions against manufacturing regions, particularly during years when tobacco supplies fell short of demand. On another level, the tobacco war involved competition among cigarette-manufacturing regions.[93] Because Chinese cigarettes were not exported in significant numbers, cigarette manufacturers in tobacco-growing regions and elsewhere depended almost exclusively on domestic sales to realize rents created by wide gaps between suppressed cured-tobacco prices and inflated cigarette prices.[94]

The tobacco war, therefore, actually consisted of concurrent cured tobacco and cigarette wars. This meant that local governments in tobacco-growing regions frequently maintained both export and import barriers, with the former designed to monopolize local cured-tobacco purchases and the latter designed to monopolize local cigarette sales. Local governments in nongrowing regions, on the other hand, engaged in a combination of offensive warfare, seeking to breach export and import barriers in tobacco-growing regions, and defensive warfare, seeking to protect local cigarette markets against imports from

---

[91] *Guizhou Ribao* (9/27/88): 2.

[92] *Jingji Cankao* (8/16/88): 2.

[93] Zhongguo Shehui Kexueyuan Gongye Jingji Yanjiusuo Diaochazu, "*Guanyu yancao zhuanmai tigaige wenti de diaocha*" (An investigation into problems in the system reform of the tobacco monopoly), *Jingji Yanjiu*, no. 11 (1985): 36–40.

[94] Customs statistics do not report any exports of Chinese cigarettes during the period of the tobacco wars. They do, however, record minor exports of cured tobacco, less than 1 percent of domestic production. *Zhongguo Tongji Nianjian, 1990*: 647–9. Competition for exports did not, therefore, play a role in triggering and fueling interregional conflicts, as was the case in the cotton war.

tobacco-growing regions. Tobacco-growing regions also engaged in offensive warfare, hoping to breach import barriers on cigarettes raised by nongrowing regions and gain access to export markets. The lines of conflict in the tobacco war were, therefore, complex and crisscrossing.

The tobacco war began before the partial deregulation of internal trade in 1984. The early stages of the war were dominated by conflicts between central and local cigarette manufacturers. Although the central government claimed a de facto monopoly on cigarette production and marketing, during the early 1980s local governments in tobacco-growing regions set up their own factories and began to produce cheap cigarettes and "native tobacco."[95] Out-of-plan plants soon outnumbered in-plan plants and by 1982 their consumption of raw tobacco had reached a point where in-plan plants could not obtain sufficient inputs.[96] In addition, because unauthorized factories run by communes, brigades, and townships sold their cigarettes at prices below those charged by state-owned factories, they quickly captured a significant share of the domestic market. State-owned factories thus found themselves not only short of inputs, but also deprived of outlets for their products. As a result, their profits, and, hence, state revenues, began to fall. In 1982, the State Council attempted to solve this problem by ordering local governments to shut down or restructure out-of-plan plants.[97] Although some illegal plants shut down, many continued to operate under the protection of local governments or went underground.[98]

After local governments failed to retrench local tobacco manufacturing, the State Council declared a formal monopoly on tobacco in September 1983.

[95] In 1960, the central government established a tobacco industry trust supervised by the Ministry of Light Industry, which regulated production and allocation by mandatory planning. "Report on the Tobacco Monopoly System."

[96] *Xinhua* (Domestic Radio Service), in *FBIS, China* (2/6/84): K6–8; *Renmin Ribao* (10/6/84), in *FBIS-China* (10/14/84): K12–13; and *Anhui Ribao* (9/8/84): 1.

[97] *"Guowuyuan pizhuan Guojia Jihua Weiyuanhui deng bumen guanyu dui waijihua yanchang tiaozheng yijian de baogao de tongzhi"* (State Council's comment on the report by the State Planning Commission and other ministries regarding the restructuring of out-of-plan tobacco factories) (5/3/82), in *Zhongyao Jingji Fagui Ziliao Xuanbian*: 417–18; *"Qinggongye Bu, Shangye Bu, Caizheng Bu, Guojia Wujia Ju, Zhongguo Yancao Zonggongsi guanyu kongzhi juanyan shengchan he tiaozheng bufen buheli pinzhong bi jia wenti de baogao"* (Report of the Ministries of Light Industry, Commerce, and Finance; the State Materials Bureau; and the China Tobacco Corporation regarding control of cigarette production and product prices) (6/17/82), in *Zhongyao Jingji Fagui Ziliao Xuanbian*: 419–20; and *"Guowuyuan pizhuan Qinggongye Bu guanyu jihua wai yanchang tiaozheng yijian de baogao de tongzhi"* (State Council comments on the Ministry of Light Industry's report on restructuring of out-of-plan tobacco factories) (5/14/83), in *Zhongyao Jingji Fagui Ziliao Xuanbian*: 422–4.

[98] "Report on the Tobacco Monopoly System," *Jingji Yanjiu* (11/20/85), as cited in *BBCSWB, Far East* (1/22/86).

According to regulations, the new State Tobacco Monopoly Bureau and its commercial representative, the China Tobacco Corporation, would exercise unified
control over the cultivation, purchase, distribution, allocation, and wholesaling
of tobacco and tobacco-related products. Provincial-level governments were
ordered to establish tobacco-monopoly bureaus to administer the new tobacco
monopoly and bring local purchasing agents, factories, and wholesalers under the joint leadership of the Tobacco Monopoly Bureau, the China Tobacco
Corporation, and provincial tobacco bureaus.[99]

Establishment of a formal state tobacco monopoly failed to reduce the size of
the out-of-plan sector and, by 1984, reported cigarette manufacturing capacity
exceeded domestic demand by 25 percent.[100] As a result, the State Council
issued further instructions, ordering 300 out-of-plan plants closed down (up
from the 200 it had ordered closed in 1982).[101] The State Council General
Office also reiterated its orders that all local tobacco companies be placed under
the dual leadership of the China Tobacco Corporation and local governments,
with the tobacco corporation assuming the role of senior partner.[102] Seeking
to solidify the power of the tobacco corporation, the State Tobacco Monopoly
Bureau issued additional regulations granting the China Tobacco Corporation
control over the planting, production, distribution, and allocation of flue-cured
tobacco as well as the production, allocation, and sale of cigarettes, cigars, and
cut tobacco. The corporation also received the authority to set production quotas
for local tobacco-processing plants and set all tobacco product prices. Finally,
the monopoly bureau granted the tobacco corporation the right to license all
interprovincial transfers of cigarettes, cigars, and flue-cured tobacco.[103]

Once again, local governments failed to abide by the new regulations and
continued to protect out-of-plan factories.[104] In fact, six years after the State

---

[99] *"Yancao zhuanmai tiaoli"* (Regulations for the tobacco monopoly) (9/23/83), in *Zhongyao Jingji Fagui Ziliao Xuanbian*: 1330–3.

[100] According to *Xinhua*, in-plan and out-of-plan plants had a total productive capacity of 25 million cases while total domestic consumption was only 20 million cases. "Circular Issued on Tobacco Corporation Problems," *Xinhua* (9/2/84), in *FBIS-China* (9/6/87): K13–14.

[101] *Jingji Ribao* (2/16/84): 1 and *"Guowuyuan Bangong Ting zhuanfa Guojia Jingji Wei guanyu Zhongguo Yancao Zonggongsi dangqian jidai jueding de jige zhuyao wenti de qingyu de tongzhi"* (Notice of the State Council General Office forwarding to the State Economic Com-mission the China Tobacco Corporation's request for decisions regarding urgent problems) (8/24/84), *Guowuyuan Gongbao*, no. 442 (9/20/84): 728–30.

[102] *Xinhua* (9/2/84), in *FBIS-China* (9/6/87): K13–14.

[103] *"Yancao zhuanmai tiaoli shixing xize"* (Detailed rules and regulations for the implementation of the tobacco monopoly) (9/10/84), in *Zhongyao Jingji Faqui Ziliao Xuanbian*: 1333–40 and *China Daily* (9/12/84), in *FBIS-China* (9/12/84): K13.

[104] *"Guojia Jingji Weiyuanhui guanyu jianjue guan ting jihua wai yanchang de tongzi"* (Notice of the State Economic Commission regarding immediate implementation of the State Council's

---

Council first ordered out-of-plan cigarette factories closed the head of the State Tobacco Monopoly Bureau was still demanding that local governments shut them down.[105]

In addition to operating illegal cigarette factories, local governments frequently obstructed cigarette imports, including those authorized by the China Tobacco Corporation. In 1984, for example, county governments in Jiangxi banned sales of cigarettes produced in neighboring Hunan and set up roadblocks to prevent traders from bringing cigarettes across the border. In Shandong, local officials in Ye County refused to allow imports from neighboring counties. Commercial officials in Liulin County (Shaanxi) impounded trucks transporting cigarettes from Shanxi province on grounds that it was illegal to import cigarettes into Shaanxi.[106] In 1985, investigators from the Academy of Social Sciences reported that various provincial governments had not only failed to transfer control over local cigarette factories to the China Tobacco Corporation but, instead, had set up local tobacco monopolies and blocked imports from state-owned factories. Some local governments also subsidized local cigarette manufacturers by rebating a portion of their taxes, thus allowing them to undercut prices charged for cigarettes produced by state-owned factories. Two years later, *Jingji Cankao* reported that many localities had erected regional blockades to prevent cross-border trade in cigarettes. Various provinces used campaigns against illegal peddlers to prevent sales of imported cigarettes. In Guizhou, Kaiyang County organized a major drive against sales of cigarettes imported from other provinces. Qufu County (Shandong) also took action to prevent illegal imports of cigarettes.[107]

At the same time, conflicts occurred between provincial governments that "owned" in-plan factories, and subordinate local governments operating out-of-plan factories. Seeking to prevent local out-of-plan factories from cutting into their rents, provincial governments sought to limit sales of illegally produced

---

decision to close down out-of-plan tobacco factories) (7/5/85), in *Zhongyao Jingji Fagui Ziliao Xuanbian*: 440.

[105] *CEI Database* (8/5/88), in *FBIS-China* (8/8/88): 46. In 1987, according to an official of the tobacco monopoly, thirty illegal factories continued to operate with local governments' connivance, producing 1.4 million cases of cigarettes worth ¥2 billion. Six years later, the bureau announced that it had recently shut down 266 illegal factories, many of which were reincarnations of factories ordered closed in 1983. Before being shut down, these illegal factories had produced 20 million cartons of cigarettes annually. *Xinhua* (11/17/87) and *South China Morning Post* (3/17/93).

[106] *Jingji Ribao* (5/14/84): 4; "Report on the Tobacco Monopoly System," *Jingji Yanjiu* (11/20/85), in *BBCSWB, Far East* (1/22/86); *Jingji Cankao* (9/25/87): 4; *Zhongguo Fazhi Bao* (7/19/86): 2.

[107] During this period, Australian Sinologist David Kelly recalls police forcing travelers to throw away packages of cigarettes when trains crossed provincial boundaries. Interview, April 1993.

local cigarettes. In 1984, the Anhui provincial government, for instance, outlawed the sale of "local cigarettes."[108] Two years later, the government of Guizhou condemned local governments for blocking imports of cigarettes produced by factories in other localities within the province and ordered county governments to dismantle regional blockades and allow circulation in the province. Opening up distribution channels did not, however, include opening up the province to imports from other provinces. The following year Guizhou banned sales of cigarettes produced in neighboring Sichuan. Shanghai, on the other hand, suffered a shortage of locally produced name-brand cigarettes as a result of massive outflows to neighboring Jiangsu at the same time that the municipal government had to station inspectors at railway stations to prevent cheap cigarettes from Guangzhou and Xiamen from flooding the local market.

While the cigarette war dragged on, competition for cured-tobacco supplies escalated in the mid-1980s as production of tobacco leaf began to fluctuate wildly. After hitting a peak of 1.85 million tons in 1982, production fell to 1.15 million tons in 1983, but then increased back up to 2.08 million tons in 1985, creating a temporary glut.[109] The following year, however, production dropped to 1.37 million tons, but then began to climb to 2.34 million tons in 1988 and 2.41 million tons in 1989.[110] The sown area also oscillated during these years. While supplies of inputs varied, cigarette production increased steadily, rising from 15.20 million cases in 1980 to 31.95 million cases in 1989. In contrast to the cotton sector, where supply consistently lagged behind demand after 1987, supplies of raw tobacco tended to fall below demand only periodically.[111]

Periodic shortages triggered stiff interregional conflict. In 1984, local governments in twenty counties in Anhui had to move decisively to prevent outflows of tobacco, which threatened fulfillment of state purchase quotas.[112] The following year, even though a surge in tobacco production produced a glut of cured tobacco, export embargoes and the diversion of supplies into illegal cigarette

---

[108] *Anhui Ribao* (9/8/84): 1; *Guizhou Ribao* (10/5/86): 1 and (7/7/87); and *Jiefang Ribao* (8/7/88): 2.
[109] The State Tobacco Monopoly and State Price Bureau blamed the 1985 glut on local governments, charging that: "Currently, the major problem in flue-cured tobacco production is that some localities are not strictly following relevant regulations set by the state. . . . As a result, output of flue-cured tobacco has greatly surpassed market demand. . . ." *Beijing Domestic Service* (8/16/85), in *FBIS-China* (8/19/85): K9.
[110] *Zhongguo Tongji Nianjian, 1992*: 352, 360, and 438.
[111] Production of cured tobacco had, in fact, increased 3.35 times between 1980 and 1989, during which time production of cigarettes increased only 2.10 times. *Zhongguo Tongji Nianjian, 1992*: 360 and 439.
[112] *Anhui Ribao* (9/8/84): 1.

production left major state-owned factories in Shanghai chronically short of needed raw materials.[113]

The tobacco war did not, however, really get underway until 1986, when total production fell from 2.08 million tons in 1985 to 1.37 million tons. Even though production had decreased significantly, local authorities in many major tobacco-growing areas refused to raise prices, thus opening up gaps between official and black-market prices. In Guizhou, where production fell 33.56 percent (from 289,000 tons to 192,000 tons), local authorities in Bijie Prefecture threw up roadblocks after farmers began to ship large quantities of tobacco across the border into Sichuan and Yunnan, where prices were higher.[114] Export barriers, however, only worsened the situation as local authorities failed to purchase farmers' crops, forcing them to destroy them.[115] Similarly, tobacco-growing regions in western Hubei experienced massive outflows after purchasing stations in Hunan and Sichuan raised their prices while local prices remained so low that farmers were forced to burn their crops to minimize their losses. Hoping to prevent outflows of cured tobacco, local governments took steps to prevent illegal purchasing before the 1987 harvest. The government of Anhui banned exports. Guizhou ordered local governments to form "tobacco purchasing and allocation coordination small groups" to prevent renewed conflict in tobacco-growing areas and smuggling. Kaiyang County (Guizhou) "divided its force to the three routes" deploying several county cadres in each tobacco-purchasing station in hopes of preventing illegal activity. The central government, meanwhile, ordered local governments to stop all forms of price competition and banned factories from purchasing tobacco directly from farmers. Cadres from the State Tobacco Monopoly specifically warned that local governments must not engage in cross-border scrambles for tobacco.

Preventive measures quickly failed. As soon as the new crop came onto markets, Henan was engulfed in conflict. Purchasing stations along county boundaries were caught up in a spiral of price increases. Price increases in one village threw entire counties into chaos and price increases in one county threw whole areas into chaos.[116] Zunyi, Jinsha, and Xifeng counties (Guizhou) were hard hit as local supply and marketing cooperatives vied with each other "like the eight

---

[113] Henan allegedly failed to provide 60 percent of its delivery quota of the cured tobacco, Guizhou 65 percent, and Yunnan 70 percent. "Report on the Tobacco Monopoly System."

[114] *China Statistical Yearbook, 1986* (Beijing: Zhongguo Tongji Chubanshe, 1986): 146 and *Zhongguo Tongji Nianjian, 1987*: 173.

[115] *Guizhou Ribao* (9/20/86): 1, (6/26/87): 1, and (7/15/87): 1; *Hubei Ribao* (12/4/86): 1; *Anhui Ribao* (5/7/87): 2; *Jingji Ribao* (8/17/87): 1; and *Nongmin Ribao* (9/2/87): 1.

[116] *Henan Ribao* (7/25/87): 1; *Guizhou Ribao* (8/3/87): 1, (8/17/87): 1, and (9/1/87): 2; *Zhongguo Gongshang Bao* (10/13/87): 1.

immortals soaring over the sea, each showing his prowess" for control of the tobacco crop. Some localities covertly increased prices. Some offered farmers from other counties a free meal if they would bring their tobacco across county lines. Others "sealed" their borders to prevent outflows of tobacco. Cadres appealed to farmers' "love of home and village" to discourage smuggling. After watching 110 tons out of a total of 120 tons of locally grown tobacco flow over into Yunnan and Guangxi in 1986, cadres from the commercial bureau and local tobacco bureau in Xingyi County (Guizhou) sought out and "hunted down" smugglers. As conflicts mounted, major cigarette factories found that embargoes by tobacco-growing regions had left them chronically short of inputs. The Changde Cigarette Factory in Hubei, for example, was able to obtain less than half the cured tobacco it had received the previous year and could only obtain tobacco from localities within Hunan because local governments in other provinces refused to honor existing delivery contracts.

The 1987 war left tobacco markets in disorder, and both central and provincial governments took steps to prevent a new war in 1988. After suffering losses in excess of ¥600 million (U.S.$162 million) in 1987, the central government ordered all purchasing stations to obtain permits from provincial bureaus of the tobacco monopoly and forbade any purchases by unauthorized units, including factories located outside major tobacco-growing areas.[117] The government of Henan, which lost more than ¥140 million (U.S.$38 million) in the 1987 tobacco war, ordered tobacco-growing counties to set up joint inspection committees to ensure that local purchasing policies were compatible and sent provincial cadres to monitor and coordinate purchasing in border areas.[118]

Hoping to prevent a renewal of conflict along its borders, Anhui unveiled "three must nots": local authorities must not allow tobacco to flow out of their localities, must not drive up prices, and must not allow outsiders to meddle in local purchasing. All imports and exports of cured tobacco were explicitly prohibited.[119] Meitan, Fenggang, and Yuqing counties (Guizhou) abandoned the policies that had triggered panic buying during previous years in favor of a

---

[117] "*Guojia Wujia Ju Zhongguo Yancao Zonggongsi guanyu tiaozheng kaoyan shougou jiage de tongzhi*" (Notice of the State Price Bureau and the China Tobacco Corporation regarding regulation of tobacco purchase prices) (2/10/87), in *Wujia Wenjian Xuanbian (1987–1988)*: 240–1; "*Guojia Yancao Zhuanmai Ju Guojia Wujia Ju guanyu zhizhi jia jiage qiangshou yanye de tongzi*" (Notice by the State Tobacco Monopoly and the State Price Bureau regarding curbing price increases and panic buying of tobacco) (6/4/87), in *Wujia Wenjian Xuanbian (1987–1988)*: 246–8; and "*Guowuyuan Bangong Ting guanyu zhizhi jia jia qiangshou he ti ji shougou yanye de tongzhi*" (State Council General Office notice prohibiting price increases, purchase scrambles, and excess purchasing of tobacco) (9/1/87), *Guowuyuan Gongbao*, no. 22/545 (9/30/87): 736.
[118] *Henan Ribao* (6/2/88): 1.
[119] *Anhui Ribao* (6/27/88): 1 and *Guizhou Ribao* (8/11/88): 1.

policy of intercounty cooperation. Each county agreed to harmonize purchasing policies, to erect no purchasing stations along its boundaries, to dismantle illegal stations, and to send representatives to neighboring areas to ensure cooperation.

Despite these measures, conditions worsened in 1988, even though production of tobacco had increased substantially. In southern Hunan, strict price controls implemented by Lingling Prefecture collapsed almost immediately, setting off bitter intercounty competition. In Ningyuan County (Hunan) local cadres closed off the county, raised roadblocks, set up purchasing stations along its boundaries, and deployed patrols. Cadres lurked along roads, in fields, and on hills to catch farmers trying to cross into neighboring Dao County, where prices were higher.[120] In western Hubei, buyers from Badeng, Hefeng, and Zhangyang counties (Hunan) "raided" Wufeng County (Hubei) taking 250 tons of tobacco back with them. Chenzhou and Lingling prefectures (Hunan) collapsed into chaos as prices rose rapidly, triggering panic buying and speculation. Conflict erupted along the Yunnan-Sichuan border.

In July, a five-county war erupted along the Henan-Hubei border after Laohekou and Xiangyang counties (Hubei) violated state policies and raised tobacco prices.[121] In response, Deng County (Henan) "snatched up the gun." It threw up roadblocks and banned exports of tobacco. Soon local cadres in these counties and nearby Xichuan and Xinye counties (Henan) were guarding their borders day and night "with guns on their shoulders and live ammunition." Gunfire shattered the quiet of the border as cadres shot out the tires of farmers trying to sneak across the border and cadres confiscated the farmers' tobacco. Seeking to create a *cordon sanitaire*, local officials in Henan banned the cultivation of tobacco within fifteen to twenty kilometers of the provincial border. Nevertheless, during July and August, 7,500 tons of Henan-grown tobacco slipped across the border into Hubei. In the process, two people died and 125 were injured. Growers, meanwhile, began to withhold stocks from markets in anticipation that purchase prices would continue to increase.

As the situation deteriorated, the State Tobacco Monopoly again ordered unauthorized purchasing stations closed and price competition and cured-tobacco exports halted.[122] Central orders came to naught and, in September, bitter conflicts erupted in Guizhou. After tobacco supplies began to flow into

---

[120] *Nongmin Ribao* (7/26/88): 2 and (10/14/98): 1; *Jingji Ribao* (9/9/88): 1; and *Renmin Ribao* (9/26/88): 2.

[121] *Henan Ribao* (8/22/88): 1; *Jingji Cankao* (9/2/88): 2; *Nongmin Ribao* (7/26/88): 2 and (11/28/88): 2; *Jingji Cankao* (8/16/88): 2; and *Xinhua* (9/7/88), in *FBIS-China* (9/13/88): 36.

[122] *Jingji Ribao* (9/7/88): 1 and *Guizhou Ribao* (9/27/88): 2 and (10/10/88): 2.

Dafang County, cadres in Qianxi County threw up roadblocks and fined farmers ¥25 if they were caught returning to Qianxi County with empty carrying baskets or ¥300 if they were driving an empty horse cart. Nanyang, Dafang, Zhijin, and Hezhang counties suspended exports after local processing factories complained they could not afford to buy tobacco at prices being offered by outsiders. Yuqing and Siqian counties found themselves locked in a war after Yuqing erected barriers to prevent farmers from shipping their tobacco into Siqian. Weng'an, Zunyi, Meitan, Yuqing, Huangpin, Fuquan, and Kaiyuan fought a bitter seven-county war. As the chaos in Guizhou deepened, officials of the State Tobacco Monopoly estimated that illegal price increases would cost the state more than the ¥100 million lost the previous year.

As prices climbed and competition intensified, farmers began adulterating stocks with bricks, metal, and dirt. Even so, buyers snapped up whatever farmers offered for sale.[123] Declining quality and increased prices were extremely costly. Total losses in the 1987–8 tobacco wars reportedly ran as high as ¥2.2 billion (U.S.$591 million).[124] Henan reportedly lost ¥206 million (U.S.$55 million) and Hunan ¥400 million (U.S.$107 million).[125]

Seeking to avoid a repeat of the 1988 tobacco war, the central government convened a meeting of representatives of major tobacco-growing provinces in May 1989. At this summit, the State Tobacco Monopoly unveiled a new system of permits designed to prevent unauthorized purchasing and to control exports from tobacco-growing regions and imports into nongrowing areas. The State Council, meanwhile, approved measures strengthening the State Tobacco Monopoly, mandating unified purchase and imposing strict price controls and outlawing purchasing by units other than those authorized by the tobacco monopoly and ordered farmers not to ship tobacco out of their home areas or to sell tobacco to any purchaser except officially authorized purchase stations.[126]

---

[123] *Jingji Ribao* (7/29/89): 2.

[124] *Renmin Ribao* (2/12/92): 2. According to Du Yuxiang total losses in the tobacco wars were more than ¥600 million (U.S.$161.82 million). Du Yuxiang, *"Nongcun shangpin liutong tizhi gaige sishi nian"* (Forty years of reform in the rural commodity circulation system), *Jingji Yanjiu Ziliao*, no. 4 (1989): 11–18. In 1989, *Renmin Ribao* put state losses and those of cigarette factories at ¥340 million for 1987–8. *Renmin Ribao* (7/25/89): 1.

[125] *Renmin Ribao* (2/12/92): 2. Other sources put Henan's losses at ¥140 million in 1987 and ¥300 million in 1988. *Henan Ribao* (1/23/89): 2.

[126] *"Guojia Yancao Zhuanmai Ju, Zhongguo Yancao Zonggongsi guanyu renzhen gaohao yanye shougou gongzuo de yijian"* (Proposal of the State Tobacco Monopoly and the China Tobacco Corporation on earnestly conducting tobacco purchasing) (6/15/89), *Guowuyuan Gongbao*, no. 15/596 (9/12/89): 589–91; and *"Guowuyuan Bangong Ting zhuanfa Guojia Yancao Zhuanmai Ju, Zhongguo Yancao Zonggongsi guanyu renzhen gaohao yanye shougou gongzuo*

The governments of Henan, Shandong, Hubei, Anhui, Yunnan, Guizhou, and Sichuan promised to implement these new controls.[127] Henan adopted a system of "tobacco-purchasing licenses," ordered 1,050 unauthorized purchasing points closed, and threatened to dismiss and punish cadres who triggered conflicts. In Guizhou, the provincial government brokered an agreement committing local governments in thirty-five counties and nine prefectures to unified price, grade, and payment policies and banning cross-border purchasing. Hunan concluded a series of agreements with Guangdong, Guangxi, and Guizhou that sought to prevent renewed scrambles for tobacco.

In conjunction with these agreements, vigorous action by provincial governments helped "abruptly lower the temperature" in major tobacco-growing regions in 1989.[128] In Henan, when trouble erupted in Xuchang, Weidi, and Xinzheng counties, provincial officials responded immediately, dismissing cadres in Xuchang and Weidi, closing illegal purchasing stations, and fining everyone involved in unauthorized purchasing ¥100, with fines doubled for those from outside the immediate county. When speculators threatened to overrun Xiangcheng County (Henan) resolute action by county authorities and the government of Pingdingshan City quickly restored order.

Elsewhere in Henan, villages in Xiping and Queshan counties illegally set up their own purchase stations and cadres in Huaibin County illegally raised prices. Prompt action by provincial authorities, however, prevented these incidents from escalating into a full-scale tobacco war.[129] Even the usually volatile Henan-Anhui border remained quiet. Other provinces also remained relatively peaceful. In Hunan, Chenzhou, Lingling, and Shaoyang prefectures enjoyed stability after two years of intense conflict, even though counties in Chenzhou and Lingling prefectures had to issue several million yuan worth of IOUs after they ran out of cash to pay for tobacco purchases.

During 1990, it became clear that the heyday of the tobacco wars had passed. Provincial governments in major tobacco-growing regions continued to expand interregional cooperation, and in early 1990 Henan renewed earlier agreements

yijian de tongzhi" (Transmittal notice of the State Council General Office regarding the proposal of the State Tobacco Monopoly and the China Tobacco Corporation on earnestly conducting tobacco purchasing) (6/27/89), *Guowuyuan Gongbao*, no. 15/596 (9/12/89): 589.

[127] *Fazhi Ribao* (5/12/88): 1; *Renmin Ribao* (5/15/89): 2, (6/4/89): 2, and (7/25/89): 1; *Henan Ribao* (6/5/89): 1; *Jingji Cankao* (11/1/89): 2; *Henan Ribao* (11/5/89): 1; and *Guizhou Ribao* (6/27/89): 2.

[128] *Henan Ribao* (7/31/89): 1 and (11/6/89): 2 and *Renmin Ribao* (7/23/89): 2.

[129] *Henan Ribao* (8/9/89): 1; *Jingji Cankao* (8/18/89): 2; *Anhui Ribao* (8/10/89): 2; *Hunan Ribao* (7/28/89): 2; and *Nongmin Ribao* (10/23/89): 2.

with Anhui and Hubei banning all forms of interregional competition.[130] Hunan, meanwhile, warned local governments that it would not tolerate local policies that might trigger a new tobacco war. Problems occurred nonetheless. In Henan, village governments in Shenqiu County illegally purchased tobacco, and purchasing agents in Suiping County violated state pricing policies. In both cases, county authorities immediately cracked down and prevented trouble from spreading to other localities. Provincial authorities also took prompt action against Xiangcheng County after it began purchasing adulterated tobacco.

Yunnan also continued to experience problems. During 1990, five prefectures along the Yunnan-Guizhou-Sichuan border region fought a cross-border tobacco war in which adulteration and illegal price increases cost the state ¥210 million in losses.[131] The following year, Shangcai County illegally set up purchasing stations along its borders and failed to dismantle them when ordered to do so by the provincial government, creating disorder in neighboring counties.

As was true in the case of the cotton war, the cooling off of the tobacco war was largely a function of changes in the supply-demand balance rather than central intervention. As the war escalated, production of cured tobacco began to increase. During 1987, the sown area increased 42.77 percent and production increased 42.85 percent after the average price per ton of cured tobacco increased 25.94 percent. The following year, sown areas increased an additional 15.29 percent and production 2.91 percent, for a net two-year increase of 64.60 percent in the sown area and a 47 percent increase in production.[132] Cigarette production, meanwhile, expanded so rapidly that, by 1987, a glut of low-quality cigarettes had emerged. Thereafter, production continued to exceed consumption, with the result that by 1993, inventories of cheap cigarettes had grown so large that Chinese tobacco manufacturers had stocks equal to two and a half years of consumption on hand.[133] Under these conditions, it simply made less and less sense for local governments to scramble for supplies of cured tobacco.

Before changes in supply and demand eased interregional conflicts, the central government attempted to solve the tobacco war by strengthening monopsony

---

[130] *Zhongguo Shangye Bao* (2/10/90): 1; *Hunan Ribao* (5/27/90): 1 and (8/31/90): 1; and *Jingji Ribao* (9/3/90): 2.
[131] *Renmin Ribao* (2/12/92): 2 and *Fazhi Ribao* (9/16/91): 1.
[132] *Zhongguo Tongji Nianjian, 1992*: 352 and 360 and *Zhongguo Guonei Shichang Tongji Nianjian, 1991*: 184.
[133] *Xinhua* (11/17/87); *Reuters* (10/13/87); *Xinhua* (6/20/90); and *Reuters* (8/12/93).

controls over the purchase of cured tobacco and monopoly controls over the production of cigarettes. Yet, neither efforts to impose a central monopoly nor attempts to broker agreements among the local agents of that monopoly proved particularly effective. In fact, the tobacco war occurred largely within the organizational boundaries of the tobacco monopoly after local governments sought to cash in on the profits generated by low cured-tobacco prices and high cigarette prices. Competition between local out-of-plan factories and factories operating under the plan resulted in the cigarette war. Competition between out-of-plan and in-plan factories then spilled over into conflicts over supplies of cured tobacco, thereby triggering the tobacco war.

The central government's initial attempt to reassert control foundered when the establishment of the State Tobacco Monopoly Bureau in 1983 and the subsequent adoption of regulations increasing the China Tobacco Corporation's power to regulate purchasing, manufacturing, and distribution failed to force local governments to close down illegal cigarette factories. Attempts to use unified purchase to prevent local governments in tobacco-growing areas from blocking exports to state-authorized cigarette factories also fell short. The tobacco war, therefore, actually escalated after the central government attempted to recentralize control.

After failing to reassert control by fiat, the center brokered a series of agreements among tobacco-growing regions. As was the case in the cotton war, the combination of an unsuccessful attempt to recentralize purchasing and nonaggression pacts put local governments in tobacco-growing regions in a position where they could set up local monopolies, block exports to manufacturing regions, and collude with other local governments to prevent fratricidal price competition.

Once again, central intervention did not bring about an immediate end to the fighting between local monopsonies; the tobacco war only began to subside after it became clear that competition was not only costly, it also rapidly dissipated rents. Once it became clear that uncontrolled competition among local monopsonies was essentially self-defeating, provincial, prefectural, and county governments threw their weight behind the interregional nonaggression pacts in an effort to cut their losses. The center indirectly assisted in their efforts by providing local governments in tobacco-growing regions with legal authority to block exports and maintain strict control over local prices. In the end, however, the center never really succeeded in forcing local governments to eliminate vertical barriers blocking the flow of cured tobacco to state-owned cigarette factories or the distribution of cigarettes produced by state-authorized manufacturers.

THE WOOL WAR

The wool war arose out of a combination of spatial maldistribution, high profits, low technical barriers to entry, and supply-demand contradictions.[134] The causes of the wool war were, therefore, similar to those of the cotton and tobacco wars. Yet, the wool war was a fundamentally different conflict. First, blind speculation rather than rent seeking, in the pure sense, fueled the war, particularly in its latter stages. Second, the center remained essentially neutral. Unlike the cotton or tobacco wars, the center did not attempt to separate the combatants. Finally, speculation and central neutrality combined to produce the most striking feature of the wool war – the defeat of rent-seeking interests. By 1989, market forces had triumphed over rent seeking, and rent-seeking wool-producing regions found themselves stuck with a glut of high-priced, low-quality wool that they could neither use themselves nor sell to other regions.

Two policy changes set the stage for the wool war. In January 1985, the central government abolished the state monopsony on wool and shifted to a system of purchase by contract and markets.[135] A year later, it changed the wool allocation system.[136] The center granted Neimenggu, Gansu, Qinghai, and Xinjiang permission to adopt what became known as the "three selfs": "self-production, self-use, and self-marketing."[137] The "three selfs" did not include a blanket ban on exports. The policy allowed these four regions to retain 53 percent of local production.[138] At the same time, the center decontrolled wool markets in other regions, allowing non–wool-producing regions to engage in wool exchanges.[139]

---

[134] *Zhongguo Xumu Gongye Tongji* (Beijing: Zhongguo Tongji Chubanshe, 1990): 614 and *Zhongguo Tongji Nianjian, 1988:* 352.

[135] Watson, Findlay, and Du, "Who Won the 'Wool War'?": 233 and *"Zhonggong Zhongyang, Guowuyuan jinyibu huoyue nongcun jingji de shi xiang zhengce"* (Notice of the Central Committee and the State Council on ten policies designed to invigorate the rural economy), *Zhongyao Jingji Fagui Ziliao Xuanbian:* 222–6. Also see Christopher Findlay, ed., *Challenges of Economic Reform and Industrial Growth: China's Wool War* (North Sydney, Australia: Allen & Unwin, 1992).

[136] Wool markets were decontrolled in the joint CCP Central Committee–State Council statement on rural policy issued as Document No. 1 for 1986. Wang Bingxiu, *"Wo guo yangmao gongqiu zhuangkuang ji qi duice de tantao"* (An inquiry into China's wool supply and countermeasures), *Nongye Jingji Wenti,* no. 3 (1987): 11–14.

[137] She Lingtang, *"Zhongguo yangmao shichang yuanxing jizhi yanjiu"* (Research on the long-term mechanisms of China's wool markets), *Nongye Jingji Wenti,* no. 2 (1992): 19–22 and Liu Delun and Li Zhengqiang, *"Wo guo yangmao gongxu maodun ji duice tantao"* (An inquiry into contradictions in the supply and demand for wool in China and countermeasures), *Zhongguo Nongcun Jingji,* no. 12 (1988): 42–6.

[138] *Jingji Ribao* (11/17/86): 2.

[139] She, *"Zhongguo yangmao shichang yuanxing jizhi yanjiu."*

Table 4-4. *Spatial Distribution of Wool Sector, 1987*

Province	Woolen Cloth (10,000 Meters)	Percentage Woolen Production	Cumulative Percent Woolens	Raw Wool Production (Tons)	Percentage Raw Wool Production	Cumulative Percent Raw Wool	Locational Coefficient
Fujian	2.05	1.03	1.03	0.00	0.00	0.00	
Hunan	2.44	1.22	2.25	0.00	0.00	0.00	
Guangxi	1.20	0.60	2.86	0.00	0.00	0.00	
Guangdong	3.88	1.95	4.80	0.00	0.00	0.00	
Jiangxi	1.67	0.84	5.64	0.00	0.00	0.00	
Shanghai	18.78	9.43	15.07	93.00	0.04	0.04	211.75
Hubei	8.57	4.30	19.37	113.40	0.05	0.10	79.24
Beijing	8.81	4.42	23.79	195.00	0.09	0.19	47.37
Tianjin	9.35	4.69	28.48	217.20	0.10	0.30	45.14
Guizhou	0.73	0.37	28.85	677.00	0.32	0.62	1.13
Anhui	4.14	2.08	30.93	1,282.00	0.61	1.23	3.39
Jiangsu	47.21	23.70	54.63	1,328.00	0.64	1.87	37.28
Yunnan	0.93	0.47	55.09	1,719.00	0.82	2.69	0.57
Sichuan	2.78	1.40	56.49	2,554.00	1.22	3.91	1.14
Zhejiang	9.53	4.78	61.27	2,583.00	1.24	5.15	3.87
Shaanxi	3.90	1.96	63.23	2,886.00	1.38	6.53	1.42
Shanxi	2.60	1.31	64.53	3,689.00	1.77	8.30	0.74
Ningxia	1.38	0.69	65.23	3,912.00	1.87	10.17	0.37
Henan	8.12	4.08	69.30	4,750.00	2.27	12.44	1.79
Jilin	4.15	2.08	71.38	5,323.00	2.55	14.99	0.82
Liaoning	10.09	5.06	76.45	6,731.10	3.22	18.21	1.57
Heilongjiang	6.64	3.33	79.78	7,085.90	3.39	21.61	0.98
Xizang	0.23	0.12	79.90	8,935.20	4.28	25.88	0.03
Hebei	4.45	2.23	82.13	9,875.00	4.73	30.61	0.47
Gansu	6.50	3.26	85.39	13,472.70	6.45	37.06	0.51
Shandong	14.22	7.14	92.53	13,932.00	6.67	43.73	1.07
Qinghai	2.91	1.46	93.99	20,100.00	9.62	53.35	0.15
Xinjiang	6.17	3.10	97.09	44,597.40	21.35	74.70	0.15
Neimenggu	5.80	2.91	100.00	52,858.00	25.30	100.00	0.12
	199.23			208,908.90			

Source: Based on data in *Zhongguo Tongji Nianjian, 1988.*

Granting Neimenggu, Gansu, Qinghai, and Xinjiang greater control over locally produced wool gave them new leverage over domestic supply. Combined, these four provinces produced 63 percent of China's wool (see Table 4-4).[140] These provinces, however, accounted for only 13 percent of total wool-spinning capacity and only 11 percent of wool cloth production in 1987. Allowing them to retain more than half of locally produced wool, therefore, gave them control over significant stocks of wool that they could export and dispose of in newly established markets in other parts of China.

[140] *Zhongguo Xumuye Tongji (1949–1989)* (Beijing: Zhongguo Tongji Chubanshe, 1990): 603 and 608.

As was the case with the cotton war, the center's decision was ill timed.[141] Prior to 1985, wool production had slowly declined from 201,837 tons in 1982 to 177,953 tons in 1985. Sheep herds had also declined, dropping from 106.57 million head in 1982 to 94.21 million head in 1985, as increasing consumer income raised consumption of meat and diverted sheep away from wool production.[142]

Demand for wool, meanwhile, rose as spinning capacity increased from 478,000 spindles in 1978, to 600,000 spindles in 1980, and to 1,900,000 spindles in 1985, including 1,300,000 spindles installed in mills operating within the plan and 600,000 spindles operating outside the plan. At the same time that wool production had declined 11.83 percent, therefore, demand for wool had increased twofold.[143] Foreign imports helped alleviate the resulting pressure on supply, but at a considerable cost in foreign exchange.[144]

Wool-producing areas were among those expanding wool manufacturing. The number of spindles in the four major wool-producing provinces of Neimenggu, Gansu, Qinghai, and Xinjiang more than doubled from 85,400 in 1980 to 191,000 in 1986.[145] For the most part, factories in these regions were technologically backward and operated outside the plan.[146] Demand from new out-of-plan mills in non–wool-producing areas, including small village and township mills in Zhejiang and Jiangsu, was also rising, thus increasing the pressure on out-of-plan supplies.[147] Wool supplies were, therefore, already tight and likely to tighten further before the central government decided to relax state controls over purchasing and allocation of wool.[148]

Moreover, there had already been problems in wool-producing areas. In October 1984, local governments began to restrict purchases of above-quota wool by individual traders. Some localities had already engaged in price wars

---

[141] Zhang, Lu, Sun, Findley, and Watson, "The 'Wool War' and the 'Cotton Chaos'": 14–15.

[142] Liu and Li, "*Wo guo yangmao gongxu maodun ji duice tantao*": 44 and Wang Xukai and Lang Zuoshi, "*Yangfangye de weiji yu yangyangye de kunjing ji chulu*" (The wool textile industry's crisis, the sheep raising industry's predicament, and ways out), *Nongye Jingji Wenti*, no. 3 (1987): 15–17; *Zhongguo Xumuye Tongji (1949–1989)*: 568–626; and *Zhongguo Tongji Nianjian, 1987*: 178.

[143] Wang, "*Wo guo yangmao gongqiu zhuangkuang ji qi duice de tantao*": 11.

[144] *Xinjiang Ribao* (8/27/88): 1.

[145] *Zhongguo Fangzhi Gongye Nianjian*, various years.

[146] *Jingji Ribao* (11/17/86): 2.

[147] *Nongmin Ribao* (6/27/85): 2. Growth in wool manufacturing outside of the four major wool-producing provinces was so rapid that installed spinning capacity in Neimenggu, Gansu, Qinghai, and Xinjiang actually declined as a percentage of total installed capacity, falling from 16.52 percent of the total in 1975, to 14.24 percent in 1980, and then 13.69 percent in 1986.

[148] *Jingji Ribao* (11/17/86) and (11/15/86): 1–2; *Jingji Cankao* (9/7/89): 1; and Paul Leung, "China: Woolen Base Rising," *Textile Asia* (March 1989): 124.

as they sought to obtain sufficient wool to fulfill their purchasing quotas.[149] Shortly after the central government abolished the state wool monopsony, wool-producing regions in Hebei and Neimenggu were hit by panic buying as wool mills in Shanghai, Beijing, and Datong competed for supplies. In Hebei, purchases doubled, pushing prices from ¥2.45 to ¥3.54 per *jin*. Stockpiles dropped from 7,000 tons to 2,340 tons. Gansu also experienced rapid price increases during 1985 as prices for cashmere rose from ¥8 to ¥28 and wool prices rose from ¥2.6 to ¥3.9 per *jin*. Yulin and Yan'an prefectures (Shaanxi) were rocked by a "war" as outsiders drove up wool and cashmere prices. In Yulin County, herders began to adulterate wool with sand as high demand drove buyers to snap up whatever stocks were available. In Neimenggu, conflicts erupted as outside buyers poured into wool-producing areas. By the summer of 1985, purchasing stations along county borders faced each other "glaring like tigers eyeing their prey." During early 1986, illegal price increases by purchasing stations along the borders of Hebei, Neimenggu, Ningxia, and Qinghai created renewed disorder, prompting the State Price Bureau to issue an urgent notice ordering local price bureaus in these provinces, as well as in Shanxi, Gansu, Liaoning, and Heilongjiang, to stabilize wool prices in accordance with policies laid down by the State Price Bureau, Ministry of Textiles, and Ministry of Commerce.

Having already received permission to adopt local-use-only policies, the major wool-producing provinces of Gansu, Qinghai, Xinjiang, and Neimenggu responded to the escalating wool war by banning exports. Restricting exports did not, however, restore order. Local governments within these provinces continued to engage in speculative price wars and battle for control over local supplies. Local governments in Xinjiang and Qinghai, in fact, used the ban on exports to extract illegal kickbacks from outsiders, demanding that they pay a 50 percent export duty, disguised as a "grassland management fee." Local governments in Xizang imposed similar export tariffs.[150] Some localities even demanded that outsiders pay for wool with foreign exchange. In Hebei, meanwhile, outside buyers scrambled across wool-producing regions searching for wool only to find "the gruel is meager and the monks many."

Export barriers were not, however, successful as local officials found they could not control each buyer and each wool-raising household, with the result that wool continued to flow out of low-price localities and into high-price localities, confronting low-price localities with the choice of either raising prices or

---

[149] *Nongmin Ribao* (12/29/86): 2 and (6/27/85): 2; *Jingji Ribao* (7/6/85): 4; *Shaanxi Ribao* (5/15/86): 2 and (10/10/85): 1; *Renmin Ribao* (7/21/86): 2; and *Zhongguo Shangye Bao* (7/8/86): 1.
[150] *Jingji Ribao* (11/15/86): 1–2 and *Hebei Ribao* (5/28/87): 1.

failing to fulfill their purchase targets.[151] Seeking to prevent costly price wars, some counties attempted to end the war by negotiating "truce agreements" but were unable to stop the fighting because other localities continued to "invade" them by raising local purchase prices.

In the short term, the wool war proved highly profitable for wool-producing regions. By 1986, herders' income from the sale of wool in Neimenggu, Gansu, Qinghai, and Xinjiang had reportedly increased ¥260 million. Local government revenues from wool sales increased from ¥18 million to ¥60 million. On average, counties in wool-producing regions obtained an additional ¥60,000 in revenues as a result of illegal price increases and ad hoc taxes.[152]

The war continued in 1987, when "a thousand armies and ten thousand horses descended on producing regions."[153] Most wool-producing areas had by now adopted various types of unified purchase and marketing policies. Seeking to prevent herders from selling their wool to outsiders, local governments in some areas refused to sell farm households fertilizer and pesticides until they had fulfilled their contractual deliveries to the state. Others erected roadblocks and required purchasers to obtain "transport permits," without which wool could not be shipped on either the railroads or highways. Zhangjiakou Prefecture (Hebei) imposed a 30 percent export duty on wool. In some areas, local regulations mandated that local mills had priority in buying wool; if they could not obtain sufficient supplies, wool previously purchased for outsiders would be confiscated.

Despite the obvious escalation of interregional conflicts, the central government adopted a hands-off approach to the wool war. It did not restore the central wool monopsony or attempt to broker interregional peace agreements, as it had done in other conflicts. In the absence of central intervention, individual provinces and localities adopted unified purchase and tried to negotiate multilateral agreements to prevent price competition and cross-border purchasing but with limited success.[154]

The central government was not entirely passive. Seeking to reduce supply-demand contradictions, the central government ordered Neimenggu, Gansu, Qinghai, and Xinjiang to increase wool exports in 1986. It reduced the amount of wool these provinces could retain from 53 percent of local production to 40 percent.[155] The central government also authorized major wool-producing regions to use auctions to regulate wool exports. Three auctions took place in 1988, one in Neimenggu, one in Xinjiang, and one in Nanjing.

---

[151] *Hebei Ribao* (7/10/87): 2 and (5/28/87): 1.
[152] *Jingji Ribao* (11/15/86): 1–2.
[153] *Renmin Ribao* (5/30/88): 2; *Nongmin Ribao* (7/29/88): 2; and *Jingji Cankao* (9/7/87): 1.
[154] *Renmin Ribao* (8/12/89): 2.
[155] *Jingji Ribao* (11/17/86): 2, (10/22/88): 3 and (10/27/88): 1; and *Neimenggu Ribao* (9/21/88): 1.

The introduction of wool auctions failed to end the wool war. If anything, auctions seemed to accelerate price increases and encourage rent seeking by local governments in wool-producing regions. In the fall of 1988, Xinjiang banned all wool exports. Soon thereafter, prefectural and county governments within Xinjiang imposed their own local export bans.[156] Nationally, prices climbed 71.63 percent, increasing from an average of ¥628.5 per 100 kilograms in 1987 to ¥1,078.7 in 1988.[157] Herders continued to adulterate their wool.[158] Along the Liaoning-Neimenggu border, local officials erected inspection posts on the main access road leading into wool-producing regions in Neimenggu to prevent speculators from invading, only to see them bypassed as speculators overran border markets.[159] Nationwide, the war dragged on into a fourth year.

Despite signs of continuing trouble, by 1988 the wool war had reached a critical juncture and conditions were changing. Although supplies remained tight nationally, local governments in wool-producing regions were not restricting exports to ensure supplies for local mills. In many cases, they were using export barriers to engage in profiteering. Export barriers enabled supply and marketing cooperatives to keep purchase prices well below prices outside wool-producing areas.[160] By imposing unified purchase, local governments could then obtain rents by reselling local wool on markets elsewhere.

During 1987, local governments moved beyond profiteering and began to engage in headlong speculation. Having witnessed rapid increases in prices as the wool war escalated, cadres came to anticipate further increases and thus began to hoard wool rather than export it. By 1988, stockpiles in wool-producing regions had hit a record 104,000 tons, much of it badly adulterated to increase its weight.[161] In early 1989, supply and marketing cooperatives in Neimenggu and

---

[156] *Zhongguo Tongxun She* (9/11/89), in *FBIS-China* (8/11/89): 31.

[157] *Zhongguo Tongji Nianjian, 1988*: 794 and *Zhongguo Tongji Nianjian, 1990*: 283.

[158] In Xinjiang, farmers not only added sand, they also used syrup to add additional weight. *Xinjiang Ribao* (8/14/88): 1.

[159] *Dongbei Jingji Bao* (11/22/88): 1; *Jingji Ribao* (8/12/88): 1; *Nongmin Ribao* (8/15/89): 1; and *Jingji Cankao* (11/12/89): 2.

[160] Farmers charged that unified purchase allowed "the supply and marketing cooperatives to wipe the oil off the bodies of the farmers and act as a covert organization opposing the farmers." Local cadres complained that they were not responsible: "When the farmers eat losses, they blame the cadres but it's the [state commercial bureaus] that are profiting; this stupid situation cannot be worse." *Nongmin Ribao* (7/28/88): 2.

[161] Thirty-two kilograms of wool purchased in Neimenggu in 1988, for instance, contained 26.8 kilograms of dirt. That year, on average, after washing Neimenggu wool proved only 5.11 percent pure versus 35 percent in 1986. In Heilongjiang, the purity rate dropped from 30 percent to 15 percent. *Dongbei Jingji Bao* (11/22/88): 1; *Heilongjiang Ribao* (9/5/90): 2; *Renmin Ribao* (11/13/89): 2; and Liu and Li, *"Wo guo yangmao gongxu maodun ji duice tantao"*: 42.

Xinjiang were holding more than 57,000 tons. Herders also began to hoard wool in expectation of further price increases. Herders in Neimenggu, for example, were reportedly withholding some 15,000 tons.[162]

Hoarding was not limited to wool-producing regions. Fearing future price increases and uncertain supplies, wool mills had bought up large stocks of wool during 1987 and continued to add to their reserves in 1988. By 1989, many had reserves well in excess of short- and medium-term requirements and had begun to cut back on purchasing.[163] Moreover, because their capital was tied up in existing inventory, wool mills that did make new purchases could not pay in cash but had to rely on IOUs.[164]

Speculation had also reduced demand for domestic wool. As domestic prices rose, the price differential between domestic and imported wool decreased, prompting coastal wool manufacturers to switch to imported supplies.[165] By the late 1980s, some wool manufacturing centers had largely ceased to rely on domestic supplies. In 1989, for example, mills in Beijing imported 71.4 percent of their supplies of wool, and mills in Tianjin imported 97.5 percent of their wool.[166] Mills in Zhejiang and Jiangsu also began to import large quantities of wool from Australia. As coastal manufacturers shifted to imported wool, demand for high-priced, low-quality Chinese wool fell. Finally, the economic slowdown following retrenchment in September 1988 had begun to push up stockpiles of woolen products. By late 1989 recession had begun to cut demand for woolen products, leaving mills with ¥1.7 billion worth of unsold inventory and forcing them to cut back production.

In the summer of 1989, the bottom dropped out of the Chinese wool market. The average price for lamb's wool declined from ¥1,078.7 per 100 kilograms in 1988 to ¥907.1 in 1989 and then to ¥663.8 in 1990, a net decline of 38.46 percent.[167] In northern Shaanxi, prices for high-grade white down fell 44 percent and prices for common wool plummeted 72 percent. In Neimenggu, prices for top-quality wool fell to the state-guaranteed minimum of ¥554 per 100 kilograms. Even then, many supply and marketing cooperatives refused to pay full price. The extent of deflation in the wool market was

---

[162] *Zhongguo Shangye Bao* (4/14/90): 1.

[163] *Heilongjiang Ribao* (9/5/90): 2.

[164] *Jingji Cankao* (9/17/90): 1.

[165] Even though imported wool remained more expensive per 100 kilograms, higher purity and longer fibers meant that the imported wool produced more wool cloth than Chinese wool and was thus actually cheaper. *Heilongjiang Ribao* (9/5/90): 2.

[166] *Jingji Cankao* (11/12/89): 2; *Zhongguo Tongxun She* (8/11/89), in *FBIS-China* (8/11/89): 31; and Hu Yang, "China: Wool Piles Up," *Textile Asia* (January 1990): 86–7.

[167] *Zhongguo Tongji Nianjian, 1990*: 283; *Zhongguo Tongji Nianjian, 1991*: 263; *Jingji Cankao* (9/16/90): 2; and *Zhongguo Shangye Bao* (6/23/90): 3.

amplified by the fact that the period 1988–9 was one of significant inflation, with prices increasing 18.5 percent in 1988 and then 17.8 percent
in 1989.

Having been able to sell everything they produced, even adulterated wool, for
¥2,200–2,300 per 100 kilograms in 1988, herders in Ihju League (Neimenggu)
suddenly found that the local supply and marketing cooperative would buy
only 350 kilograms of the 1,000 kilograms they brought to market and then
would pay only ¥600–700 per 100 kilograms.[168] Adding insult to injury, the
cooperatives paid for half of what they bought with IOUs, with the result that
herders came away with only ¥300–400 in cash, 15 percent of what they got
in 1988. Throughout Neimenggu, cooperatives stopped buying wool, with the
result that half the wool shorn in 1989 remained in the hands of herders.[169]

Provincial cadres, on the other hand, complained that the cooperatives already
had 46,000 tons of wool in stock and had already lost ¥11 million as a result
of interest charges.[170] When Neimenggu sent agents to Shanghai, Beijing, and
elsewhere in search of buyers, they found themselves confronted with agents
from Xinjiang, Qinghai, Gansu, and Ningxia, all of whom were saddled with
large stocks of wool. By late 1989, Neimenggu reportedly lost approximately
¥100 million (U.S.$27 million), and a third of textile mill workers in Huhehaote
were furloughed. The wool war was over.

The almost overnight end of the wool war was largely a result of blind speculation. Fixed purchase prices may have created rents before 1986. Speculation,
however, pushed prices beyond market-clearing levels. In the short term, speculation fueled itself, creating a bubble. If local governments had been able to
control wool supplies and manipulate rents, they might have succeeded in maintaining the bubble. But they could not corner the market for wool because they
did not control foreign imports. Even at the height of the wool war, rent-seeking
local governments in wool-producing regions controlled only about a quarter
of the total wool supply.[171] Thus, potential local monopsonies had to confront a
market whose prices they could not control, either individually or collectively.
Even though they could not control prices, local monopsonies could have created

---

[168] A league is an administrative unit found in Neimenggu and corresponds to a prefecture. Ihju
is the Mongol pronunciation. In *putonghua* (Mandarin) Ihju would be rendered as Yikezhao.
Zhongguo Fen Sheng Shi Xian Da Cidian (Dictionary of China's provinces, cities, and counties)
(Beijing: Zhongguo Luyou Chubanshe, 1989): 206.

[169] *Renmin Ribao* (11/13/89): 2.

[170] *Jingji Cankao* (11/12/89): 2 and *Jingji Ribao* (1/26/90): 3.

[171] According to the Minister of Textiles, total demand for washed and processed wool (as opposed
to raw wool) in 1987 was 240,000 tons, of which only 50,000 tons came from domestic sources.
Imports totaling 175,000 tons made up most of the difference. *Jingji Ribao* (10/22/88): 3.

rents by driving artificial wedges between local purchase prices and prevailing market prices. Uncontrolled speculation and adulteration,[172] however, pushed domestic prices so high that Chinese wool simply could not compete with imported wool.

Wool auctions, paradoxically, proved to be the nail in the coffin of unbridled speculation. Convinced that prices would increase as a result of auctions, local governments in wool-producing regions bought heavily in early 1989. When auctions opened, however, it became clear that a glut existed, and buyers quickly pushed prices down, confronting local governments that had speculated on rising prices with the choice of selling their wool at a loss or letting it remain unsold. Even then, few buyers were willing to purchase available stocks. In Chifeng Prefecture (Neimenggu), for example, the local supply and marketing cooperative bought 9,300 tons of wool only to see prices at the Beijing auction drop and leave it with 8,300 tons of inventory and large outstanding debts to the bank. Unable to command a price it deemed fair, the government of Xinjiang banned exports of wool, even though the local livestock products corporation had accumulated 13,300 tons in surplus inventory worth ¥220,000.[173]

After 1989, local governments in wool-producing regions struggled to cope with the "great depression." Xinjiang, where supply and marketing cooperatives owed sheep herders ¥64 million for wool purchased in 1988 and 6,600 tons of wool remained in herders' hands, the provincial government sought to stabilize markets by easing credit and encouraging continued purchases.[174] In Neimenggu, the government imposed a floor price of ¥500 per 100 kilograms, less than half the 1988 price. Many supply and marketing cooperatives, however, lacked the cash to buy wool and simply shut down. Purchases rebounded somewhat in 1990, but intervention proved marginally effective and wool prices continued to slide in 1991.[175]

In general, the central government took a hands-off approach to the wool war. After issuing regulations calling on local governments to tighten market controls in 1986, it remained on the sidelines until June 1989. When wool markets began to collapse, the central government issued a notice stating that wool markets had become too chaotic in recent years. Too many channels had been allowed to open up. The central government, therefore, called on local

---

[172] Adulteration increases the real cost. As purity declines, manufacturers have to purchase more raw wool to obtain the same amount of usable wool. Thus, if the price doubles and purity falls 50 percent, the real price increases four times, even though the nominal price only doubles.

[173] She, "*Zhongguo yangmao shichang yuanxing jizhi yanjiu*": 21.

[174] *Jingji Cankao* (1/21/90): 2 and *Nongmin Ribao* (7/23/90): 4.

[175] *Statistical Yearbook of China, 1993*: 244 and *Zhongguo Guonei Shichang Tongji Nianjian, 1992*: 175.

governments to restore control and crack down on adulteration. Purchasing units in neighboring areas must not engage in "scalping," illegally reselling wool bought at monopsony prices. They should not scramble with each other, force up market prices, covertly raise prices, or "suppress grade to suppress price" when buying wool from herders. To ensure proper implementation of regulations, provincial-level commercial, textile, price, and technical control bureaus were ordered to set up small groups and tighten controls on local purchasing.[176]

The June 1989 notice was not a major policy shift. It simply ordered local governments to stop the wool war. It was also essentially irrelevant. Market forces had already ended the war.

The center's response to the escalating wool war was not necessarily one of inattention or neglect. Its response was neutrality. As previously noted, by the time the war reach its peak, major textile mills owned by the state had already shifted over to imported wool, not domestic wool. That meant that when wool-producing regions embargoed exports or pushed black-market prices up, state-owned mills were largely unaffected. Instead, collective mills, particularly those in areas that produced little wool, such as Jiangsu and Zhejiang, bore the brunt of shortages and price inflation during the wool war. Insulated by foreign imports, the central government had no immediate incentives to intervene when wool-producing regions raised export barriers. Nor did it have incentives to support collective wool mills outside wool-producing regions. Because its interests were neither advanced nor harmed by rent seeking in wool-producing regions, the central government could remain neutral, occasionally calling on local governments to stop the worst abuses but doing little to prevent rent seeking by wool-producing regions.

Provincial governments in wool-producing regions also had little reason to prop up inflated wool prices or abet rent seeking by local supply and marketing cooperatives. Speculation had hurt mills in both manufacturing and major wool-producing regions. The profits of the Number 1 and Number 3 Wool Textile Mills in Lanzhou, for example, were cut by ¥2.11 million in 1986 as a result of rising costs.[177] In Xinjiang, profits in the local textile sector fell by ¥500,000 while profits in Neimenggu's fell by ¥1.85 million. By 1987, profits on each meter of wool cloth produced in Xinjiang had fallen from ¥5 to ¥0.8. Rent

---

[176] *"Shangye Bu, Guojia Ji Wei, Fangzhi Bu, Guojia Gongshang Xingzheng Guanli Ju, Guojia Wujia Ju, Guojia Jishu Jiandu Ju 'Guanyu jiaqiang mianyang mao, shanyang rong shichang guanli de tongzhi"* (Notice of the Ministry of Commerce, State Planning Commission, Ministry of Textiles, State Commercial Administration Management Bureau, State Price Bureau, and the State Technical Control Bureau on strengthening controls on wool and down markets) (6/16/89), *Wujia Wenjian Xuanbian (1989)*: 287–8.

[177] *Jingji Ribao* (11/15/86): 1–2 and *Jingji Cankao* (9/9/87): 1.

seeking by local supply and marketing cooperatives and speculation by herders, in short, had begun to cut into profits earned by higher-level governments within wool-producing regions, creating new contradictions within these provinces.

Central neutrality outlived the wool war. When wool markets collapsed, the center did not intervene in any major way. It allowed prices to fall nearly 50 percent and allowed inventories to pile up in wool-producing regions, forcing herders, local governments, and speculators to bear the long-term costs of the wool war. Even if it was willing to tolerate rent seeking, or found itself unable to prevent it, the center was clearly unwilling to bear the costs or pick up the pieces when uncontrolled rent seeking backfired on raw material–producing regions.

The outcome of the wool war thus confirms one of the propositions advanced in Chapter 3: that uncontrolled rent seeking will ultimately dissipate rents. In the case of the wool war, headlong speculation quickly pushed prices above both domestic market-clearing levels and, in combination with declining quality, prevailing world prices. Once this occurred, demand for domestic wool dropped and so did the efficacy of export protectionism. Paradoxically, therefore, whereas central intervention in the form of unified purchase failed to end the cotton and tobacco wars, central neutrality succeeded in ending the wool war, but only after any semblance of state control over the purchase and allocation of domestic wool supplies had all but collapsed.[178]

THE SILK COCOON WAR

The silk cocoon war differed in a number of critical ways from the preceding conflicts. Some basic sectoral facts were similar: high profits, low technical barriers to entrance, and so forth.[179] The silk sector, however, was not as spatially maldistributed as the cotton, tobacco, and wool sectors. Most silk cocoons were produced and processed in the same province, with three provinces (Zhejiang, Jiangsu, and Sichuan) dominating both raw silk production and

---

[178] Five years after the wool war ended, signs of trouble reappeared in 1994, when cashmere prices rose dramatically, increasing from ¥70 per kilogram to ¥240 in northern Shaanxi after a renewed spurt of growth in the wool-spinning sector again pushed demand beyond supply. Speculation and adulteration reportedly reached such levels at this time that sugar, which herdsmen used to increase the weight of their cashmere, disappeared from local stores. *Reuters* (8/4/94).

[179] Start-up costs were low and profits high. A basic silk filature that cost ¥10,000 to build and equip could reportedly produce returns of between ¥100,000 and ¥200,000. Sun Ziduo, "*Nongchanpin maoyi dazhan xiancheng de yuanyin, weihai he jiejue tujing*" (Causes of trade wars over rural products, their harmful effects, and suggested solutions), *Zhongguo Nongcun Jingji*, no. 11 (1988): 36–40 and Lardy, *Foreign Trade and Economic Reform in China*: 76–7.

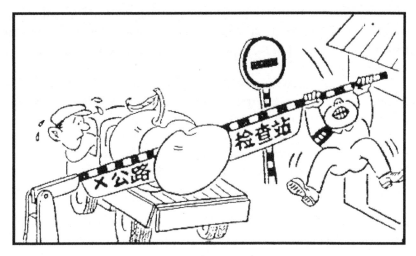

Unknown
"Slicing the apple"

manufacturing.[180] On the surface, therefore, contradictions between manufacturing and raw material–producing regions do not appear to provide an explanation for the silk cocoon war.

Although detailed data on silk-reeling capacity are not available, excessive expansion of silk-reeling capacity nevertheless appears to have been a primary contributing factor. According to Chinese press figures, by 1987 domestic silk filatures had the capacity to process more than 450,000 tons of raw silk. Domestic production totaled only 353,500 tons, leaving a 27.30 percent gap between supply and capacity.[181] By 1989, the gap between supply and demand had widened because supply remained constant at 353,500 tons while reeling capacity increased to 500,000 tons, leaving a 41 percent shortfall.[182]

The gap was even larger in key silk regions. In 1987, Jiangsu produced 20.63 percent of China's raw silk and 22.49 percent of its finished silk.[183] Local filatures, however, had an installed capacity 33 percent greater than the provincial supply. The following year, Wujiang County, one of Jiangsu's major

---

[180] In 1989, these three provinces produced 73.46 percent of total silk cocoons and 77.63 percent of total silk cloth. *Zhongguo Tongji Nianjian, 1990*: 369 and 464.

[181] *Jingji Ribao* (5/28/88): 2 and (7/9/88): 3.

[182] *Jingji Ribao* (4/17/89): 3. According to one 1988 report, silk-reeling capacity was actually three times the supply of silk cocoons. This report, however, is so far out of line with other reports that its veracity must be questioned. *China Daily* (11/2/88), in *FBIS-China* (11/2/88): 39.

[183] *Zhongguo Tongji Nianjian, 1988*: 252 and 352; *Jingji Ribao* (2/1/89): 2; *Renmin Ribao* (2/26/89): 5; and *Anhui Ribao* (2/3/89): 5.

silk-reeling centers, produced only half the raw silk demanded by local filatures. Anhui's silk filatures faced a 40 percent shortfall in supply. The Zhujiang Delta region in Guangdong had the capacity to process 2,500 tons of raw silk but produced only 500 tons.[184]

Foreign exports exacerbated interregional competition for raw silk. With even rudimentary processing, exported silk was enormously profitable.[185] More important, silk exports earned hard currency, which could then be used to finance imports or resold on domestic swap markets at a profit. Silk-cocoon-raising localities, therefore, sought to ensure that locally produced silk was processed locally and exported by the local foreign trade departments. Traditional export entrepôts such as Shanghai, on the other hand, sought to maintain their position as middlemen, a position that not only enabled them to claim a share of export profits but also allowed them to buy raw silk domestically with soft *renminbi* and sell it to foreign buyers for hard currency.[186] New coastal trade centers in Guangdong, meanwhile, sought to muscle in and establish themselves as middlemen.[187] Even nonproducing localities that had never acted as entrepôts sought to divert exports from other localities.[188] In conjunction with shortages in supply, demand for exportable silk created an environment conducive to interregional conflict comparable to that observed in the cotton, tobacco, and wool wars.

After a series of skirmishes between 1984 and 1986, the silk cocoon war broke out in 1987 as "different armies" engaged in "tangled warfare" and civil strife.[189] Provinces fought provinces, counties fought counties, and villages fought villages in a struggle that resembled the "tangled warfare among warlords." In Henan, panic buying affected 80 percent of silk production. "Four tigers invaded Sichuan," offering double the local price and even offering to pay, illegally, in foreign exchange. In the fall, the Shandong-Jiangsu-Anhui border erupted after purchasing stations in northern Jiangsu illegally raised prices. Purchasing stations in Anhui retaliated by offering farmers a half *jin* of

---

[184] *Jingji Ribao* (1/3/89): 2. This gap was a direct result of dramatic decreases in local silk production as farmers moved into other cash crops or out of agriculture and into rural industry.

[185] Officially, silk cocoons were a "Category I" export good. This meant that export purchases by China National Silk Import and Export Corporation ("China Silk") and provincial trading corporations were made based on domestic prices. Because the domestic price for raw silk was considerably lower than the world prices, simple arbitrage trade was highly profitable.

[186] Sun, "*Nongchanpin maoyi dazhan*."

[187] *Jingji Cankao* (7/3/87): 1.

[188] *Jingji Cankao* (7/15/88): 1.

[189] *Jingji Cankao* (10/10/87), (4/24/88): 1, (6/28/99): 2, and (8/11/88): 2; *Fazhi Ribao* (4/23/88): 1; *Henan Ribao* (6/25/88): 2; and *Reuters* (5/25/88). The "four tigers" refers to buyers from Guangdong, Shanghai, Jiangsu, and Zhejiang.

urea fertilizer for each *jin* of silk cocoons, triggering an influx from Jiangsu. Along the Jiangsu-Shandong border in the vicinity of Linyi City (Shandong) silk flowed across the border out of Jiangsu, leaving local filatures chronically short of raw silk. Diversion of silk from the state purchasing channel reached such levels that a third of state-owned filatures, including 1,000 of Shanghai's 1,600 filatures, were left idle by a lack of raw silk.

The 1987 silk war proved costly. China Silk reportedly had to spend ¥250 million more than anticipated to obtain silk cocoons and lost U.S.$100 million in foreign exchange earnings.[190] Evidence also surfaced of widespread official profiteering and smuggling. Faced with a rapidly deteriorating situation, the central government intervened in February 1988 by imposing strict price controls and banned all purchases except those by authorized purchasing agents.[191] In May 1988, Zhejiang, Jiangsu, Sichuan, and Anhui responded by setting up a system whereby all units purchasing silk cocoons had to post bond in the form of an "adjustment fund" equal to 100 percent of the value of the silk based on producer prices in their province.[192] Funds would be paid to their respective provincial tax bureaus, which would hold them in escrow. After reeling the cocoons, if these units then sold their raw silk to the provincial silk corporation at state-set prices, they would receive a certificate authorizing the tax bureau to return their bond. If they failed to sell their raw silk to the provincial corporation or demanded higher prices, then the units would forfeit their bonds or have the difference between state-set prices and the sale price deducted from them.

Jiangsu tightened controls further by placing silk purchasing under the unified management of the provincial commercial bureau and ordering all units purchasing silk to receive authorization from the bureau. The provincial government banned direct purchases by individuals, units, and filatures. Authorized units were ordered to post a bond of ¥300 per *dan* that would be returned only if processed silk was then sold to the provincial silk corporation. Exports to other provinces were banned, and units caught selling to units outside the province would forfeit their bonds.[193] Zhejiang adopted unified purchase by supply and

---

[190] *Jingji Ribao* (5/28/88): 2 and *Reuters* (5/25/88).
[191] "*Guojia Wujia Ju Duiwai Jingji Maoyi Bu guanyu zhengdun canjian shougou jiage de tongzhi*" (Notice by the State Price Bureau and the Ministry of Foreign Trade regarding rectification of silk cocoon purchase prices) (2/21/88), in *Wujia Wenjian Xuanbian (1987–1988)*: 252–3 and "*Duiwai Jingji Maoyi Bu Guojia Gongshang Xingzheng Guanli Ju Guojia Wujia Ju guanyu jiaqiang canjian shougou jingguan guanli gongzuo de tongzhi*" (Notice by the Ministry of Foreign Trade, the State Commercial Management Administration, and the State Price Bureau on strengthening direction and management of silk cocoon purchases) (2/23/88), in *Wujia Wenjian Xuanbian (1987–1988)*: 254–5.
[192] *Zhejiang Ribao* (5/23/88): 1 and *Zhongguo Shangye Bao* (5/28/88): 2.
[193] *Xinhua Ribao* (5/29/88): 1 and *Zhejiang Ribao* (6/1/88): 1 and (6/2/88): 1.

marketing cooperatives and had local governments in major silk-producing regions sign agreements wherein they pledged not to engage in cross-border purchasing or compete with each other for supplies.

On June 6, 1988, the State Council issued Notice No. 305, ordering provincial silk companies in Zhejiang, Jiangsu, Sichuan, and Anhui to implement a system of unified purchase and management, shut down illegal silk-purchasing stations, implement state price policies, and sign interregional agreements harmonizing local purchase and price policies.[194] The circular, however, left the details of implementation up to the provinces, directing them to decide which departments would control purchasing and establish local price ceilings. Sichuan responded by placing all silk-cocoon purchasing under the unified control of the provincial silk corporation and banning all intercounty purchasing. Seeking to prevent "anarchy," Hunan ordered all outside buyers to register with county authorities and threatened that any buyer who illegally raised prices would have his purchases confiscated.[195]

Despite these measures, Jiangsu, Zhejiang, Anhui, and Sichuan once again felt the "lash" of war in 1988.[196] On May 27, buyers from Jiangshan and Changshan cities (Zhejiang) attacked Yushan County (Jiangxi) by setting up purchase stations along their borders with Yushan. Silk filatures in Kaihua County (Zhejiang) then invaded Yushan by sending trucks across the border to purchase silk directly from producers. Buyers from Guangfeng and Dongxiang counties (Jiangxi) then joined in the fray, which *Jiangxi Ribao* equated with the invasion of China by the imperialist powers during the 1900 Boxer Rebellion, referring to the invaders as the "eight-power allied armies."[197]

---

[194] *Renmin Ribao* (6/8/88): 2 and (6/15/88): 1; *Nongmin Ribao* (6/16/88): 2; and *Xinhua* (6/8/88), in *FBIS-China* (6/10/88): 21.

[195] *Hunan Ribao* (6/27/88): 1. The situation in Hunan, which was not specifically covered by Notice No. 305 and was not an important silk producer, was complicated. Low silk-cocoon prices had reduced production significantly and the provincial government believed it was necessary to decontrol prices. Floating prices, it hoped, would raise local production. At the same time, however, the provincial government did not want outside buyers to pour into the province and drive prices up sharply. Thus, when it allowed silk cocoon prices to rise, it imposed strict controls on purchasing and exports. Guangdong faced a similar problem with declining local production as farmers shifted into more profitable activities. *Jingji Ribao* (1/3/89): 2.

[196] *Zhongguo Shangye Bao* (10/18/88): 3.

[197] *Jiangxi Ribao* (7/27/88): 1. Ironically, in the weeks just before Yushan County was invaded, local cadres had decided to tear down roadblocks set up the previous year to block exports of silk, concluding that they would not work. In place of export barriers, they had adopted a system of providing farmers with incentives based on compensation for their costs in bringing silk cocoons to county purchase stations, a bonus of fertilizer upon delivery, and the right to buy additional fertilizer at reduced prices.

Elsewhere, buyers from Hubei, Henan, Zhejiang, and Jiangsu invaded Anhui.[198] "Anhui armies fought Anhui armies" in a "civil war," while war raged between Hubei and Anhui. Huoshan County saw a third of locally produced silk cocoons flow across the border into Hubei, even though local cadres erected roadblocks to prevent outflows. In parts of Anhui, the conflict reached such intensity that cadres who manned checkpoints by day dared not go out at night for fear that the farmers would retaliate against them, and several deaths were attributed to the war.

In Henan, a war erupted between Huaiyang and Lushan counties after local commercial, price, foreign trade, agricultural, and public security bureaus ignored State Council and provincial regulations.[199] Linqu County (Shandong) suffered through a second year of warfare as village and township filatures scrambled for silk cocoons. In Mengyin and Yiyuan counties (Shandong) village cadres engaged in official profiteering, buying silk cocoons locally at state-fixed prices and then smuggling them out of their respective counties for resale. In Sichuan, the fighting resumed even before the smoke of the 1987 silk cocoon war had cleared. After local governments in silk-raising areas threw up defense lines, erecting customs posts and checkpoints and ordering local security forces to patrol the roads in an effort to seal their borders, buyers counterattacked. Buyers from Guangdong, for example, hired transportation units of the People's Liberation Army to run the blockade, hoping that local officials would not dare stop trucks belonging to the army.

As the war heated up, prices skyrocketed. During the spring purchasing season, prices nationwide averaged ¥520 per *dan* compared with ¥244 in 1987.[200] By late June, prices averaged ¥600 in Jiangsu, ¥580 in Zhejiang, ¥550 in Anhui, and ¥354 in Sichuan. By mid-July, prices in Jiangsu and Zhejiang provinces had reached ¥610. In Luotian County (Hubei) prices oscillated between ¥700 and ¥800. In She County, southern Anhui, prices rose from ¥450 to ¥550 in just three days. Buyers from Henan, Hubei, Zhejiang, and Jiangsu reportedly pushed prices as high as ¥1,300 in parts of western Anhui, four times the official price of ¥320 set by provincial authorities. By mid-summer, as suggested by these price changes, "fixed" prices had ceased to exist, except in official writs, and the market had effectively displaced the state in determining actual prices.

---

[198] *Fazhi Ribao* (5/8/89): 1; *Anhui Ribao* (7/24/98): 2; *Jingji Cankao* (7/15/88): 1.
[199] *Henan Ribao* (6/23/88): 2; *Dazhong Ribao* (5/27/88): 2 and (8/2/88): 1; *Jingji Cankao* (6/28/88): 1; and *Far Eastern Economic Review* (10/27/88): 38.
[200] *Jingji Cankao* (8/11/88): 2; *Zhongguo Wujia Tongji Nianjian, 1989*: 315; *Nongmin Ribao* (7/1/88):1 and (7/12/88): 1; and *Jingji Cankao* (7/15/88): 1.

After the "spring silk cocoon war" began, provincial and prefectural governments tried to bring the situation under control. When township and village filatures in Huzhou City (Zhejiang) violated "gentlemen's agreements" concluded with localities in neighboring Jiangsu and triggered a round of panic buying, the Zhejiang government publicly rebuked municipal authorities, which then fined the units involved.[201] After a two-month cease-fire along the Jiangsu-Zhejiang border collapsed in August, the Zhejiang provincial government brought leading cadres from Jiaxing City, Haining City, Tongxiang County, Deqing County, Yuhang County, and, once again, Huzhou City to a summit meeting in Hangzhou, where they agreed to a single uniform price for silk in northern Zhejiang and a ban on purchasing by all units except supply and marketing cooperatives.

In Sichuan, the government of Luzhou Prefecture fined supply and marketing cooperatives in Naxi County after they illegally raised prices.[202] Several provinces ordered the police to patrol their borders and directed their tax, commercial, and price bureaus to tighten market regulations. Individual provinces imposed export duties, labeled "product adjustment fees," and implemented strict licensing systems.

After Notice No. 305 failed to halt the silk cocoon war, the State Council issued a second notice on September 22, reiterating that China Silk had a monopoly on silk exports and purchases of raw silk for export.[203] To tighten China Silk's control, the State Council imposed an 80 percent export tax on silk fabrics and a 100 percent export tax on raw silk, silk cocoons, silk waste, and spun silk effective October 26 and stipulated that this duty would be rebated only to China Silk and approved joint ventures.[204] Exports by joint ventures, however, were also subjected to a new system of export licenses. China Silk, in

---

[201] *Renmin Ribao* (6/11/88): 1 and (2/26/89): 1; *Zhejiang Ribao* (6/3/88): 1; and *Jiefang Ribao* (8/20/88): 3; and *Jingji Ribao* (8/31/88): 2.

[202] *Renmin Ribao* (6/14/88): 2 and *Jingji Ribao* (9/5/88): 3.

[203] Before 1988, silk-cocoon-raising regions had been allowed some leeway to use agents other than China Silk to export silk produced above China Silk's purchase quota. Notice No. 305 sought to clamp down on an increasing tendency to divert exports away from China Silk, which paid lower prices for domestic silk than competing provincial export corporations and smugglers. In western Anhui, for instance, the state paid ¥83,000 a ton for silk purchased under the plan. At that time, out-of-plan prices stood at around ¥160,000 per ton. Units wishing to sell silk outside the plan, however, had to pay a ¥83,000 to an "adjustment fund," with the result that in-plan and out-of-plan prices were effectively the same. Smuggling silk out of the provinces allowed sellers to avoid paying the ¥83,000 adjustment fund, thereby almost doubling their income from the sale. *Jingji Cankao* (7/15/88): 1.

[204] *Jiefang Ribao* (9/25/88): 3; *China Daily* (11/2/88), in *FBIS-China* (11/2/88): 38; *Far Eastern Economic Review* (3/23/89): 82–93; *Xinhua* (9/25/88), in *FBIS-China* (9/26/88): 30–1; *Jingji Ribao* (11/2/88): 1; and *Jingji Cankao* (11/2/88): 1.

turn, worked with the Customs Administration to tighten export controls and with the Bank of China to block commercial lending to units engaged in illegal silk exporting. The State Council also ordered the bank to curtail all loans to silk filatures that could not prove they had legal access to supplies.

In some areas, new regulations seemed to work. In the "black triangle" of northern Zhejiang, local officials "showed mutual understanding and sympathy." They set up a "joint four-county inspection group" to regulate prices strictly and managed to prevent renewed conflict.[205]

In other areas, such measures failed and a "fall silk-cocoon war" followed hard on the heels of the 1988 spring silk-cocoon war.[206] In Shanxi, war broke out when Qinshui and Yicheng counties set up purchase stations along their borders with Yangcheng County and raised prices from ¥205 to ¥250 and then to ¥300. Cadres in Yangcheng erected roadblocks in an effort to prevent farmers from smuggling silk cocoons into Qinshui and Yicheng. Roadblocks, however, failed as farmers snuck across the county line at night and used back roads instead of the main roads. As silk began to pour across the border, prices rose further, rising to ¥375, then climbing to ¥400 and ultimately ¥450.[207] In Liaoning, state and collective filatures seeking to purchase silk cocoons illegally from farmers directly pushed prices for tussah silk cocoons, which produce a lower grade of silk than the mulberry silk cocoons more common in other parts of China, from ¥68 per *dan* to ¥147.[208] The Anhui-Hubei border war resumed in September, when Luotian County (Hubei) jacked prices up from ¥370 to ¥470 and sent smugglers to infiltrate Jinzhai County (Anhui) where they beat up two police officers. Langxi County (Anhui), meanwhile, "stole" 2.9 tons of silk cocoon from Liyang County (Jiangsu) by illegally raising prices. Along the Jiangsu-Zhejiang border, when Wujiang County (Jiangsu) illegally raised prices, Tongxiang County

---

[205] *Jingji Cankao* (10/22/88): 2. The black triangle included Deqing, Yuhang, Haining, and Tongxiang counties. As noted below, this four-county effort did not, however, prevent a border war as Tongxiang County found itself engaged in a fight with neighboring Wujiang County, Jiangsu.

[206] The sericulture cycle results in two distinct periods highly conducive to conflict. In most areas of central China, two crops of silkworms are raised a year, with the first crop appearing in April or May and a second crop appearing in late summer. Lillian M. Li, *China's Silk Trade: Traditional Industry in the Modern World 1842–1937* (Cambridge, MA: Harvard University Press, 1981): 18–30.

[207] *Nongmin Ribao* (9/28/88): 1. Silk cocoon prices vary naturally according to seasons, with spring cocoons commanding the highest prices and summer and fall cocoons commanding lower prices. *Nongmin Ribao* (5/29/89): 1.

[208] *Jingji Cankao* (10/25/88): 2; *Renmin Ribao* (11/2/88): 1 and (11/5/88): 1; and *Jingji Ribao* (9/20/88): 1 and (9/24/88): 1. Tussah silk is produced by silkworms fed on oak leaves instead of mulberry leaves and is of lower quality and commands lower prices.

(Zhejiang) countered by raising prices above those in Wujiang, thus triggering a border war.

Elsewhere in Zhejiang, cadres in Yuhang County managed to buy up silk cocoons by illegally raising prices. They obtained additional cocoons in the same manner from farmers in Fuyang County. They then sold them to Xiaoshan City's local specialties company for a net profit of more than ¥52,000 – ¥41,000 of which they pocketed.[209] Cadres in Xiaoshan, meanwhile, engaged in illegal purchasing, buying cocoons directly from farmers in Yuhang and Deqing counties. They then sold their entire haul to a filature in Hangzhou for a profit of ¥74,000. Factories in Shangwu engaged in illegal purchasing and sales. Jiaxing City illegally exported raw silk earmarked for delivery to state filatures in the Shenzhen and Zhuhai special economic zones.[210]

As new fighting erupted, the State Council sent cadres into the field to help keep the peace.[211] When Luotian County (Hubei) and Jinzhai County (Anhui) tangled during the fall cocoon-purchasing season, cadres from the State Council and the Hubei provincial government were immediately dispatched to investigate and put a stop to illegal price competition. The cadres ordered the Hubei provincial government to make a self-criticism and immediately return all silk worms illegally purchased in Anhui. A similar team was sent to Langxi County (Anhui) after it attacked Liyang County (Jiangsu). Under pressure from the team, the Anhui provincial government ordered Langxi County to give back 2,907 kilograms of silk cocoons illegally purchased in Liyang.

Despite last-minute peacekeeping efforts, the 1988 silk cocoon war proved costly. According to some reports, the state was forced to allocate an additional ¥470 million for silk purchases and state-owned silk filatures lost an estimated ¥190 million.[212] Other reports put the total cost of the 1988 silk cocoon war as high as ¥1 billion.[213] Anhui reportedly suffered economic losses of ¥77.75 million. In Suzhou City (Jiangsu) shortages of raw silk idled a third of local filatures, and the provincial silk industry reportedly lost ¥190 million. Zhejiang was also hard hit. Conflicts along its border with Jiangsu reduced the

---

[209] As noted previously, local protectionism often shaded off into official profiteering. In this particular case, the two seem to have coexisted, with official profiteering claiming the lion's share.

[210] *Zhongguo Shang Bao* (6/26/89): 1.

[211] *Jingji Ribao* (11/2/88): 1; *Renmin Ribao* (11/2/88): 1 and (11/5/88): 1; and *Xinhua* (11/4/88), in *FBIS-China* (11/8/88): 32.

[212] *Jingji Cankao* (8/11/88): 2 and *Renmin Ribao* (2/28/89): 2. According to Du Yuxiang, by the end of 1988 the state had suffered total losses in excess of ¥200 million (U.S.$53.73 million) in the silk cocoon war. Du, "*Nongcun chanpin liutong tizhi gaige sishi nian.*"

[213] *Xinhua* (1/29/89), in *FBIS-China* (2/1/89): 48; *Fazhi Ribao* (5/8/89): 1; and *Renmin Ribao* (2/26/88): 1 and (2/28/89): 2.

value of silk reeled by ¥30 million, and Jiaxing, Tongxiang, Dehai, and Haining counties lost ¥2.8 million in tax revenues and U.S.$10 million in export earnings as a result of illegal purchases.

Diversion of supplies away from state purchasing channels also starved state-owned filatures. Filatures in Wuxi City (Jiangsu), for example, received only 46 percent of the 10,200 tons of the raw silk allocated to them by the state plan, forcing them to close down for half the year and idling a third of local silk workers.[214] Filatures in Shanghai, a traditional silk-manufacturing center, received just 13 out of 2,200 tons of silk allocated to them by China Silk after silk-cocoon-raising regions embargoed exports. Moreover, the imposition of unified purchase threatened to intensify shortages because the suppression of prices caused farmers to cut back on silk cocoon production or "go underground," raising and reeling cocoons at home rather than selling them to authorized filatures.

In light of continued shortages, central authorities remained "pessimistic" about the prospects that new regulations could maintain the peace as the 1989 purchasing season approached, according to Huang Jianmo, the president of China Silk. As a result, on April 25, 1989 the State Council issued a "supplemental notice" reiterating its September 1988 policies.[215] The notice, which was relayed to responsible cadres in a telephone conference on April 27, stated that China Silk would continue to have a monopoly on the purchase of silk cocoons, reeled silk, and coarse silk. It forbade farmers from reeling silk themselves and ordered that all cocoons be sold to the state. Direct purchases of raw silk or coarse silk by filatures were banned. The notice called on major producing areas to set up joint local-provincial "coordination groups" and to adhere strictly to state price regulations. Local governments were specifically ordered not to raise price subsidies or provide price markups. The State Council warned that units that engaged in illegal purchasing would be subject to fines and confiscation. It banned provincial branches of China Silk from engaging in interprovincial purchasing and threatened them with disciplinary action if they sent buyers into other areas. Finally, the notice imposed a ban on new filature construction and ordered areas with excess reeling capacity to close down underutilized, unprofitable, inefficient, and backward filatures. Previous

---

[214] *Jingji Ribao* (9/5/88): 3; *Far Eastern Economic Review* (10/27/88): 38; *Zhongguo Shang Bao* (4/16/89): 1; and Jingji Cankao (4/17/89): 1.

[215] *Xinhua* (1/29/89), in *FBIS-China* (2/1/89): 49; *Renmin Ribao* (4/27/89): 2 and (5/14/89): 2; *Jingji Cankao* (5/16/89): 2; and *"Guojia Wujia Ju, Jingmao Bu guanyu wanshan canjian zuigao xianjia de tongzhi"* (Notice by the State Price Bureau and the Ministry of Trade regarding comprehensive price ceilings for silk cocoons) (3/8/89), in *Wujia Wenjian Xuanbian (1989)*: 139–40.

regulations had already imposed strict price ceilings and banned foreign exports except by China Silk.

In accordance with the State Council's April 25 notice, the provincial governments of Hubei, Henan, and Anhui signed agreements calling for unified purchase under the direction of provincial silk corporations, a ban on all cross-border purchasing, price controls, and a system of licensing.[216] A seven-county agreement among Luotian, Macheng, and Yingshan counties (Hubei); Shangcheng County (Henan); and Jinzhai, Huoshan, and Yuexi counties (Anhui) supplemented the provincial-level agreement by establishing a *cordon sanitaire* five kilometers deep on either side of the provincial borders within which purchasing stations were banned. Further negotiations resulted in a second agreement that incorporated Sha, Jixi, and Ningguo counties (Anhui) as well as making Chun'an and Lin'an counties (Zhejiang) parties to the agreement. This second agreement added the stipulation that if farmers crossed county boundaries and attempted to sell silk cocoons, they were to be turned away and ordered home. Lingbi, Si, and Tianchang counties (Anhui) signed similar agreements with counties in Jiangsu. To prevent renewed conflicts along the Anhui-Hubei, Anhui-Jiangsu, and Anhui-Zhejiang borders, cadres from the State Council and the Anhui provincial government set up four inspection teams. Finally, Anhui dispatched cadres to Hubei, Jiangsu, and Zhejiang to help coordinate policy, and the provincial government warned that it would hold county and village leaders responsible for any instances of illegal price increases in their jurisdictions, even if they were committed by subordinates. Elsewhere, Hai'an County (Jiangsu) set up a "silk cocoon purchasing and curing association" to help coordinate policy within its boundaries and increase cooperation with neighboring Nantong, Yangshou, and Yancheng cities. Municipal and village cadres in Danyang City (Jiangsu) agreed that whoever triggered a new silk war would be fined immediately.

Despite these measures, problems began to occur as soon as the 1989 spring silk-cocoon–purchasing season got underway. Trouble erupted in Huzhou City (Zhejiang) after buyers from other provinces offered prices above those set by the state.[217] Conditions were ripe in Huzhou. The state-fixed price of ¥530 per *dan* was not only lower than prices paid in 1988 and lower than prices being offered by illegal buyers, it was also ¥58 less than farmers' costs, which ran to ¥588 per *dan*. Moreover, party and state cadres had become so deeply

---

[216] *Jingji Cankao* (6/16/89): 1; *Hubei Ribao* (5/22/89): 1; *Anhui Ribao* (5/25/89): 1; *Zhongguo Shangye Bao* (8/10/89): 1; *Fazhi Ribao* (5/8/89): 1; *Renmin Ribao* (5/31/89): 2; and *Xinhua Ribao* (6/14/89): 1.

[217] *Jingji Cankao* (5/25/89): 4; *Nongmin Ribao* (5/29/89): 1; and *Renmin Ribao* (7/22/89): 2.

involved in illegal speculation that the farmers called them "cocoon buying officials." Despite these factors, the conflict in Huzhou did not spill over into other regions and in mid-July, the Zhejiang provincial government was prepared to claim success in containing and preventing a new silk cocoon war because only isolated incidents of illegal buying were reported.

Other areas also reported calm. In marked contrast to 1988, when Wujiang County (Jiangsu) triggered a bitter cross-border conflict, the Jiangsu-Zhejiang border remained quiet as silk purchasing moved into high gear in Tongxiang County, Huzhou City, and Jiaxing City (Zhejiang) and across the border in Wujiang (Jiangsu).[218] Jinzhai County (Anhui) and Luotian County (Hubei) reported that a new system of "silk cocoon purchasing contract permits" had brought an end to the bitter conflicts that had wracked these counties in previous years.

Behind the scenes, however, the silk cocoon war dragged on in a number of areas. In October, the State Council summoned officials from Zhejiang and Jiangsu to Beijing and warned them that they must take immediate action to contain price wars along their mutual borders.[219] The State Council subsequently issued a public reprimand to Zhejiang and imposed fines after it failed to abide by the terms of the agreements hammered out in Beijing. Trouble was also reported in Danyang County (Jiangsu) where cadres had agreed earlier to a system of immediate fines if anybody was caught raising prices, and in neighboring Dantu, Jintan, and Wujin counties. Parts of Huzhou City (Zhejiang) managed to fulfill less than half their purchasing targets as a result of smuggling into Jiangsu.

Filatures also continued to suffer from serious shortages. In Hangzhou, shortages of raw silk idled 82.53 percent of its 6,000 silk looms in fall 1989. As of the end of 1989, Shanghai had received none of the 1,600–2,000 tons of raw silk promised its filatures by the state in 1988.[220] Nevertheless, 1989 was a better year than 1988. Purchases of mulberry silk cocoons increased 12.58 percent.[221] Average purchase prices, meanwhile, increased only 0.60 percent.[222]

In spring 1990, the system of interprovincial treaties continued to grow. Provincial silk corporations in Guangdong and Guangxi signed an agreement banning cross-border purchasing. To minimize problems in border areas,

---

[218] *Xinhua Ribao* (7/12/89): 2 and *Renmin Ribao* (8/8/89): 2.

[219] *Renmin Ribao* (10/4/89): 2; "*Guowuyuan Bangong Ting jiu chuli Zhejiang sheng weifan guojia guiding shougou chun jian fachu tongbao*" (Circular of the State Council General Office regarding the handling of Zhejiang province's violation of state regulations on the purchase of spring silk cocoons) (9/25/89), in *Wujia Wenjian Xuanbian (1989)*: 145–6; *Xinhua Ribao* (10/19/89): 2; and *Zhejiang Ribao* (6/13/90): 1.

[220] Hu Yang, "China: Silk Still Short," *Textile Asia* (January 1990): 90–1.

[221] *Zhongguo Guonei Shichang Tongji Nianjian, 1991*: 185.

[222] *Zhongguo Tongji Nianjian, 1990*: 283.

they agreed to operate joint purchasing stations where representatives of each province would be responsible for purchasing silk cocoons from residents of their respective provinces.[223]

Some trouble occurred during 1990. A deputy village chief in Tongxiang County (Zhejiang) was injured when he confronted illegal purchasers.[224] In October, the Zhejiang provincial government rebuked cadres in Yuhang and Deqing counties for raising prices and purchasing silk cocoons from farmers in other counties. Yizheng City (Jiangsu) also experienced serious outflows of silk cocoons when purchasing stations in neighboring counties in Anhui raised prices ¥50 per *dan* above those being offered in Yizheng. The following year *Nongmin Ribao* reported that some unidentified localities continued to fight with each other for supplies. The formerly volatile Jiangsu-Shandong, Sichuan-Hubei, Guangdong-Guangxi, and Zhejiang-Anhui borders, though, remained quiet throughout the spring and summer purchasing seasons.

In many ways, the silk cocoon war replicated the pattern seen in the other resource wars discussed previously. The search for high profits resulting from suppressed input prices led to a combination of overexpansion of reeling capacity and fierce competition for supplies. Once again, the center responded to the war in an essentially defensive manner: it reasserted China Silk's monopsony to ensure supplies for state-owned filatures and to ensure that export quotas were met. China Silk, however, was not a monolith and it clearly had difficulty preventing its provincial and subprovincial branches from competing with each other. Thus, a series of cease-fires had to be negotiated between provinces and counties.

Granting China Silk unified control over purchases and working out a series of interregional treaties did not instantaneously end the silk cocoon war. Local purchasing agents in some areas continued to fight for supplies long after the State Council issued Notice No. 305, and skirmishes continued to be reported three years after the State Council intervened. Major actors, including the provincial government of Zhejiang, violated central government policies.

At the same time, the central government acted more forcefully than it had in other resource wars. Local governments, including provincial governments, that violated state directives were not only threatened with fines but were also publicly rebuked. Superior levels were held accountable for illegal acts committed by subordinates. Provincial governments also acted relatively forcefully, either in conjunction with central cadres sent to pacify silk-cocoon-raising

---

[223] *Guangxi Ribao* (5/16/90): 1.
[224] *Zhejiang Ribao* (6/11/90): 2 and (10/17/90): 1; *Xinhua Ribao* (11/1/90): 2 and (11/22/90): 2; *Nongmin Ribao* (10/17/91): 3; and *Zhongguo Shangye Bao* (8/18/90): 3.

regions or on their own. Coercive measures and threats, however, never provided a panacea and violations continued. As a result, the central government never entirely brought silk-cocoon purchasing under control.

As was true in other resource wars, conflicts began to die down after war-induced price increases increased production. By 1991, production of mulberry silkworm cocoons had increased 51.37 percent over 1987 levels.[225] More important, the silk cocoon war created a speculative bubble like that found in the case of the wool war. After increasing 102.09 percent from ¥4,628.57 per ton in 1987 to ¥9,355.83 per ton in 1988, and then an additional 40.09 percent to ¥13,106.27 per ton in 1989, silk cocoon prices began to tumble in 1990. That year, the price per ton fell to ¥9,785.71, a drop of 25.34 percent. The following year, the price fell to ¥9,547.24, a 2.44 percent decrease.[226]

CONCLUSION

In the cases of the cotton, tobacco, wool, and silk sectors, we observe a common pattern wherein an initial relaxation of restrictions on the purchase and sale of commodities over which the state had previously enforced either a monopsony (in the case of cotton) or had relied on a system of compulsory deliveries at state-fixed prices (tobacco, silk, and wool) was soon followed by the eruption of serious conflicts for control over markets and supplies. In the course of these conflicts, fixed prices quickly collapsed as rival bidders pushed them up well beyond those set by the state. As prices began to rise and conflicts over supplies began to increase, producers responded by seeking to evade deliveries to the agents of the state monopsony so they could sell their produce to either nonstate buyers or to the agents of the state monopsony in other areas who were willing to pay premium prices. Once supplies began to flow toward the highest bidder, local governments attempted to block outflows by issuing bans on outside sales and erecting roadblocks to prevent exports. Ostensibly, the purpose of these export barriers was to ensure deliveries of supplies to the official state monopsony and ensure that prices did not rise above those fixed by the state. Yet it is quite evident that much of the stocks that were purchased by local supply and marketing cooperatives at official prices never made it into the state allocation system. Officially designated consumers did not receive their quota, as specified by the plan, and supplies either went to local consumers or ended up on black markets, where they were bought by out-of-plan consumers in manufacturing regions.

[225] *Zhongguo Tongji Nianjian, 1992*: 360.
[226] *Zhongguo Guonei Shichang Tongji Nianjian, 1992*: 175.

We also observe that, in these cases, the breakdown of the old state monopsony system and subsequent rapid price increases led to high levels of speculation, as those with supplies of a scarce commodity withheld stocks in anticipation of further price increases and consumers rushed to buy up supplies out of fear of further price increases. As speculation pushed prices upward, producers responded by expanding production, which increased total supply. The latter behavior is, of course, exactly that anticipated by a simple supply and demand model. Such a model also anticipates speculation because speculation arises out of short-term uncertainty about supply, demand, and price.

A simple supply and demand model also explains the latter stages of each of these commodity wars in which we see a common pattern of market collapse and retraction. In all four cases, and most obviously in the case of the wool war, because in the short term demand will exceed supply in a system of depressed prices and given that in the case of agricultural commodities supply cannot respond immediately to changes in demand, the first stage of a commodity war will be characterized by shortages. These shortages will, in turn, push prices up rapidly. Rising prices, however, will lead to increases in supply and concurrent decreases in demand. If we assume that producers plant or increase herds based on the inflated prices created by the shortages during the first phase of the conflict, this will result in an overexpansion of supply. Demand is subject to negative pressures as price increases; however, as production expands, demand will fall, leading to an oversupply of the commodity in the next phase of the conflict. The second phase of a commodity war is, therefore, likely to witness gluts and the resulting sudden collapse of prices. Falling prices will then cause contractions in supply and an expansion in demand. To some extent, speculation may delay the shift from shortage to glut conditions as buyers continue to bid up prices believing that even though supply has increased, demand will remain strong. Ultimately, however, a drop in demand will burst the speculative bubble and prices will begin to tumble.

Although one might interpret the resulting boom-bust pattern as evidence of market failure, the pattern actually is consistent with the operation of market forces as supply and demand move from an administratively contrived disequilibrium characterized by contrived shortages and skewed prices to a balanced equilibrium. The length of the production cycle in agriculture means that the adjustment process will be prolonged and thus characterized by repeated periods of disequilibrium. Agricultural commodity markets are thus likely to be more unstable than markets for other commodities (e.g., industrial commodities) where supply can be more easily varied.

In general, we see raw material–producing regions usurping the central monopsony's right to monopolize the purchase of undervalued raw materials and adopting mixed strategies of local industrialization and black marketeering. Faced with reductions in supply and demands for higher prices, consumers in manufacturing regions respond by seeking to bypass raw material–producing regions' monopsonies and buy raw materials directly from producers. Competition between the local monopsony and outside buyers leads to a generalized price war in which prices are rapidly bid up by all sides.

As these price wars escalated, we observe a surprisingly ineffectual response by the center that, because it was the formal owner of the rents that others were seeking to capture, ought to have responded defensively to protect its financial interests. What we observe in three of the four cases is issuance of proclamations ordering a halt to the price war, followed by efforts to negotiate nonaggression pacts among the local governments in regions affected by the price war. Other dictates demanded that unofficial buyers stop encroaching on the state's prerogatives and that both the supply and marketing cooperatives and farmers stop selling to them. The goal of these pacts and dictates was to prevent rivalry among the local agents of the state's monopsonies and, thereby, to halt price increases and to ensure that the state received its mandated share of output and supplies for its factories. In the case of both the tobacco and cotton wars, orders from the center proved of little consequence. Local governments typically agreed to cease-fires at the end of one purchasing season, then resumed the fighting as soon as the next season opened. In the case of the silk cocoon war, central intervention seems to have been rather more effective, at least in bringing an end to the worst periods of price instability and fighting for control over supply. This strategy did not succeed, however, until after prices had shot up rapidly and large stocks of cocoons had flowed out of the state monopsony system.

In the fourth case (the wool war), the center took little action. Having ceded its claims on rents from wool and textile production, the center had little immediate reason to intervene to prevent price wars from dissipating rents that now belonged to others. Nor did it have any interest in protecting and preserving local monopsony institutions, particularly once it became obvious that these institutions were, in fact, heavily engaged in the speculation that was driving up wool prices.

Abstractly, we would anticipate the failure of mutual-restraint regimes such as those proposed by the center whenever we assume that the center cannot ensure opportunistic defection from the proposed cease-fire regime. So long as demand remains greater than supply and prices are below market-clearing levels, those involved in the contest for control over supply and rents will all have incentives to defect. If they believe that others will defect, they have incentives to defect before they end up with the sucker's payoff of unrequited cooperation/exploitation. Barring assurance that the center can prevent opportunistic defection, a combination of opportunism and defensiveness should lead to the swift repudiation of any promises to cooperate as soon as competition begins to intensify.

Clearly, neither the center nor provincial governments were able to prevent opportunistic rent seeking. Provincial governments, for example, were quick to adopt measures designed to stop commodity wars and local governments "willingly" signed on to mutual nonaggression pacts. But provincial-mediated truces generally only lasted through the end of the slack season and quickly collapsed as the harvest approached. Similarly, the dispatch of central "cease-fire monitors" proved ineffective and once a scramble began their mere presence did little to prevent headlong opportunism.

Although provincial governments were not particularly successful in preventing commodity wars it is noteworthy that areas along provincial boundaries frequently experienced the most intense conflicts. We need to recognize that a provincial boundary is not simply a boundary between two geographic entities but is also between two hierarchies. In the case of the various state monopsonies involved in the resource wars, the chain of responsibility and subordination passed down from the center to the province, from the province to the prefecture or municipality, from there to the county, and then on down to the grassroots level. Purchasing stations along provincial boundaries were, therefore, the agents of different segments of the monopsony. Mutual suspicion and institutional rivalry are thus likely to undermine effective cooperation between provinces, particularly when it may not be clear which side triggered a price war.

Provincial boundaries were, however, only one fault line and resource wars were not really interprovincial conflicts. Instead, they were generally intense conflicts among rival local monopsonists in which the primary protagonists were purchasing agencies. Raw material–producing localities thus tended to fight each other. In fact, it is frequently hard to identify "outside" aggressors (i.e., buyers from manufacturing regions) because so much of the reporting focuses on competition between purchasing stations within growing regions. Outsiders were present, however, because, without them, prices would not have been forced upward. Certainly it may have been true that speculation led some purchasing stations to vie with each other for control. In the end, consumers, exerting pressure through their demand function, were the driving force behind price increases. The "aggressive" role of manufacturing regions is thus cloaked and operates through emerging market mechanisms.

Despite the repeated breakdown of cross-border cooperation, the center's attempt to impose unified purchase did not fail entirely, as is clearly evidenced by the rather dramatic shift in the terms of trade against many of the Category II goods over which resource wars were fought. After wartime highs several times the levels the center sought to enforce during the early stages of the wars, as will be shown in detail in Chapter 6, prices for many of these goods fell rapidly, dropping below prewar levels in some cases. In most cases, prices not only fell, but the state regained monopsony control over these commodity markets, with the net result that the *status quo ante* was frequently restored.

I think it is wrong, however, to conclude that these wars failed to result in systemic change. Even though the institutions of state monopsony may have survived and continued to dominate segments of the rural economy, the structure of these surviving monopsonies had changed. Whereas the prewar monopsonies were vertically integrated, albeit somewhat imperfectly, with the center acting as principal and the local supply and marketing cooperatives acting as its grassroots agents, the new monopsony was hierarchic in form, but not necessarily in substance. The center, after all, ultimately succeeded – belatedly and only after repeated failures – in reconstituting the state monopsony, not by reimposing top-down authority but rather by having its first-order agents broker cooperation among its lower-order agents. In structural terms, therefore, the new unified purchase system may have been a monopsony in form, but it was a shadow of its predecessor because it was based on a horizontally fragmented structure held together in large part by voluntary cooperation, rather than coercion-based compliance, and was thus vulnerable to egoistic defection. Unified purchase was, therefore, an unstable system.

Zhongguo Gongshang Bao, 2/2/89:1
"No more obstacles"

5

Import Protectionism

EXPORT protectionism and interregional resource wars characterized the initial stages of local protectionism. Born out of rents created by the underpricing of raw materials and persistent shortages created by the same underpricing, export protectionism arose shortly after the adoption of commercial reforms in 1984. Import protectionism took longer to reach critical levels because investment priorities before 1978–9 limited productive capacity in many rent-producing sectors and created persistent shortages, forcing the state to ration many overvalued goods.

Economic reforms adopted in 1984 afforded local governments new opportunities to invest in sectors characterized by rents. Investment in consumer durables, such as televisions, refrigerators, and washing machines, began to increase during the early 1980s.[1] Combined urban collective and rural TVE investment in fixed industrial assets increased from ¥722 million in 1978 to ¥48.38 billion in 1988, a thirty-five fold increase (adjusted for inflation) in just ten years, with the bulk of this investment going to light industrial production.[2] State investments in light industry, meanwhile, grew from ¥2.93 billion in 1978 to ¥12.33 billion in 1988, thus pushing total investment from ¥3.45 billion at the start of the reform period to ¥60.71 billion ten years later.

Despite the rapid expansion of light industrial production during the early and mid-1980s, shortages persisted until 1987–8, when supply began to catch

---

[1] Although fixed-asset investment in the manufacturing sector increased 55.04 percent between 1980 and 1985, fixed investment in washing machine, refrigerator, and hot-water heater production increased 63.01 percent. Fixed investment in television, radio, and tape recorder production increased 77.58 percent. *Zhonghua Renmin Gongheguo 1985 Nian Gongye Pucha Ziliao*, vol. 4: 236, 316, and 318.

[2] Based on data in *Zhongguo Guding Zichan Touzi Tongji Ziliao, 1950–85*: 349 and 351; *Zhongguo Guding Zichan Touzi Tongji Ziliao, 1986–1987* (Beijing: Zhongguo Tongji Chubanshe, 1989): 272 and 274; and *Zhongguo Guding Zichan Touzi Tongji Ziliao, 1988–1989* (Beijing: Zhongguo Tongji Chubanshe, 1991): 257 and 260.

up to demand. So long as supply lagged behind demand, both infant and mature industries were able to expand without necessarily infringing on each other's markets. Import protectionism, therefore, was not necessary, even though infant industries undoubtedly profited from administrative measures that gave them an added competitive edge. As growth in investment pushed markets toward saturation, however, pressures for increased import protectionism grew and finally exploded in 1989, when a combination of inflation followed by recession cut demand for a wide range of consumer goods. Thus, even as the period of resource wars sputtered to a close, a new period of intense local protectionism erupted as local governments raised "bamboo walls" (*libaqiang*) and "brick ramparts" (*zhuanbilei*) to keep outside goods off saturated local markets.

Illegal tolls, which had been around since the early 1980s, also exploded during 1989. Illegal tolls did not grow out of the price scissors or supply-demand contradictions caused by price distortions. Instead, illegal toll taking arose out of a combination of fiscal need and greed. Illegal tolls represented a quick, low-cost way of raising revenues, not just for cash-strapped local governments in poor areas or those stuck with a tax base dominated by sectors on the wrong side of the price scissors, but also for any local government. As the 1989–90 recession cut into legal revenues, more and more local governments found themselves forced or lured into illegal toll taking. As a result, the number of illegal tolls began to increase dramatically at the same time that import barriers proliferated. As import barriers proliferated and illegal customs posts sprung up "like trees in a forest," making interregional trade more expensive and difficult, China's economy seemed to lurch toward disintegration.

In this chapter, I describe the rise of import protectionism, focusing on the role of skewed prices in creating the "crisis of overproduction" that left domestic markets saturated and led local governments to erect import barriers. I also describe the concurrent rise of illegal toll taking and its impact on interregional trade. Although I shall defer analyzing the logic of import protection and illegal toll taking until Chapter 6, as well as analyzing the central government's response to this new outbreak of generalized economic warfare, it is important to note in advance that the growth of import protectionism signaled a major change in the nature of local protectionism and, in conjunction with the proliferation in illegal tolls, a significant intensification in local protectionism during the winter of 1989–90.

The transition from a period dominated by export protectionism to one dominated by a combination of import protectionism and illegal toll taking not only involved a shift in the dominant forms of local protectionism, it also involved changes in the lines of conflict. Export protectionism pitted raw material–producing regions against manufacturing regions. Import protectionism and illegal toll taking, on the other hand, were essentially wars of "all against all." Because local governments fought as defenders of local industry, it made little tangible difference whether they were raw material–producing regions defending struggling infant industries or manufacturing regions defending mature industries.

In the case of illegal tolls, developmental cleavages mattered only in the sense that less-developed raw material–producing regions were presumably more likely to resort to illegal toll taking out of fiscal need than were wealthier manufacturing regions, which were presumably more likely to resort to illegal toll taking out of fiscal greed. In a context of falling legal revenues, however, even relatively developed manufacturing regions could find themselves forced to engage in illegal toll taking simply to make ends meet. The transition from export protectionism to import protectionism-cum-illegal toll taking, therefore, relegated sectoral divisions to a secondary level of importance and gave way to a more generalized form of interregional economic conflict.

BAMBOO WALLS AND BRICK RAMPARTS

The incidence of import protectionism began to rise sharply in fall 1989. In part, import protectionism arose out of the economic slump brought about by Li Peng's 1988 austerity program and accompanying tight-money policies.[3] Austerity alone did not, however, trigger import protectionism. Instead, a combination of austerity and long-term structural problems pushed China's economy into recession and triggered import protectionism.

Like export protectionism, import protectionism had its roots in price distortions left in place by partial reform. Artificially high profits in certain industrial sectors led local governments to overinvest in these sectors following the liberalization and decentralization of investment and economic decision making. Import protectionism, however, had a longer gestation period than export protectionism because a combination of pent-up demand and strong growth in per capita income allowed growth in demand to outpace growth in supply, thus delaying the crisis of overproduction predicted by the model of skewed prices in Chapter 3. Before 1989, in fact, although some cases of import protectionism

---

[3] Wu, *"Lun 'kuai-kuai jingji' chansheng, houguo, zhili"* and Barry Naughton, "The Chinese Economy: On the Road to Recovery?" in William A. Joseph, ed., *China Briefing, 1991* (Boulder, CO: Westview, 1992): 77–95.

occurred (e.g., the cigarette war), sellers' markets minimized the need for import barriers.

In 1988–9, demand for consumer goods began to level off at a time when supply continued to grow. As a result, by 1989–90 markets had become saturated. Market saturation and local governments' desire to protect sales by local producers led to a combination of aggressive consumer goods export expansion and import protectionism as local governments sought to monopolize local markets and concurrently encouraged local producers to dispose of excess stocks elsewhere. The result was a period of intensified conflict, not only between infant industries in raw material–producing regions and mature industries in manufacturing regions but also between mature industries.

The advent of recession in the fall of 1989 brought the crisis of overproduction to a head. The 1989–90 recession[4] affected all but three provinces.[5] After years of steady, sometimes explosive growth, national income fell for two consecutive years in established manufacturing centers,[6] the rapidly growing coastal provinces of Jiangsu and Zhejiang, and seven interior provinces.[7] Fourteen provinces experienced declines in 1989 but rebounded the following year to surpass 1988 levels. Double-digit inflation during 1988, meanwhile, cut real income for both urban and rural residents and reduced consumption. Per capita urban consumption fell 7.34 percent in real terms during 1989 and remained 3.40 percent below 1988 levels through 1990. Rural consumption fell 8.64 percent in 1989 and another 2.34 percent in 1990, with the result that rural consumption declined 10.78 percent during the two-year period from 1988 to 1990. Retail sales fell 5.95 percent in 1989, rose 0.62 percent in 1990, but remained 5.37 percent below 1988 levels. As the recession deepened, however, industrial activity continued to grow.[8]

As supply and demand diverged, inventories began to mount rapidly, doubling to ¥50 billion by the end of 1989, according to the Industrial and Commercial

---

[4] "Recession" defined as a real decline in national income. Overall, national income fell 5.45 percent in 1989. There was a slight recovery in 1990 as national income grew 1.22 percent over 1988 levels. Data from *Zhongguo Tongji Nianjian, 1992*: 32 and 235.

[5] Only Shanxi, Guangxi, and Ningxia escaped formal recession. Even so, growth in these provinces fell to levels well below the go-go years of 1987–8.

[6] Beijing, Tianjin, Liaoning, and Shanghai.

[7] Jilin, Anhui, Hubei, Hunan, Guizhou, Xizang, and Qinghai.

[8] Industrial activity decreased marginally (less than 1 percent) in eight provinces (Jilin, Heilongjiang, Shanghai, Jiangsu, Zhejiang, Jiangxi, Hubei, and Hunan) whereas it increased in the remaining provinces during 1989. The following year, all provinces except Xizang surpassed 1988 levels of industrial activity. *Zhongguo Tongji Nianjian, 1992*: 54, 236, 276, and 598.

Bank of China and the State Statistical Bureau.[9] Enterprise revenues and, hence, profits and taxes handed over to both central and local governments began to fall precipitously. In 1989, enterprise profits and taxes fell 9.40 percent compared with 1988 levels.[10] In 1990, profits and taxes declined again, falling 16.13 percent and dropping 22.65 percent below 1988 levels. An 8.80 percent rebound in 1991 boosted profits and taxes relative to 1989. Nevertheless, enterprise profits remained 17.05 percent below 1988 levels through 1991.

Afraid that "soft markets" would cut their revenues, increase unemployment, and undermine social stability, local governments resorted to import protectionism.[11] By erecting import barriers, they hoped to shore up sales of locally produced goods, thereby maintaining local revenues and preventing locally owned factories from shutting down.[12] As one official explained:

> When markets soften and products don't sell, localities want to protect production and local revenues. I purchase what I produce, sell what I produce, and outside goods do not enter my markets.[13]

According to the Chinese press, import protectionism intensified dramatically beginning in November 1989, when cities in Sichuan banned imports of nineteen types of goods.[14] Guizhou retaliated by banning imports of more than 100 products, including bicycles, tape recorders, televisions, and refrigerators.[15] Immediately thereafter, localities in the north, northeast, central south, and east adopted "blockade policies."[16] In the process, local protectionism spread

---

[9] *China Daily* (3/16/90), in *FBIS-China* (3/16/90): 25. Well after the recession began, the State Council tried to deal with the problem of excess production of automobiles, ethylene, refrigerator compressors, color television tubes, video recorders, and cotton textiles by ordering a moratorium on new plant construction and the expansion of existing production lines in August 1990, a move that would have, at best, prevented the construction of additional excess capacity. *Xinhua* (8/7/90), in *FBIS-China* (8/9/90): 45.

[10] *Zhongguo Tongji Nianjian*, various years.

[11] This concern with social stability probably reflects the fact that the 1989 recession and softening of markets occurred just months after the widespread antigovernment agitation that culminated in the events of June 4 in Beijing.

[12] *Jingji Cankao* (6/4/90): 1.

[13] *Jingji Cankao* (7/20/90): 1.

[14] *Hong Kong Standard* (8/10/90) and "Chinese Communist Terms," *Inside China Mainland* (October 1990): 29.

[15] *Jingji Cankao* (7/20/90): 1.

[16] *Jingji Cankao* (6/8/90): 1. Unfortunately, the identity of these localities cannot be determined from the available data. In general, although the amount of detail on import protectionism is fairly good, a frustratingly large number of reports do not identify the localities involved by name.

downward through the administrative hierarchy, moving from provincial to local levels as the recession deepened.[17]

Import protection took a variety of forms. In Xinjiang, for example, the regional government publicly banned imports of forty-eight types of products, including bicycles, color televisions, bicycle tires, soap, detergent, light bulbs, batteries, hot water bottles, alcohol, paint, prepared Chinese medicines, cough suppressants, and wool products.[18] Provincial regulations required prior approval from the regional planning commission, price bureau, industrial department, and finance bureau for all other imports. Units importing goods without approval faced stiff fines. These measures cut Xinjiang's imports by 50.1 percent during the first quarter of 1990.

Other areas followed Xinjiang's lead. Jilin banned beer imports from Liaoning and Heilongjiang.[19] Tianjin banned imports of beer from Hebei.[20] Beijing and Tianjin restricted imports of washing machines and bicycles. Wuhan and Shanghai found themselves locked in a bitter battle over razor blades as each tried to block imports from the other. Chu County, Anhui, and Nanjing City, Jiangsu, fought an "eye for an eye, tooth for a tooth" struggle after Nanjing banned beer imports from Chu County and Chu County retaliated by banning imports of a wide variety of consumer goods from Nanjing. Officials in Shangrao Prefecture, Jiangxi, ordered local supply and marketing cooperatives to purchase and sell only local products.

---

[17] *Jingji Cankao* (5/29/90): 1. The assertion that import protectionism began at the provincial level is as reported by the Chinese news media. Hard evidence of provincial-level protectionism prior to 1989 is limited. During the resource wars, for example, the primary antagonists were originally subprovincial governments in raw material–producing regions and buyers from manufacturing regions, and later competing local monopsonies. Provincial-level governments appeared most often as mediators seeking to disengage local governments. More cases involving explicit involvement of provincial governments in the erection of local trade barriers appeared during 1989–90. Ambiguity exists, however, in many instances whether import bans ascribed to a province were in fact enacted by the provincial government or by subordinate governments within the province. My sense is that subprovincial governments probably moved first by banning specific imports. Provincial governments then followed with bans on imports from other provinces. Finally, as market conditions worsened, local governments banned imports from other areas within the same province. The available evidence does not, however, prove conclusively that local protectionism spread in this sequential manner and assertions that it did remain conjectural.

[18] *Zhongguo Shang Bao* (7/3/90): 1 and *South China Morning Post* (3/9/90).

[19] *Wen Wei Pao* (7/9/90): 3, in *Inside China Mainland* (September 1990): 11.

[20] *Christian Science Monitor* (10/17/90): 5; *Washington Post* (11/7/90); *Jingji Cankao* (7/15/90): 1; and *Zhejiang Provincial Service* (12/21/90), in *FBIS-China* (12/26/90): 55.

Many localities banned imports of bicycles, tape recorders, televisions, refrigerators, aluminum products, shoes, and woolen blankets.[21] One unspecified city in East China designated fifty products as "essential and protected" and 122 products as "critical and protected." In the northeast, one local government ordered that water pumps needed for a drought relief project be purchased locally, even though locally produced pumps were considered unreliable. In Hubei, Tongcheng County imposed monopolies on retail sales of candy, cakes, tableware, and twelve other types of common products, banning all imports of such goods and imposing fines equal to 30 percent of the retail price on any outside goods sold within the county. In Hebei, the provincial government granted the provincial farm machines company a monopoly on sales of tractors and diesel engines and local commercial departments monopolies on the purchase and sale of matches, soap, detergent, washing machines, and a variety of other small consumer goods. All imports that might compete with products produced in Hebei required government authorization. Fearing increased local unemployment, some localities restricted the employment of nonresidents.

Various localities imposed import duties on outside products. Counties in South China, for example, imposed a 20 percent "dumping tax" on all sales of nonlocal beer.[22] Local governments in East China imposed a ¥50 per ton "local product protection tax" on imported cement, banned purchases of outside cement for key construction projects, ordered local banks to withhold loans to units purchasing outside cement, and had local supply departments withhold steel from construction projects using imported cement. County governments in northern Jiangsu (Subei) levied fines of ¥200–300 on trucks transporting cement from plants located in neighboring Shandong province and banned all sales of cement except through the locally controlled building-materials supply unit. Yushan County, Jiangxi, imposed a 3 percent "import regulatory tax" on commodities imported from Zhejiang and other provinces. Localities in Jilin, Liaoning, and Hubei issued regulations imposing fines on commercial departments and department stores that sold beer, liquor, detergent, bicycles, and color televisions imported from other areas. Jiangsu province levied heavy ad hoc taxes on a wide variety of imports.

---

[21] *Jingji Cankao* (4/27/90): 1, (6/4/90): 1, (6/8/90): 1, and (9/6/90): 4; *Ching Chi Tao Pao* (March 1990), in *FBIS-China* (3/16/90): 24; and *South China Morning Post* (3/9/90).

[22] *Jingji Cankao* (4/27/90): 1, (5/29/90): 1, (6/8/90):1, and (9/6/90): 4; *Gongren Ribao* (11/24/90): 1; *Zhejiang Provincial Service* (12/21/90), in *FBIS-China* (12/26/90): 55; and *Asian Wall Street Journal* (11/9/90): 4.

Pingjiang County, Hunan, levied multiple taxes on imported cement, bricks, tiles, and other building materials, raising prices on these products 20 to 30 percent.

Rather than impose import duties, some areas relied on post hoc confiscation of profits to discourage purchases of outside goods. According to regulations enacted in one unnamed area, commercial units had to turn over all income earned from sales of unauthorized imports to the local government's "price subsidy fund." Elsewhere, local governments seized profits from sales of imported goods and then fined units importing products. Still other localities ordered that all above-normal income from the sale of imported goods be turned over to the local price bureau.[23] Cities in Heilongjiang, meanwhile, imposed heavy taxes on imported beer while rebating taxes on locally produced beer.

Other localities used administrative "levers" to restrict imports.[24] Some cities implemented a system of "special and controlled purchasing" for televisions, refrigerators, bicycles, washing machines, sound equipment, and copiers, whereby only purchases of locally produced goods were authorized. In East China, some cities ordered units selling imported products to obtain production permits, certificates of product inspection, weight certificates, drug-inspection certificates, and public health inspection certificates. An unnamed provincial government in this same region issued regulations directing price and commercial administration bureaus to ensure that the retail markup rate for local products was 2 to 3 percent higher than that for imported products, thus making sales of local products more profitable for retailers. Other areas used ad hoc "management fees" to raise the price of outside products.

Some localities used "heavy rewards and heavy punishments" to encourage sales of local products and discourage sales of outside products. One locality issued regulations stipulating that:

> If commercial, materials, or supply and marketing departments have already signed purchasing contracts with places outside the province, they must negotiate with the latter to cancel the contracts, if possible, and cease all deliveries. If contracts have not yet been signed, all state distributors and enterprises are prohibited from ordering from outside the province. Those that are discovered doing so will be severely dealt with.[25]

---

[23] *Jingji Cankao* (6/8/90): 1 and (7/2/90): 1.

[24] *Zhongguo Shangye Bao* (6/2/90): 1; *Jingji Cankao* (6/8/90): 1; and *Renmin Ribao* (7/9/89): 5.

[25] Li, *"Diqu fengsuo de xianzhuang ji jiejue wentide jianyi."*

In the southwest, local cadres warned that if local units bought imported electrical equipment, their electricity would be cut off.[26] Local governments in two provinces issued regulations stating that units purchasing local products could retain 2 percent of gross revenues and use 1 to 3 percent of sales revenues to pay bonuses. Bonuses on sales of local products were also declared a cost rather than a charge against profits and, thus, exempted from taxes. Certain cities in south-central China waived taxes on bonuses paid by commercial units selling local products, ordered commercial units to increase sales of local products 10 percent over the previous year's sales, and mandated that local products constitute a minimum of 60 percent of total sales.

During 1989–90, local protection extended beyond the trade and commercial systems. Local governments subverted and usurped control of the banking and legal systems, transforming them from agents of the central government into instruments of "localist policies."[27] Local banks were used to erect "monetary blockades." In mercantilist fashion, monetary blockades let funds "enter but not leave," "maximizing inflows while minimizing outflows," and "collecting much while paying out little." Various localities ordered local banks to give preferential commercial loans to units buying local products, extend loans only to local enterprises, and refuse payment to outside accounts. Banks dishonored checks issued to outsiders, refused payment to outside accounts, or delayed transferring funds claiming that "delaying payment is reasonable and advantageous." Other local banks enacted secret "internal regulations" stipulating that checks from enterprises holding accounts in other localities should not be honored. In some areas, local banks limited the amount of payments per day to outside accounts. Even where bank officials recognized the need to handle interregional transactions properly, they blocked transfers to avoid offending local governments.

Infected by "departmentalism" and local protectionism, local financial authorities frustrated efforts to settle debts between regions.[28] In Shenyang City, Liaoning, the municipal electrical corporation found that it could not collect outstanding debts because local governments in other cities had issued orders forbidding local banks from making payments on outside obligations.

---

[26] *Jingji Cankao* (6/8/90): 1.

[27] *Fazhi Ribao* (8/22/91): 3; *Hubei Ribao* (6/16/90): 1; *Jingji Ribao* (7/19/91): 1, and (9/8/91): 1; *Jingji Cankao* (4/27/90) and (5/31/89): 1; and *Xinhua* (7/25/91), in *BBCSWB, Far East* (7/30/91): b2/1.

[28] *Jingji Ribao* (7/12/91): 1, (7/22/91): 1, (8/9/91): 1, and (9/5/91): 1; *Jingji Cankao* (3/10/91): 4 and (4/27/90): 1; *Wen Wei Po* (7/9/90): 3, in *Inside China Mainland* (September 1990): 12; and *Dazhong Ribao* (5/31/89): 1.

In Neimenggu, the regional government suspended loan payments to outside lenders, arguing that the center's tight money supply necessitated retention of all available cash within the region. In Shandong, local banks refused to honor commercial credits issued by local enterprises for purchases of agricultural commodities, leaving farmers holding over ¥10 million of worthless IOUs. Elsewhere, banks and responsible cadres refused to help outside enterprises collect bad debts from local enterprises. Many banks found themselves caught in a catch-22 situation as local governments directed them to pay outside accounts only after all debts to local accounts had been settled by outside banks. Yet, debts to local accounts could not be cleared because other localities had the same sorts of policies in place. Bank officials and local cadres, therefore, rationalized monetary embargoes on the grounds that "he who pays first, eats the loss."

The Hubei counties of Honghu, Puqi, and Tongcheng went still further. Seeking to prevent local residents from buying goods across the border in Hunan, they issued their own local currency. Purchases of consumer goods and agricultural commodities, cadres' wages, and bonuses were all paid with local currency.[29] Because only these three Hubei counties honored this new currency, its issuance effectively severed economic ties between markets in Hubei and Hunan.

Localism was not the only source of monetary trouble during 1989–90. Cutbacks in government appropriations and loans for capital construction ordered during late 1988 and early 1989 had left many construction projects and their suppliers unable to pay their debts.[30] Tight monetary policies enacted by the Bank of China in the battle against inflation reduced liquidity further. In combination, rather than singularly, these factors fueled an explosion of "triangular debt" (*sanjiao zhai*) and "debt chains" (*lianhuan zhai*). By 1990, total bad debt stood at a staggering ¥160 billion (U.S.$30.02 billion). Despite repeated intervention by the People's Bank of China, bad debt had surged to ¥225 billion (U.S.$42.21 billion) by mid-1991.[31]

Local governments also used the courts to protect local interests, arbitrarily interfering in legal cases, undermining the independence of the courts, and converting them into instruments of local protectionism. Local officials

---

[29] *Jingji Cankao* (9/6/90): 4.

[30] *Jingji Ribao* (8/13/91): 3.

[31] *Gongren Ribao* (8/31/91): 1. Paradoxically, the growth of triangular debt occurred despite an end to the center's tight money policies, renewed spending on capital construction, and a general improvement in economic conditions during 1991. That triangular debt outlived the period of austerity suggests that monetary blockades played a considerable part in causing the problem in the first place.

obstructed justice, challenged the authority of the courts, slandered legal cadres, falsified evidence, and "even went so far as to invert truth and lies, connive with criminals, and illegally arrest legal cadres and hold them hostage."[32] Some county and subcounty-level cadres "openly declare[d] that the local court is not allowed to accept entrustments from another court and to grant local property to a non-local litigant." In Henan, local officials illegally dismissed the president and two vice presidents of the local court after they ruled against local interests. (Shortly after the president appealed to higher authorities for redress, he suddenly died in a "traffic accident.") Court officials "shirked" their responsibility to enforce the law impartially and "scrambled" to protect local interests. Local courts frequently ruled in favor of locals regardless of the evidence. According to a senior judge in Hubei, considerable bias could be found in one-third of local court rulings. Sixty percent of unresolved disputes, he asserted, arose out of interference in court procedures.

As local governments subverted the courts, enterprises discovered that courts in other areas could not or would not enforce contracts if they hurt local interests. In some areas, local courts refused to accept or repeatedly delayed cases brought by outsiders. Local court officials often failed to act impartially, blatantly ignoring the facts in ruling in favor of locals. Even if a decision favorable to outsiders was reached, local authorities might not enforce it or might enforce it halfheartedly.[33]

In 1989, for example, courts in Ziyang County and Neijiang City, Sichuan, ruled in favor of local interests in a two-year-old case involving a contractual dispute between enterprises in Ziyang County and Yinchuan City, Ningxia, even though the evidence clearly supported the claims of the Yinchuan-based plaintiff.[34] In Shanxi, the county procurator of Zhangzi County and local banking officials repeatedly blocked the transfer of funds to a Shandong-based enterprise after courts in Shandong ruled against the Shanxi-based defendant.[35] In Heilongjiang, local police officials and lawyers stymied efforts to settle a contractual dispute involving a factory in Shandong and a department store in Mudianjiang City. In Shandong, when cadres demanded monies owed an enterprise based in Penglai County by enterprises based

---

[32] *Jingji Ribao* (1/5/91): 1; *Jingji Cankao* (4/7/91): 4 and (8/8/91): 1; and *Jingji Cankao* (4/1/90), in *FBIS-China* (5/3/90): 28. Local protectionism not only disrupted the enforcement of contractual and economic law, but also civil and even criminal law.

[33] *Fazhi Ribao* (5/15/89): 1.

[34] *Fazhi Ribao* (8/7/91): 2. The case was later settled in favor of the Yinchuan enterprise by the Sichuan high court.

[35] *Fazhi Ribao* (1/6/89): 1.

in Weifang City, officials of the Weifang credit cooperative assaulted and beat them.

The combination of import barriers, financial blockades, and the subversion of local courts threatened to all but cripple the interregional trade system by undermining property rights. Traders not only had to contend with administrative restrictions, tariffs, and embargoes, they could never be sure that outside purchasers would honor contracts or that local authorities would enforce contracts. Even if a contract was honored, local banks might refuse to settle claims or might embargo payments.

Although the 1989–90 recession undoubtedly played a critical role in softening markets, the roots of import protectionism can be traced back to price distortions. Skewed prices encouraged excess production of overpriced goods. Analyses of the goods affected by import protectionism, changes in the spatial distribution of production, and supply-demand parameters support the hypothesis that excess production played the major role in triggering import protectionism. Arguably, in fact, the 1989–90 recession only exacerbated a growing gap between production and consumption by temporarily reducing final consumption and thus sharpening a preexisting contradiction rather than creating a new one.[36]

The overwhelming majority of products specifically identified as subject to import restrictions by various localities were consumer goods.[37] Some localities did restrict imports of producer goods. As noted previously, local governments in northern Jiangsu banned imports of cement and other building materials. Markets for automobiles and trucks were also reportedly fragmented into a dozen or more regional markets as a result of collusion between provincial governments and local vehicle manufacturers.[38] Hengyang City, Hunan, banned imports of acetylene gas in June 1990 after local producers experienced serious losses.[39] Explicit import protectionism was, however, concentrated on consumer goods/finished products, not raw materials, as was the case with export protectionism.[40]

Production of commodities frequently subjected to import protectionism – beer, bicycles, refrigerators, televisions, and washing machines – tended to be

---

[36] *Jingji Cankao* (7/20/90): 1.
[37] Of thirty-three specifically named products, thirty were consumer goods.
[38] Kim Woodward, "The Automotive Sector," *The China Business Review* (March–April 1989): 40.
[39] *Jingji Ribao* (8/14/90): 1.
[40] This should not be surprising because banning imports of scarce raw materials would be clearly illogical and irrational, just as would banning exports of overstocked finished products.

widely distributed.[41] By 1989, twenty-nine provinces produced beer, twenty-seven manufactured tape recorders, twenty-six built televisions, twenty-four produced bicycles, and twenty-three turned out washing machines.[42] Moreover, the spatial pattern of production of these products had changed during the early reform period as production increased rapidly outside the traditional industrial centers of Beijing, Tianjin, Liaoning, and Shanghai.[43] The spatial shift of production created a twofold loss of markets for these industrial centers. First, they lost market share in both coastal and interior areas as a result of rising local production. Second, they lost market share in the interior to new competitors based in the coastal provinces of Jiangsu, Zhejiang, and Guangdong. Dispersion of manufacturing, therefore, closed off markets on which traditional industrial centers could dispose of their products and increased friction between traditional centers and emerging manufacturing centers along the coast for export markets in the interior. Because local production was also increasing in the interior, competition between imports from the coast and local products was also increasing in that region. The dispersion of manufacturing during the mid-1980s thus served to heighten interregional competition and conflict, particularly as markets approached saturation.

In addition to changing the spatial distribution of production, headlong growth during the mid-1980s led to excessive production.[44] Although direct data on commodity demand are unavailable, proxy estimates of the supply-demand relationship suggest that, even before the onset of the 1989–90 recession, supplies of many products had begun to move in the direction of excess supply. Comparing changes in the gross value of sales to production shows that before 1987 growth in sales generally exceeded production. Thereafter, growth in production began to exceed growth in sales for a variety of consumer goods. Output, therefore, continued to grow even as sales leveled off. Although admittedly rough, calculations suggest that the acute shortages typical of the

---

[41] Hong Kong sources list these products, plus knitted goods, matches, soap, detergents, building material, plastics, tires, tractors, diesel engines, light trucks, and mini-trucks, as commonly subjected to import protectionism. *Ching Chi Tao Pao* (Hong Kong) (March 1990), in *FBIS-China* (3/16/90): 24.

[42] Based on data in *Zhongguo Tongji Nianjian, 1990.*

[43] Based on data in *Zhongguo Tongji Nianjian, 1981; Zhongguo Tongji Nianjian, 1982;* and *Zhongguo Tongji Nianjian, 1990.*

[44] Questioned about the 1990 recession, Minister of Commerce Hu Ping responded that its cause "lies in the overproduction and stockpiling of unmarketable, out modeled goods." *China Daily* (11/1/90), in *FBIS-China* (11/1/90): 36.

prereform period had disappeared before inflation led to decreases in consumption in 1989.[45]

The competition for markets that led many areas to ban imports of refrigerators in what became known as the "refrigerator war" illustrates the dynamics of excess production and import protectionism.[46] During the early 1980s, refrigerator manufacturing had been highly profitable. A factory capable of turning out 100,000 units per year could earn profits of between ¥30 and ¥50 million a year, sufficient to allow investors to recoup their initial investment in just two years. Lured by high profits and a seemingly limitless demand for household refrigerators, local governments built more than 100 new factories during the mid-1980s, including 60 using expensive imported technology. By 1985, productive capacity had surpassed two million units per year.

Concerned about the cost of imported technology and worried by the headlong expansion of refrigerator production, the central government convened a meeting of factory managers and provincial officials at the Friendship Hotel in Beijing in 1985. At this "summit," representatives of the various provincial governments agreed that each province would limit itself to one or two major factories and would limit future investments in refrigerator plants. With demand continuing to grow, however, local authorities soon reneged on the pact and continued to build new refrigerator plants and expand existing plants. As a result, output rose from 1.4 million units in 1985 to 2.3 million units in 1986, and to 4.0 million units in 1987.[47] In 1988, production shot up to 7.6 million units, surpassing the 1990 target of 6.5 million units agreed upon at the 1985 Friendship Hotel summit. The following year, production hit nine million units. Refrigerator factories, however, were capable of producing thirteen million units a year.[48]

Just as output peaked in 1989, the bottom fell out of the refrigerator market as the recession deepened. Sales plummeted, falling from 7.34 million units in 1988 to 6.04 million units in 1989, and to only 4.36 million units in 1990.[49]

---

[45] Based on data in *Zhongguo Guonei Shichang Tongji Nianjian, 1992*: 133–44 and *Zhongguo Tongji Nianjian, 1992*: 438–43. Bicycle markets, for example, had clearly reached the point of "saturation" (*baohe*) by 1988. During the first half of 1989, factories churned out 19.72 million bicycles. Sales, however, reached only 12.26 million. As a result, commercial inventories increased from 822,200 to 8.38 million. An additional five million unsold bicycles remained stockpiled in factories. The bicycle sector, in other words, had built up total inventories in excess of an entire year's sales. *Jingji Ribao* (10/21/89): 3.

[46] *Gongren Ribao* (6/22/90): 4 and *Jingji Ribao* (4/13/90): 1.

[47] *Zhongguo Tongji Nianjian, 1991*: 424.

[48] *Jingji Ribao* (4/13/90): 1.

[49] *Zhongguo Guonei Shichang Tongji Nianjian, 1991*: 151. Comparisons of 1988 and 1989 sales figures are potentially misleading. In 1988, rumors of price deregulation and 20–30 percent

170

Profits sagged. By 1990, seventeen of forty-three refrigerator manufacturing corporations were operating in the red. Faced with slow sales, excess inventory, falling profits, and declining tax revenues, local governments in many areas banned imports during 1989–90.

Sichuan's "beer war" provides a second example of how high profits led to excess production and import protection. In 1975, the province had a single brewery located in Chongqing.[50] Seeking to cash in on high profits from beer production and faced with what seemed to be limitless demand for beer, localities invested heavily in beer production. During the mid-1980s, breweries "sprang up like bamboo shoots after a spring rain." By 1988, the province had twenty-six breweries. A year later, the number had increased to thirty-seven. In 1990, forty-three breweries with a productive capacity of 500,000 tons of beer per year were in operation.

Sichuan's beer manufacturers quickly found themselves in deep trouble. Although Sichuan's breweries could turn out half a million tons of beer a year, provincial consumption was only half that amount, around 250,000 tons a year.[51] Unused capacity could not be used to produce beer for export to other provinces because excess capacity existed elsewhere and local governments had banned beer imports.[52] Sichuan's breweries thus found themselves fighting for control over a saturated provincial market.

Sichuan's beer war, however, was not only about markets for bottled beer. Like the tobacco war, the beer war actually consisted of two wars involving concurrent conflicts over beer markets and the raw materials used in brewing beer. Shortages of grain, hops, and other ingredients limited annual production of beer to approximately 220,000 tons of beer a year, forcing Sichuan breweries to operate at half capacity and leaving local demand unfulfilled even as breweries fought for markets.

---

inflation in the major cities triggered a wave of panic buying (*qiang gou*). As a result, sales of major consumer goods, including refrigerators, jumped dramatically in 1988 (sales of refrigerators doubled). Thus, although significantly lower than 1988 sales, sales of many consumer goods were actually higher in 1989–90 than they had been in 1987. Nevertheless, significant gaps existed between supply and demand during 1989–90.

[50] *Sichuan Ribao* (9/16/90): 2.

[51] After reaching 212,400 tons in 1987, beer production in Sichuan grew just 2.35 percent over the next two years, reaching 217,500 tons in 1989. In 1990, output grew faster, increasing 15.77 percent to 251,800 tons, and then shot up 25.69 percent in 1991, hitting 316,500 tons. *Zhongguo Tongji Nianjian*, various years.

[52] As early as 1987, brewery capacity in Zhejiang, for example, was double provincial demand, and many localities had banned imports or severely restricted sales of nonlocal beer. *Renmin Ribao* (8/8/87): 2. A second beer war occurred in Heilongjiang in the early 1990s. See *Fazhi Ribao* (2/28/95): 3.

Sichuanese breweries and their local government owners thus found themselves struggling concurrently for scarce supplies and access to overcrowded markets. Faced with rising input prices as a result of competition, local governments banned exports of materials used in making beer. At the same time, they banned imports of bottled beer in hopes that shortages would keep local prices high, thus inflating brewery profits. Neither import nor export protection protected breweries from the negative effects of excess expansion; by 1991, only four breweries remained profitable.

Income effects also helped trigger import protectionism. As their incomes and the availability of goods increased, Chinese consumers became more discriminating in their purchases. Except for the period of panic buying during the summer of 1988, when even inferior goods found ready buyers, by the late 1980s consumers were refusing to purchase poor quality goods – including many that had sold well in the past.[53] Demand for cheap textiles, black-and-white televisions, refrigerators, and bicycles fell off sharply, leaving factories with large unsold inventories.[54] With markets already in transition from scarcity to saturation and sales of inferior quality products beginning to decline, the 1989–90 recession hit technologically backward infant industries particularly hard, forcing their political allies to use administrative means to protect them from more advanced competitors.[55] Because many of the infant industries thrown up during the mid-1980s relied on outdated technology, this meant that producers in newly industrializing areas were particularly hard hit by declining sales during 1989–90.[56]

Although import protectionism appears to have been designed mainly to protect local producers from all outside competition, in some instances trade barriers were specifically aimed at established industrial centers and newly emerging producers along the coast. Certain interior provinces, for example, imposed a ¥200 surcharge on color televisions imported from Shanghai and

---

[53] In Zhejiang, for example, consumption of cheap, general-purpose soap declined sharply after the introduction of higher quality products. As sales declined, local commercial departments and soap factories found themselves locked in a "soap war" (*feizao dazhan*) when commercial departments refused to buy up stocks of soap they could not sell. *Renmin Ribao* (10/4/91): 2.

[54] *Far Eastern Economic Review* (8/1/91): 49. Demand for black-and-white televisions became so weak that in the summer of 1991 factories in Sichuan were selling components through storefront retailers in Chongqing. Customers could then either pay to have the components assembled or could put them together themselves, Heath-Kit fashion. Author's interviews, May 1991.

[55] *Jingji Ribao* (7/14/90): 2.

[56] Ironically, some of these infant industries had purchased equipment scrapped by established manufacturers when they upgraded their productive technologies. White, *Shanghai Shanghaied?*

Beijing, boosting the price well above that of locally produced sets.[57] Other localities specifically banned imports of refrigerators from Tianjin.

Many localities singled out Guangdong as market conditions deteriorated. The municipal government in Wuhan, for instance, banned imports of Huabao air conditioners from Guangdong on the pretext that shortages of electricity in the city necessitated a ban on the sale of air conditioners – power shortages that did not, however, necessitate a concurrent ban on sale of locally made air conditioners.[58] In the northwest, various provinces banned imports of fountain and ballpoint pens made in Guangdong. In other areas, local commercial authorities ordered cancellation of contracts to purchase monosodium glutamate (MSG) from Guangzhou-based companies. In one city, local authorities imposed strict controls on sales of nineteen beverages, all of which were imported from Guangdong. Other barriers were more subtle. Some localities allowed retailers a 9 percent markup on locally produced alcohol but allowed only a 5 percent markup on alcohol imported from Guangdong. Still other areas levied ad hoc fees on products from Guangdong. Certain cities levied a three jiao "educational fee" on each bottle of Guangdong-produced beverages imported by local retailers. Other areas demanded additional retailing fees. In some cities, local authorities restricted the quantity of Guangdong goods that could be displayed by local retailers.[59]

Conflicts were not limited to a single interior-coastal axis. Guangdong and Beijing, for example, found themselves at odds over the sale of Guangdong-produced hot-water heaters.[60] Arguing that imports would run them out of business, Beijing manufacturers convinced the municipal government to ban sales of Guangdong hot-water heaters. Consumers, mostly hotels and guest houses (i.e., units that earned foreign currency) fought back, arguing that locally produced hot-water heaters were unreliable; ultimately they got the city government to replace the ban with a tariff, thinly disguised as a ¥100–150 "special installation fee." Makers of plastic packing materials based in Zhongshan City, Guangdong, complained that a conspiracy by cadres in Shanghai prevented them from breaking into markets in that city.[61] "North-south" conflicts among developed areas, therefore, coexisted with the "east-west" conflicts between developed and underdeveloped areas witnessed during the resource wars before 1989.

---

[57] *Jingji Cankao* (5/24/90): 1 and (7/2/90): 1.
[58] *Far Eastern Economic Review* (4/2/92): 77–8.
[59] *Jingji Cankao* (5/14/90): 1.
[60] Author's interview, Hong Kong, May 1993.
[61] *Eastern Economic Review* (4/2/92): 77–8.

Import protectionism exploded in a chain-reaction pattern. As markets became saturated and trade barriers went up in one area, other localities found themselves forced to retaliate or adopt defensive protectionism.[62] One deputy mayor in the northeast complained that, although the municipal government knew that protectionism was an incorrect policy in the long term, what alternative did it have when local products could not penetrate outside markets while outside products flooded local markets? If you don't raise barriers, he said, then you must eat the loss:

> When your products are refused entry into other markets, then isn't it hard to be radiant with smiles while outsiders have access to your markets? Who then will take care of your production and employment problems? Who then will take care of local revenue problems?[63]

Another official in the northeast demanded, "Why should we open markets when everybody else gives us a cold shove?"[64] When asked why his county had restricted imports of cement, even though local production was only 15 percent of local demand, an official in Jiangsu declared:

> At present, all counties are engaging in [local protectionism], whoever doesn't, eats the loss. If other areas don't engage [in protectionism] then we will dismantle our [barriers]. This is only a temporary measure.[65]

Fear of unrequited cooperation (continuing to allow unrestricted trade when other areas resorted to "beggar-thy-neighbor" trade policies) thus helped push some areas into import protection although local markets might not have been distressed.

Even absent any immediate fear of exploitation by outsiders, some local officials felt that, without immediate protection, local industries would fail. Long-term relief in the form of improved market conditions, they believed, would come too late.[66] As one mayor explained:

> When dealing with a seriously ill person, the first thing to do is to revive the heart, afterward you can check the pulse. But if the person is dead, then why talk about how to control the disease or its cause?[67]

---

[62] Li, "*Diqu fengsuo de xianzhuang ji jiejue wentide jianyi*" and *China Daily* (11/6/90).

[63] *Jingji Cankao* (4/27/90): 1.

[64] *China Daily* (8/19/90).

[65] *Gongren Ribao* (11/24/90): 1.

[66] The Chinese phrase used herein means literally, "Distant water cannot quench current thirst" or figuratively, aid will be too slow in coming to be of any help.

[67] *Jingji Cankao* (5/8/90): 1.

In other words, protection might not be the optimal policy, but it was preferable to allowing other areas to flood local markets with their goods and force local producers to cease production.

As a result, localities that claimed to prefer trade resorted to hidden protectionism. As captured by the somewhat convoluted slogan "open the nation, restrict the bureau, seal off the province,"[68] they voiced support for interregional cooperation, then blocked imports from centrally controlled enterprises and pursued provincial autarky. Others acted deviously, secretly "moving bricks to build walls" or appeared to move in the direction of opening up local markets while in fact raising new defenses. Some localities claimed that import controls were necessary to stop sales of counterfeit goods. Others produced counterfeit copies of name-brand goods produced elsewhere and claimed they were imported.

To summarize, the 1989–90 recession precipitated an upsurge in local protectionism. Faced with mounting stockpiles of unsold goods and declining enterprise revenues, afraid that the recession would undermine local employment and trigger social unrest, and caught in a spiral of escalating protectionism by other regions, localities threw up defensive walls and ramparts around their economies. As import protectionism increased, Minister of Commerce Hu Ping complained that "local protectionism has become more and more serious."[69] Some months later, an official in the Ministry of Commerce, stated:

> The current wave of local protectionism is the worst in the last forty years in terms of the variety of barriers and scope of products involved. . . . It exists to a certain extent in every province.[70]

Although we have no clear way to measure the level of local protectionism and, thus, cannot independently verify Hu's and Zhang's statements, the fact that we see local protectionism moving from the grassroots to higher levels of the administrative apparatus, including the provincial level, and moving on into the banking and legal systems, certainly suggests that local protectionism was markedly worse during the winter of 1989–90 than it had been in previous years.

The upsurge in import protectionism was significant not simply because it signaled an increase in local protectionism and, hence, greater internal economic

---

[68] *Zhongguo Shangye Bao* (6/2/90): 1; *Jingji Cankao* (6/17/90): 1 and (12/19/91); *Fazhi Ribao* (3/3/92): 3; and *Renmin Ribao* (4/3/92): 2.

[69] *Hong Kong Standard* (9/10/90).

[70] *Christian Science Monitor* (10/17/90): 5.

fragmentation. Import protectionism involved a fundamentally different set of interactions and conflicts from those involved in export protectionism, even though both import and export protectionism grew out of the same set of market distortions that led to shortages of cheap inputs and excess investment in the production of overvalued outputs. In contrast to export protectionism, in which two distinct sets of actors (raw-material producers and raw-material consumers/manufacturers) faced each other, import protectionism involved conflicts among like actors. Hence, whereas export protectionism pitted one set of preferences and options against another, import protectionism pitted identical preference sets against each other.

As a result, regardless of whether they may have been long-established manufacturing centers (e.g., Beijing, Tianjin, or Shanghai), newly emerging industrial centers (e.g., Guangdong, Zhejiang, or Jiangsu), or newly industrializing regions, all localities in the end faced the same set of problems when demand contracted and sellers' markets disappeared. All faced the problem of excess supply. Certainly newly industrializing areas were at a competitive disadvantage because their products were often inferior to those produced in other regions. As a result, local governments in these areas may have had the most acute incentives to throw up import barriers. But neither newly emerging industrial centers nor established industrial centers were invulnerable. In fact, industries in old industrial centers, particularly in the rust belt in Northeast China, were often also at a severe disadvantage because locally produced products were frequently of poor quality or obsolete. Thus, it is not surprising that to the extent the data reveal a temporal pattern to the spread of import protectionism, they suggest that import barriers first appeared in the less developed hinterland and the old industrial provinces of the northeast. Nor is it surprising that we find little evidence of import protectionism in provinces such as Guangdong but rather import barriers that specifically targeted products from these areas. Ultimately, therefore, the contraction of demand brought on by the 1989–90 recession triggered an economic war of all against all, in which local governments throughout the country were under significant pressure to raise import barriers to protect "their" industries from outside competition and, hence, to limit the negative impact of the recession.

But import protectionism was not a solution to the underlying problem of excess supply. Sealing local markets off may have protected locally owned industries and potentially allowed them to continue to extract rents by preventing competition from driving down prices.[71] Import barriers could not, however,

---

[71] Although consumer prices in general continued to rise during 1990, albeit at a modest 2.1 percent compared to 17.8 percent in 1989, prices for major consumer durables fell. The price of a

force demand up; thus, excess local production could not be easily disposed of on local markets alone. As a result, local governments as a group had a common interest in reviving the national economy and thereby stimulating consumer demand. Moreover, they had a common interest in reviving interregional trade because exports to other areas offered the most realistic long-term solution to the problem of excess inventory. Whereas we might characterize export protectionism as a zero-sum game in which the primary question was the division of rents created by depressed raw-material prices, import protectionism was a game more akin to a prisoners' dilemma in the sense that the actors would be made better off if they cooperated by lowering their trade barriers – but only if they could be sure that others would follow suit and not resort to opportunistic protectionism and beggar-thy-neighbor export polices. Before considering the implications of the differing structures of export and import protectionism, we need to examine a third threat to the growth of markets – illegal toll taking – that intensified during the same period that import protectionism was rapidly increasing.

ILLEGAL TOLLS

As if the center's problems were not great enough, the upsurge in import protectionism occurred alongside an upsurge in the number illegal tolls. These tolls were hardly new, and reports of illegal trade barriers go back to the early 1980s. By 1989–90, however, illegal tolls had become ubiquitous as localities throughout China erected local "customs posts."

Strictly speaking, illegal tolls were not a form of local protectionism. Although checkpoints were often used to block exports and imports, most illegal tolls, known variously as "customs posts," "roadblocks," "inspection stations," or simply "barriers," were set up to extract ad hoc supplementary taxes on trade passing through a particular jurisdiction. Inspection stations were not necessarily illegal or contrary to central regulations. Public security and transportation departments had the authority to conduct inspections of vehicle safety, collect tax payments, examine licenses, and so forth. Forestry management departments were authorized to conduct inspections of lumber shipments as a way of clamping down on illegal logging. Commercial departments were authorized

bicycle, for example, which had increased 21 percent in 1989, fell 5 percent, washing machine prices declined 2 percent, color televisions declined 13 percent, and black-and-white televisions declined 7 percent. *Zhongguo Guonei Shichang Tongji Nianjian, 1990, 1991,* and *1992.*

to conduct checks to ensure that traders had paid taxes and fees mandated by central and provincial regulations.[72]

On paper, other departments had the authority to conduct inspections and assess fines and fees. They were not, however, authorized to set up their own inspection stations or to set fine and fee schedules unilaterally. Regulations issued before 1990 and reiterated afterward stipulated that bureaus and local governments wishing to conduct inspections must, to paraphrase various regulations:

(a) Receive prior authorization from the provincial public security bureau;
(b) Have an "inspection station permit" or "road inspection permit" (also known as a "road inspection station permit");
(c) Conduct inspections only at "unified inspection stations" supervised by representatives of the provincial public security bureau;
(d) Use approved schedules of fines and fees; and
(e) Issue receipts for all payments, using authorized receipt books.[73]

In accordance with these regulations, provincial and local governments erected inspection stations and conducted checks of vehicles. In 1990, for instance, the Hubei provincial government legally maintained checkpoints at points of entry into the province, cities, intersections of major traffic arteries, points of entry into forestry areas, bridgeheads, ferries, wharves, truck stops, airports, and distribution depots. Similarly, neighboring Hunan operated inspection stations at all major points of entry into the province. Fujian maintained a system of twenty-three checkpoints that allowed it to control traffic both within the province and across provincial boundaries.[74]

Local authorities, however, flagrantly and routinely disregarded central and provincial regulations in their desire to prey on trade. When challenged about the legality of charges levied against a shipment of lumber, for example, officials in Donghai County, Jiangsu, retorted that they listened to instructions

---

[72] "*Guowuyuan guanyu gaige daolu jiaotong guanli tizhi de zhi*" (Notice of the State Council on reform of the road and transportation management system) (10/7/86), *Guowuyuan Gongbao*, no. 26/516 (10/10/86): 820; *Hunan Ribao* (7/11/85); and *Jiefang Ribao* (6/6/89): 3.

[73] "*Guowuyuan guanyu gaige daolu jiaotong guanli tizhi de zhi*" (Notice of the State Council on reform of the road and transportation management system) (10/7/86), *Guowuyuan Gongbao*, no. 26/516 (11/10/86): 820; *Guizhou Ribao* (1/25/86): 1; *Fujian Ribao* (2/10/88): 1; *Jiangxi Ribao* (8/13/90): 1; *Dazhong Ribao* (11/26/89): 1; *Fazhi Ribao* (1/17/90): 1; *Henan Ribao* (12/1/90): 1; and *Fazhi Ribao* (12/12/91): 1.

[74] *Hubei Ribao* (8/8/90): 1; *Fazhi Ribao* (12/12/91): 1; and *Fujian Ribao* (10/11/84): 2.

from the county government, not the State Council.[75] As a result, a plethora of units erected their own checkpoints during the 1980s. In 1984, for instance, transportation, safety, commercial, tax, public security, highway administration, forestry, local products, agricultural machinery, and antismuggling departments had set up roadblocks along roads leading into Hunan from northern Guangdong. The following year, tax, commercial, quarantine, supply, food products, scrap materials, insurance, village, street, transportation, supervision, agricultural machinery, and road maintenance bureaus in Hengyang County, southern Hunan, maintained inspection stations. Before 1988, a dozen different bureaus in Fuyang Prefecture, Anhui, conducted inspections and levied nearly three dozen different fines and fees on trade goods.

During 1989, public security, transportation, commercial, tax, forestry, public health and epidemic diseases, urban administration, environmental protection, insurance, tobacco, and grain bureaus in Hunan were found to be illegally levying fees and fines.[76] That same year in Fang County, Hubei, farmers transporting local bamboo products had to pass through barriers maintained by village, county, and provincial bureaus. In 1990, 2,000 personnel representing twenty different local and provincial bureaus manned 263 inspection stations at twenty-eight different locations in Canzhou Prefecture, Hebei. In Huaiyin City, Jiangsu, twenty-two bureaus maintained 100 illegal inspection stations. In Jiangxi, investigators found a dozen different departments engaged in improper inspections.

At these toll stations, local authorities demanded a blizzard of ad hoc taxes and fees, to which they frequently added numerous fines. Levies might include "local specialty products taxes," "agricultural and forestry specialty products taxes," "lumber industry specialty products taxes," "market and trading taxes," "product taxes," "business taxes," "income taxes," "commercial taxes," and "product subsidy taxes."[77] Traders might find themselves forced to pay "management fees," "market management fees," "individual household management fees," "commercial management fees," "purchasing fees," "production management fees," "supply unit management fees," or "agricultural machinery management fees."

---

[75] *Fazhi Ribao* (12/27/90): 1; *Nongmin Ribao* (9/4/84): 1 and (6/6/88): 2; *Nanfang Ribao* (1/18/84): 1 and (5/7/84): 1; *Hunan Ribao* (8/16/85): 1; *Anhui Ribao* (4/24/88): 2; *Jingji Cankao* (6/1/88): 1; *Jingji Cankao* (6/2/88): 1; and *Renmin Gong'an Bao* (6/17/88): 1.

[76] *Jingji Ribao* (4/8/89): 2; *Hubei Ribao* (7/27/88): 2; *Renmin Ribao* (9/15/91): 2; *Xinhua Ribao* (12/23/90): 2; and *Jiangxi Ribao* (8/13/90): 1.

[77] *Fujian Ribao* (6/28/88): 1; *Nongmin Ribao* (8/21/91): 3; *Jiefang Ribao* (10/10/90): 3; *Jingji Cankao* (6/2/88): 1; *Fazhi Ribao* (10/21/88): 1 and (9/23/88): 2; *Henan Ribao* (10/12/88): 1; and *Jingji Ribao* (5/30/84): 3.

Truckers might have to pay fees for "road maintenance," "road damage," "urban parking," and "engaging in transportation."[78] Livestock traders faced a host of quarantine fees.[79] Lumber and bamboo traders were asked to "contribute" to "reforestation funds," "forest industry development funds," and "spring bamboo renewal funds," as well as paying "tree and fruit seedling fees" and "bamboo resources development fees." On top of these fees, miscellaneous charges could include "quality inspection fees," "production support funds," "urban construction fees," "educational fees," "educational surcharges," "environmental protection fees," "sanitation protection fees," "public health fees," "livestock spraying fees," "public safety fees," and "agricultural development funds." Some localities demanded a "resource compensation" fee for products shipped to other areas.

In addition, traders might have to pay a variety of "tolls," including "bridge tolls," "scales/weighing tolls," "ferry tolls," "barrier-passing transaction fees," "exit tolls," "border-crossing tolls," "large and medium city entry and transportation fees," and "provincial boundary–crossing tolls." [80] Truck drivers could find themselves fined for bringing produce into a town during the daytime, for using their bright headlights, excessively dim headlights, broken headlights, speeding, failure to pay road maintenance fees, carrying excess weight, or improper loading.

Local officials in some areas came up with truly creative, even bizarre, charges. Fan County, Henan, levied charges for "assistance to people injured by vehicles" on trucks passing through it.[81] Shaoyang County, Hunan, imposed a "first-aid fee" on trucks passing through its territory. Xinning County, Hunan, demanded that farmers transporting citrus pay "bamboo basket taxes" and "bamboo basket value added taxes" on grounds that their oranges were packed in bamboo baskets and bamboo was a forest product liable for specialty products taxes. Local authorities in Beijing, Tianjin, and Hebei reportedly forced trucks carrying coal from mines in Shanxi to the coast to pay "rainy-day driving fees," "night transport fees," and an "uncultured and

---

[78] *Fujian Ribao* (6/28/88): 1; *Dazhong Ribao* (11/22/85): 1 and (12/1/85): 1; and *Jingji Ribao* (5/30/84): 3.

[79] *Jingji Cankao* (6/2/88): 1; *Fujian Ribao* (10/7/87): 1, (6/28/88): 1, (9/23/88): 2, and (6/25/90): 1; *Henan Ribao* (9/25/87): 3 and (10/12/88): 1; *Fazhi Ribao* (12/27/90): 1; and *Nongmin Ribao* (8/6/90): 4 and (8/21/91): 3.

[80] *Shanxi Jingji Bao* (7/28/90): 1; *Nongmin Ribao* (12/13/85): 2, (8/21/91): 3, and (11/8/91): 1; *Jingji Ribao* (5/30/84): 3; *Gongren Ribao* (7/11/90): 1; and *Fazhi Ribao* (8/27/91): 2 and (7/13/90): 1.

[81] *Henan Ribao* (9/25/87): 3; *Fazhi Ribao* (8/29/89): 4 and (12/6/88): 4; *Renmin Ribao* (8/27/88): 2; *Dazhong Ribao* (11/10/89): 2; and *Nongmin Ribao* (8/6/90): 4.

impolite behavior" fee. In southern Shandong, localities required trucks to purchase special local license plates. Anque County, Sichuan, simply imposed a "no-name tax."

In addition to fees and taxes, traders had to obtain multiple licenses and permits. Truckers in Henan, for instance, had to carry drivers licenses, "vehicle operating licenses," "safety check certificates," "proof of payment of road maintenance certificates," "proof of vehicle purchase certificates," "business licenses," "payment of highway bonds certificates," "certificates of insurance," and "border entry permits."[82] In Fujian, loggers seeking to ship lumber to Fuzhou had to obtain a "provincial unified lumber delivery ticket," an "intraprovincial lumber transport permit," and a "unified lumber inspection ticket." In Henan, traders had to carry "transit permits" granting them permission to cross county boundaries. Farmers wanting to engage in interprovincial trade in Hunan had to get a "border-crossing pass" while farmers in Qu and Lanxi counties (Zhejiang) had to get "exit permits" authorizing them to cross county boundaries. Failure to obtain permits, many of which were idiosyncratic to a particular jurisdiction or authorized by secret regulations, and produce them on demand could result in delays, fines, or even the confiscation of vehicles and goods. Moreover, by the late 1980s, traders had to pass through a maze of illegal customs posts (see Table 5-1).

In some areas, the density of customs posts, as measured by the number of kilometers of roads per illegal tolls, reached considerable levels. Heilongjiang had an average of one toll for every four kilometers of road within the province,[83] Henan every 8.7 kilometers, and Jiangxi every 30 kilometers. Handan City (Hebei) had fourteen customs posts in just 10 kilometers. Shuyang County (Jiangsu) maintained ten tolls along a 10-kilometer stretch of the Shu River. Hengyang County (Hunan), located at the junction of major roads linking Hunan, Guangxi, and Guangdong, had six tolls in 22 kilometers, one every 3.7 kilometers. Fuyang Prefecture (Anhui) averaged one toll per 10 kilometers. Xiangfan City in north-central Hubei had roadblocks every 9.4 kilometers of road within its boundaries, Shaoyang County (Hunan) every 6 kilometers, and Huiyang Prefecture (Guangdong) every 30 kilometers.

---

[82] *Henan Ribao* (9/25/87): 3 and (9/23/88): 1; *Fujian Ribao* (9/23/88): 2; *Jingji Ribao* (5/30/84): 3; and *Nongmin Ribao* (11/8/91): 1.

[83] *Heilongjiang Ribao* (11/30/90): 2; *Nongmin Ribao* (6/6/88): 2 and (12/5/88): 1; *Fazhi Ribao* (9/4/90): 1; *Gongren Ribao* (7/11/90): 1; *Xinhua Ribao* (8/8/90): 1; *Anhui Ribao* (4/24/88): 2; *Jingji Cankao* (6/1/88): 1, (6/2/88): 1, and (3/9/91): 1; *Renmin Gong'an Bao* (6/17/88): 1; *Hunan Ribao* (11/7/88): 1; and *Nanfang Ribao* (1/18/84): 1 and (5/7/84): 1.

Table 5-1. *Number of Illegal Tolls*

Province	Year	Number of Authorized Tolls	Number of Illegal Tolls
Hebei	1990	543	1,536
	1991	200	1,596
Shanxi	1990		1,000
Heilongjiang	1990		2,000
Fujian	1984	82	118
	1988	162	425
	1990		300
Jiangxi	1990	166	1,200
Henan	1987	156	480
	7/1988	156	841
	9/1988	156	1,271
	10/1988	156	1,700
	1989	156	1,270
	1990	156	288
	1991	60	1,000
Hubei	1990		1,827
	Early 1991		1,018
	Late 1991		2,600
Hunan	1991	425	2,600
Guangxi	1990		2,000
Guizhou	1990	85	340
Yunnan	1990	132	570
Shaanxi	Early 1990		2,280
	Late 1990		3,000

Sources: Renmin Ribao (9/15/91); *Fazhi Ribao* (1/17/90), (9/4/90), (10/18/90), (1/15/91), (12/17/91), and (4/20/92); *Jingji Ribao* (4/8/89) and (12/13/90); *Jingji Cankao* (9/10/90) and (5/27/91); *Zhongguo Shang Bao* (9/27/90) and (10/11/90); *Nongmin Ribao* (12/5/88), (9/27/91), (2/19/92), (4/15/92), and (5/12/92); *Renmin Gong'an Bao* (3/8/88), (12/11/90), and (11/29/91); *Tianjin Ribao* (11/29/90); *Heilongjiang Ribao* (11/30/90); *Fujian Ribao* (4/11/84), (2/26/88), (4/21/88), (1/11/88), and (12/2/90); *Jiangxi Ribao* (8/30/90); *Henan Ribao* (11/26/86) and (12/22/90); *Hunan Ribao* (2/28/90); and *Guizhou Ribao* (11/19/90).

The 620-kilometer Liaoning section of the Beijing-Harbin highway had 45 permanent and 120 temporary inspection stations, one every 3.8 kilometers.[84] Thirty customs posts lined the 78-kilometer section of Highway 104 linking

[84] *Fazhi Ribao* (8/29/91): 1; *Fujian Ribao* (11/11/90): 1 and (12/2/90): 1; *Henan Ribao* (11/22/88): 2; *Renmin Ribao* (7/25/88): 4; *Xi'nan Gongshang Bao* (7/18/88): 2; *Renmin Gong'an Bao* (12/11/90): 1; *Jingji Cankao* (3/9/91): 1; *Gongren Ribao* (7/11/90): 1; *Sichuan Ribao* (10/21/86): 1; and *Xi'nan Jingji Bao* (5/6/91): 1.

Wenzhou in Zhejiang with Fuzhou, the capital of Fujian province. In Henan, six inspection stations impeded traffic between the provincial capital of Zhengzhou and Xinxiang County, 82 kilometers north of the city, and five tolls lined the national highway in Xinzheng County, central Henan. The 75-kilometer section of the Gui-Huang highway linking Guilin, Guizhou, with the Hunan border averaged a toll every 5.8 kilometers. In Zhao'an County (Fujian) six barriers stood along a single kilometer stretch of the Xiamen-Guangzhou highway. Local authorities set up thirteen checkpoints along a single kilometer in the northern Hubei town of Guangshui. Eight inspection stations blocked the road between Changzhi City and neighboring Changzhi County in Shanxi. Not content with their ability to collect tolls at fixed checkpoints along the main roads, local authorities in Ziyang County (Sichuan) mounted patrols to catch farmers seeking to bypass tolls by using back roads. A shipment of noodles from Xingwen County in southeast Sichuan had to pass through thirty-seven checkpoints during a 376-kilometer trip to Chongqing.

As goods ran the gauntlet, customs posts in each locality "plucked a feather as the wild goose passed."[85] As a result, transit costs mounted quite rapidly. In 1985, for example, trucks loaded with hogs had to pay ¥600 in tolls, fees, and fines between Hengyang in southern Hunan and Shaoguan in northern Guangdong.[86] A load of lumber shipped from the southern Hunan county of Shuangpai to Hengyang City incurred ¥408 in "road costs." Three years later, a shipment of nine tons of bamboo shoots bound for Zhejiang paid a total of ¥2,000 in taxes, surcharges, and fees, 46.6 percent of the shipment's total value, as it passed through Jian'ou County, Fujian. In Fujian, a load of lumber moving 396 kilometers from Taining County to Fuzhou City paid ¥805 in tolls and fines. In Hunan, a 140-kilometer trip from Xinning County to Shaoyang City cost ¥240. Illegal transit taxes on a truckload of hogs from Liuyang County in Hunan to Guangzhou totaled ¥879, versus legal taxes and fees of only ¥497.5. Commercial authorities in Quanzhou County (Guangxi) demanded a ¥2,200 "barrier-passing transaction fee" for a single shipment of 31 hogs.

In 1989, truckers traveling between Shandong and Guangzhou reported having to pay ¥1,500 in local tolls, taxes, and fines – approximately half their gross

---

[85] Although "plucking a feather as the wild goose passes" was the most common metaphor, other sources also used the phrase "as the pig passes, everyone plucks a bristle" (*zhu guo ba mao*). *Hubei Ribao* (8/2/87): 2.

[86] *Jingji Ribao* (7/3/85): 2; *Hunan Ribao* (6/26/85): 2; *Fujian Ribao* (6/28/88): 1 and (9/23/88): 2; *Fazhi Ribao* (12/6/88): 4 and (10/21/88): 1; and *Guangxi Ribao* (6/13/88): 2.

profits.[87] A trip across Henan that year resulted in ¥274 in assorted taxes, fees, fines, and tolls. The following year, a truck loaded with five tons of grapes had to pay ¥1,200 in "road-buying money" as it traveled from Shandong to Fujian.[88] Six tons of bamboo shoots shipped from Fujian to Zhejiang incurred ¥2,077 worth of taxes, fees, tolls, and fines, ¥205 more than their original cost.[89] Transit charges on a ton of charcoal shipped from Anhua County (Hunan) to Changsha amounted to ¥14.5 per kilo, compared with an original purchase cost of ¥15.5 and a retail value of ¥25.5 per kilo. A load of lumber originating in that same county ran up ¥5,228 in fees, fines, and taxes while traveling just 40 kilometers.

Ad hoc taxes and fees in Sichuan, meanwhile, amounted to an average of 23 percent of the sale price of local specialty crops.[90] In 1991, farmers transporting apples from Shanxi to Hunan had to hand over ¥700 in the course of their 1,100-kilometer trip, whereas another load of apples shipped from Mianyang in northern Sichuan to Xi'an incurred ¥1,200 in charges. A truck carrying two tons of bamboo shoots worth ¥2,240 was forced to hand over ¥1,234 in fees, 55.1 percent of its original value, upon entering Quzhou City (Fujian). According to the head of a trucking company in Handan City (Hebei), his firm paid ¥2.14 million in ad hoc fines during 1988, a sum equal to ¥1.27 per ton kilometer of freight. During the first four months of 1990, a Shanxi-based coal transport company claimed to have paid ¥220,000 in fines and an additional ¥40,000 in tolls during the first half of May alone.

Fines and fees were often levied in an arbitrary manner. In Shen County (Shandong) for example, a policeman asked a driver for his license. When it was produced, he announced, apparently with a straight face, "So you didn't bring it, twenty yuan fine!"[91] When a truck loaded with pigs bound for Wuhan passed through Jingshan County (Hubei) local officials imposed a ¥300 fine without so much as looking at the driver's licenses or permits. In Hebei, police in Gu'an County stopped 90 percent of all vehicles along the highway from Beijing and

---

[87] *Dazhong Ribao* (11/10/89): 2 and *Jingji Ribao* (4/8/89): 2.

[88] *Nongmin Ribao* (11/15/90): 1. To add injury to insult, the grapes rotted before they reached their destination in Fujian because of the repeated delays caused by numerous "inspections" and shakedowns.

[89] *Fujian Ribao* (6/25/90): 1; *Nongmin Ribao* (12/10/90): 4; *Hunan Ribao* (11/30/90): 4; and *Fazhi Ribao* (8/14/90): 2.

[90] *Zhongguo Shang Bao* (8/4/90): 1; *Fazhi Ribao* (7/13/90): 1 and (9/24/91): 2; *Xi'nan Jingji Bao* (5/6/91): 1; and *Gongren Ribao* (7/11/90): 1 and (2/11/91): 2.

[91] *Gongren Ribao* (7/11/90): 1; *Renmin Ribao* (11/7/87): 5 and (8/27/91): 2; *Shanxi Jingji Bao* (7/28/90): 1; *Hunan Ribao* (12/18/89): 2; *Nongmin Ribao* (12/5/88): 1; and *Jingji Cankao* (2/15/90): 2.

fined half of them. In Hebei, police in Xinji City routinely fined all privately owned trucks, while police in Xian County automatically fined every truck passing through the county, as did police in Yanggao County (Shanxi). Village cadres in Xupu County (Hunan) imposed a ¥60 fine on all trucks carrying local citrus. Lumber inspectors in Xincheng County (Henan) automatically fined tractors and trucks transporting lumber ¥20–30, ¥100 if they carried more valuable mine props. Having been authorized to charge a toll to pay for repairs to the Xi'an-Lanzhou highway, Xianyang City (Shaanxi) decided to erect additional toll stations along the more-traveled Xi'an-Baochi highway and charge the same tolls.

Illegal tolls generated considerable revenues. In 1988, police officers in Xinzheng County (Henan) told the provincial governor that they brought in a daily quota of ¥100 in fines per man.[92] In 1992, a policeman in Ninghe County (Tianjin) responded to complaints that he was imposing fines on trucks arbitrarily by claiming that he had no choice because he had been ordered to bring in ¥2,000 a day, as had all policemen in the county. During 1990, barriers created by stretching steel cables across the Shu River in Shuyang County (Jiangsu) collected an estimated ¥390,000 in tolls from passing barges in just four months. Illegal local customs posts in Sihong County (Jiangsu) cost local farmers ¥20,000 a year. A single barrier on the main route between coal fields in Shanxi and the coast brought in ¥200,000–300,000 a year. Illegal customs posts in Shuangcheng City and Wuchang County (Heilongjiang) allegedly generated ¥941,000 in 1990. Sixteen roadblocks between the cities of Changde and Yiyang in Hunan allegedly produced more than ¥300,000 a month that same year. Individual customs posts in other parts of Hunan reportedly brought in between ¥10,000 and ¥2 million per month. Ten inspection stations along roads in Yulin County (Shaanxi) generated ¥100,000 during three years of operation.

By 1990, illegal tolls were yielding so much income that officials in some areas reportedly considered checkpoints a "smokeless industry."[93] In Hunan, illegal customs revenues had actually become so large that a number of localities had the audacity to demand compensation for lost income when the central and provincial governments ordered unauthorized roadblocks torn down.[94]

---

[92] *Jingji Ribao* (4/8/89): 2; *Renmin Ribao* (11/13/88): 2 and (8/26/91): 2; *Fazhi Ribao* (11/19/90): 2 and (8/4/92): 2; *Xinhua Ribao* (8/8/90): 1; *Shanxi Jingji Bao* (7/28/90): 1; *Heilongjiang Ribao* (11/30/90): 2; *Hunan Ribao* (8/15/90): 1; and *Nongmin Ribao* (1/3/91): 1.

[93] *Christian Science Monitor* (10/17/90): 5.

[94] *Renmin Ribao* (8/26/91): 2.

How much of the income from illegal taxes, fees, and fines ended up in local government coffers is not clear. Some portion presumably went directly into the pockets of those conducting "inspections." Farmers and truckers repeatedly complained, for instance, that inspectors and police refused to issue receipts for fines, fees, and taxes, implying that the monies collected were not handed over to the local government or were never recorded as official revenues.[95] In some cases, police and inspectors accepted bribes in lieu of fines, fees, or taxes. For a "fee" of ¥80 paid to certain individuals in Xinning County (Hunan) a battery of fines, fees, and taxes might be conveniently "forgotten." At one roadblock in Sichuan, farmers paid bribes, which inspectors described tongue in cheek as a "fallen-to-the-ground tax."

Opportunistic inspectors and policemen took advantage of their positions to engage in petty corruption. Inspectors in Xubao County (Shanxi) "picked the pockets" of each farmer passing through the local coal inspection station for ¥5.[96] Fines might be paid in kind: a few pigs, a couple of packs of cigarettes, a watch or two, or perhaps even spare parts. Taxes, fines, and fees were also subject to negotiation. Truckers in Luan County (Hebei), for example, bargained a ¥1,100 fine for "unpaid" road-maintenance fees down to ¥500. A ¥90 fine for "excess" weight in Lanxi County (Zhejiang) was reduced to ¥45 after prolonged haggling. A subsequent ¥150 fine for the same offense by the same truck was cut to ¥75.

Some localities engaged in "tax farming." Two policemen in Datong County (Shanxi), for example, claimed that they had been given an annual quota of ¥10,000 per inspector. After handing in ¥20,000 per post, they could keep 30 percent of the gross.[97] Based on an annual reported take of between ¥200,000 and ¥300,000, this would have worked out to a yearly income of between ¥146,000 and ¥230,000 for the county and ¥54,000 to ¥70,000 for the inspectors.

To sum up, although illegal tolls existed throughout the 1980s, by 1989-90, local authorities in many areas had erected a complex and unregulated system of tolls, fines, and fees. The problem was not that local authorities consciously sought to block trade, even though roadblocks were frequently used to prevent exports of scarce agricultural commodities. In most cases, the primary purpose

---

[95] *Gongren Ribao* (7/11/90): 1; *Renmin Ribao* (12/23/89): 2; and *Nongmin Ribao* (8/6/90): 4 and (11/8/91): 1.

[96] *Shanxi Jingji Bao* (7/28/90): 1; *Renmin Ribao* (11/7/87): 5; *Fujian Ribao* (9/23/88): 2; *Fazhi Ribao* (7/13/90): 1 and (9/24/91): 2; *Jingji Ribao* (5/30/84): 3; *Hunan Ribao* (6/26/85): 2; and *Nongmin Ribao* (11/8/91): 1.

[97] *Shanxi Jingji Bao* (7/28/90): 1.

of these illegal tolls was to generate income.[98] In fact, the "profitability" of illegal tolls depended on the continuation of trade and would increase as the volume of trade grew.

Unregulated toll taking, however, soon created a "tragedy of the commons" that threatened trade. Each locality might extract only a small percentage of the potential profits from trade, but with each locality "plucking a feather," the "wild goose" was soon plucked naked as total extractions stripped away all profits. Illegal toll taking tends to kill trade not by design but rather by accident. Yet, as illegal tolls exploded, the result was the same as if local governments had consciously set out to halt trade. The significance of illegal tolls, in fact, lies less in the details of who, when, how, and why local governments taxed and harassed trade than in the aggregate effect on trade. Viewed in aggregate terms, domestic trade in China had begun to resemble trade in medieval Europe[99] or in pre-1911 China[100] as local governments "fed off the

---

[98] I found only one unambiguous case of the erection of illegal tolls for objectively economic reasons. In that instance, roadblocks went up in retaliation for export protectionism. In July 1986, localities in western Hebei erected customs posts after localities in Shanxi blocked exports of coal. Trade between the two provinces had grown rapidly during the previous years. Hoping to force coal prices up, officials in Shanxi set up checkpoints along roads leading into Hebei and fined any shipments priced below levels fixed by the Shanxi provincial government. After failing to convince Shanxi to stop interfering with coal exports, officials in Shijiazhuang retaliated by imposing a 30 percent export duty, disguised as a charge to support a new "agriculture products development fund" (*nongye chanpin fazhan jijin*) on grain, vegetables, and edible oils shipped to Shanxi. Hebei officials also refused to allow coal trucks bound for Beijing and Tianjin to enter the province from coal fields in Shanxi. *Renmin Ribao* (9/22/86): 2.

[99] In medieval Europe, local lords imposed a complex variety of transit taxes and tolls on trade, often crippling commerce. See James Westfall Thompson, *Economic and Social History of the Middle Ages (300–1300)* (New York: Century, 1928): 565–9; M.M. Postan, *Medieval Trade and Finance* (Cambridge: Cambridge University Press, 1973): 107–10; and Fernand Braudel, *Civilization and Capitalism, 15th–18th Century*, vol. 2: *The Wheels of Commerce* (New York: Harper & Row, 1982): 357–9.

[100] From the Ming period onward, Chinese governments relied on internal tariffs and tolls to tax the movement of goods between market regions. Prior to the mid-nineteenth century, the central government operated a system of internal customs (*neidi guanshui*) collecting transit taxes at major ports and transportation hubs. During the Taiping Rebellion, the Qing government authorized local authorities to establish a second internal tariff system. Known as the *lijin*, the new system of local tariffs was supposed to support militias fighting the Taiping rebels. In theory, tariffs were fixed at relatively low levels and were formally under central control. Unlike the previous internal tariff system, the new *lijin* system was relatively dense and taxed the movement of trade commodities not only as they passed through major wholesale centers, but also along transportation routes throughout the countryside. With each locality collecting tariffs – often at rates above those set by the central government – the cumulative burden of transit taxes (*xingli*) collected by *lijin* bureaus strung out along transportation arteries quickly became a significant barrier to domestic commerce. Both the *lijin* and the internal customs system, often known collectively in the West as the "native customs," remained in operation

---

roads" and created "chaos on the roads."[101] Thus in the winter of 1989–90 illegal tolls threatened to become the straw that broke the back of a camel already heavily burdened by mounting import protectionism and ongoing export protectionism.

CONCLUSION

By 1989–90, China's internal trade was in disorder. Ongoing export protectionism blocked the flow of raw materials. Import protectionism fragmented consumer goods markets into a myriad of "feudal economies" and "city-state economies."[102] Predatory "road-blocking tigers" arbitrarily extorted illegal taxes and tolls from individual traders, making it "hard for traders to take to the roads."

The problem in 1989–90 was not just the existence of multiple forms of local protectionism. The advent of widespread import protectionism and the escalation of illegal tolls had transformed the structure of interregional economic conflict. Conflicts over raw materials and export protectionism had split localities into two distinct groups: established manufacturing centers and newly industrializing/raw material–producing regions. Raw material–producing regions used export protectionism to block exports of undervalued inputs that they either rechanneled into local infant industries in hopes of moving up the chain of production and cashing in on rents recreated by China's skewed price system or onto black markets. In manufacturing regions, consumers (primarily manufacturers) "resisted" export protectionism by launching price offensives aimed at capturing scarce raw materials or by resorting to the black market. Conflict, thus, occurred along relatively simple lines and had direct links to structural factors, particularly price distortions.

Import protectionism, on the other hand, pitted manufacturing regions, including newly emerging manufacturing areas located in traditional raw

---

until 1910. After the fall of the Qing in 1911, a de facto system of internal customs reemerged during the warlord period and continued to exist throughout the Republican period. See Susan Mann, *Local Merchants and the Chinese Bureaucracy, 1759–1950* (Stanford, CA: Stanford University Press, 1987): ch. 6 and *Zhongguo Gongshang Shuishou Shi* (History of Chinese commercial taxation) (Beijing: Zhongguo Caizheng Jingji Chubanshe, 1990): 265–72, 313–15, and 346–66.

[101] *Jingji Ribao* (4/8/89): 2.
[102] Literally, "castle city economies."

material–producing regions, against each other. As inventories of unsold goods piled up during the 1989–90 recession, local governments in both manufacturing and raw material–producing regions erected import barriers to protect local producers, thereby propping up local production, profits, revenues, and employment and, optimally, limiting the local impact of deteriorating market conditions. Because excess supply resulted partly from the growth of redundant infant industries in less developed regions, interregional conflict continued to occur along the original cleavages defined by the price scissors. Import protectionism, however, was not a conflict simply between regions on either side of the price scissors. Instead, import protectionism pitted manufacturers and their local government allies in all regions against each other. As import protectionism escalated, local governments in both manufacturing and raw material–producing regions erected import barriers. For manufacturing regions, though, this was often the first time that local governments engaged in extensive local protectionism.

Although the combatants were not split along input-output price lines, import protectionism nevertheless arose out of the same price distortions that gave rise to earlier interregional conflicts. Price distortions not only created shortages of inputs and fueled competition for the rents that could be captured by converting undervalued inputs into overvalued outputs, they also encouraged excessive investment in the manufacture of rent-producing consumer goods, ultimately leading to overproduction and market saturation. When this occurred in the context of a recession, local governments in regions on both sides of the price scissors had parallel incentives to engage in import protectionism.

When import barriers began to go up, the concurrent proliferation of illegal tolls created a situation of generalized warfare. Unconnected to structural factors, illegal tolls could develop in any area. Although less-developed regions might have had stronger incentives to erect tolls and charge ad hoc taxes, incentives to use trade restrictions to exact a portion of the profits generated by trade were not limited to raw material–producing regions. On the contrary, manufacturing regions also had incentives to engage in illegal tolls. In fact, producing regions, consuming regions, and those simply located along major transportation arteries all had incentives to tax trade. Moreover, they had incentives to do so without regard to the aggregate impact of their actions. Illegal tolls, therefore, were not only potentially ubiquitous, they were also uncontrolled and unregulated.

Perhaps the most important effect of the escalation of local protectionism during 1989–90, however, lay in its impact on property rights. The co-optation of the courts and banks by local governments seriously undermined property rights. When courts and banks obeyed orders from local officials rather than laws and regulations, contracts became unenforceable, credit became unreliable, and long-term investments across regional lines became insecure and risky.[103] Even in the absence of conscious local protectionism, trade could not flourish without secure property rights extending across administrative lines. As a result, mounting "localism," of which trade protectionism constituted one aspect and illegal tolls another, critically weakened the foundations upon which even a semimarketized economy had to rest. The transition from export protectionism to a combination of ongoing export protectionism, import protectionism, and illegal tolls, therefore, appeared to act at direct cross purposes to marketization and regional economic integration.

The central government did not passively acquiesce in the rise of import protectionism and illegal tolls. In the fall 1990, it initiated a major campaign to eradicate local protectionism. On September 16, a joint Central Committee–State Council decision ordered a sweeping attack on the "three disorders" (*san luan*).[104] On November 10, the State Council published a second notice

---

[103] Soon after the implementation of the coastal development strategy in 1988, Guangdong Vice Governor Kuang Ji complained that it was risky for his province to help build resource bases in other provinces. *Far Eastern Economic Review* (10/27/88): 39. Shenyang City, Liaoning, came face-to-face with the uncertainty surrounding investments in 1990 when local authorities in various North China provinces refused to deliver coal and aluminum produced by interprovincial "joint ventures" in which Shenyang-based enterprises had sunk considerable sums. *Ta Kung Pao* (5/9/90), in *Inside China Mainland* (September 1990): 12. That same year, textile mills in Shenyang contracted with suppliers in Shandong and Hebei for 3,080 tons of raw cotton. These suppliers, however, reneged, delivering just 310 tons on grounds that new provincial policies forbade exports. Previously, enterprises in Zhejiang had confronted much the same problem. In 1984–5, they invested ¥290 million to develop coal mining in the northeast and were to receive 1.6 million tons of coal in repayments in 1986. By the end of that year, however, the coal producers had delivered just 48,000 tons, 3 percent of their contractual obligations. Institutional investors elsewhere in the Shanghai region also complained that resource producers did not feel obligated to live up to the terms of agreements wherein coastal enterprises provided investment capital for joint projects in return for repayment in kind. See *Renmin Ribao* (2/9/87): 2 and *Jingji Cankao* (4/27/90): 1. When asked what recourse was available in such instances, one expatriate involved in various business ventures in China explained that it was best to do nothing because seeking legal redress would only antagonize supplies. Author's interviews, Beijing, March 1991.

[104] *"Zhonggong Zhongyang, Guowuyuan guanyu jianjue zhizhi luan shoufei, luan fakuan he gezhong tanpai de jueding"* (Decision of the Central Committee and State Council regarding putting a firm stop to illegal collection of fees, illegal fines, and all kinds of sharing of expenses) (9/16/90), *Guowuyuan Gongbao*, no. 23/632 (1/15/91): 838–42. The decision was not published until November 16, when *Renmin Ribao, Jingji Cankao,* and *Jingji Ribao* carried it on their front pages.

attacking regional blockades.[105] *Renmin Ribao* followed up on November 30 with a front-page editorial attacking regional blockades.[106]

In the months that followed, provincial, prefectural, and county governments throughout China responded vigorously, and the center's new antiprotectionism campaign appeared to progress with amazing ease and rapidity. Having reached new heights in 1990, local protectionism appeared to recede, suddenly giving way to a relatively open domestic economy. The extent to which the reality conformed to appearances will be dealt with in the following chapter, as will be the factors contributing to the overt success of the central government's campaign.

---

[105] "*Guowuyuan guanyu dapo diqu jian shichang fengsuo jinyibu gaohuo shangpin liutong de tongzhi*," November 10, 1990 (State Council notice on breaking down interregional market blockades and encouraging commodity circulation), *Guowuyuan Gongbao*, no. 26/635 (1/28/91): 956–8. The text of this notice was published on the front pages of *Jingji Cankao* (11/23/90): 1 and *Jingji Ribao* (11/23/90): 1 and as a second-page story by *Renmin Ribao* (11/23/90): 2. Most provincial and specialized papers carried the notice on or about November 23.

[106] *Renmin Ribao* (11/30/90): 1.

Hubei Ribao, 11/25/84: 1
"Opening up"

6

Marketization

THUS far, my analysis has focused on the origins and development of local protectionism. Based on this discussion, it would appear that by 1989–90 little progress had been made toward transforming China's internal economy from one characterized by the coexistence of markets and the plan. Resource wars had undermined the old system of commodity monopsonies left in place after reforms in the early 1980s. But movement toward effective marketization appeared stalled by the adoption of the new unified purchase system and the reduction in interregional economic conflict brought about by centrally brokered cease-fires. If anything, the new system appeared to represent retrogression because it was a system of fragmented local monopsonies rather than a centrally controlled and regulated monopsony. Illegal import barriers blocked the flow of consumer goods. Predatory taxation threatened to stifle whatever trade managed to continue in the face of export and import protectionism. Monetary embargoes and the subversion of local courts exacerbated the situation by undermining property rights and prompting the explosive growth of interregional debt chains.

Despite this upsurge in local protectionism, China did not split into warring economic fiefdoms. Instead, China's internal trade system weathered the crisis of 1989–90, emerged from that crisis, and began to move in the direction of reduced local protectionism. Specifically, after the central government initiated a major antiprotectionism campaign in November 1990, provincial, prefectural, and county governments embarked on a sustained campaign to lower internal trade barriers. As the campaign progressed, local governments seemed to throw open the doors they had slammed shut in previous years.

The center's new campaign did not target all forms of local protectionism. The 1990 antiprotectionism campaign concentrated on import protectionism and fiscal predation. The center did not move against export protectionism. On the contrary, the State Council continued to support the system of unified purchase that served as a vehicle for export protectionism. In the case of cotton, the center actually legitimated export protectionism by issuing regulations granting producing regions the right to levy export tariffs.

Nevertheless, an important transition began in the fall of 1990. For the first time since 1984, the overt trend in interregional economic interaction ceased moving toward increasing protectionism. The State Council's 1990 proclamations, in fact, seemed to cut through the Gordian knot of import protectionism with remarkable ease – even though the proclamations were arguably little more than mere slips of paper. The sudden growth of antiprotectionism in 1990 therefore raises the question: why did the center government's 1990 antiprotectionism diktat succeed in evoking a positive response from local governments?

In the pages that follow, I will argue that antiprotectionism succeeded because shifting from import protectionism to more open interregional trade benefited most local governments. Whereas export protectionism pitted dissimilar actors with contradictory interests against each other in a contest for control over rents originating in one locality but monetized in another locality, import protectionism pitted actors with symmetric interests against each other in what was essentially a form of prisoners' dilemma. On the surface, import protectionism appears to be a battle for control over local markets, with local governments seeking to ensure local manufacturers have preferential, if not exclusive, access. In reality, import protectionism has its roots in the excessive investment associated with inflated consumer goods prices. Seeking to cash in on highly profitable consumer goods manufacturing, many localities built productive capacity far in excess of local demand. As a result, local manufacturers became dependent on outside sales to ensure profits. Without exports, they would either have to curtail production and operate at less efficient levels or would face steadily growing inventories and hence declining profits. When the 1989–90 recession cut demand throughout China, the pressure to "export" surplus production increased, as did the pressure to shore up demand by restricting access to local markets. In other words, the recession and the resulting shift from a sellers' to a buyers' market created incentives to restrict access to local markets while aggressively exporting surplus production to other localities.

The problem facing local governments throughout China was that whereas import protectionism yields considerable benefits if excess local production could be dumped onto other markets, if import protectionism became generalized and surplus production could not be dumped elsewhere, local manufacturers would be worse off. Thus, while opportunistic import protectionism yields benefits, the payoff from mutual import protectionism was worse than the payoff from mutual trade. Yet, local governments faced a dilemma: absent central intervention, the threat of opportunistic defection greatly lowered the chances of affecting a generalized shift from mutual import protectionism to mutual trade. Thus, just like two prisoners who can escape punishment if neither rats on the other, but who will suffer a greater punishment if one refuses to cooperate with the police while the other turns state's evidence (and escapes with a lower punishment), local governments caught up in import protectionism needed a hedge against opportunism. The center, though, had incentives to facilitate interregional cooperation because state-owned industries were directly hurt by discriminatory local trade policies that closed local markets to outsiders. As a result, helping local governments move away from mutual import protectionism was not only congruent with the center's long-term goal of opening China's inner doors, it also served its short-term financial interests by helping state-owned enterprises gain access to markets. Thus, whereas export protectionism was a preferable outcome under all conditions for raw material–producing regions, for most regions import protectionism was only preferable under certain conditions and highly unfavorable once it became generalized. Thus, whereas the growth of export protectionism begat an upward spiral in interregional economic conflict, the growth of import protectionism begat pressures to move toward interregional cooperation.

Predatory toll taking, which exploded during the 1989–90 recession, operated by a different logic. Like import protectionism, opportunistic toll taking tended to yield diminishing returns as it became increasingly widespread because it involved a form of the tragedy of the commons. So long as trade continued, toll taking allowed localities to scrape off a share of the gains from trade in the form of ad hoc transit taxes. As the total take from illegal tolls increased, however, the profitability of trade decreased and with it the flow of goods between localities. The geese from which local governments plucked feathers were apt to grow fewer as more and more hands plucked feathers and might ultimately disappear if the plucking got too bad. When combined with the general falloff in trade resulting from the recession and the spread of import protectionism, rapid growth in illegal toll taking quickly became an economic liability, particularly for provincial governments faced with faltering economies.

As with import protectionism, it is one thing to say that illegal toll taking is an economic liability and another thing to find a way out of the tragedy of the commons. Once again, the problem lies in the fact that whereas excessive toll taking is undesirable, opportunistic toll taking can be highly profitable if others eschew toll taking. But unlike import protectionism, illegal toll taking lacks the retaliatory mechanism that helps drive local governments toward greater cooperation. Quite simply, if my neighbor imposes illegal taxes on trade passing through his jurisdiction, I cannot punish him by setting up tolls of my own. If I do and trade drops, we are both left worse off. But if I tear down my tolls and he does not, then he benefits while I continue to suffer the negative effects of diminished trade and the extortion of illegal taxes from my goods passing through his tolls. Moreover, unlike export protectionism, which tends to become obsolete as prices, supply, and demand equilibriate, illegal toll taking does not tend to eliminate itself over time. Illegal toll taking thus represents a much more intractable control problem than either import or export protectionism. Nevertheless, once it reaches excessive levels, some localities, and particularly those that do not benefit from ad hoc local taxes, will have incentives to move against illegal local tolls, at least in the short run.

I argue in the pages that follow that having reached the nadir of local protectionism during the spring and summer of 1990, China witnessed a sudden rise in antiprotectionism when the central government issued new policies calling for the elimination of illegal local trade barriers in the fall of 1990. Antiprotectionism during 1990–1 did not eliminate local protectionism. So long as prices remain at disequilibrium and local governments can manipulate regulations, local protectionism remains a constant threat. As a result, the problem of local protectionism did not simply disappear when import protectionism reached a point where central intervention made it possible for local governments to escape the prisoners' dilemma of mutual protectionism and move toward greater interregional economic cooperation. The complex nature of local protectionism, the vast number of localities involved, and the covert (and often illegal) nature of much of the concrete activity involved mitigated against a clean end to local protectionism. In the years following the center's 1990 campaign against local protectionism, in fact, opportunistic protectionism continued to recur. The "crisis of local protectionism" had nevertheless begun to pass because by the time that local protectionism appeared to spiral out of control, opportunistic rent seeking, both in the form of export and import protectionism, had already eliminated many of the macroeconomic conditions that gave rise to it in the first place.

TWO SLIPS OF PAPER

Two State Council notices published in late 1990 set the stage for the reduction of import protectionism and illegal toll taking. On August 23, officials of the State Council held a telephone conference with provincial governments on various problems relating to trade.[1] Three and a half weeks later, on September 16, the State Council approved a notice ordering an immediate crackdown on the "three disorders" (*san luan*) – illegal levying of fees (*luan shoufei*), illegal imposition of ad hoc fines (*luan fakuan*), and illegal sharing of expenses (*luan tanpai*).[2]

---

[1] *Yunnan Ribao* (12/18/90): 1.

[2] "*Zhonggong Zhongyang, Guowuyuan guanyu jianjue zhi luan shoufei, luan fakuan, he ge zhong tanpai de jueding*" (Joint CCP Central Committee and State Council notice on immediately

196

Despite repeated warnings, the notice declared, numerous localities continued to engage in multifarious forms of illegal fiscal activity and extortion. Citing threats to government finances, economic development, and the party's relationship to the masses, the notice condemned cadres for focusing on the parochial interests of their localities and departments and ordered a sweeping campaign against fiscal irregularities. To combat the three disorders, the State Council authorized joint committees composed of representatives of the State Council, provincial governments, provincial party committees, local party organizations, and local governments to inspect and rectify all units engaged in the collection of fees and fines. All ad hoc, ambiguous, and unauthorized fines and fees, including those collected by local customs barriers, were to be immediately abolished and a uniform system set up. To ensure that no ad hoc fines and fees were subsequently imposed, a new nationwide system of receipts was to be established and regularly audited. Henceforth, only units possessing a "fee collection permit" were authorized to assess fees. The number of inspection stations was to be reduced and all stations were to come under the direct supervision of the Ministry of Public Security.

Two months later, on November 10, the State Council followed up with a notice attacking market blockades and calling for the elimination of regional trade barriers.[3] The recent appearance of market blockades, the notice stated, contributed to the current market slump, hampered rectification of the economy, and threatened economic development and stability. Henceforth, the notice ordered, local governments must stop interfering with markets. As a first step, the notice ordered the eradication of all illegal roadblocks along roads, on wharves, and along borders, and an immediate end to the practice of using such checkpoints to block the flow of commodities. Only checkpoints duly authorized by provincial authorities in accordance with central regulations and supervised by county-level public security bureaus should continue to operate. Inspectors were ordered to abide strictly by published regulations governing fines.

The notice went on to forbid commercial management, quality control, and health-inspection authorities from using pretexts such as cracking down on

---

stopping the illegal levying of fees, illegal imposition of fines, and all forms of sharing of expenses), no. 16 (9/16/90), in *Guowuyuan Gongbao*, no. 23/632 (1/15/91): 838–42. "Sharing of expenses" refers to the practice of forcing nongovernmental units and individuals to cover local governments' expenses. *Nongmin Ribao* (7/15/91): 2.

[3] *"Guowuyuan guanyu dapo difang jian shichang fengsuo, jinyibu gaohuo shangpin liutong de tongzhi"* (State Council notice on smashing interregional market blockades and expanding commodity circulation), no. 61 (11/10/90), in *Guowuyuan Gongbao*, no. 26/635 (1/28/91): 956–8. Also see *Renmin Ribao* (11/30/90): 1.

bogus and shoddy goods to exclude outside products. Local officials were forbidden to raise taxes arbitrarily or tax imported products more heavily, penalize enterprises selling or buying outside goods, confiscate income earned from the sale of outside products, or reduce taxes on local products. Banks were ordered not to restrict loans for purchases of outside goods or raise interest rates on such loans. Price bureaus were told not to manipulate purchase-sale price differentials or wholesale-retail differentials to block sales of outside goods. Price bureaus and commercial bureaus were ordered to stop imposing mandatory sales quotas for local goods. Local governments and bureaus were ordered to annul all regulations inconsistent with the spirit of the State Council's November 10 notice, including any administrative measures that improperly promoted the sale of local products and blocked imports. Party and state cadres were admonished to oppose resolutely unhealthy tendencies in commodity circulation. Finally, provincial authorities were given until December 25 to report back to the State Council on efforts to eradicate blockades.

Despite their firm tone, nothing in either the September 16 notice on the three disorders or the November 10 notice on market blockades was substantively new. In fact, both notices repeated earlier prohibitions on local protectionism. On July 5, 1985, for example, the State Council published a notice ordering the immediate dismantling of all roadblocks except those properly authorized by the Public Security Bureau and a nationwide crackdown on illegal tolls.[4] In October 1986, the State Council again ordered all unauthorized highway inspection stations dismantled and authorized the Ministry of Public Security to assume direct control over all inspections.[5] On April 28, 1988, the State Council ordered local governments to crack down on the "three disorders" and halt the collection of illegal fees, indiscriminate fining, and illegal sharing of expenses. Two months later, the Minister of Transportation reiterated that existing regulations stated that only the Ministries of Public Security and Transportation could authorize the establishment of inspection stations. He threatened serious action if all unauthorized stations were not abolished immediately. In October, the Minister of Commerce denounced regional blockades that restricted the flow of scarce commodities. In December 1989, the State Commercial Management Administration Bureau issued a notice ordering the immediate removal of all unauthorized roadblocks. Although some provinces responded to these

---

[4] *"Guowuyuan guanyu liji zhizhi zai gonglu shang luan she qia, luan fakuan, luan shoufei"* (Immediately curb illegally constructed roadblocks, indiscriminate fines, and indiscriminate fees) (7/5/85), in *Zhongyao Jingji Fagui Ziliao Xuanbian*: 740–1.

[5] *Zhongguo Fazhi Bao* (10/25/86): 1; *Zhongguo Shangye Bao* (7/9/88): 2; *Jingji Cankao* (6/5/88): 1; *Renmin Ribao* (11/5/88): 2; and *Zhongguo Gongshang Bao* (12/21/89): 1.

directives by implementing campaigns against illegal customs posts,[6] in most cases the number of illegal customs posts continued to increase.[7]

Even though the September and November notices may have been little more than old wine in new bottles, mere slips of paper, they produced a noticeably different response from that of their predecessors. Whereas in the past the local response to central campaigns against illegal trade barriers had often been largely pro forma, in 1990 local governments jumped on the center's antiprotectionism bandwagon. Local governments[8] had actually begun campaigns to eradicate illegal roadblocks before the September 16 State Council notice. In January 1990, Guangxi announced that it would rectify the more than 2,000 inspection stations erected in violation of central and provincial regulations promulgated in 1988.[9] In March, the government of Sichuan ordered all illegal customs posts eliminated. In December, it issued regulations prohibiting units other than the tax bureau, forestry department, public security bureau, tobacco monopoly, and silk cocoon control authorities from setting up checkpoints. These new regulations also eliminated duties on citrus exports. On May 30, the Henan commercial bureau initiated a campaign to eliminate illegal roadblocks. Guizhou also began a campaign to rectify customs posts. In June, the Hunan provincial government declared that all barriers to trade within the province must be eliminated. Shanxi moved against tolls blocking coal exports. In July, the government of Jiangxi announced it would begin a program to eliminate illegal checkpoints. On August 2, the Hubei provincial government initiated

---

[6] In 1986, for instance, Guizhou issued a directive prohibiting the erection of inspection stations without prior approval from the provincial government. *Guizhou Ribao* (1/25/86): 1. In July 1988, the government of Guangxi ordered local governments to implement the central government's June 1988 notice banning local customs posts immediately. *Renmin Gong'an Bao* (7/5/88): 1. Fujian, meanwhile, fought a running battle against local customs posts throughout the 1980s. See *Fujian Ribao* (4/23/84): 1, (10/11/84): 2, (2/10/88): 1, and (11/16/88): 2; *Zhongguo Nongmin Ribao* (5/20/84): 1; and *Renmin Gong'an Ribao* (3/8/88): 1.

[7] The number of illegal customs posts in Henan, for example, grew from a base of 156 authorized by the provincial government in 1985 to 480 in 1987. The following summer, the number mushroomed to 841 in July, 1,271 in August, and 1,700 in October. A provincial campaign in late 1988 shut down more than 1,000 illegal roadblocks but by early 1989 more than 1,200 were again reported in operation. *Henan Ribao* (11/26/86): 1, (11/9/88): 1, and (12/22/90): 1; *Nongmin Ribao* (12/5/88): 1; *Jingji Ribao* (4/8/89): 2; and *Fazhi Ribao* (1/17/90): 1.

[8] Although in the interest of space I focus on provincial governments in the pages that follow, prefectural and county governments also actively participated in the campaign against illegal roadblocks and import barriers.

[9] *Fazhi Ribao* (1/10/90): 1, (1/17/90): 1, (9/10/90): 1, (10/18/90): 2, and (10/25/90): 2; *Xi'nan Gongshang Bao* (3/15/90): 1; *Sichuan Ribao* (12/5/90): 1; *Henan Ribao* (7/7/90): 1; *Guizhou Ribao* (11/19/90): 1; *Hunan Ribao* (6/18/90): 1 and (12/28/90): 1; *Tianjin Ribao* (11/29/90): 6; *Jingji Cankao* (7/15/90): 1 and (9/10/90): 1; *Jiangxi Ribao* (8/30/90): 1; and *Hubei Ribao* (8/8/90): 1.

a campaign to clean up the "three disorders" and eradicate unauthorized inspection stations. On September 10, Shandong announced that public security officials had shut down illegal customs posts.

After publication of the two State Council notices, provincial, prefectural, and county governments responded with vigorous campaigns against illegal roadblocks. In December 1990, local governments in Hebei began a concerted effort to shutdown illegal tolls.[10] The provincial government of Heilongjiang announced that it would undertake a strenuous investigation of unauthorized checkpoints within the province. Jiangsu promulgated strict new regulations governing the erection of barriers along major interprovincial arteries. Zhejiang Vice Governor Gao Dezheng ordered local cadres to shut down all illegal roadblocks. Bureaus in Anhui were ordered to conduct a thorough investigation of all roadblocks and shut down any unauthorized posts. Fujian announced a new system of permits and registration of inspection stations as part of its ongoing effort to eradicate illegal tolls. Guangdong ordered all inspection stations shut down immediately, with the sole exception of 51 antismuggling checkpoints maintained by provincial authorities. Yunnan announced that it had dramatically reduced the number of inspection posts within the province. Based on progress during early 1991, Premier Li Peng was ready to claim preliminary success in eradicating illegal customs posts in June 1991, when he addressed a national conference on the elimination of the "three disorders."

The campaign to eliminate illegal customs posts nevertheless continued into the summer of 1991. In September, Shaanxi announced that it had eliminated several thousand illegal roadblocks in a forty-day campaign.[11] According to Shaanxi Governor Bai Qingcai, the province would henceforth pursue a policy of immediately dismantling any and all illegal custom posts. Concurrently, the provincial government lifted restrictions on trade in all agricultural products except grain, cotton, edible oils, silk cocoon, tobacco, and specific medicinal herbs. Hubei, Henan, Hebei, Qinghai, and Liaoning also continued to crack down on illegal customs posts during late 1991.

Although the dismantling of illegal customs posts received the bulk of public attention, local governments also had begun to eliminate import barriers. Once again, some localities moved before the formal beginning of the central government's antiprotectionism campaign. In January 1990, well before the State

---

[10] *Fazhi Ribao* (1/15/91): 1; *Renmin Ribao* (6/18/91): 1 and (8/27/91): 2; *Heilongjiang Ribao* (11/14/90): 1 and (11/30/90): 2; *Jingji Cankao* (12/17/91): 1; *Xinhua Ribao* (12/29/90): 1; *Anhui Ribao* (12/16/90): 1; *Fujian Ribao* (12/2/90): 1 and (12/5/90): 1; *Nanfang Ribao* (1/6/91): 1; *Yunnan Ribao* (12/18/90): 1; and *Zhongguo Shang Bao* (10/11/90): 1.

[11] *Jingji Cankao* (2/15/90): 2 and (5/23/91): 1; *Nongmin Ribao* (9/27/91): 1 and (10/23/91): 1; *Renmin Ribao* (9/15/91): 2; *Jingji Ribao* (8/15/91): 1; and *Renmin Gong'an Bao* (11/29/91): 1.

Council's attack on local protectionism got underway, the leading Guangdong daily, *Nanfang Ribao*, condemned the growth of market barriers, asserting that protection of backward producers only retarded local economic development.[12] In April, Beijing Mayor Chen Xitong told representatives of local commercial departments and retailers that the municipal government would not tolerate local protectionism and that they should not buy local products if they were inferior and more expensive than imported goods.[13] Two months later, representatives from Beijing, Tianjin, Hebei, Shanxi, and Neimenggu met in Beijing to hammer out a comprehensive agreement calling for the elimination of interprovincial trade barriers. After local protectionism caused markets to stagnate, the government of Tianshui City (Gansu) adopted aggressive protrade policies by seeking renewed economic cooperation with localities in Sichuan, Xizang, and Xinjiang. In August, the municipal government of Pingdingshan (Henan) announced that it would welcome imports of products from other areas. In parts of eastern Jiangxi, low-level commercial cadres, meanwhile, circumvented import restrictions imposed by their superiors and continued to import goods from Zhejiang.

Once the center began to attack local protectionism, support for ending import protectionism increased. On October 2, the leading Shanghai newspaper *Jiefang Ribao* denounced import barriers, declaring that they only served to protect backward local enterprises and weaken the local economy.[14] An editorial in *Henan Ribao* called for the removal of the "bamboo walls" that hindered the formation of a united national market.[15] In November, *Fujian Ribao* reported that textile wholesalers in Sanming City had resumed importing cloth from North China after the municipal government renounced local protectionism. Commercial authorities in the city of Shaowu, Fujian, implemented new credit policies that placed local and outside products on an equal footing. In February 1991, the government of Yunnan abolished all price distinctions between local and imported products. Qinghai, meanwhile, announced a provincial export promotion policy modeled on the coastal development strategy and ordered the elimination of all internal trade barriers.

[12] *Nanfang Ribao* (1/9/90): 1. Guangdong's early support for antiprotectionism comes as little surprise, of course, because import barriers had been aimed specifically at that province's products (see Chapter 5).

[13] *Xinhua* (4/10/90), in *FBIS-China* (4/20/90): 43; *Jingji Cankao* (6/22/90): 1; *Gansu Ribao* (6/6/90): 2; *Henan Ribao* (8/17/90): 1; and *Zhejiang Provincial Service* (12/21/90), in *FBIS-China* (12/26/90): 55.

[14] *Jiefang Ribao* (10/2/90): 2. Like Guangdong's early support for open markets, *Jiefang Ribao's* call for the elimination of import barriers was obviously consistent with Shanghai's position as a leading producer and exporter of consumer goods.

[15] *Henan Ribao* (10/12/90): 3; *Fujian Ribao* (11/29/90): 2; *Fujian Ribao* (1/23/91): 2; *Jingji Cankao* (2/3/91): 1; and *Qinghai Ribao* (11/3/90): 2.

Other localities had gone against the tide and had never resorted to import protectionism. Cadres in Qingyuan City (Guangdong), for example, steadfastly resisted pressure from local enterprise managers to raise import barriers, arguing that barriers would hurt consumers and result in a devastating combination of flooded markets and rising prices.[16] Despite pressure from local producers saddled with large stockpiles of unsold consumer goods, the municipal government of Jingmen City (Hubei) not only refused to raise import barriers but implemented an open-door trade policy instead. Municipal authorities in Changde City (Hunan), meanwhile, refused to limit imports of outside goods and instead authorized unfettered trade in all products except cotton, silk, and urea fertilizer. While seeking to promote sales of local products, the municipal government of Chongqing refused to block imports of consumer goods even after imported products captured 75 percent of local markets. The Sichuan provincial government, meanwhile, ordered the "provincial gates" thrown open and ordered local governments to stop using locally issued "transit permits" and "passes" to block exports. It also relaxed restrictions on exports of grain, edible oils, citrus, phosphorus fertilizer, soda ash, caustic soda, pork, and hog hides.[17] Believing that trade rather than protectionism would improve soft markets, Tongren Prefecture in northern Guizhou embarked on a campaign to expand trade with counties across the border in Sichuan, Hunan, and southwestern Hubei.[18]

The public vigor of local government in implementing the antiprotectionism campaign notwithstanding, illegal customs posts continued to be a problem. In January 1992, reporters from *Nongmin Ribao* revealed that localities in Shandong, Hebei, and Tianjin continued to maintain illegal customs posts.[19] When questioned by reporters, the director of the State Commercial Administration claimed that local bureaus of his department in Zhejiang, Guizhou, Hebei, and three other unidentified provinces had eliminated 612 illegal barriers. Commercial bureaus in Neimenggu, Liaoning, and twelve other unidentified provinces had eliminated 1,310 illegal barriers since the beginning of the antiprotectionism campaign in 1990. Nevertheless, he admitted that local protectionism remained a serious problem in many areas. According to the Minister of Agriculture, the failure to eradicate local trade barriers still threatened to stunt the development of rural commerce and imperil the deepening of

---

[16] *Jingji Ribao* (11/6/90): 1; *Hubei Ribao* (10/31/90): 1; *Jingji Cankao* (10/1/90): 1; and *Zhongguo Shang Bao* (7/21/90): 1.

[17] *Jingji Cankao* (10/14/90): 2 and *Sichuan Ribao* (12/5/90): 1. The government of Sichuan had previously said that it would pursue an open-door export policy and expand raw-material exports rather than engage in local industrialization and import substitution. *Los Angeles Times* (4/6/88).

[18] *Guizhou Ribao* (12/10/90): 1.

[19] *Renmin Ribao* (1/30/92): 2 and *Nongmin Ribao* (1/27/92): 1, (1/29/92): 1, and (1/31/92): 1.

reform. The Minister of Commerce denounced continued local protectionism as a "stumbling block" and praised the governments of Shaanxi and Sichuan provinces for adopting tough antiprotectionism policies. The head of the transportation management department of the Ministry of Public Security denounced local police for failing to uphold regulations and engaging in illegal activity, particularly the arbitrary collection of "attitude fines." The State Council, therefore, implemented a second antiprotectionism campaign in early 1992.

Provincial governments dutifully followed up with renewed attacks on local protectionism. In early February 1992, Sichuan ordered the immediate removal of all customs posts except those authorized for the control of tobacco, silk, and forestry resources.[20] Hebei announced that it had reduced the number of local inspection posts from 1,796 to just 200 and the number of officials engaged in inspecting the flow of commodities from more than 8,000 to 3,500. Henan reported it had shut down more than 1,000 customs posts (most of which it had presumably shut down during the 1990 antiprotectionism campaign), leaving just sixty inspection posts in place. Shandong initiated a campaign to reduce the number of local inspection stations and, after a two-month investigation, ordered 166 unauthorized posts closed, thereby cutting the number of checkpoints in the province from 288 to 122. After admitting that it had set up a network of customs posts in 1986, the municipal government of Tianjin ordered them dismantled. Shaanxi, which had eliminated internal trade barriers with considerable fanfare the previous summer, conceded that illegal roadblocks had become a problem once again and launched a renewed effort to eradicate them. The Jiangxi provincial government also clamped down on signs of resurgent local protectionism in the early summer of 1992.

Reports of import protectionism became less frequent after the 1991–2 campaign. Nevertheless, evidence of trade barriers continued to appear. Some localities continued to block imports of goods that might compete with local products and to pursue local autarky.[21] According to *Fazhi Ribao*, even though the blockades and customs posts may have disappeared, local governments continued to block imports by erecting dense thickets of regulations and red tape and often rendered local markets all but impenetrable. Localities in Fuming and Muyang counties (Jiangsu), for instance, imposed arbitrary "inspection" fees on beer produced in other areas and required each bottle to carry "anti-forgery stickers." Local protectionism was so bad in the domestic beer market that the

---

[20] *Nongmin Ribao* (2/11/92): 1, (2/19/92), (4/15/92): 1, (5/12/92), (6/30/92): 1, and (12/25/92): 1; *Hebei Ribao* (2/28/92): 1 and (2/20/92): 1; *Dazhong Ribao* (2/24/92): 1; *Renmin Ribao* (2/25/92): 2; *Gongren Ribao* (3/27/92): 1; and *Jingji Ribao* (4/27/92): 1.
[21] *Jingji Ribao* (9/3/93): 3; *Fazhi Ribao* (3/4/93): 3 and (10/27/93): 1; and *Asiaweek* (12/7/01).

Qingdao Brewery found that it was necessary to buy shares in local breweries in Wuhan, Beijing, and Shenzhen in order to break into these markets while the Beijing-based Yanjing Beer Group found it necessary to buy up a dozen local breweries to gain access to markets in other cities.[22] Bass Breweries, on the other hand, found itself forced to abandon its China operations after it was refused bottling licenses in key cities.[23] Foreign soft drink manufacturers reported that local autarky and protectionism had forced them to construct a series of regional bottling plants and distribution systems.[24] China's electrical power system was also reportedly fragmented into a series of regional monopolies between which no sales occurred, even when prices were much lower in one locality than the other.[25]

Local efforts to control import protectionism also continued. In late 1993, leading cadres from Shanghai, Jiangsu, Fujian, Beijing, Tianjin, Heilongjiang, Hebei, Henan, and Guangdong, along with officials from twenty major cities, met in Shanghai to discuss how to eliminate trade barriers and improve economic cooperation, including cooperation in eradicating the manufacture of counterfeit goods.[26] In 1996, authorities in Ningxiang County (Hunan) were accused of protecting local factories engaging in the illegal manufacture of counterfeit goods. Investigators found evidence of similar illegalities in various localities in Zhejiang, Jiangxi, and Shandong. In 1997, *Hebei Zhengfa Bao* reported that some localities in the province continued to bar imports of certain goods. Three years later in 2000, *Xinhua* reported that local governments in some areas still refused to allow imports of construction materials, fertilizer, and instant noodles.

Local protectionism remained a major problem within the legal system. Litigants continued to complain about biases on the part of local courts. In some areas, local protectionism was so serious that companies complained that it was pointless to even sue in cases of breach of contract and fraud because local courts would never provide redress.[27] Dishonest judges might refuse to hear lawsuits or accept false evidence from locals. Some local courts continued to refuse to carry out judgments against locals handed down by other courts. In other localities,

---

[22] *Asiaweek* (12/7/00) and *Shenzhen Daily* (3/11/02).

[23] China Online (4/10/00).

[24] China Online available at http://www.chinaonline/estoreNew/Consumer_Goods/Em1009_sample.htm.

[25] *Asiawise* (7/12/01).

[26] *Jingji Cankao* (11/26/93): 1; *Hunan Ribao* (3/27/96): 1 and (3/11/96): 1–2; *Zhejiang Ribao* (9/18/93): 1; *Jiancha Ribao* (7/30/96): 1; *Shanghai Fazhi Bao* (9/11/96): 3; *Hebei Zhengfa Bao* (1/22/97): 4; and *Xinhua* (7/3/00).

[27] *Jilin Ribao* (10/28/93): 2; *Fazhi Ribao* (3/31/93), (2/21/94): 1, (4/13/94): 2, (7/26/94): 1, and (8/15/94): 1; and *People's Daily* (English edition) (1/29/00).

outsiders bringing lawsuits against locals were illegally detained and jailed. When courts did rule in favor of outsiders, local cadres in some areas reportedly scolded and cursed judges for betraying their localities. Local protectionism remained so entrenched, according to officials of the Supreme People's Court in Beijing, that as of early 2000 local courts had blocked upward of 850,000 lawsuits involving close to ¥260 billion in order to protect local interests.

Monetary blockades also persisted. After the beginning of the 1990 campaign against local protectionism, it was reported that local governments continued to order local banks to refuse payment to outside accounts, thereby "pouring fuel on the fires" of what the deputy director of the State Council's Triangular Debt Clearance Small Group described as a still chaotic commodity trading system.[28] Other banks remained infected by the false belief that "payment of debts would result in losses" and that "he who repays first is the one to eat the loss."

In June 1991, Li Peng publicly warned that the banking system must strengthen enforcement of existing regulations, that enterprises must not refuse to pay their debts or raise regional blockades, and that local governments must assume greater leadership in the campaign to clear triangular debts.[29] The following month, the State Council issued a notice ordering local finance bureaus to adhere strictly to state regulations in conducting interregional transactions and called on local branches of the People's Bank of China to ensure that debts were settled promptly and correctly. In December 1992, Ren Jianxin, a member of the CCP Central Committee and secretary of its committee on legal and political affairs, admitted that local protectionism remained a problem in the court system. He warned local courts and legal departments that they must not automatically side with local interests in resolving legal disputes, exact revenge against officials who properly enforced judgments against local interests, use anticorruption measures as a cover for conducting attacks on outsiders, block the settlement of debts owed to enterprises in other localities, or take hostages in legal disputes.

The 1990–2 campaign against local protectionism, in short, did not eradicate the problem.[30] But it marked a turning point. By the fall of 1990, more provincial

---

[28] *Renmin Ribao* (8/16/91): 2, (8/23/91): 2, (8/28/91): 2, and (8/31/91): 2.

[29] *Renmin Ribao* (6/20/91): 1–2; *Jingji Ribao* (7/26/91): 1; and *BBCSWB, Far East* (12/23/92): B2/3.

[30] It must be acknowledged that although press reports suggest a dramatic decrease in interregional trade during 1989–90 and an increase after the advent of the November 1990 antilocal protectionism campaign, hard evidence of such a shift is lacking. Working with data on commercial transactions, Kumar finds that imports increased for all provinces, except Tianjin, between 1985 and 1992, while exports increased for all but four provinces during this same period. Relative to total retail sales, however, interprovincial trade decreased throughout these years

and subprovincial governments in both manufacturing and raw material–producing regions were clearly more inclined toward trade than they had been earlier, and they moved more vigorously to clamp down on illegal local trade barriers. The response to the central government's fall 1990 policies thus raises the question: why would local governments suddenly embrace antiprotectionism? Does the fact that provincial governments jumped on the antiprotectionism bandwagon suggest that the central government suddenly wielded considerably more power than it had in previous periods?[31] Or does the shift to antiprotectionism reflect a change in the attitudes of local governments toward interregional cooperation?

I argue that local governments' dismantling of import barriers and customs posts can be explained in terms of rational self-interest rather than coerced compliance or a sudden change in attitudes. To the extent that central intervention made a difference, I assert that it facilitated a transition from protectionism to trade that was already underway. I will begin by examining how the structural foundations of import protectionism and illegal toll taking affected (a) the probability that the central government could or would move decisively and (b) the probability that local governments would support central efforts to eradicate these forms of local protectionism. I shall then analyze how economic development and industrialization changed local governments' incentives to engage in export protectionism. Finally, I shall examine how linkages between different forms of local protectionism, particularly export and import protectionism, affected the probability that local governments would opt to pursue more open-trade policies.

IMPORT PROTECTIONISM AND PRISONERS' DILEMMA

Differences in the nature of export and import protectionism explain why even a relatively weak center could affect a rapid shift from high levels of import

and in absolute terms it decreased between 1988 and 1990. Unfortunately, most provincial statistical bureaus stopped publishing data on interprovincial trade in the early 1990s. As a result, there are no data to confirm that the preliminary trend toward increased interprovincial trade observed by Kumar in the 1992 data and implied by anecdotal reports continued. Kumar also finds little structural differentiation among China's provinces, which suggests a continued tendency toward regional autarky. Young also concludes that regional autarky has increased since the 1980s. Anjali Kumar, "Economic Reform and the Internal Division of Labour in China," in Goodman and Segal, eds., *China Deconstructs: Politics, Trade and Regionalism*: 104 and 113, and Alwyn Young, "The Razor's Edge: Distortions and Incremental Reform in the People's Republic of China," *The Quarterly Journal of Economics* 65, no. 4 (November 2000): 1091–11.

[31] On the relationship between central power and local bandwagoning, see Avery Goldstein, *From Bandwagon to Balance-of-Power Politics: Structural Constraints and Politics in China, 1949–1978* (Stanford, CA: Stanford University Press, 1991).

protectionism to greater interregional economic cooperation. As noted at the beginning of this chapter, export protectionism and import protectionism, while rooted in the same price scissors – induced macroeconomic contradictions — were fundamentally different conflicts. Export protectionism arose because local governments in raw material–producing regions were able to make themselves better off by blocking exports of undervalued inputs and either diverting them into newly constructed local processing industries or onto the black market. Faced with a loss of needed raw materials and demands for higher prices, consumers in traditional manufacturing centers responded by seeking to bypass raw material–producing regions' export barriers and thus triggered bidding wars. As argued in chapters 3 and 4, the center experienced great difficulty in trying to contain resource wars, managing at best in most cases to patch together "cease-fire" deals that quickly became a cover for ongoing export protectionism and black marketeering. More critically, the center's inability to halt opportunistic rent seeking meant that successive bidding wars pushed prices upward toward market levels, thus progressively reducing the scale of rents that fueled export protectionism while also reducing the contradictions between supply and demand that gave rise to the need for administrative allocation.

There is also little question that the center was largely unable to prevent the spread of import protectionism during the recession of 1989–90. It seems implausible to assume, therefore, that the center was strong enough to force a sudden reduction in the level of import protectionism in the fall of 1990. Analysis of the structure of import protectionism and predatory toll taking, however, reveals that even limited central intervention could bring about such a shift, not because the center was able to force local governments to abandon import protectionism and predatory toll taking, but rather because it served local governments' own interests to back away from endemic import protectionism and predatory toll taking.

To illustrate why this should be true, let us begin by remembering that the center could not deter or stop export protectionism because local governments in raw material–producing areas had a "dominant" strategy of rent seeking. That is, regardless of what local governments in manufacturing regions did, local governments in raw material–producing regions could make themselves better off by throwing up export barriers. Given imperfect information and enforcement problems that degraded the center's ability to sanction those engaged in export protectionism, the result was a pattern of conflict in which the combatants became locked into conflicts that the center could not halt nor which the combatants themselves were likely to abandon unless the center could insure them against opportunism. Even then, they still had incentives to resort to opportunism. The result was a vicious cycle in which attempts by the center to bring export protectionism under control actually set the stage for continuation of the resource wars because whenever the center managed to halt bidding wars, it perpetuated the conditions that gave rise to them: skewed prices and supply-demand contradictions.

By contrast, until the 1989–90 recession hit, both newly industrializing areas, including those in raw material–producing regions and established manufacturing areas, benefited from trade. So long as demand for consumer goods exceeded supply, all manufacturers preferred trade. Trade allowed developed regions to export surplus local production, thereby maximizing revenues and profits. Exports of finished products allowed less-developed regions to earn monies to pay for imports of capital goods from developed regions and helped sustain the development of local infant industries. Sellers' markets, meanwhile, meant that both superior and inferior products found ready markets, thus reducing friction between established and emerging producers. Local governments may have resorted to local protectionism in this environment, seeking opportunistically to tilt the playing field in favor of local manufacturers by discriminating in favor of "their" enterprises. Opportunistic barriers need not, however, have triggered massive retaliation because sellers' markets ensure that inventories can be disposed of elsewhere.

Once overproduction, which results in part from the adoption of ISI/FPI by raw material–producing regions, occurs and buyers' markets replace sellers' markets, the underlying preference of all manufacturers for trade remains unchanged. Ironically, market saturation actually initially increases the imperative to trade because expanding exports allows local enterprises to dispose of excess inventory. At the same time, however, local governments have incentives to begin restricting access to local markets. Restricting access, in theory, allows local manufacturers to increase local market share at the expense of outside competitors, thus inflating sales, while also preventing outsiders from dumping their excess production onto the local market. However, unless excluding outsiders opens up enough market space such that all local manufacturers can dispose of their excess inventories, local manufacturers will still benefit from continued access to other markets. If local demand is contracting, local manufacturers are, in fact, likely to find their dependence on exports increasing at the same time that pressure to raise local import barriers is increasing. Thus, as markets approach saturation, a combination of import barriers and aggressive export promotion is necessary to help shore up local manufacturers' sagging sales. This combination of policies, particularly when coupled with beggar-thy-neighbor price cutting and dumping, however, will soon force all local governments to raise import barriers, thereby pushing the system toward closure.

The preceding applies to both newly industrializing regions and established manufacturing centers. To the extent that differences exist, they are primarily differences in timing. Because their infant industries are less competitive and, thus, more vulnerable to softening demand, local governments in newly industrializing areas[32] will have incentives to raise import barriers earlier than local governments in manufacturing regions. If demands continue to soften, eventually established manufacturing centers will be tempted to wall off local markets as export markets disappear, excess inventories build up, and dumping begins. Differences in timing are not, however, the same as differences in preferences because under conditions of local market saturation both newly industrializing and established manufacturing regions will become increasingly export dependent.

Once raw material–producing regions have begun to industrialize, therefore, both these newly industrialized and established manufacturing regions have similar preferences. Both will engage in opportunistic import protectionism whenever they can get away with it because this allows local producers to gain an artificial competitive edge. But because rents will lead to the construction of excess capacity, as industrialization deepens, both established manufacturing regions and newly industrializing regions will come to depend on exports to dispose of "surplus" output. As a result, both prefer mutual trade over mutual protectionism. Both are averse to exploitation by the other. The preferences of different localities are thus symmetric. Because retaliation by others prevents any region from obtaining its maximal payoff (unilateral exploitation, i.e., enjoying unfettered access to other markets while restricting access to local markets), the best possible outcome is mutual trade, not mutual protection.

A mutual trade equilibrium, however, is unstable. Local governments will trade only so long as demand for finished products exceeds supply. Unable to dispose of excess local production on export markets and faced with the threat that other localities will dump their excess production on local markets, local governments find themselves forced to raise trade barriers under these conditions. As a result, as markets approach saturation, cooperation (mutual trade) breaks down, and the outcome shifts to that of mutual protection.

Mutual protection is, however, less desirable than mutual trade even in conditions of local saturation. In the short term, closing local markets off and blocking imports may give local producers some relief. In the long term, closing off

---

[32] Although the distinction between raw material–producing and manufacturing regions retains some salience, to the extent that this cleavage matters in the context of import protectionism it serves to distinguish between newly industrialized areas and established manufacturing centers or between areas with infant industries and areas with mature industries.

local markets does not solve the problem of excess production. Local producers, particularly those in developed regions, should find that the loss of export markets more than offsets the gains from import protectionism. Noncooperation also leaves local governments vulnerable to secondary retaliation, particularly to the taking of "fiscal hostages" as local governments refuse to pay existing debts, erect monetary embargoes, and block cash exports. Import protectionism is thus a poor substitute for trade. Nevertheless, once import barriers begin to proliferate, local governments are apt to find themselves on a slippery slope and become trapped by the need to prevent other regions from exploiting them by engaging in beggar-thy-neighbor trade policies.

Increased demand and a return to sellers' markets would, of course, lessen the need to protect local markets and push the outcome back toward a mutual-trade equilibrium. Getting from point A to point B can, however, prove problematic, as was evident in the statements of various local cadres (see Chapter 5). First, import protectionism tends to exacerbate soft market conditions and undermine efforts to reinvigorate the economy. Second, local governments may fear that whoever makes the first move will suffer if others fail to reciprocate. So long as there is uncertainty about the willingness of others to cooperate, therefore, it does not pay to take the lead because the leader is likely to pay a high cost because others can exploit it. This implies that once trade has broken down, local governments will find themselves in a form of prisoners' dilemma, wherein all would be better off if trade revived but pervasive fear of unrequited cooperation prevents them from moving in that direction.

Import protectionism will lead to a suboptimal outcome absent effective central intervention. The center, however, is unlikely to remain passive in the face of increasing import protectionism. The center is itself a major economic actor and its enterprises are heavily – if not exclusively – dependent on export markets. Enterprises owned by the center lack the territorial base enjoyed by locally owned collective enterprises. All sales by state-owned enterprises are in a very real sense exports because markets are de facto controlled by local governments, not the center. When local governments intervene on behalf of "their" enterprises, therefore, their barriers will tend to fall particularly hard on state-owned enterprises.[33] If local trade barriers deny state-owned enterprises access to markets, their inventories will mount, profits will fall,

---

[33] Although this statement implies a black-and-white distinction between local industries and state-owned industries, the distinction is, in fact, not so clear-cut. Local governments frequently share responsibility and quasi-ownership of locally based, state-owned enterprises with the central ministries. As a result, they may well intervene on behalf of "their" state-owned industries as well as "their" collective industries. Import protectionism will, however, deny access to state-owned enterprises in other regions.

and revenues will decrease. The growth of import protectionism will therefore inflict direct losses on the central government, giving it strong incentives to come to the aid of state-owned enterprises by actively opposing local import protectionism.

The logic of import protectionism thus stands in almost direct contrast to that of export protectionism. All actors, including those in less developed raw material–producing regions, developed manufacturing regions, and the central government, benefit more from mutual trade than from mutual protection, and all have symmetric preferences. The real difficulty in solving import protectionism, therefore, lies in reviving the economy and rebuilding trust among localities. Reviving the economy will ease market saturation, stimulate demand, and thus reduce the pressures to protect local producers. Rebuilding trust will convince local governments that cooperation will not go unrequited. Rent-seeking interests do not, therefore, stand in the way of mutual trade, as was the case with export protectionism, and the structure of the import-protection game favors, rather than obstructs, movement toward the mutual trade outcome. The real need is thus not a change in local governments' preferences but for the center to step into the role of honest broker and use its good offices to convince local governments that lowering import barriers will not result in unrequited cooperation and hence exploitation.

In the context of late 1990, opportunities existed for the center to assume the role of honest broker. Specifically, local governments needed central assistance in clearing "triangular debts." By the summer of 1991, enterprises had accumulated debts totaling ¥160 billion (U.S.$30.02 billion), including ¥142 billion (U.S.$26.64 billion) in circulating capital debts and ¥18 billion (U.S.$3.38 billion) in debts related to capital construction projects, plus an additional ¥80 billion (U.S.$15.01 billion) worth of enterprise capital tied up in unsold inventory.[34] Because interenterprise debt was triangular (i.e., A owes B, who owes C, who owes A) and resulted in part from shortages of cash, settlement required a combination of cash injections and an honest broker who would assure that the complex debt transfers were properly carried out. Only the central government had the authority to issue loans sufficient to reliquidate the system.[35] The center was also in a position to allocate moneys directly to debt

---

[34] *Renmin Ribao* (8/18/91): 2.

[35] According to the center's debt-clearance plan, all debt clearances would be handled by banks rather than by individual enterprises. Creditor enterprises would submit their claims to their banks, which would then forward them to the banks of the debtor enterprises. The latter banks would then either obtain funds from debtors or issue loans in the name of the debtor enterprises and disburse these funds to creditors' banks. Any debts owed by "creditor" enterprises would then be settled by the bank. *Xinhua* (8/5/90), in *FBIS-China* (8/15/90): 26–7.

repayment, thus avoiding the potential pitfalls inherent in circuitous triangular debt settlement.

The central government had, in fact, begun to assume this role in 1989, when the People's Bank of China set up three interbank debt-clearance groups, one in the northeast, responsible for clearing debts in Liaoning, Jilin, and Heilongjiang; a second one for western China responsible for clearing debts in Sichuan, Yunnan, Guizhou, Xizang, Shaanxi, and Gansu; and a third for East China responsible for clearing debts in Fujian, Hubei, Henan, Guangdong, Guangxi, Hainan, Jiangsu, Anhui, and Jiangxi.[36] When the bank experienced difficulty in implementing this system, the State Council set up the "State Council Debt Clearance Leadership Small Group" to provide overall coordination and direct central oversight. In September 1990, the small group brought provincial representatives together for a debt summit in Beijing. The following month, the State Council put Vice Premier Zhu Rongji in charge of debt clearance. Using loans from the People's Bank of China totaling ¥28.4 billion and ¥2.2 billion in local funds, the Debt Clearance Small Group was able to settle a total of ¥101.1 billion in triangular debts during the fall of 1991, mostly by transferring credits among accounts held by the People's Bank of China. The central government also urged state-owned wholesalers to buy unsold inventory from manufacturers and provided credits for such transactions.

Even though the problem of triangular debt was never entirely resolved, central intervention in 1991 provided important confidence-building support for a movement away from the suboptimal mutual protection equilibrium in which localities found themselves during 1989–90. Central loans and mediation had effectively brokered a nationwide exchange of fiscal hostages and bought up excess production, thus allowing local governments to reopen their economies to trade without fear of unrequited cooperation. When bust turned to boom after 1992, moreover, the underlying problem of too many products chasing too few buyers was also largely eliminated, thus giving local governments yet another set of incentives to lower their import barriers.

ILLEGAL TOLLS AND THE TRAGEDY OF THE COMMONS

In many ways, the illegal toll taking is the least complicated aspect of local protectionism, in both its origins and its logic. Illegal tolls arise out of fiscal need or a combination of greed and opportunism. Local governments erect illegal

---

[36] *Jingji Cankao* (1/7/90): 1; *Jinrong Shi Bao* (5/10/90): 1; *Renmin Ribao* (9/21/91): 1 and (11/11/91): 1; and *China Daily* (9/4/91).

customs posts and levy illegal taxes on trade passing through their jurisdictions, either because a weak tax base makes it difficult for them to cover local public expenditures or because they see an opportunity to make a quick profit. Price distortions and a lack of local industry may play a role in that they affect the strength of the local tax base and, thus, may increase or decrease a local government's fiscal hunger. In the end, however, they merely serve to differentiate between crime driven by need and crime driven by greed. Thus, we might conclude that local governments in poor, backward localities may have had greater justification for erecting illegal tolls than those in wealthy areas. That normative distinction does not, however, alter the logic of illegal toll taking by creating asymmetric preference orderings. Whether from need or greed, we may assume all local governments are predisposed to engage in opportunistic behavior.

There are thus really only two possible outcomes: illegal toll taking works or it fails. It works so long as trade continues and local governments can skim a percentage of the gains from trade. Unregulated toll taking, however, tends to kill trade. Unless local governments can accurately estimate the optimal weight of tolls the traffic will bear, negotiate agreements that apportion tolls equitably among all localities through which a commodity will pass, and strictly enforce such agreements, illegal tolls will tend to produce persistent tragedies of the commons as individual tolls add up to excessive levels. Even though each locality may only pluck a feather or two from the wild goose, to use the Chinese analogy, by the time the wild goose runs the gauntlet of localities it is likely to find itself plucked clean. When traders discover that toll fees eat up their entire gains from trade (or even more, as was true in several of the cases discussed in Chapter 5), traders are unlikely to continue to journey to distant markets. As the number of tolls increases, therefore, trade is likely to decrease. As the volume of trade decreases, local governments may try to compensate for reduced volume by increasing their squeeze. The likely result is that trade will decrease more rapidly. Ultimately, when tolls become ubiquitous and the sum of fees traders must pay becomes exorbitant, trade will drop off to the point at which local governments will find they have plucked the wild goose to death.

The center derived little direct benefit from illegal toll taking, although individual bureaus and departments of the center may have obtained some benefits from illegal fines and fees. The illegal nature of these tolls meant that the center received no "cut" from ad hoc taxes. Instead, the proceeds flowed into local coffers – or into the pockets of local cadres. Because the center lacked a stake in illegal tolls, central interests posed no insurmountable obstacles to efforts to control or eradicate local tolls. On the contrary, the fact that toll taking was illegal, and, hence, a fairly serious violation of discipline, meant that the center had positive incentives to crack down.

Although the logic of illegal toll taking may be simple and straightforward, eliminating such tolls is far from simple. First, local governments have little incentive to dismantle illegal tolls until illegal toll taking reaches crisis levels. Because opportunity costs are low, tolls pay until trade dies out. Second, although the tragedy of the commons may kill trade, thereby denying all local governments the benefits of predatory tolls, if other localities dismantle tolls, then individual local governments will have renewed incentives to erect or re-erect tolls. Third, enforcing a comprehensive ban on tolls will be difficult, both initially and increasingly as the volume of trade, and hence the opportunities to make quick illegal profits by erecting tolls, revives.

Fourth, and perhaps quite counterintuitively, the central government may find it advantageous to allow local governments to engage in a certain amount of predatory toll taking. If it bans all local tolls, the central government is likely to find itself confronted with new fiscal burdens as local governments turn to it for funds to cover expenses formerly financed by illegal tolls and taxes. Tolerating a "reasonable" level of toll taking thus relieves fiscal pressures on the central government – a not unimportant consideration for a central government that faced mounting budgetary deficits from the mid-1980s onward.[37] The dependence of large numbers of local governments on budgetary subsidies from higher levels, on the other hand, gives the center leverage by enabling it to use the threat to withhold subsidies as a means of deterring local governments from engaging in excessive toll taking.

The preceding factors suggest that the toll taking will have a rather distinct rhythm. First, the center and local governments are most likely to throw their support behind campaigns to eliminate illegal tolls only after illegal toll taking begins to spiral out of control. Second, after the acute tragedy of the commons has been solved, local governments are likely to revert to their old ways and begin engaging in illegal toll taking once again. As a result, it is not surprising that it was not until 1989–90, when the "density" of illegal tolls had reached critical levels, that we see concerted action to re-open the blocked arteries of trade. Nor is it surprising that even though thousands of illegal tolls were eliminated in vigorous provincial cleanups, many

---

[37] Between 1986 and 1991, the real budgetary deficit increased from ¥21.18 billion to ¥64.41 billion. Although shortfalls in revenues were partially offset by borrowing, "red ink," the difference between revenues plus borrowing and expenditures, rose from ¥5.47 billion to ¥47.59 billion. Where: Revenues = (Taxes) + (Enterprise Profits) + (Royalties and Surtaxes) + (Other); Adjusted Outlays = (Outlays) + (Enterprise Subsidies); Deficit = (Revenues) − (Adjusted Outlays); Red Ink = (Deficit) − (Borrowing). Based on data in *Zhongguo Tongji Nianjian, 1992*: 215 and 218.

localities had rebuilt their tolls within a matter of months as trade – and the economy – rebounded. Illegal toll taking, in short, will rise and fall without ever entirely disappearing.

The incidence of illegal toll taking and, ironically, pressure to bring toll taking under control will also increase as economic conditions deteriorate. On the one hand, deteriorating economic conditions may force local governments to look to predatory tolls as a means of offsetting decreased income from legal sources, and, on the other, the increasing number of tolls and the resulting squeeze on trade will accelerate economic deterioration.

Because the tragedy of the commons associated with illegal tolls will increase in hard times, the burden of illegal tolls will tend to increase at the same time that soft market conditions fuel increased import protectionism. The resulting coincidence of uncontrolled toll taking and deepening import protectionism will tend to create a "crisis of local protectionism."

The point of maximum crisis, however, should trigger antiprotectionism at both the central and local levels. This shift does not occur because local governments suddenly renounce rent seeking or fiscal predation. On the contrary, antiprotectionism grows because opportunistic import protectionism (blocking imports while dumping excess inventory on export markets) becomes an untenable strategy once other localities retaliate by closing off export markets. Faced with the prospect of the a undesirable outcome of mutual protectionism, local governments have incentives to support efforts to restore mutual trade. The explosive growth in illegal tolls and damage to property rights associated with local protectionism gives local governments additional reasons to support antiprotectionism.

Local governments' shift to antiprotectionism dovetails with the interests of the central government. Hurt by import protectionism and cut off from the gains from local tolls, the center has positive incentives to assume the role of honest broker and lender of last resort necessary to solve the prisoners' dilemma of import protectionism. Its basic inclination to oppose local protectionism gives the center additional reasons to support and co-opt local governments' campaigns against local tolls. Paradoxically, therefore, the crisis of local protectionism ought to lead to a transition from increasing protectionism to increasing antiprotectionism.

RENEWED EXPORT PROTECTIONISM

Although the 1990 antiprotectionism campaign may have reduced import protectionism and the number of illegal local tolls, it did not end local protectionism.

While attacking import protectionism and tolls, the central leadership did not move to end export protectionism. Neither the September notice on the three disorders nor the November notice on regional blockades explicitly called for the eradication of export barriers. Both concerned themselves with the "recent" growth of local protectionism and directed local governments to remove import barriers and dismantle illegal customs posts.

Some pressure to eliminate export barriers and liberalize interregional trade regulations was evident. A joint Central Committee–State Council notice on agricultural policy issued in December 1990, for example, called on local governments to dismantle illegal tolls that blocked the flow of agricultural commodities.[38] The central government also approved the establishment of a series of regional wholesale markets during 1990.[39] In ordering illegal customs posts dismantled, a number of provincial and local governments called for a relaxation of restrictions on the flow of agricultural products. As noted previously, both Sichuan and Shaanxi used their campaigns against illegal customs barriers as vehicles to liberalize rural trade.

Over the next several years, central policy moved in two divergent directions. At the same time it formally deregulated a considerable part of the rural economy, it stubbornly clung to its claim to monopsony rights over cotton, silk cocoons, and tobacco procurement. So long as the center continued to block the marketization of these commodities, rent seeking continued and hence these sectors continued to witness periodic wars.

In late 1991 and early 1992, as supplies of grain, cotton, sugar, tea, tobacco, and other key commodities began to exceed demand, the center announced a new round of deregulation.[40] In a November circular, the State Council decontrolled grain markets, with the proviso that state purchase quotas must be met. It also loosened restrictions on edible oil and oil-bearing crops, sugar, hogs, wool, jute, and hemp, which would henceforth be subject to limited price regulation using a system of purchase by contract to ensure that prices remained stable. State purchases of these commodities would be reduced, thus allowing the bulk of production to be sold on the market. To ensure the free circulation of these

[38] *Nongmin Ribao* (12/5/91): 1.
[39] The first wholesale market was set up in the city of Zhengzhou (Henan) and dealt in wheat. Provincial governments subsequently authorized establishment of a corn wholesale market in Changchun (Jilin); rice wholesale markets in Haikekou (Jilin) and Wuhe (Anhui); grain wholesale markets in Jiujiang (Jiangxi) and Wuhan; and a pork wholesale market in Chengdu. *Nongchanpin Liutong Tizhi Gaige yu Zhengce Baozhang*: 110. For a discussion of how the Zhengzhou market worked, see Hang Chang, "Stabilizing Agricultural Prices," *The China Business Review* (May–June 1991): 32–6.
[40] *Xinhua* (2/30/92), in *BBCSWB, FE* (6/10/92) and *Xinhua* (11/13/91), in *FBIS* (11/19/91): 44–6.

commodities, the State Council banned all local restrictions on exports, ordered all unlicensed checkpoints dismantled, and forbade the levying of export duties and other unlawful fees and fines.

Soon thereafter, the Central Committee issued a document on rural work in which it reiterated the basic thrust of the November 1991 State Council circular on regional blockades. The document also stipulated that, in the short term, price ratios between commodities subject to state purchase controls and those no longer subject to state regulations were to be "rationalized." As supplies of regulated goods increased, the circular indicated that the state should gradually shift these commodities over to market regulation.[41] In March 1992, in the wake of Deng's Southern Tour, the State Council once again endorsed the deregulation of grain, edible oils, and sugar, as did Premier Li Peng in his Work Report to the National People's Congress's annual session in April. At that time, wool markets were effectively deregulated.[42] Deregulation of the wool market was, however, essentially a symbolic reform because the center had all but formally ceded monopsony power to the provinces in 1985 and made no effort to reclaim that power once the wool war broke out.

Three key commodities remained subject to tight state regulation. As discussed previously, cotton remained subject to a state monopsony. Purchases by individuals and units other than duly authorized supply and marketing cooperatives were outlawed. The only exception allowed was in instances where cotton consumers financed the development of new production bases, in which case they could buy directly for a period of five years.

Tobacco remained subject to a state procurement monopsony whereas tobacco products, including cigarettes, remained a state monopoly. In 1991, amid the chaos of the tobacco war, the National People's Congress approved a new tobacco monopoly law that tightened central control by allowing the state tobacco monopsony to set the amount of acreage planted and to fix prices.[43] Only the monopoly had the right to buy tobacco (with the sole exception of some low-grade types of sun-cured tobacco). All interregional sales had to be approved by the monopoly, which also had the power to regulate the production and import of all products (filters, papers, machinery, etc.) used in the production of cigarettes, cigars, and so forth. Finally, the monopoly was to regulate production by establishing quotas for individual provinces for the production of

---

[41] *Xinhua* (12/24/91), in *BBCSWB-FE* (1/3/92); *Xinhua* (3/26/92), in *BBCSWB-FE* (3/28/92); and *Xinhua* (4/3/92), in *BBCSWB-FE* (4/7/92).

[42] Andrew Watson, "Market Reform and Agricultural Growth: The Dynamics of Change in the Chinese Countryside in 1992," in Joseph Cheng Yu-shek and Maurice Brosseau, eds., *China Review 1993* (Hong Kong: Chinese University Press, 1993): 14–12.

[43] *Xinhua* (6/29/91), in *BBCSWB, FE* (7/6/91).

tobacco products. Provincial-level authorities were then to distribute the quota among individual factories. Any unit or individual trading in tobacco without proper authorization could be fined and, under some circumstances, could be imprisoned for up to three years.

Silk cocoons also remained subject to unified purchase under the terms of the regulations issued by the State Council in June 1988 wherein only China Silk, acting through its provincial-level subsidiaries, had the right to buy silk cocoons and had a monopoly on silk exports. As it had claimed since the mid-1980s, the central leadership continued to argue that monopoly regulation of these commodities was a temporary measure and that over time the state monopsony should be phased out. The center also continued to claim that the purpose of state control was to maintain stability and balance in supply and demand by preventing wild swings in prices.[44]

The failure to deregulate the cotton, tobacco, and silk cocoon markets partly reflected deep-seated opposition to full-scale marketization and a profound concern that total deregulation might lead to economic instability and social unrest in the countryside. A commentary published by the *Xinhua* agency in early 1992, soon after Deng's Southern Tour, for instance, argued that even though supply and demand appeared to have equilibrated in recent years, the current equilibrium was partially the result of the depression of demand during the 1989–90 recession. Under existing conditions, the authors contended, further reforms could destabilize the rural sector.[45]

Conditions during 1992 were also not particularly favorable to deregulation. The boom unleashed in the wake of Deng's Southern Tour created unstable conditions in the countryside as banks illegally diverted funds earmarked for agricultural procurement into speculative investments in coastal boomtowns. Starved for cash, procurement agencies issued large numbers of paper IOUs to farmers. In conjunction with excessive and predatory taxation, the widespread use of IOUs triggered a wave of unrest in the countryside during late 1992 and early 1993.[46] Declining farm incomes, meanwhile, unleashed a flood of rural migrants into the cities, creating concern about uncontrolled urbanization, crime, and potential urban unrest.[47]

---

[44] Liu Jiang, "Strive to Achieve Further Development of China's Rural Economy," *Qiushi*, no. 19 (10/1/93), in *BBCSWB, FE* (11/25/93).

[45] *Xinhua* (2/23/92), in *BBCSWB, FE* (2/27/92).

[46] See Andrew Wedeman, "Stealing from the Farmers: Institutional Corruption and the 1992 IOU Crisis," *The China Quarterly*, no. 152 (December 1997): 805–31.

[47] See Yan Yun-xiang, "Dislocation, Reposition and Restratification: Structural Changes in Chinese Society," in Maurice Brosseau and Lo Chi Kin, eds., *China Review 1994* (Hong Kong: Chinese University Press, 1994).

With an eye obviously focused on the prospect of rural unrest and instability in the agricultural sector, the 1993 Agricultural Law maintained the state's right to regulate markets, including those previously deregulated. Under the terms of the law, the State Council could authorize provincial-level governments to engage in direct purchase of major commodities on behalf of the state and to set procurement prices for specific crops.[48] Deregulated commodities, therefore, could be subject to reregulation if prices became unstable or if the state saw a need to reimpose mandatory sales quotas. The tenuous nature of deregulation became clear in 1994 when the state suspended grain markets and reimposed mandatory delivery quotas after prices began to climb dramatically, causing significant increases in the urban cost of living.[49] Thus, in both theory and practice, three of the commodities over which major resource wars had been fought during the 1980s remained state monopsonies after the 1991–2 round of agricultural reforms.

The decision to put off marketization and retain monopsony controls over these products all but ensured a new round of resource wars. As argued in Chapter 3, any system of state-fixed prices will have a propensity to oscillate between periods of acute shortage, during which resource wars are likely to erupt, and periods of glut, during which "peace" will prevail. This pattern is a function of the iterative effects of distorted prices. At the outset, the depression of input prices combined with the inflation of output prices will cause demand for the input to increase while decreasing its supply. As controls over allocation weaken, competition for scarce resources will drive up prices, inducing increases in supply and decreases in demand. Rising prices will thus dissipate rents and increase production costs. As rents decrease, the trade-off between the benefits from egoistic rent seeking and compliance with the center's monopsony regulations will decease, thus leading to an expectation that compliance will become more likely with each increment of time. This suggests that eventually an equilibrium, in which the centralized monopsony is restored but in which the level of monopsony rents extracted is reduced as the gap between the monopsony price for the input and its market-clearing price decreases, will emerge.

If supply and demand adjust to changes in price automatically, then a gradual evolution toward such an equilibrium might be theoretically possible. The twin facts that agricultural commodities generally have long production cycles and their producers are likely to possess highly imperfect information all but

---

[48] "The Agricultural Law of the PRC," *Xinhua* (7/3/93), in *BBCSWB-FE* (7/21/93).

[49] Claude Aubert, "The Chinese Rural Economy in 1996," in Maurice Brosseau, Suzanne Pepper, and Tsang Shu-ki, eds., *China Review 1996* (Hong Kong: Chinese University Press, 1996): 326–7.

assure that the markets will remain unstable for some time. Long production cycles and imperfect information imply that farmers are apt to base production decisions on current prices and beliefs about prices derived from recent changes. Because shortages will tend to drive the current market price above that likely once expanding supply and decreasing demand have equilibriated, farmers are likely to base production decisions on unrealistically high future prices. Moreover, they are likely to believe that prices will continue to increase rapidly, as they have done in the recent past, and thus significantly overestimate future price levels. As a result, they are likely to overexpand production and thus create a glut.

Glut conditions will, of course, create downward pressure on prices and in extreme cases may cause the black-market price to drop below the state's fixed price. If the black-market prices fall below the fixed price, monopsony is likely to find itself in the position of a buyer of last resort and under pressure to buy more stocks that it can resell to consumers, many of whom may have built up their reserves in previous periods as a buffer against further price increases. Under these conditions, supply is likely to contract as farmers cut back on production and shift over to other crops, and the erstwhile monopsonist will have incentives to lower the monopsony price to the prevailing market price or to abandon her claim to monopsony rights. Glut conditions are, therefore, favorable to marketization.

Falling prices, however, are also likely to lead farmers to cut back on production, thus causing supply to drop and creating potential shortages as declining prices stimulate demand – and, of course, increases in prices. Under these conditions, the erstwhile monopsonist will have incentives to try to reclaim her monopsony rights and use these rights to extract rents. This implies that so long as monopsony structures remain in place, the resulting cycle of shortage and glut will create conditions favorable to the perpetuation of the monopsony – and the shortage-glut cycle. The destabilizing effects of this monopsony-price induced shortage-glut cycle will be amplified by stochastic shocks caused by weather. Should poor weather conditions (drought and/or flooding) coincide with periods of depressed production, then shortages will be exacerbated. Should good weather conditions coincide with periods of excessive production, then glut conditions will be worsened. The inherently unpredictable nature of the weather, therefore, becomes yet another destabilizing factor under monopsony conditions.

It was, therefore, rather predictable that new resource wars erupted over all three commodities over which the state continued to claim monopsony rights as the Chinese economy began to shift into high gear following Deng's January 1992 Southern Tour.

The cotton sector remained the most unstable. After the 1987–9 cotton war drove procurement prices up, doubling them from ¥3,218 per ton in 1985 to ¥6,473 per ton in 1991, production of cotton increased significantly. Between 1986 and 1992 the area sown with cotton increased from 4.31 million to 6.84 million hectares, while output increased from 3.54 million tons in 1986 to a peak of 5.68 million tons in 1991. Domestic supplies of cotton, therefore, rose 60.5 percent during the cotton war. In 1991, supply and marketing cooperatives were able to overfulfill the state procurement quota for the first time in six years, and peace prevailed in the long-troubled cotton-producing regions along the Hebei, Shandong, Henan, Jiangsu, and Anhui borders.[50] Despite these favorable conditions, the State Council ordered the localities to maintain a tight grip on cotton markets, calling on them to adhere strictly to state-fixed prices, to fulfill central purchase quotas before allocating cotton to local out-of-plan consumers, and threatening to fine units violating regulations. The State Council also warned that individual cadres could be held liable for violations committed by units under their command.

With supply exceeding demand, prices fell slightly in 1992, dropping 5 percent from ¥6,473 per ton to ¥6,119 per ton. The following year, production began to fall. Sown area decreased by close to a third, falling to 4.99 million hectares in 1993. Total acreage in key cotton-producing provinces fell even more dramatically. Farmers in Shandong, for example, reduced acreage by 69 percent in two years. Their counterparts in Hebei cut back by 62 percent. Bad weather during 1992–3, including heavy rains in some cotton-producing regions, and the spread of boll weevils cut output per hectare.[51] As a result, total output fell from 5.68 million tons in 1991 to 4.51 million tons in 1992 and to 3.74 million tons in 1993, for a total decrease of 34 percent in just two years.[52]

Nevertheless, a number of localities moved to deregulate cotton markets. In early 1993, the Shandong provincial government announced that it would immediately eliminate mandatory delivery quotas and allow prices to be set by negotiation between sellers and buyers, although the province would continue to guarantee a minimum price and regulate maximum prices.[53] Shandong's decision proved ill conceived; as supplies dropped, the center quickly denounced localities that relaxed controls and countermanded local initiatives to deregulate the market informally.

---

[50] *Xinhua* (12/21/91); *Jingji Ribao* (1/14/92): 2; and *Xinhua* (8/10/91), in *BBCSWB, FE* (8/19/91).
[51] *Jingji Cankao* (11/15/93); *Jingji Ribao* (3/21/93): 2; *Financial Times* (London) (8/19/94); and *Zhongguo Tongji Nianjian, 1997*.
[52] *Zhongguo Tongji Nianjian, 1997*: 381 and 384.
[53] *Xinhua* (1/13/93), in *BBCSWB, FE* (1/27/93); *Jingji Ribao* (3/13/93): 1; and *Renmin Ribao* (9/2/94), in *BBCSWB, FE* (9/18/94).

When chaos erupted in Hebei, Jiangsu, Anhui, Jiangxi, Shandong, Henan, Hubei, and Shaanxi during the fall purchasing season, the center ordered an immediate strengthening of the unified purchase system, fixed the purchase price at ¥6,600 per ton (a 10 percent increase over the previous year), and deployed inspection teams to troubled areas.[54] Provincial governments quickly complied with the spirit of the center's orders. Shandong deployed inspection teams to troubled areas and banned all purchases by units other than the supply and marketing cooperatives, as did Jiangsu and Henan. The government of Liaoning offered farmers a ¥30 bonus for each *dan* sold to the state, plus 15 kilograms of fertilizer at discount. Henan offered a similar bonus of ¥25–30 for each *dan* above the contracted amount and banned exports of above-quota cotton.

Despite central intervention, an increase in production (up from 3.74 million tons in 1993 to 4.35 million tons in 1994), and an increase in the official procurement price to ¥10,000 per ton (up from a preliminary increase to ¥8,000 in early 1994), conflicts continued the following year. Problems were reported in Hebei, Jiangsu, Anhui, Jiangxi, Shandong, Henan, Hubei, and Shaanxi as black-market prices reached ¥15–16,000 in some areas and rose to ¥20,000 in key industrial centers.[55] Once again, the center imposed unified purchasing, banned direct purchasing by textile mills, demanded strict adherence to the officially set procurement price, and threatened to punish any unit or individual caught engaging in cotton trading outside officially approved channels.[56] Central inspection teams were once again sent to border areas to monitor the procurement process and prevent cross-border wars.[57] Most provinces also deployed their own inspection teams, often creating interdepartmental teams composed of personnel

---

[54] *Zhongguo Shang Bao* (8/24/93): 1, (8/26/93): 1, (9/5/93): 1, (10/17/93): 1, (10/28/93): 1, (12/26/93): 1, (12/14/93): 2, and (12/26/93): 1; *Zhongguo Gongshang Bao* (10/9/93): 1 and (10/10/93): 1; *Renmin Ribao* (12/23/93): 1, (8/24/93): 1, and (9/17/93): 2; *Nongmin Ribao* (9/14/93): 1 and (10/14/94): 1; *Dazhong Ribao* (9/3/93): 1, (10/7/93): 1, and (10/19/93): 2; *Xinhua Ribao* (9/9/93): 1; *Henan Ribao* (9/14/93): 1, and (10/27/93): 1; and *Liaoning Ribao* (9/28/93): 1.

[55] *Nongmin Ribao* (8/1/94): 1, (9/24/94): 1, (10/8/94): 1, (10/10/94): 1, (10/13/94): 1, (10/14/94): 1, (11/1/94): 1, and (12/23/94): 1; *Fazhi Ribao* (8/5/94): 1, (10/13/94): 1, (11/4/94): 5, (11/16/94): 1, and (12/9/94): 2; *Reuters* (2/24/94); *Jingji Ribao* (7/23/96); *Zhejiang Fazhi Bao* (11/1/94): 1; *Xinhua* (8/29/94), in *BBCSWB, FE* (8/31/94); *Xinhua* (9/1/94), in *BBCSWB, FE* (9/7/94); and *Xinhua* (10/9/94), in *BBCSWB, FE* (10/14/94).

[56] In some areas, the center's policy became known as the "three nos": no decontrol of the cotton management system, no opening up of cotton markets, and no deregulation of cotton prices. See *Zhejiang Fazhi Bao* (11/1/94): 1 and *Nongmin Ribao* (10/10/94): 1.

[57] *Nongmin Ribao* (10/10/94): 1, (10/17/94): 1, (10/18/94): 1, and (10/19/94): 1; *Hubei Provincial Broadcasting Station* (11/2/94), in *BBCSWB, FE* (11/15/94); *Jiangsu People's Broadcasting Station* (10/10/94), in *BBCSWB, FE* (10/26/94); *Fazhi Ribao* (10/12/94): 1; and *Reuters* (11/1/94).

from the commercial, supervisory, public security, and tax bureaus, as well as officials from the local government and the supply and marketing cooperatives. A number imposed additional restrictions. Shandong barred purchasing across county and village lines. Several provinces moved to shut down illegal textile mills and confiscate illegally purchased stocks. Officials from Hebei, Shandong, and Henan hammered out a mutual nonaggression pact committing each province to strictly police purchasing and prevent cross-border buying, while localities in Hubei set up round-the-clock checkpoints to halt illegal shipments of cotton.

In a number of localities, local cadres obstructed procurement efforts. In Wannian County (Anhui), for example, party cadres seized half a ton of cotton seed from the local supply and marketing cooperative, fought with local government cadres after they sided with the cooperatives, fined farmers ¥200 who sold their cotton to the cooperative, and seized household goods.[58] In Wuxu City (Hubei) local party cadres threw up roadblocks and threatened to fine farmers ¥500 per *dan* if they sold their cotton to the cooperative. The cadres then took the cotton and sold it on the black market. When ordered by the municipal government to cease and desist, they refused. In Hubei, a gang of farmers beat a cadre to death after he attempted to force them to sell their cotton at the state-set price; officials from a state farm assaulted cadres who attempted to seize cotton stocks and threatened farmers who sold cotton to the cooperatives. In many areas, farmers withheld their stocks, believing that black-market prices would continue to increase and that the state price would ultimately be adjusted upward.

In anticipation of more trouble in 1995, the center moved early in the year to shore up the unified purchase system. After the end of the 1994 procurement season, it raised the official state price for cotton to ¥13,000, then increased it to ¥14,000 in mid-1995.[59] In March, local officials were told that there would be no deregulation of the cotton sector and ordered to roll back prices to those fixed by the center, policies that the center repeatedly articulated throughout the remainder of the year. As the purchase season approached, however, it became clear that a new cotton war was unlikely. Even though the amount of land sown with cotton had fallen slightly between 1994 and 1995, favorable weather boosted output per hectare and total output increased 10 percent to 4.77 million tons.[60] As supply increased, demand was dropping. Textiles had been piling

---

[58] *Nongmin Ribao* (10/14/94): 1; *Reuters* (9/13/94), (10/30/94), (11/1/94), and (11/8/94); *Xinhua* (10/28/94), in *BBCSWB, FE* (11/4/94); and *Hebei Ribao* (11/2/94), in *BBCSWB, FE* (11/24/94).

[59] *Xinhua* (3/12/95), in *BBCSWB, FE* (4/1/95); and *Xinhua* (8/16/95), in *BBCSWB, FE* (8/23/95).

[60] *Zhongguo Tongji Nianjian, 1997.*

up in warehouses during the past year while foreign imports had increased as domestic prices moved closer to world prices and the quality of Chinese cotton declined because of extensive adulteration. Aggregate demand was, therefore, estimated to be 10 percent less than total supply in early 1995.[61] Later that year, supply and demand were believed to be in rough equilibrium and downward pressures on prices were reported. The procurement season progressed with relatively limited conflicts reported.

By 1996, supply was reported to exceed demand, but the center did not relax the regulations granting it and its local agents monopsony rights over the purchase and allocation of cotton in 1996.[62] On the contrary, the center actually tried to tighten its controls by implementing a new "governor's responsibility system" that made the individual governors liable for shortages in deliveries to the state. The center, however, also relaxed its price policy by allowing prices to fluctuate within an 8 percent band. The following year, with supply still exceeding demand, the state was again faced with the prospect that its fixed price might actually become higher than the black-market price. The center thus relaxed its price policy further, broadening the band within which prices could fluctuate to 12 percent. Unified purchase, though, remained and the supply and marketing cooperatives would continue to purchase cotton on behalf of the state, but they would not act as a monopsony; instead they would assume the role of price regulators, with the primary responsibility of ensuring the stability of prices and, thus, supply and demand.

In early 1998, the state cut its fixed price from ¥14,000 to ¥13,000 and then lowered it to ¥10,000 in early 1999.[63] In December 1998, after two years of partial deregulation, the center announced that it would no longer set procurement prices beginning with the 1999 cotton marketing season. Instead, the state would announce nonbinding guidance prices. To maintain domestic price stability, state-owned cotton and jute companies would engage in countercyclical purchasing, building up reserves during periods of excess production and selling stocks when declining production threatened to push prices above the guidance price. So long as prices fluctuated within a band fixed by the state around its

---

[61] *Xinhua* (6/6/95), in *BBCSWB, FE* (6/14/95); *Xinhua* (8/16/95), in *BBCSWB, FE* (8/23/95); and *Nongmin Ribao* (10/28/95): 1.

[62] *Jingji Ribao* (9/16/96) and (8/29/97); *Nongmin Ribao* (11/6/96); and Shi Jianwei, "The New Direction of China's Cotton Policy," Agricultural Outlook Forum 1999, available at http://www.usda.gov/agency/oce/waob/outlook99/speeches/055/shi.txt.

[63] *China Daily* (1/12/99); *Jingji Ribao* (9/16/96); *Jingji Cankao* (9/1/96), in *BBCSWB, FE* (10/14/96); *Xinhua* (4/17/98), in *BBCSWB, FE* (9/30/98); *Xinhua* (4/17/98), in *BBCSWB, FE* (4/22/98); Shi, "The New Direction in China's Cotton Policy"; *Jingji Cankao Bao* (1/12/99); and *Renmin Ribao* (12/25/98).

guidance price, authorized dealers and consuming units could purchase cotton directly from growers. The supply and marketing cooperatives would, according to these new regulations, continue to trade in cotton but would no longer have an exclusive right to the harvest.

As was true in 1985, deregulation came at a time of glut and in 1999 cotton prices fell to ¥7,800 per ton soon after the state lifted price controls. Nationally, average prices then inched up to ¥8,000 per ton in early 2000, 20 percent below the ¥10,000 per ton price set by the state in early 1999, with the prices ranging from a low in some areas of ¥7,800 and a high of ¥8,400 in other areas.[64] A 1.2 million ton shortage, however, developed in the fall of 2000 after bad weather cut production, causing prices to shoot up 70 percent to ¥13,600, well above the target price of ¥11,000 set by the All-China Federation of Supply and Marketing Cooperatives, and panic buying was reported in some areas. As called for by the 1999 deregulation policy, when prices rose above the guidance price, the state began to pump reserve stocks into the market rather than resorting to unified purchase. The state also initiated significant cuts in cotton textile-processing capacity, ordering the elimination of 5.2 million spindles in 1998 and an additional 4.4 million in 1999.

While the cotton sector lurched between shortage and glut and finally toward marketization, the tobacco sector remained mired in chronic oversupply in the years that followed the tobacco wars. Seeking to cash in on the high profits created by the state monopoly on tobacco products, localities in tobacco-producing regions seriously overexpanded cigarette production. As of mid-1993, excessive production of cigarettes had led to a buildup of stockpiles equal to two and a half years' demand. With more than 5 million tons of cured tobacco worth ¥20 billion piled up in inventory, factories were not interested in buying more than a fraction of the nearly 3.5 million tons of tobacco grown in 1992 and 1993.[65] Because demand for tobacco was down, local procurement agencies frequently lacked the cash needed to pay for deliveries of tobacco. In many cases they refused to buy more stocks. As a result, large amounts of tobacco remained in the hands of growers. In those localities where state procurement continued, growers frequently found purchasing agents forced prices down to below the state-set price. To cope with these problems, the tobacco monopoly tried to cut production of cured tobacco, both by reducing the amount of acreage

[64] *Zhongguo Jingji Shibao* (4/24/00); *Wenhui Bao* (9/22/00); *China Daily* (11/30/00); and *Diaoyan Shijie* (7/10/99).
[65] *Xinhua* (10/10/92), in *BBCSWB, FE* (10/21/92); *Reuters* (8/12/93); *Nongmin Ribao* (8/21/92): 3; *Henan Ribao* (10/19/93): 5; *Xinhua* (1/18/93), in *BBCSWB, FE* (1/27/93); *Xinhua* (2/17/93), in *BBCSWB, FE* (2/24/93); and *Xinhua* (8/3/93), in *BBCSWB, FE* (8/25/93).

it contracted for and by cutting the price it paid for deliveries above those specified in advance.

Nevertheless, tobacco markets remained unstable as a result of competition between the tobacco monopoly and buyers representing factories operating (often illegally) outside the plan. Cigarettes remained highly profitable, particularly for factories and localities that did not pay taxes to the central monopoly, and these producers continued to "invade" tobacco-growing regions to buy directly from farmers. As a result, local tobacco wars continued to erupt.[66] Local purchasing stations along a long stretch of the Guizhou-Sichuan border found themselves locked in a protracted struggle in the summer of 1993 after buyers in Sichuan began offering higher prices. The following year, a tobacco war erupted along the Sichuan-Guizhou-Hunan border after local authorities increased prices above those set by the tobacco monopoly.

In 1994, production began to drop. Sown area fell from 2.09 million hectares to 1.49 million heetares. Total output of tobacco decreased from 3.45 million tons to 2.24 million tons. Production of flue-cured tobacco dropped from 3.04 million tons to 1.94 million tons. Production remained at about the same level the following year.[67] As production decreased, the state pushed prices upward, raising the average price per ton from approximately ¥6,000 in 1993 to ¥6,800 in 1994, then to ¥9,800 in 1995. In 1996, output increased, with sown area increasing to 1.83 million hectares and total output to 2.92 million tons, about the same level as 1993. Procurement prices, meanwhile, rose to approximately ¥11,850 per ton, almost twice that paid during the glut of 1993.

With production down and factory stockpiles reduced, the center foresaw the possibility of a major tobacco war in the summer of 1995 and ordered local authorities to tighten controls when buyers from out-of-plan factories began to buy stocks at prices above those set by the state.[68] The following year, the tobacco monopoly increased the acreage contracted for tobacco production, thus raising total supply while continuing to restrict markets. Teams of officials from the central monopoly bureaus were deployed to monitor purchasing in volatile border regions, and a renewed crackdown on illegal cigarette factories and wholesalers was launched. As a result, although instances of illegal purchasing

---

[66] *Guizhou Ribao* (8/27/93): 1, (9/23/93): 2, and (10/8/93): 1; *Fujian Ribao* (8/30/93): 1; and *Nongmin Ribao* (9/13/94): 4.

[67] *Zhongguo Tongji Nianjian, 1997*: 281, 382, and 385.

[68] *Fazhi Ribao* (6/29/95): 2 and (8/5/95): 1; *Jiangsu Fazhi Bao* (7/15/95): 3; *Jingji Ribao* (6/25/96), (12/31/96), and (6/6/97); *Xinhua* (11/20/96), in *BBCSWB, FE* (11/21/96); *Xinhua* (3/31/98), in *BBCSWB, FE* (4/8/98); and *Nongmin Ribao* (8/23/97); and Muzi News (5/25/98), available at http://latelinenews.com/ll/english/4082.shtml.

continued, a full-scale tobacco war did not erupt in 1996 and the sector remained relatively stable thereafter. Seeking to curb excess production of cigarettes, including counterfeit brands, the State Tobacco Monopoly Administration ordered a consolidation of the tobacco industry in 1998. China's 180 cigarette manufacturers would be merged into a series of conglomerates, according to the plan.

The silk sector, meanwhile, experienced serious new instability during 1994–5. The stability witnessed in the early 1990s after the center granted China Silk greater authority over purchasing, reeling, and marketing of silk products proved illusory. As Yu Xiaosong, Vice Minister of the State Economic and Trade Commission later admitted, China Silk's monopoly had, in fact, been broken in 1988 and large quantities of raw silk continued to flow into illegal local filatures and de facto prices remained well above those fixed by the state.[69]

As the 1993 procurement season approached, authorities in Jiangsu reported that buyers were "poised with daggers drawn." The center therefore reiterated that China Silk continued to hold a monopoly and ordered local authorities to maintain the system of unified purchase.[70] That year, however, state purchases shrank 13 percent as war erupted and, perhaps, as much as 30–40 percent of total production flowed onto illegal markets, with the result that China Silk could not meet authorized filatures' demand for raw silk.[71] The following year, despite an increase in the state price, the war continued as localities and individual speculators illegally increased prices by as much as 25 percent during the first quarter. By the end of 1994, silk cocoon prices had risen more than 55 percent, according to official statistics.[72] Widespread withholding of supplies by farmers anticipating that the state would have to raise its price to match black-market prices exacerbated the situation and helped push prices up further.[73] As the cost of raw silk rose, the state-owned silk sector suffered serious losses. In 1994, the industry reportedly suffered ¥490 million in losses. In 1995 enterprise losses in Sichuan, Jiangsu, Zhejiang, and Anhui alone topped ¥1.16 billion.

As it had in 1988, the center responded to the deteriorating situation by issuing new regulations augmenting China Silk's authority. It first ordered a comprehensive rectification of the silk industry in an effort to cut back on capacity.

---

[69] *Xinhua* (5/15/96), in *BBCSWB, FE* (5/16/96).
[70] *Nongmin Ribao* (6/9/93): 2 and *Xinhua* (5/27/93), in *BBCSWB, FE* (6/23/96).
[71] *Jiangsu Fazhi Bao* (6/23/94): 1.
[72] Based on data in *Zhongguo Tongji Nianjian*, various years.
[73] *Nongmin Ribao* (7/14/94): 3; *Reuters* (7/17/94) and (8/4/94); *Xinhua* (4/26/94), in *BBCSWB, FE* (4/6/94); and *Xinhua* (1/22/96), in *BBCSWB, FE* (1/31/96).

Spurred on by high prices, local filatures had expanded by the mid-1990s to a point at which total demand stood at 950,000 tons versus total domestic supplies of approximately 680,000 tons. To close the resulting gap, the center ordered unauthorized local filatures shut down and centralized control over the entire silk industry. At the same time, control over procurement and prices was shifted from the provincial affiliates of China Silk to a new national silk corporation.[74] Markets in national border regions, which had formerly fallen outside of China Silk's control, were also ordered shut in an effort to prevent the diversion of supplies from other regions.

Over the next several years, the silk sector became noticeably less volatile. The extent to which tighter central controls helped stabilize the sector is questionable. As had been true of the wool sector during the 1980s, black market – driven price increases for raw silk and excessive expansion of reeling capacity had plunged the silk industry into serious financial trouble. Unable to operate profitably, many local firms either shut down or cut back on production. As a result, prices began to fall in 1995, dropping from more than ¥230,000 per ton in 1994 to ¥186,000 in 1995, then to ¥160,000 in 1996. By 1997, demand and supply had reportedly equilibriated at about 760,000 tons.[75]

In 1998, however, falling demand for exports resulting from the Asian Economic Crisis reportedly created a surplus of 6,000 tons of silk cocoons. Continued weak demand was expected to push the surplus up to 15,300 tons in 1999.[76] Total losses for the silk industry were estimated at ¥600 million in 1998, with 58 percent of silk filatures suffering losses. As of mid-1999 the silk industry had suffered losses of ¥586 million, with Zhejiang alone suffering ¥243.89 million in losses. As a result, in early 2000, the central government announced plans to cut silk production capacity by 20 percent.

In key respects, the procurement system remained relatively unchanged through the late 1990s. The state continued to claim monopsony rights over a variety of key commodities and to maintain an institutional and regulatory structure that sought to limit, if not negate, the effects of market forces on these commodities. Thus, the state cotton, tobacco, and silk monopsonies all remained in place through the late 1990s and only the wool monopsony was formally abolished. By 1999, however, the state had partially deregulated the cotton sector, while both the tobacco and silk cocoon sectors remained mired in financial difficulties.

---

[74] *Xinhua* (5/17/96), in *BBCSWB, FE* (5/20/96) and *Reuters* (9/23/96).
[75] *Xinhua* (5/29/97), in *BBCSWB, FE* (6/4/97).
[76] *Qiye Bao* (7/20/99); *Zhongguo Jingji Shibao* (11/12/99); and Muzi News (3/31/00), available at http://latelinenews.com/ll/english/64242.shml.

Despite the lack of formal marketization by the mid-1990s, the cotton, tobacco, and silk sectors had, in fact, become partially and de facto marketized. Its formal claims notwithstanding, the center was no longer an effective monopsonist in a definitional sense. Its control over the various monopsony institutions was imperfect at best and subject to rapid deterioration, with shortages in supply creating large gaps between state-fixed prices and black-market prices. The monopsony institutions themselves, and particularly their grassroots structures where procurement actually took place, were in fact apt to prove the single most serious threat to the center's claims to monopsony rights in this situation.

Nor did the center exercise sufficient control over supply and demand to enable it to control prices. Although the state continued to fix procurement prices each year, price movements were driving up market forces. When supply fell short of demand, black markets emerged and supplies flowed onto these markets rather than into the state monopsony. As black-market prices rose, the state found itself forced to raise its prices. When supply exceeded demand and black-market prices fell, farmers rushed to dump excess supply onto the state monopsony at above black-market prices. When this occurred, the state cut its purchases and forced the monopsony price downward. As such, the monopsony price shifted in accordance with changes in supply and demand, albeit in a highly imperfect manner. So long as state prices did not quickly adjust to fluctuations in market conditions, rents continued to exist and, hence, the quest for rents by both local governments and individuals continued to generate market instability, particularly when price differentials increased. But for all intents and purposes, the state had ceased to act as a price setter, even in the absence of formal institutional changes that would have led to full marketization of these sectors.

Even though the center did not radically restructure those parts of the rural economy over which it claimed monopsony rights in the early 1990s, a second round of fairly serious economic conflicts during 1993–5 further undermined its control over these commodities. As its control declined, the center found itself faced with a choice between adjusting its prices to bring them more closely in line with black-market prices, which were themselves determined by supply and demand, or risking a hemorrhaging of supplies out of legal markets and onto the black market. Thus, even though the center did not alter the formal institutional structures of the cotton, tobacco, and silk cocoon sectors, its inability to resist market forces resulted in a transformation in the way these institutions functioned. By the late 1990s the state monopsonies were arguably operating in a semimarketized environment, one in which the center had to fix prices based on the interplay of supply and demand.

PRICE WARS

As noted previously, the fading of import protectionism after 1991 can be explained both as a function of the center's role in mediating a lowering of local import barriers and shifting macroeconomic conditions. Whether designed to shelter struggling infant industries or to protect local manufacturers from "unfair" outside competition, import barriers are most likely to proliferate during economic downturns, particularly when demand drops more rapidly than supply and leaves local producers with mounting inventories of unsold goods. Conversely, during boom times, particularly when growth in demand surges ahead of growth in supply and creates inflationary pressures, sellers' markets tend to make import protectionism less critical and, given the risks associated with the erection of illegal import barriers, less attractive for local governments.

Given the countercyclical nature of import protectionism, it is not surprising that import protectionism seemed to move to the margins during the mid-1990s. During these years, growth surged, rising from a low of 3.8 percent in 1990 to 9.2 percent in 1991 and then to double digit rates between 1992 and 1994.[77] Industrial output increased even more rapidly, shooting from 3.4 percent in 1990 to 14.4 percent in 1991, 21.2 percent in 1992, and 20.1 percent in 1993 before slowing to 18.4 percent in 1994 and then 14.0 percent in 1995. Prices, meanwhile, began to climb as inflation first edged up from a modest 2.1 percent in 1990 and 2.9 percent in 1991 to 5.4 in 1992 and then jumped to 13.2 percent in 1993, 21.7 percent in 1994, only to then fall back to 14.8 percent in 1995. Average per capita consumption for urban residents rose dramatically as inflation fell from 18 percent in 1989 to 3.1 percent in 1990, jumping 22.6 percent, and continued to increase at double-digit rates even as inflation increased, rising 11.6 percent in 1992, 12.8 percent in 1993, and then a startling 29.5 percent in 1994. Thereafter, consumption continued to rise, with increases of 18.3 percent in 1994, 10.2 percent in 1995, and 26.2 percent in 1996. Under such conditions, trade barriers thus tended to devolve back into sorts of "discriminatory practices" that may have helped boost sales of local products by giving them a price advantage over imports or predatory taxes that allowed local governments to siphon off a share of importers' profits during the post-1992 boom.

The post-1992 boom, however, began to fade in 1996 when the central government sought to dampen inflationary pressures and ensure a "soft landing." Growth rates began to slow, dropping down to 9.6 percent in 1996, 7.8 percent in

---

[77] *Zhongguo Tongji Nianjian, 2000.*

1997, and then 7.1 percent in 1998.[78] Industrial production also slowed, falling to 10.5 percent in 1997, 8.9 percent in 1998, and then 8.1 percent in 1999. Growth in per capita urban consumption, meanwhile, also slowed, dropping to 12.4 percent in 1997, 7.1 percent in 1998, and then 7.0 percent in 1999. Prices, however, began to plummet, as inflation dropped to 6.1 percent in 1996 and then fell to a marginal 0.8 percent the following year. In 1998, China entered a period of deflation as prices fell 2.6 percent and then fell an additional 3 percent in 1999, according to the State Statistical Bureau.

With deflation pushing prices down and consumer demand cooling off, conditions should have favored a return of widespread import protectionism in 1998. Initially, import protectionism did appear to be on the rise. In 1998, for example, the Shanghai municipal government effectively mandated that all taxicabs in the city must be locally produced Volkswagen Santanas and then tried to block sales of the Xiali produced by Tianjin Automotive Industries in a joint venture with Daihatsu and the Fukang produced by Dong Feng Motors–Citroen in Hubei by imposing extra taxes and fees totaling upward of ¥80,000 per vehicle, almost doubling the costs of the Xiali and the Fukang.[79] Authorities in Hubei retaliated by slapping a variety of taxes on the Santana, including a ¥70,000 fee for the "relief of enterprises in extreme difficulty," which drove its retail price from ¥172,000 to ¥326,000. The Hubei government, however, offered to withdraw the fee if Shanghai cut its de facto tariff on the Fukang.[80] Faced with the possibility of losing access to Hubei, where sales of the Santana amounted to 55 percent of total sales, Shanghai announced in December 1999 that it would eliminate the higher licensing fee for cars produced outside of the city. The following year, Hubei-based Sanjiang Renault had to halt sales of its minivans in Jiangxi after the provincial authorities imposed fees that increased their sale price 15 percent and left them unable to compete with minivans produced within the province. In the spring of 2000, the municipal government in Xi'an was reportedly using discriminatory taxes to block sales of "imported" taxis and ensure sales of locally produced automobiles.

---

[78] These are official estimates, which have been strongly questioned by a variety of economists. Rawski, for example, argues that growth rates dropped off much more dramatically after 1997, falling to between 2 and 3 percent in 1998. Thomas G. Rawski, "What's Happening to China's GDP Statistics?" *China Economic Review* 12, no. 4 (December 2001).

[79] Licensing fees for a privately owned Santana, meanwhile, cost ¥20,000. *Zhonghua Gongshang Shibao* (12/17/99) and *Zhongguo Qiche Bao* (9/8/98).

[80] *Asia Times* (1/15/00); *Zhonghua Gongshang Bao* (12/17/99); *Zhengquan Shibao* (12/19/99); *Far Eastern Economic Review* (10/14/99); and U.S. Embassy, Beijing, "Western Development and the End of Xi'an Taxicab Protectionism," available at http://www.usembassy-china.org/english/sandt/xian-taxi.htm.

In early 2000, a series of "car wars" erupted as producers began to cut prices in hope of expanding market share and disposing of excess inventory. In January, Dong Feng–Citroen cut the price of its Fukang cars. Tianjin Automotive responded by reducing prices for its Xiali cars.[81] Several months later, Shanghai General Motors cut the price of its Buick Sail while Chang'an Suzuki cut the price of its cars. Soon thereafter, Shanghai Volkswagen knocked ¥10,000 off the price of its Santana and lowered prices for the Passat, leading Dong Feng–Citroen to further reduce the price of the Fukang and First Automotive to cut the price of its Volkswagen Jetta. Tianjin Automotive also dropped the price of the Xiali still further.

China's television market was also hit by a series of bitter price wars. Several years earlier, domestic manufacturers had used price cuts to grab market share from foreign imports. In 1999, however, they turned on each other as sales fell and productive capacity far outstripped demand.[82] By the late 1990s, domestic manufacturers could reportedly produce upward of fifty million units a year, even though domestic demand had leveled off at approximately twenty million units a year, with little room for further growth due to saturation. Although exports siphoned off ten to twelve million units a year, production levels remained high, with domestic manufacturers churning out 34.97 million sets in 1998 and 42.62 million sets the following year. Inventories thus increased from 6.21 million sets in 1998 to 9.34 million sets in 1999.[83] Fearing ruinous competition, China's eight leading television manufacturers attempted to form a cartel and announced they would halt production for a month in May 1999. The following June, amid a new price war, an alliance of nine manufacturers, which accounted for 80 percent of retail sales, unsuccessfully attempted to establish a floor price. In July, the competition increased when foreign producers also began cutting prices. As of early 2001, Chinese television manufacturers had reportedly lost ¥14.7 billion as a result of repeated price wars, with individual firms suffering losses ranging from ¥300 million up to ¥1 billion.

Air-conditioner manufacturers also found themselves locked in a bitter price war in 2000, even though the five major producers who accounted for 60 percent of sales had agreed not to cut prices the year before. Like the television sector, air-conditioner manufacturers had overexpanded during the boom years, pushing annual productive capacity to ten million units as of

---

[81] *China Daily* (1/07/00), (1/20/00), (4/20/00), (6/08/00), (7/19/00), (7/25/00), (7/26/00), (7/28/00), (8/23/00), (8/28/00), (8/29/00), (9/06/00), and (12/21/00).

[82] *China Daily* (4/22/99), (4/30/99), (5/7/99), (6/3/99), (8/7/00), (8/11/00), (8/14/00), (10/24/00), (12/28/00), and (1/3/00).

[83] *Zhongguo Tongji Nianjin 2000.*

the mid-1990s, only to find that demand was only six to eight million units. By 2000, production had reportedly reached twenty-two million units, while sales stood at just twelve million units.[84]

Prices for personal computers, DVD players, jewelry, student insurance, washing machines, refrigerators, Internet access, telephone calling cards, and microwave ovens also fell sharply during 1999–2000.[85] Oversupply and cut-throat competition triggered an "ice cream" war as producers cut prices 25–30 percent. An "underwear war" erupted after the number of firms producing thermal underwear jumped from 10 in 1998, to 70 in 1999, and then 500 in 2000. Although sales jumped from seven million pairs in 1999 to thirty million pairs in 2000, producers began cutting prices as much as 65 percent, driving the sale price below cost for many producers. Movie theaters joined the fray in late 2000, cutting prices to just ¥5 in some cities. Faced with a glut of outlets and sluggish consumer sales, retailers in Shanghai were routinely slashing prices 70 percent in early 2000 for new merchandise, even though many were already losing vast sums. Beer manufacturers, meanwhile, faced a market where production stood at thirty million tons a year by 2001 but demand remained only twenty million tons. By then, a five-year price war had driven the average cost per bottle from ¥1.7 in 1996 to ¥1 in 2000, even though costs had risen significantly during the interim and vicious competition had culled the number of breweries to 400 and led to the formation of twenty-seven major brewery groups. Even insurance companies and hospitals began to cut prices. The Tongji Medical Health and Care Center in Wuhan, for example, reduced its daily charges from ¥360–380 to ¥120–160 and lowered the cost of a physical from ¥800 to ¥300, while the Wuhan Concord Hospital knocked ¥2,000 off the price of coronary artery radiological examinations and cut the fee for a quadruple bypass operation in half. Other hospitals in Wuhan began offering free examinations and diagnoses. In Hangzhou, competition between Chinalife Insurance and China Pacific Insurance reportedly drove the cost of student health insurance programs from ¥45 to ¥40 and then ¥35 per month.

A price war erupted among China's domestic airlines after the Civil Aviation Administration of China (CAAC) loosened controls over ticket prices.[86] Within a year, some airlines were reportedly selling tickets at below cost. Despite new regulations banning discounts, the following fall airlines operating in the highly

---

84 *China Daily* (3/2/00), (3/16/00), (3/22/00), (4/11/00), and (2/19/00).
85 *China Daily* (6/4/99), (3/31/00), (5/4/00), (5/12/00), (8/4/00), (8/25/00), (8/31/00), (9/11/00), (11/23/00), (11/24/00), (12/7/00), (12/14/00), (12/28/00), (1/23/01), (2/18/01), and (3/11/02).
86 *China Daily* (4/16/99), (11/17/99), (7/27/00), and (12/15/00).

competitive South China market began discounting tickets 30 to 40 percent off prices approved by CAAC. By the summer of 2000, discounting had reportedly cut the price of tickets between Shanghai and Hainan by a third as China Southern, China Eastern, Xiamen, and Hainan Airlines battled for passengers. By the end of the year, tickets from Kunming to Beijing were selling at 30 percent off face value, while airlines were knocking 50 percent off official prices in Hainan, and 10 percent off in Wuhan and Harbin, this despite a new ban on discounts and the approval of a 15 percent fare increase meant to offset rising fuel prices.

The 1998–2000 price wars reveal the extent to which the Chinese economy had changed since 1989–90. First, whereas local governments tried to maintain prices in 1989–90 by throwing up import barriers and locking out imports, in 1998–2000 we see manufacturers, not local governments, responding to market saturation by cutting prices. In other words, whereas local governments resorted to antimarket mechanisms in 1989–90, in 1998–2000 manufacturers, wholesalers, and retailers resorted to market mechanisms. The price wars of 1998–2000 were thus market-driven conflicts among companies, rather than battles between local governments as was true in 1989–90.

Second, when competition led to price wars, the central government responded not by trying to fix prices, but rather by imposing antidumping legislation. In a variety of cases, agencies of the central government did try to impose price floors, as was the case when CAAC banned the discounting of airline tickets. Some local authorities also attempted to negotiate "cease-fire agreements" among competing manufacturers, as was the case in the fall of 2000 when the Shanghai Rag Trade Association formed a commission to regulate the city's thermal underwear market.[87] Representatives of beer manufacturers and distributors in Hubei also attempted to negotiate a settlement of the province's beer war, while major television manufacturers actually formed a cartel in an attempt to prevent competition from driving prices further down.

Such moves were, however, opposed by the center. New regulations issued by the State Development Planning Commission in the fall of 1999, for example, imposed fines for companies found to have cut prices below cost or to have offered hidden discounts.[88] When television manufacturers tried to fix prices in the summer of 2000, officials of the State Development Planning Commission warned that price fixing violated laws governing fair competition and warned that any manufacturers found colluding to fix prices could be fined ¥30,000 to ¥300,000 and have any income from illegal sales confiscated. When some

---

[87] *China Daily* (12/7/00) and *Shenzhen Daily* (3/11/02).
[88] *China Daily* (8/2/99), (8/5/99), (2/18/00), and (8/11/00).

providers cut the cost of Internet telephone calls, the Ministry of the Information Industry, which had recently brokered a price deal among China Telecom, China Unicom, and Jitong Network Communications, warned that it would not allow any further cuts. By and large, however, the center remained passive, with government officials warning against cutthroat competition but also noting that price wars benefited consumers and were likely to restimulate sluggish sales – this even though falling prices clearly threatened state-owned enterprises.

The absence of overt import protectionism can be ascribed to several factors. First, whereas local governments often had direct proprietary interests in local enterprises at the time of the 1989–90 recession, reforms initiated in the mid-1990s had weakened that link. In 1988, a new law governing state-owned enterprises ordered ownership transferred from government agencies to "state asset management bureaus" and state-owned holding companies. Over the next decade, the transfer created a complex and often tangled system of ownership that tended to shift control away from an enterprise's nominal owners and into the hand of managers, who increasingly determined the allocation of "profits."[89]

Second, the 1994 Tax Reform effectively greatly reduced direct transfers of corporate profits as a source of public revenues. Thereafter, enterprise profits accrued to local financial institutions, which, in turn, transferred part of their income to the state, but in the form of taxes, not profits, while individual enterprises continued to pay a corporate tax on their net profits. Moreover, after 1994 the bulk of tax revenues came from the new value-added tax (VAT) that local bureaus of the central tax authority collected, not local tax bureaus that had collected taxes on behalf of the center prior to 1994, which then split the VAT, with 75 percent going to the central treasury and 25 percent going to local governments. Because the VAT was paid at the point of sale or transfer, both "imports" and "local" products were subject to the same tax structure, with the result that local governments did not necessarily obtain higher revenues from sales of local products. Thus, although local governments undoubtedly continued to have a strong vested interest in their local economy, they were less tied to local producers, at least financially, than had been true ten years earlier.

The price wars of 1998–2000 and the passive response of local governments to the distress caused to firms by slumping sales reveal, perhaps as well as any other indictor, the extent to which markets had displaced administration. Whereas when the economy slumped in 1989–90, local governments had quickly thrown up defensive bulwarks to cordon off local markets and protect local manufacturers, when the economy slumped in 1998–2000 manufacturers simply cut

---

[89] See Andrew Wedeman, "Corporate Capitalism and Socialist China," in Edmond Terence Gomez, ed., Chinese Enterprise, Transnationalism, and Identity (New York: Routledge, forthcoming).

prices and fought for market share. Local protectionism, while still present, was at best a marginal factor and when localities such as Shanghai tried to erect import barriers they were generally forced to quickly tear them down. Finally, the 1998–2000 price wars were not so much battles for monopoly control over local markets, but rather battles involving large manufacturers fighting for shares of national markets. The price wars of 1998–2000 were, in other words, market wars among corporations, not feuds among "economic warlords."

CONCLUSION

The early 1990s witnessed both a sudden rise and decline in import protectionism. Import protectionism, which exploded after Li Peng's 1988 retrenchment program pushed the Chinese economy into a recession and caused a sharp drop in consumer demand, declined rather quickly after the center intervened in the fall of 1990 and Deng's 1992 Southern Tour led to a new economic boom. Import protectionism was itself a second-best alternative to trade, given that localities raising import barriers were apt to suffer retaliation by other regions and, hence, the loss of export markets for surplus local production. Moreover, the booming economy increased consumer demand, leading to a shift from a buyers' market to a sellers' market. In this situation, the rationale for import protectionism decreased. Economic conditions, therefore, favored a shift away from widespread import protectionism to much more limited and covert forms of discrimination against imports.

The same economic conditions that favored decreased import protectionism, however, led to a revival of export protectionism. Boom conditions pushed up demand for raw materials, leading to shortages and causing a surge in black-market prices and a renewed scramble for rents. The level of chaos during 1993–5 did not reach that witnessed during 1987–8, in part because the resource wars of the 1980s had ended with the effective marketization of a wide range of commodities over which the center had relinquished its monopsony claims in 1985. In the case of the much more limited range of commodities over which the center continued to claim monopsony rights, creeping marketization forced the center to fix procurement prices based on fluctuating supply and demand and hence changes in black-market prices. When increasing gaps between demand and supply forced black-market prices above the fixed procurement price, the state responded by increasing the fixed price. When demand fell below supply and black-market prices fell below the fixed procurement price, the state responded by cutting the fixed price. As a result, although the state continued to claim monopsony rights over cotton, tobacco, and silk, the state could no longer impose its price by administrative fiat.

The contrast between the rather surprisingly rapid decline in import protectionism and the much more protracted decrease in export protectionism reflected fundamental differences in these two forms of local protectionism. Although the origins of both can be traced to market distortions created by the center's failure to enact price reform at the same time that it allowed partial deregulation of the economy, the logic underlying export and import protectionism was quite distinct.

Export protectionism derived from the rents and shortages created by the suppression of raw-material prices. Because shortages – that is, a combination of artificially reduced supply and inflated demand – were a natural by-product of depressed prices and predated the partial reform of China's rural economy, egoistic rent seeking by localities located on the "wrong" side of the price scissors emerged quickly. This, in turn, created vertical conflicts between the center, which laid legal claim to rents, and the localities, upon which the center relied to collect and monetize its rents. From the outset, therefore, export protectionism involved a zero-sum conflict between the center and the agents of its monopsonies, with locally owned industrial consumers in other regions as well as individual traders and speculators serving to create and sustain black markets.

The presence of black markets, in turn, served to push prices upward as supplies tended to flow toward buyers willing to pay higher prices, but also helped undermine the integrity of the state's monopsony institutions as they became increasingly involved in black marketeering and, hence, in direct competition with each other for control over scarce supplies. Vertical conflict between the center and its monopsony agents coexisted alongside horizontal conflicts between the center's monopsony agents. Decollectivization complicated the situation because producers became increasingly sensitive to price signals thrown off by the black market. The net result was a multisided conflict in which the interaction between prices, supply, and demand caused oscillations between periods of glut, during which the state could force prices downward and had incentives to pull back from its monopsonist role as automatic buyer, and periods of acute shortage, during which black marketeering undermined the state's ability to maintain an effective monopsony.

Because most undervalued raw materials were agricultural commodities, weather served as a random destabilizer while the production cycle meant that conflicts tended to be of relatively short duration, reaching their peaks during the harvest season, but then cooling off during the slack season. Resource wars, therefore, were relatively short-lived conflicts. Their intensity could not be predicted with certainty in advance because of uncertainty about the harvest, during which chaos might reign for a few weeks or perhaps a couple of months – if production fell short of demand—or might not erupt – if production exceeded demand. The propensity of the center's agents to forsake their responsibilities can be viewed as a function of the size of rents created by gaps between the monopsony price and the black-market price. That gap can be seen as a function of unpredictable contradictions between supply and demand. The net result is a situation in which the center could not accurately predict whether existing institutional arrangements would succeed in maintaining its "order" or if markets would collapse. So long as the center sought to retain some semblance of a monopsony, therefore, its ability to prevent and control resource wars was necessarily uncertain. In the long run, the state could best stabilize markets and ensure access to inputs for its firms by reducing the gap between the monopsony price and the black-market price and allowing changes in the black-market prices to determine changes in the monopsony price. Export protectionism and resource wars thus drove a form of creeping price reform wherein the state may have continued to fix prices, but had to fix them at levels dictated by market forces.

Import protectionism, on the other hand, arose out of the inflation of finished goods' prices. Before the advent of reform, however, the state had underinvested in many sectors characterized by these rents. As a result, at the outset of reform the supply of these goods was frequently less than demand and local governments could expand production of rent-producing goods without coming into direct conflict with the center – except, of course, to the extent that local efforts to secure undervalued inputs interfered with central efforts to obtain supplies of these same goods. Once local markets became saturated, local governments had incentives to block imports, thus artificially reducing local supply. At the same time, local governments had to look to exports as a means of dumping excess local production onto other markets. As dumping began to occur, other localities had incentives to throw up import barriers to avoid falling victim to the beggar-thy-neighbor trade politics adopted by others. Because market saturation occurred at the same time that central policy and inflation had cut demand, the result was a sudden crisis of excess supply and a dramatic upsurge in import protectionism. Thus, whereas export protectionism tended to intensify during periods of rising demand and hence inflation, import protectionism was countercyclical, rising during periods of contraction (see Figure 6-1).[90]

Yet, even before the 1989–90 crisis of overproduction, overinvestment had made manufacturers in many localities export-dependent and so the loss of access to outside markets and the pain of fiscal retaliation proved greater than the benefits derived from import barriers. Nevertheless, because individual

---

[90] Price data from *Zhongguo Tongji Nianjian, 2000.*

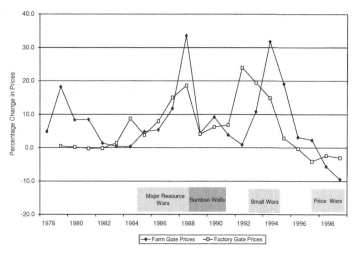

Figure 6-1. Inflation, Deflation, and Local Protectionism.

localities had good reason to fear that opening up local markets to free trade would leave them even worse off as a result of dumping, the crisis evolved into a standoff in which local governments might prefer to abandon import protectionism, but could not out of fear that they would suffer the consequences of unrequited cooperation. Because it had a direct financial interest in opening local markets, the center had strong incentives to break the stalemate by stepping in in the role of honest broker. As a result, when the center launched a new campaign against regional trade barriers in the fall of 1990, it was able to induce a surprisingly quick shift from pervasive import protectionism to "free trade," with relatively little effort.

The center's switch from a policy of constraining demand and growth to one that stimulated demand and growth also helped transform the macroeconomic environment in ways that were highly favorable to an end to import protectionism. Increasing demand alleviated a saturated market and hence reduced the incentives to block imports. The boom that began in early 1992 thus rendered import protectionism temporarily unnecessary. When demand once again fell below supply in 1998, marketization was sufficiently well entrenched that the result was deflation because producers had to resort to price cutting rather than turning to local governments to raise protective import barriers.

Nongmin Ribao, 6/3/91: 1
"Dismantling the checkpoint"

7

Escaping from the Pitfalls

WHEN we analyze a particular aspect of structural change, we are interested in explaining the causes, dynamics, and consequences of that change. But we are also interested in what change in one area tells us about broader processes of change and transformation. In other words, we are not interested only in the microcosm; we are also interested in what the microcosm tells us about the macrocosm – the "big picture."

Given its focus on conflicts over access to local markets and supplies of cotton, silk, tobacco, and wool, this book may seem to some to be about a relatively narrow and highly technical aspect of China's transition to a market-based economy or simply a tantalizing story about one of many unintended consequences of reform. That is, in fact, how local protectionism has generally been viewed in the past. But when we place rent seeking and local protectionism in the larger framework of price reform, it becomes clear that local protectionism was part of a critically important process. Moreover, analysis of the dynamics of rent seeking, local protectionism, and price reform reveals a great deal about the process of systemic change more generally in post-Mao China and helps explain why China's reforms did not become bogged down halfway between the plan and the market.

Studies of reform in post-Mao China have tended to stress either top-down, policy-driven processes or bottom-up, "spontaneous" reform. Top-down approaches stress the political debates over how to alter existing institutions and how formal changes in existing institutions reverberate through the system as a whole. Bottom-up approaches stress the breakdown of existing institutions when confronted with new demands and pressures. My study of rent seeking, local protectionism, and price reform suggests that rather than treating top-down and bottom-up explanations as rival explanations, we can view them as interconnected facets of a process of change that is shaped both by deliberate reform and the unanticipated consequences of deliberate reform. Top-down and bottom-up explanations are thus two sides of the same coin and worked together to move China's economy from one system to another.

The impetus for change can come either from the top or the bottom. Thus, for example, if a system is in equilibrium, top-down change may trigger a process of transformation by altering existing institutions and structures. In some cases, top-down change might be sufficient to move the system instantaneously from one equilibrium to another. In most cases, top-down change simply initiates a process that evolves as the system responds to some initial change with a series of bottom-up changes that, in turn, evoke further top-down changes. This interactive process continues until some new equilibrium, one that may not correspond to that initially envisioned by the instigators of the original top-down change, is reached.

Bottom-up pressures may also initiate a process of transformation, in which case we might see existing institutions becoming dysfunctional as a result of some exogenous change or as a result of evolutionary institutional decay. As existing institutions crumble under pressure from below, those in charge may attempt to defend or modify them or build new institutions. Presumably, each attempt at top-down action evokes a bottom-up response, and the process continues until a new equilibrium is reached.

In the case of rent seeking, local protectionism, and price reform in China, the process began with a series of top-down changes that loosened the center's grip on a series of institutions responsible for procuring, monetizing, and allocating rents derived from a system of fixed prices that tended to depress input prices – and supplies of those inputs – and inflate output prices. Although the center did not intend to eliminate the monopsony institutions through which the state collected and monetized rents or fully marketized industrial production and commerce, once the center's grip on the economy was loosened, bottom-up forces unleashed a scramble for rents. This scramble manifested itself almost immediately in the agricultural sector, where a series of interregional resource wars erupted as different localities fought for control over rent-bearing commodities. The consequences of rent seeking took longer to become evident in the industrial sector because it took more time for productive capacity to increase to the point at which glut conditions replaced shortage. By 1989–90, however, rent seeking in both sectors had pushed agricultural prices from the level fixed by the state to levels that, in many cases, actually exceeded market-clearing levels and put serious downward pressure on industrial prices.

As bottom-up pressures forced prices – and along with them supply and demand – toward a new market-based equilibrium, top-down reform stalled. Faced with what policymakers viewed as reform-induced economic chaos and mounting social unrest, the center's first response was to halt reform and retighten the state's grip on the economy. Beijing was not, however, in a position to simply stop the transformative processes set in motion by economic reforms in the early and mid-1980s. As a result, rather than freeze the transformation process in place, the conservatives' antireform policy of retrenchment only succeeded in increasing the gap between formal policy and economic reality.

In the remainder of this chapter, I shall demonstrate how the combination of a cautious top-down reform strategy and a bottom-up dynamic that was largely uncontrollable drove the Chinese economy toward the market. In my analysis, I juxtapose top-down and bottom-up processes rather than treat them as rivals. I thus view price reform and marketization as a dialectic process in which both top-down and bottom-up forces contributed to systemic transformation. Because it was an iterative dialectic rather than a simple thesis-antithesis-synthesis, the process appeared erratic and unpredictable. The logic of the dialectic becomes clear when we make a conscious distinction between the formal and informal processes driving rent seeking, local protectionism, and disguised price reform. By juxtaposing the caution and conservatism that characterized top-down policymaking with the loss of control that resulted from the limited reforms possible, the centrality of rent seeking, local protectionism, and disguised price reform become evident.

CAUTION IN COMMAND

Price reform is arguably both the most critical and most difficult systemic change necessary to move an economy from the plan to the market. In many areas, it was possible to grow out of the plan in an evolutionary fashion. Reformers could spawn private agriculture by emancipating Mao's peasants. In some areas, the peasants had already emancipated themselves. In other areas, emancipation was a quick means for the party to divest itself of a host of problems and costs. In the case of industry, communal industries set up during the Cultural Revolution could be transformed into "collectives," then leased to their managers. Many had lost money under the old system and letting go of these communal industries allowed the state to cut its losses. Private entrepreneurs could move into the gaps left by the state-owned and collective sectors. The managers of state-owned enterprises could be given new incentive packages that encouraged them to operate their enterprises profitably. These sorts of reforms would ultimately radically reshape the way the economy worked, but they could be enacted in a piecemeal manner and without necessarily causing serious and immediate macroeconomic and political instability.

Prices were a different matter. First, regardless of how production was accomplished, whether farm production was organized and controlled by the brigade or the individual household, if the state could set the price it paid for the commodities it wanted, it could extract rents and transfer value from producers to its coffers. Price distortions thus operated as a form of hidden tax that allowed the state to reallocate value across economic sectors and extract value from society. Eliminating rents, therefore, entailed a potentially significant reduction in the state's grip on the economy.

Second, rents were integral to the viability of the state-owned industrial sector. Cheap inputs allowed state-owned industries to operate at a profit, or at least helped reduce the losses of the more grossly inefficient enterprises. Decontrolling prices would have reduced the profitability of state-owned industries or, alternatively, forced the regime to implement additional reforms aimed at forcing these industries to operate according to the demands of the market rather than the dictates of the plan. Cheap grain, edible oil, and other foodstuffs also enabled the state to provide urban residents, including the employees of the state and state-owned enterprises, with food at below-market prices. Rents thus subsidized both the state-owned industrial sector and the urban economy in general. Price reform, therefore, would have resulted in a significant reallocation of value to the rural sector and hence away from the sectors more tightly controlled by the state.

Third, and most critically, even if the state was not interested in using prices to extract value from the economy and subsidize the urban-industrial sectors, closing a price scissors is inherently dangerous. Distorted prices, inefficiency, and poor planning and investment, all of which were characteristic of the socialist economies of the Soviet bloc and Maoist China, create chronic shortages. Without incentives to work hard and subject to the whims of politically motivated policymakers, agricultural production tends to stagnate. With investment flowing into heavy industry, including defense-related production, or allocated on the basis of political and ideological considerations, industry tends to churn out insufficient supplies of poor-quality consumer goods. Given chronic shortages and a system of rationing that limits purchases to levels below those possible given even the limited cash incomes of most workers, unspent cash tends to pile up. Socialist economics, thus, tends to create a combination of depressed supply and pent-up demand that leave consumers with surprisingly large amounts of cash but nothing to buy.

The presence of chronic shortages and pent-up demand creates a situation in which a quick shift from fixed prices to floating prices is likely to result in intense inflation. Economies cannot instantly adjust to changes in prices. Output and supply cannot be increased overnight. Fields have to be prepared, seeds and fertilizers produced and distributed. Transportation systems must be created or expanded. New factories have to be built and new sources of raw materials

244

developed. Wholesale and retail systems must be expanded and improved, managers trained, and new laws and regulations drafted and implemented. All of this takes time. The problem is that while all of these new structures are being built, shortages continue. With demand greater than supply, inflation will be the result. Even in the absence of actual inflation, fear of inflation has the potential to trigger panic as consumers and savers seek to protect themselves against possible price increases.

In fact, inflation is a necessity. Rising prices and the expectation of rising prices create powerful incentives to invest. Not only does the expectation that prices will continue to rise help sustain potential investors' beliefs that in the long run their investments will prove profitable, it also reduces capital costs because debts can be repaid in inflated currency. If the rate of inflation surges past the interest rate, the cost of capital will be negative. Born of chronic shortages, inflation thus helps spur investment in the new capacity that is necessary to boost output and ultimately eradicate shortages. Inflation, meanwhile, also cuts excess liquidity by devaluing cash holdings and lowering demand. Even short-term panic buying provides potential benefits by helping to stimulate demand and, thus, induces new investment in production and capacity. In the long run, inflation triggered by price reform will help move the economy from its initial socialist disequilibrium to a new, market equilibrium.

In the short run, however, inflation is politically explosive. High rates of inflation are generally seen as evidence of policy failure and a loss of control. Advocates of price reform are thus likely to find themselves facing serious challenges from rival factions within the leadership and a general erosion of support for reform. Moreover, because inflation cuts into the public's purchasing power, reduces real income, and diminishes savings, the people are likely to see themselves as being made worse off by reform. Mass discontent with the negative consequences of inflation not only has the potential to explode into antigovernment agitation but, even if mass discontent does not erupt, antireform forces are likely to use the threat of unrest to bash the reformers.

The short-term negatives associated with inflation are thus apt to outweigh the abstract, long-term benefits derived from swift and decisive price deregulation. In politics long-term benefits matter only if you survive the short term. Political leaders, particularly those whose positions are insecure and those who are faced with serious political rivals and threats, must operate in the here and now. If the short-term consequences of a policy lead to ouster and disgrace, the long-term efficacy of any policy is politically irrelevant. Similarly, if a policy cannot muster sufficient political support today, its efficacy tomorrow is irrelevant. Political realities, not the efficacy of alternative policies, therefore, dictate policy choices.

Deng Xiaoping seems to have sensed the dangers associated with price reform as well as anybody. Deng understood the need for economic reform and was willing to experiment with capitalism. But he was clearly averse to reforms that might have threatened the CCP's monopoly on power. Given the historic connection between hyperinflation and the collapse of support for the Guomindang, inflation was a hot bottom item, particularly for conservatives whom Deng could not afford to alienate. In ousting Hua Guofeng, Deng had cobbled together a heterodox coalition. On the one hand, Deng's coalition included economic conservatives such as Chen Yun, who saw the solution to China's chronic economic and political malaise in a return to the "rational socialism" of the mid-1950s. On the other hand, it included bolder reformers, such as Hu Yaobang, who were more willing to push rapidly into an unknown they came to call "Socialism with Chinese Characteristics." Although recognized as the first among equals and the supreme arbiter, Deng was never in absolute control and thus had to constantly play coalition politics, balancing Hu's reformist faction off against Chen's conservative faction. Thus, although Deng pushed reform whenever poor economic performance weakened the position of Chen's conservative faction, he was quick to throw his weight behind retrenchment whenever inflationary pressures weakened the position of Hu's reformist faction.[1] Moreover, even absent inflation and inflation-fueled social unrest, there was considerable opposition to price reform from entrenched bureaucratic interests, many of whom feared that price reform would reallocate value in ways adverse to their particularistic interests.[2]

In retrospect, it comes as little surprise that a strategy of incrementalism won out over radical price reform. Rather than face the potential of serious dislocations associated with sweeping price reform, many within the leadership hoped that they could some how muddle through by adopting policies that would stimulate production and gradually close the gaps between supply and demand, thereby minimizing the threat of inflation. Thus, prices were raised, often considerably during the early years of reform, and the number of commodities subject to strict price controls was reduced. Even so, the regime continued to retain control over the most important prices, those that allowed it to retain control over

---

[1] See Lowell Dittmer and Yu-shan Wu, "The Modernization of Factionalism is Chinese Politics," *World Politics* 47, no. 4 (July 1995): 467–94; Ruan, *Deng Xiaaping*; Baum, *Burying Mao*; David S.G. Goodman, *Deng Xiaoping and the Chinese Revolution: A Political Biography* (New York: Routledge, 1994); and Shirk, *The Political Logic of Economic Reform in China*.

[2] See Shirk, *The Political Logic of Economic Reform in China*: 301–5; Naughton, *Growing Out of the Plan*: 129–31; Yan Sun, *The Chinese Reassessment of Socialism, 1976–1992* (Princeton, NJ: Princeton University Press, 1995): 75–7; and Chan, "China's Price Reform in the Period of Economic Reform," *The Australian Journal of Chinese Affairs*, no. 18 (July 1987): 85–108.

the commanding heights of the economy and that had the most direct impact on state-owned enterprises and urban consumers. By the mid-1980s, incremental price adjustments had created a convoluted price system consisting of a combination of floating market prices, fixed prices, and negotiated prices and had segregated commodity markets into planned and market subeconomies, creating a situation in which the same commodity could command either a market price or a depressed fixed price depending on the buyer. Complex, contradictory, inefficient, and inherently unstable, this mixed system of prices was nonetheless politically preferable to the danger of short-term instability that might result from sweeping price reform.

When it came to price reform, therefore, caution clearly was in command and those who failed to abide by the principle of caution quickly discovered that incaution could be politically fatal. Thus, Hu Yaobang found himself ousted as general secretary when he pushed too hard in 1986 and Zhao Ziyang found himself taking the fall for Deng's own lack of caution on the question of price reform in 1988. With Zhao's demotion, the forces of ultracaution led by Chen Yun and Li Peng took over and even cautious, incremental price reform came to a halt.

LOSING CONTROL

A cautious, incremental approach to price reform may have been politically preferable but once controls have been loosened it becomes difficult to halt the process midway between the plan and market. As the analysis of the price scissors I presented in Chapter 3 showed, it is only possible to sustain a system of fixed prices if a single actor – the principal – has near total control over the actions of the other economic actors. Absent tight control, the existence of artificially induced gaps between the economic value of commodities and their nominal price will induce some actors to go after the rents claimed by the principal. Conflict among rival rent seekers will then lead to price wars, price wars will bid prices up, and rising prices will stimulate production, causing an increase in supply while dampening demand. Left to its own devices, this process will ultimately bring supply and demand into rough balance and thereby return prices to market levels.

As argued previously, the very structure of the Chinese state, with its multi-layered principal-agent–cum–principal hierarchy, hinders effective top-down control. Given the inevitable problems of agency, the center's writ naturally declines at each successive node in the hierarchy and thus affords local cadres considerable leeway to pursue their own interests at the expense of the center. The structure of China's economy also encouraged rent seeking and limited the center's ability to prevent it. Suspicious of the highly bureaucratized and centralized Soviet system and convinced that local self-reliance was a virtue, Mao encouraged the formation of a complex system of decentralized property rights. Rather than vest the center with ownership over industry and agriculture, Mao vested ownership in a variety of levels and entities. The central ministries, the People's Liberation Army, provincial governments, prefectural governments, county governments, communes, and brigades all owned industrial and commercial enterprises. The economy was rendered so complex that rather than attempt to guide production on a unitary basis, state planners instead relied on a system of "concentric balancing," wherein each level and each ownership system was encouraged to internalize production as much as possible.[3] Only when demand could not be satisfied locally were commodities transferred between systems. China's economy, thus, came to consist of a collection of semiautarkic local economies rather than a single, unified national economy.[4]

Not only did Mao encourage the cellularization of the Chinese economy, he also encouraged industrial deconcentration and the creation of new industrial centers and bases. During the First Five-Year Plan, economic planners concentrated industrial development in the interior. To this end, a majority of the industrial centers built with Soviet aid were located outside of China's prewar industrial core (i.e., Shanghai, Tianjin, and the northeast). Some factories were also moved out of traditional centers and relocated to these new industrial bases. After the collapse of the Sino-Soviet Alliance, Mao redoubled this effort for strategic reasons. A string of new industrial bases were constructed in what was known as the "Third Front," an area that encompassed parts of Hubei, Hunan, Sichuan, Guizhou, Yunnan, Shaanxi, Gansu, Qinghai, and Ningxia.[5]

From a purely economic perspective, Mao's stress on industrial deconcentration was inefficient because deconcentration led to reduplication. Mao's stress on moving industry to the interior exacerbated the problem by locating industries in remote areas while his stress on self-sufficiency led enterprises to internalize all aspects of production (e.g., factories maintaining machine shops to manufacture screws and nails rather than buying them from factories specializing in their production).

---

[3] See Thomas P. Lyons, *Economic Integration and Planning in China* (New York: Columbia University Press, 1987) and Lyons, "Planning and Interprovincial Coordination in Maoist China," 36–60.

[4] See Audrey Donnithorne, "China's Cellular Economy: Some Economic Trends since the Cultural Revolution," *China Quarterly*, no. 52 (October 1972): 605–19 and Thomas P. Lyons, "China's Cellular Economy: A Test of the Fragmentation Hypothesis," *Journal of Comparative Economics* 9, no. 2 (June 1985): 125–44.

[5] Naughton, "The Third Front: Defence Industrialization in the Chinese Interior": 351–86.

Yet, Mao's inefficiency yielded hidden advantages when the shift from a command to a market economy began. Rather than a highly centralized system of monopolies or oligopolies, China's diversified and redundant economic structure meant that, for any given product, a multiplicity of independently owned and operated firms existed. Moreover, fiscal decentralization and a property-rights system that allowed the direct owners to claim a share of enterprise income meant that the owners of these enterprises had an interest in maximizing the profits of their firms. In a sense, therefore, China had one element of a market economy in place even before the advent of reform: multiple profit-oriented firms operating in competition with each other. The industrial reforms of 1984 that led to rapid increases in the size and diversity of the collective, township and village, and private sectors further increased the number of competing firms as local governments took advantage of their increased discretion over investment decisions to construct or expand capacity in sectors where depressed input prices or inflated output prices increased profits and returns on investment.

The existence of a fragmented economy was critical to the process of rent seeking. When the center relaxed its grip on the economy during the mid-1980s, local governments already had incentives to seek rents. They had the means, and to an extent the need, to compete actively for control over rent-producing commodities and access to markets. Thus, the resource wars were essentially a concerted attack on the center's monopsony on cheap inputs by a multiplicity of competing consumers, many of who were backed by powerful owners (i.e., local governments, bureaus of the central government, units of the People's Liberation Army, etc.). In the case of local industries seeking access to cheap inputs, their owners were also charged with supervising the local agents of the central monopsony. There were thus fundamental contradictions between the fiscal interests of local governments, whose enterprises would have profited from usurping control over cheap inputs and would have increased local governments' revenues, and their responsibility to ensure delivery of these inputs to the center and its enterprises. Even when local enterprises depended on inputs produced in other localities, the interests of local governments were served by attacking the central monopsony because the monopsony was geared to allocate cheap inputs to state-owned enterprises rather than locally owned enterprises.

At the same time that fragmentation and duplication encouraged competition for cheap inputs, these factors also spurred growth in the production of finished products. As argued in Chapter 3, given an initial condition of shortage, the growth in output at first did not pit the interests of one locality and its enterprises against other localities and their enterprises. But once market saturation had been reached, local governments gained a direct interest in trying to protect local markets and enterprises from outside competition.

One of Mao's economic legacies was, therefore, a system composed of a host of rival consumers and producers. Moreover, the sheer complexity of the economy, with its multiple ownership systems and duplicative structures, made it difficult for the center to exert a high degree of control over these potential rivals. Rather than creating a single top-down hierarchy through which the center could monitor and supervise, fragmentation resulted in a system that insulated many enterprises from direct central oversight or control. To an extent, of course, rivalry among those enterprises officially designated by the center to receive and process rent-producing goods and other enterprises seeking to encroach on their prerogatives gave the "victims" of unauthorized rent seeking incentives to report illegal activity to the center. Even when it received reports of violations, the center frequently had only indirect influence and had to go through a series of levels before it could get to the offending units. In many such cases, enforcement efforts ran up against the same conflicts of interest that dogged the center's efforts to control the local agents of its monopolies because the owners of these units might well be the local government to which the center had to turn for action against them.

The structure of the state and the economy, therefore, militated against efforts to freeze in place the remnants of the old system of fixed prices and monopsony control. The same institutions on which the survival of that system depended had interests that led them to attack the system. Herein, it is critical to point out once again that the primary attack on the price system came not from outside the state, but from within. Nonstate actors played a role in the attack. Without farmers willing to evade their obligations to deliver commodities to the state monopsony and speculators willing to break the law by going directly to farmers and offering black-market prices for their produce, the resource wars would not have evolved into full-blown bidding wars. But the real breakdown of the monopsony system occurred when segments of the monopsony fell to fighting among themselves for control over the harvest and agents of state-owned enterprises and locally owned collective enterprises began to rely on black markets to obtain inputs. If monopsony institutions had remained cohesive, attacks from the outside might have been beaten back. But once the cohesion of the monopsonies collapsed and the agents of the monopsony in one locality attacked those in other localities, the doors were wide open to outsiders seeking to make inroads against the monospony. The breakdown of cohesion also created opportunities for outsiders to forge alliances with rogue elements within the monopsony.

In the case of finished products, the center did not lose control because its institutions collapsed. Rather, it lost control because decentralization and deconcentration had reduced the scope of the planned economy and allowed the growth of out-of-plan production of goods. The center thus created conditions in which its own goal of promoting rapid economic growth quickly eliminated the shortages that had plagued the economy before reform. Having set in motion an expansion of production, the center had few means to prevent that expansion from continuing to the point of excess production. The center, after all, had ceded control over output decisions to the localities and enterprises, including its own state-owned enterprises. In some cases (e.g., refrigerators, televisions), the center tried to limit investment in new capacity when it believed that excess capacity existed or would result from headlong investment. But so long as it did not allow prices to float, the underlying incentives for excess investment – high profits and seemingly limitless demand – continued to make further investment attractive. Appealing for cuts in investment under these conditions ran up against the dilemma that even though all those involved might have benefited from a common agreement to scale back and avoid excess investment, individually each actor had incentives to violate the agreement by increasing investments.[6]

Objectively, therefore, by the time politics blocked further price reform, the structures necessary to freeze the ad hoc system of mixed prices in place were either too weak to sustain a system of fixed prices or had actually become threats to the maintenance of a system of fixed prices. Between roughly 1987 and 1992, therefore, changes set in motion by earlier reforms continued apace despite policymakers' efforts to halt them. Reforms during the early 1980s had loosened the center's grip on commodity markets and devolved a degree of power down to the local level. When these changes led to fierce and illegal competition for rents, the center responded with a series of policy announcements that sought to freeze the old monopsony systems in place. But unified purchase failed to halt local encroachment on the center's rents. To the extent that the center was able to assert a degree of control, it was primarily as a mediator between rival rent seekers. Playing this role, however, undermined central authority further because it facilitated local rent seeking by dampening interjurisdictional competition without necessarily ensuring that the center received its share of rents. Moreover, by driving up prices, local rent seeking had already stimulated an increase in production sufficient to trigger a shift from a condition of shortage to one of glut. Once glut set in, policy makers in Beijing suddenly found the role of the central monopsonies redefined from extracting rents and maintaining control over scarce commodities, to that of buyer of last resort for distressed goods. Because policy makers had been forced to allow official prices to rise

---

[6] See Huang, *Inflation and Investment Controls in China*: ch. 1.

during the resource wars, they found producers not only seeking to dispose of surplus commodities by selling them to the state, but also demanding that the state monopsony pay the fixed state price even when the fixed price was below market prices. When this occurred, rather than allow the state to scrape off rents, fixed prices forced it to pay rents to producers.

Whenever fixed prices became a financial liability, the center's best option was to relinquish control and cut its losses. As matters turned out, the center did not opt for decontrol. Instead, it opted to retain the state purchasing system. However, rather than revert to a system of fixed prices, policy makers opted for a system of floating prices, with the "fixed" price set by supply and demand rather than administrative fiat. To an extent, the center was still able to cream off rents. The volume of rents, however, was cut significantly because differences between market-clearing prices and fixed prices shrank. Moreover, rents could only be obtained in periods of shortages and only if the state was able to force producers to sell at depressed fixed prices.

It is in the context of the center's inability to stop local rent seeking that the reasons for the differences between China's and Russia's reform experiences become clear. Unlike China, the former Soviet Union had evolved from a centralized economy characterized by high levels of concentration in key sectors. Whereas the Chinese economy was characterized by a multiplicity of producers, 30 to 40 percent of manufactured products in the Soviet Union had a single monopolistic producer. Single producers accounted for 77 percent of the "product groups" distributed by the state Committee for Deliveries and Supplies.[7] Where multiple producers existed, they were frequently organized into cartels as a result of common ownership by a single ministry.[8] A relatively small number of enterprises, therefore, dominated many sectors of the Soviet economy.[9] Privatization thus transferred these monopolies and oligopolies from the state to, in most cases, the firms' managers who were then positioned to extract monopolistic rents.[10] In theory, firms that accounted for more than 35 percent of output were subject to price and profit regulation. Close ties between the ex–"red directors" turned "businessmen" and the ministries responsible for

---

[7] World Bank, *Russian Economic Reform: Crossing the Threshold of Structural Change* (Washington, DC: World Bank, 1992): 82.

[8] Jim Leitzel, *Russian Economic Reform* (New York: Routledge, 1995): 100–2.

[9] Some sectors were, however, more fragmented. There were, for example, 237 beer manufacturers, 111 shoe manufacturers, 147 makers of farm machinery, 235 flour and grain processors, and 122 cotton textile makers. Annette N. Brown, Barry W. Ickes, and Randi Ryterman, "The Myth of Monopoly: A New View of the Industrial Structure in Russia," World Bank, working paper, August 1993. Also see Anders Aslund, *How Russia Became a Market Economy* (Washington, DC: The Brookings Institution, 1995): 153–4.

[10] Shleifer and Treisman, *Without a Map*: 33 and 107–8.

enforcing antimonopoly regulations, however, created conditions in which collusive relationships were likely to stifle new entries and limit competition.[11]

Reform of the banking and financial sectors, on the other hand, led to a proliferation of banks, with over 2,000 new private banks formed in the early 1990s. Many of these banks were strictly fly-by-night operations.[12] The most successful banks were those with close ties to the Central Bank that were able to reap windfall profits from Russia's hyperinflation.[13] In most cases, these banks were either the descendents of segments of the old Soviet banks or were established by major Soviet-era economic institutions.[14] These "core" banks quickly came to dominate the emerging Russian banking system and it was from their management that many of the best known "oligarchs" emerged. Other members of the new "oligarchy" emerged from the ranks of the "red directors" who took over key oil and gas enterprises.[15]

The structure of the Soviet economy thus tended to concentrate the benefits of partial reform in the hands of a relatively small set of winners who were then able to parlay their economic power into considerable political influence and hence the leverage over the policy process needed to bend the reform process to their rent-seeking ends.[16] The less concentrated structure of the Chinese economy and the emphasis on decentralization rather than privatization, by contrast, dispersed the benefits of partial reform much more widely. Rather than shifting monopolistic control from the central planning apparatus to a new set of private oligarchs, decentralization split up the old system and vested greater control over its elements in the hands of provincial, prefectural, county, township, and

---

[11] Peter J. Boettke and Bridget I. Butevich, "Entry and Entrepreneurship: The Case of Post-Communist Russia," *Journal des Economistes et des Etudes Humaines* 11, no. 1 (2001): 91–114. In actuality, however, existing Russian firms found themselves quickly stripped not only of monopoly rents but driven to the wall by competition from foreign imports, with the net result that many sectors experienced catastrophic reductions in output and profits. The television sector, which had a single manufacturer in 1989 (Rubin), saw its share of total retail sales fall from 100 percent in 1990 to 8 percent in 1996. "Russian TV Makers Channel Their Energies: Domestic Manufacturers Hope to Capture 30 Percent of the Market," *The Russia Journal* 4, no. 16 (April–May 2001). Also see "Automobile Industry: Lowered Imports Boost Local Sales," *The Russia Journal* 3, no. 6 (March 1999) and "Russian Appliance Makers Team Up: Group Battles Western Firms with One Label," *The Russia Journal* 3, no. 11 (March–April 1999).

[12] Juliet Ellen Johnson, "The Russian Banking System: Institutional Responses to the Market Transition," *Europe-Asia Studies* 46, no. 6 (1994): 971–96.

[13] Shleifer and Treisman, *Without a Map*: 54–5.

[14] Juliet Johnson, "Banking in Russia," *Problems of Post-Communism* 43, no. 3 (May–June 1996): 49–60.

[15] See Freeland, *Sale of the Century*.

[16] See Johnson, "Banking in Russia"; Virginie Coulloudon, "Corruption and Governance in Today's Russia," paper presented at the Princeton University-Central European University Joint Conference on Corruption (Budapest, October 1999); and Klebnikov, *Godfather of the Kremlin*.

village governments; central ministries and government agencies; social organizations; enterprise managers; and private individuals. Many of China's winners were remote from the centers of political power and had little if any leverage over the policy-making process. Moreover, duplication and redundancy created divisions among these winners and rendered them rivals rather than potential allies. The fragmented, disarticulated structure of the Chinese economy thus not only thwarted central efforts to control local rent seeking, it also prevented those who stood to benefit from the contradictions of partial reform from forming a coalition capable of freezing the reform process halfway between the plan and the market.

CONCLUSION

Between 1978 and 1993, China experienced sweeping price reform. In 1978, 94.4 percent of agricultural commodities were sold at prices fixed by the state. Only 5.6 percent were sold at market prices. After the first round of reform in the 1980s, 33.9 percent of these commodities were sold at fixed prices, 33.6 percent at above-quota prices set by the state, 14.4 percent at negotiated prices, and 18.1 percent at market prices. Although the role of markets in setting prices had tripled during the early years of reform, the state continued to set prices for more than 80 percent of agricultural commodities. In 1989, by contrast, 24 percent of agricultural commodities sales were at fixed prices, 19 percent at state-guided prices, and 57 percent at market prices. Four years later, fixed prices accounted for 12.2 percent of sales, guidance prices 4.2 percent, and market prices 84.6 percent. In the process, the number of agricultural commodities subject to price controls decreased from 113 to 6.[17] In 1978, all industrial prices had been fixed by the state. By 1990, fixed prices accounted for only 44.6 percent of total sales and market prices accounted for 36.4 percent. In 1993, fixed prices accounted for just 12.2 percent of sales, whereas market prices accounted for 81 percent. Whereas the state had fixed prices for 158 different industrial products in 1978, by 1993 it fixed the prices for only seven commodities.[18]

Although the commodities over which the most intense resource wars had been fought were not decontrolled and the center continued to covet the rents created by fixed prices, by 1992–3 it could no longer fix prices by administrative fiat. Instead, the center had to adopt a system in which it floated its "fixed price"

[17] Grain, cotton, tobacco, silk, lumber, and certain grades of tea.

[18] *Zhongguo Tongji Nianjian, 1985*: 479 and *Zhongguo gaige yu fazhan baogao (1992–1993): Xin de tupo yu xin de tiaozhan* (Chinese Reform and Development Report: New Breakthrough and New Challenges) (Beijing: Zhongguo Caizheng Jingji Chubanshe, 1994): 54.

in a manner that ensured it did not get radically out of line with black-market prices. In practice, if not necessarily in form, therefore, price reform was relatively complete even before the third round of major reforms in 1992–3. This did not mean that China had a true market economy. The state continued to own all of China's agricultural land, state-owned enterprises remained a prominent force in the industrial sector, the banks were still under state control, and local governments continued to own the bulk of nonstate enterprises. De facto price reform, however, meant these state-controlled entities had to operate according to the forces of supply and demand, not the commands of central planners.

On paper, most of these reforms came before the economic chaos of 1987–90, as the center relinquished control over a wide variety of commodities and markets to lower level actors within the state or to nonstate actors. Or they came in the aftermath of Deng's 1992 Southern Tour, when the conservative camp was forced to accept the inevitability of marketization. In reality, 1992–3 was a period in which policy makers "rectified the names" because rent seeking and local protectionism had already rendered the old price system obsolete.

Rent seeking had also undermined local governments' ability to restrict outsiders' access to local markets. By inducing excess investment, rent seeking in the light industrial sector rendered local manufacturers increasingly dependent on access to other markets. This, in turn, left local governments vulnerable to retaliation if they closed off local markets. Thus, whereas China's economy might be characterized as consisting of a collection of semi-autarkic cells during the prereform period, rent seeking had actually so eroded the walls between the cells that when local governments attempted to wall local markets off during the 1989–90 recession, they actually hurt local producers. As a result, even though local governments may have had sufficient autonomy to ignore central orders to abolish interregional trade barriers, as they had done in the 1980s, large-scale import protectionism was no longer economically viable, with the result that when the center solved the prisoners' dilemma of unrequited cooperation, China's "economic warlords" were quick to dismantle the "bamboo walls and brick ramparts" with which they had only recently surrounded themselves.

Given extensive de facto marketization, "sweeping" reforms could be enacted without causing major systemic disruption when the balance of political forces in Beijing shifted back to the reform faction because to a considerable extent these reforms simply codified, legalized, and institutionalized changes that had already occurred and hence brought formal policy back into line with economic reality. This is not to imply that the third phase of reform was little more than window dressing or that market forces unleashed by partial reforms in the 1980s will inexorably move China's economy toward full marketization. Top-down policy changes were critically important. By lifting restrictions on credit and allowing the expansion of financial markets, the third phase of reforms not only restimulated the economy, they also set in motion the formation of capital markets. But at least in regard to price reform, the reforms of 1992–3 appear more as a case of rectifying the names, rather than forcing dramatic change.

In sum, the overall pattern of systemic change that we observe in the case of the price system is one in which two processes, one working from the top down and the other from the bottom up, worked together to drive the systemic transformation forward. Fearful of the consequences of a "big bang" approach to price decontrol, the leadership opted instead for incremental reductions in the role of state regulation of prices and for a series of measures designed to boost output. In the agricultural sector, price increases during the early years of reform succeeded in increasing production, but the lure of rents created by the ongoing suppression of key prices triggered a series of commodity wars. Round by round, these wars progressively drove prices up, pushing them toward market-clearing levels and, in the process, pushing output up and reducing demand. By the early 1990s, supply and demand in the agricultural sector had reached a rough equilibrium – rough because the unpredictability of the weather ensures that producers cannot realistically match supply with demand. The state's fixed prices had been forced into rough conformity with market prices.

In the case of the industrial sector, the lure of rents and easy profits lured new entrants in and output increased rapidly; so rapidly that by 1989 a glut of goods existed. Having once been able to dispose of their production locally or through exports to other regions because goods were in scarce supply, producers quickly turned to their owners – local governments – for relief when the glut led to beggar-thy-neighbor competition for control over markets. Local governments responded by throwing up dense "bamboo walls and brick ramparts" in hopes of protecting local markets. But import barriers did not solve the problem of oversupply and recession. In fact, many local producers found themselves worse off because local protectionism triggered retaliation. Faced with a clearly undesirable breakdown of internal markets, local governments were quick to respond when the center called for an end to regional trade embargoes and local protectionism. In the process, however, the easy profits and rents that had helped spur rapid industrial expansion were all but wiped out, leaving producers to contend with market forces beyond both their control and the control of their government backers.

As informal processes pushed the agricultural and industrial sectors toward de facto marketization, the top-down policy process remained deadlocked over the issue of price reform. Having shied away from radical price reforms that would have "gotten the prices right" at the outset of the reform process, the leadership settled for halfway measures in 1984. Rather than decontrol all prices, the leadership segregated the price system into controlled and market subsystems and continued to claim monopsony rights over a range of commodities. In 1988, when rumors of impending price reform and fears of mounting inflation triggered panic, conservatives backed away from further price reforms and tried to freeze in place the existing mixed-price system. As the conservatives halted change at the policy-making level and rent seeking pushed prices toward de facto market levels, the gap between policy and reality increased.

Although increasing divergence and resistance might seem to have dimmed the prospects for decisive price reform, the informal and uncontrollable processes of rent seeking and local protectionism were, in fact, increasing the chances for a break with the old system. As prices, including nominally fixed prices, approached market-clearing levels, the magnitude of the changes brought on by price reform decreased. Whereas price reform in 1984 would have required significant increases in prices and had a high probability of triggering serious inflation, by 1991–2 shortages had been replaced by glut conditions; pent-up inflationary pressures had been replaced by deflationary pressures. The political costs associated with price reform were thus significantly less in 1991–2 than they had been before the economic chaos of the late 1980s, with the result that Deng and Jiang Zemin could lean toward the reform faction and restart the reform process without running excessive political risks.[19]

[19] See Gilley, *Tiger on the Brink*: chs. 6 and 7. Although deflationary pressure may have made it politically easier to shift from a policy of opposing price reform to one favorable to price reform, the transition from a slow-growth policy to a rapid-growth policy was not smooth and 1992–3 was actually a period of rapid growth and serious economic instability.

Bibliography

Anderson, Gary M. and Peter J. Boettke. "Soviet Venality: A Rent-Seeking Model of the Communist State." *Public Choice* 93, nos. 1–2 (October 1997): 37–53.

Aslund, Anders. "Lessons of the First Four Years of Systemic Change in Eastern Europe." *Journal of Comparative Economics* 19, no. 1 (August 1994): 22–38.

_____. *How Russia Became a Market Economy*. Washington, DC: The Brookings Institution, 1995.

_____. "Why Has Russia's Economic Transformation Been So Arduous?" Paper presented at the World Bank's Annual Conference on Development Economics, Washington, DC, April 1999 (available at http:/www/ceip.org).

Aslund, Anders and Peter Boone. "How to Stabilize: Lessons from Post-Communist Countries." *Brookings Papers on Economic Activity* 1 (1996): 217–314.

Aslund, Anders and Mikhail Dmitriev. "Economic Reform versus Rent Seeking." In Anders Aslund and Martha Brill Olcott, eds., *Russia After Communism*. Washington, DC: Carnegie Endowment for International Peace, 1990.

Aubert, Claude. "The Chinese Rural Economy in 1996." In Maurice Brosseau, Suzanne Pepper, and Tsang Shu-ki, eds., *China Review 1996*. Hong Kong: Chinese University Press, 1996.

Baum, Richard. *Burying Mao: Chinese Politics in the Age of Deng Xiaoping*. Princeton, NJ: Princeton University Press, 1994.

Bhagwati, Jagdish. "Lobbying and Welfare." *Journal of Public Economics* 14 (1980): 1069–87.

Bickford, Thomas J. "The Chinese Military and Its Business Operations: The PLA as Entrepreneur." *Asian Survey* 34, no. 5 (May 1994): 460–74.

Blecher, Marc. "Development State, Entrepreneurial State: The Political Economy of Socialist Reform in Xinju Municipality and Guanghan County." In Gordon White, ed., *The Chinese State in the Era of Economic Reform: The Road to Crisis*. Armonk, NY: M. E. Sharpe, 1991: 265–91.

Blecher, Marc and Vivienne Shue. *Tethered Deer: Government and Economy in a Chinese County*. Stanford, CA: Stanford University Press, 1996.

Boettke, Peter J. and Bridget I. Butevich. "Entry and Entrepreneurship: The Case of Post-Communist Russia." *Journal des Economistes et des Etudes Humaines* 11, no.1 (2001): 91–114.

259

Bibliography

Bo Zhiyue. "Economic Performance and Political Mobility: Chinese Provincial Leaders." *Journal of Contemporary China* 5, no. 12 (July 1996): 135–54.

Braguinsky, Serguey and Grigory Yavlinsky. *Incentives and Institutions: The Transition to a Market Economy in Russia*. Princeton, NJ: Princeton University Press, 2000.

Braudel, Fernand. *Civilization and Capitalism, 15th–18th Century, Vol. 2: The Wheels of Commerce*. New York: Harper & Row, 1982.

Buchanan, James. "Rent Seeking and Profit Seeking." In James Buchanan, Robert D. Tollison, and Gordon Tullock, eds., *Toward a Theory of the Rent-Seeking Society*. College Station: Texas A & M Press, 1980: 3–15.

Burns, John P. "China's *Nomenklatura* System." *Problems of Communism* 36, no. 5 (September–October 1987): 36–51.

Byrd, William A. "The Plan and the Market in the Chinese Economy: A Simple Equilibrium Model." *Journal of Comparative Economics* 13 (1989): 177–204.

————. *The Market Mechanism and Economic Reforms in China*. Armonk, NY: M. E. Sharpe, 1991.

Chan, Anita and Jonathan Unger. "Grey and Black: The Hidden Economy of Rural China." *Pacific Affairs* 55, no. 3 (Fall 1983): 452–71.

Chan, Anita, Richard Madsen, and Jonathan Unger. *Chen Village: The Recent History of a Peasant Community in Mao's China*. Berkeley: University of California Press, 1984.

Chang, Maria Hsia. "China's Future: Regionalism, Federation, or Disintegration." *Studies in Comparative Communism* 25, no. 3 (September 1992): 211–27.

Chao Chien-min. "*T'iao-t'iao* vs. *K'uai-k'uai*: A Perennial Dispute between the Central and Local Governments in Mainland China." *Issues and Studies* 27, no. 8 (August 1991): 31–46.

Chen Jiaze. "*Tidu tuiyi he fazhanji - zengzhangdian lilun yanjiu*" (Study of the movement by echelon, development pole, and growth point theories). *Jingji Yanjiu*, no. 3 (1987): 33–9.

Chen Kang, Gary H. Jefferson, and Inderjit Singh. "Lessons from China's Economic Reforms." *Journal of Comparative Economies* 16, no. 2 (June 1992): 201–25.

Chen Yizi. *Zhongguo: Shi Nian Gaige yu Ba Jiu Minyun – Beijing Liu Si Tusha de Beihou* (Ten years of reform in China and the 1989 democracy movement – background to the June 4th massacre in Beijing). Taipei: Lianjing Chuban, 1990.

Chin, Dennis L. "Basic Commodity Distribution in the People's Republic of China." *China Quarterly*, no. 84 (December 1980): 744–54.

Chung Jae Ho. "Studies of Central-Provincial Relations in the People's Republic of China: A Mid-Term Appraisal." *China Quarterly*, no. 142 (June 1995): 487–508.

————. "Central-Provincial Relations." In Lo Chi Kin, Suzanne Pepper, and Tsui Kai-Yuen, eds., *China Review, 1995*. Hong Kong: Chinese University Press, 1995: 3.1–3.45.

Colby, W. Hunter, Frederick W. Crook, and Shwu-Eng H. Webb. *Agricultural Statistics of the People's Republic of China*. Washington, DC: United States Department of Agriculture, 1992.

de Melo, Martha and Alan Gelb. "A Comparative Analysis of Twenty-Eight Transition Economies in Europe and Asia." *Post-Soviet Geography and Economics* 37, no. 5 (May 1996): 265– 85.

Dittmer, Lowell and Yu-shan Wu. "The Modernization of Factionalism in Chinese Politics." *World Politics* 47, no. 4 (July 1995): 467–94.

Dollar, David. "Macroeconomic Management and the Transition to the Market in Vietnam." *Journal of Comparative Economics* 18, no. 3 (June 1994): 357–75.

Donnithorne, Audrey. "The Organization of Rural Trade in China since 1958." *China Quarterly*, no. 8 (October 1961): 77–91.

————. *China's Economic System*. New York: Frederick A. Praeger, 1967.

————. "China's Cellular Economy: Some Economic Trends since the Cultural Revolution." *China Quarterly*, no. 52 (October 1972): 605–19.

Duckett, Jane. "The Emergence of the Entrepreneurial State in Contemporary China." *The Pacific Review* 9, no. 2 (1996): 180–98.

————. *The Entrepreneurial State in China: Real Estate and Commerce Departments in Tianjin*. New York: Routledge, 1998.

————. "Bureaucrats in Business, Chinese Style: The Lessons of Market Reform and State Entrepreneurialism in the People's Republic of China." *World Development* 29, no. 1 (January 2001): 23–37.

Du Yuxiang. "*Nongcun shangpin liutong tizhi gaige sishi nian*" (Forty years of reform in the rural commodity circulation system). *Jingji Yanjiu Ziliao*, no. 4 (1989): 11–18.

Eastman, Lloyd E. *The Abortive Revolution: China Under Nationalist Rule, 1927–1937*. Cambridge, MA: Harvard University Press, 1990.

Erlich, Alexander. *The Soviet Industrialization Debate, 1924–1928*. Cambridge, MA: Harvard University Press, 1967.

Feng Lianggeng. "*Dui nong fuchanpin shougou 'dazhan' de sikao*" (Reflections on agricultural sideline products' purchasing wars). *Shangye Jingji Luntan*, no. 2 (1989): 18–20.

Fewsmith, Joseph. *Dilemmas of Reform in China: Political Conflict and Economic Debate*. Armonk, NY: M. E. Sharpe, 1994.

Findlay, Christopher, ed. *Challenges of Economic Reform and Industrial Growth: China's Wool War*. North Sydney, Australia: Allen & Unwin, 1992.

Fitzgerald, John. "Reports of My Death Have Been Greatly Exaggerated: The History of the Death of China." In David S.G. Goodman and Gerald Segal, eds., *China Deconstructs: Politics, Trade and Regionalism*. New York: Routledge, 1994: 21–58.

Forster, Keith. "China's Tea War." Chinese Economic Research Unit, University of Adelaide, Working Paper no. 91/3.

Freeland, Chrystia. *Sale of the Century: Russia's Wild Ride from Communism to Capitalism*. New York: Crown Business, 2000.

Friedman, Edward, Paul G. Pickowicz, and Mark Selden. *Chinese Village, Socialist State*. New Haven, CT: Yale University Press, 1991.

Gilley, Bruce. *Tiger on the Brink: Jiang Zemin and China's New Elite*. Berkeley: University of California Press, 1998.

Goldstein, Avery. *From Bandwagon to Balance-of-Power Politics: Structural Constraints and Politics in China, 1949–1978*. Stanford, CA: Stanford University Press, 1991.

Goodman, David S.G. "Provinces Confronting the State?" In Kuan Hsin-chi and Maurice Brosseau, eds., *China Review 1992*. Hong Kong: Chinese University Press, 1992: 3.2–3.19.

————. "The Politics of Regionalism: Economic Development, Conflict, and Negotiation." In David S.G. Goodman and Gerald Segal, eds., *China Deconstructs: Politics, Trade and Regionalism*. New York: Routledge, 1994: 1–20.

Bibliography

———. *Deng Xiaoping and the Chinese Revolution: A Political Biography.* New York: Routledge, 1994.

Gore, Lance L. P. *Market Communism: The Institutional Foundation of China's Post-Mao Hyper-Growth.* New York: Oxford University Press, 1998.

Griffin, Keith and Azizur Rahman Khan. "The Chinese Transition to a Market-Guided Economy: The Contrast with Russia and Eastern Europe." *Contention* 3, no. 2 (Winter 1994): 104.

Gustafson, Thane. *Capitalism Russian-Style.* New York: Cambridge University Press, 1999.

Handelman, Stephen. *Comrade Criminal: Russia's New Mafiya.* New Haven, CT: Yale University Press, 1995.

Havrlyshyn, Oleh and John Odling-Smee. "Political Economy of Stalled Reforms." *Finance & Development* 37, no. 3 (September 2000) (available at http://www.imf.org/external/pubs/ft/fandd/2000/a/havrylys.htm).

Hedlund, Stefan. *Russia's "Market" Economy: A Bad Case of Predatory Capitalism.* London: UCL Press, 1999.

Hellman, Joel S. "Winners Take All: The Politics of Partial Reform in Postcommunist Transitions." *World Politics* 50, no. 2 (January 1998): 203–34.

Hellman, Joel S. and Mark Schankerman. "Intervention, Corruption and Capture: The Nexus between Enterprises and the State." *Economics of Transition* 8, no. 3 (November 2000): 545–76.

Hinton, William. *Shenfan: The Continuing Revolution in a Chinese Village.* New York: Random House, 1983.

Hsin Ying. *The Price Problems of Communist China.* Hong Kong: Union Research Institute, Communist China Problem Research Series, 1954.

Hu Zuliu and Moshin S. Khan. "Why is China Growing So Fast?" *Economic Issues*, no. 8.(available at http://www.imf.org/external/pubs/ft/issues8/index.htm).

Huang, Philip C. C. *The Peasant Family and Rural Development in the Yangzi Delta, 1350–1988.* Stanford, CA: Stanford University Press, 1990.

Huang Yasheng. "Web of Interests and Patterns of Behavior of Chinese Local Economic Bureaucracies and Enterprises during Reforms." *China Quarterly*, no. 123 (September 1990): 431–58.

———. *Inflation and Investment Controls in China: The Political Economy of Central-Local Relations during the Reform Era.* New York: Cambridge University Press, 1996.

Ickes, Barry W. and Randi Ryterman. "The Myth of Monopoly: A New View of the Industrial Structure in Russia." World Bank, working paper, August 1993.

Ishikawa Shigeru. "Resource Flow between Agriculture and Industry – The Chinese Experience." *The Developing Economies* 5, no. 1 (March 1967): 3–49.

———. "Patterns and Processes of Inter-Sectoral Resource Flows: Comparison of Cases in Asia." In Gustav Ranis and T. Paul Schultz, eds., *The State of Development Economics.* New York: Basil Blackwell, 1988: 283–331.

Jia Hao and Wang Mingxia. "Market and State: Changing Central-Local Relations in China." In Jia Hao and Lin Zhimin, eds., *Changing Central-Local Relations in China: Reform and State Capacity.* Boulder, CO: Westview, 1994: 35–65.

Jin Dengjian and Kingsley E. Haynes. "Economic Transition at the Edge of Order and Chaos: China's Dualist and Leading Sectoral Approach." *Journal of Economic Issues* 31, no. 1 (March 1997): 79–108.

Johnson, Juliet Ellen. "The Russian Banking System: Institutional Responses to the Market Transition." *Europe-Asia Studies* 46, no. 6 (1994): 971–96.

———. "Banking in Russia." *Problems of Post-Communism* 43, no. 3 (May–June 1996): 49–60.

Kelliher, Daniel. *Peasant Power in China: The Era of Rural Reform 1979–1989.* New Haven, CT: Yale University Press, 1992.

Klebnikov, Paul. *Godfather of the Kremlin: Boris Berezovsky and the Looting of Russia.* New York: Harcourt, 2000.

Kleinberg, Robert. *China's "Opening" to the Outside World: The Experiment with Foreign Capitalism.* Boulder, CO: Westview, 1990.

Koo, Anthony Y. C. and Norman P. Obst. "Dual-Track and Mandatory Quota in China's Price Reform." *Comparative Economic Studies* 37, no. 1 (Spring 1995): 1–17.

Kornai, Janos. "The Affinity between Ownership Forms and Coordination Mechanisms: The Common Experience of Reform in Socialist Countries." *Journal of Economic Perspectives* 4, no. 3 (Summer 1990): 131–47.

Krueger, Anne O. "The Political Economy of the Rent-Seeking Society." *American Economic Review* 65 (June 1974): 291–303.

Kueh, Y. Y. "Economic Reform in China at the *Xian* Level." *China Quarterly*, no. 96 (December 1983): 665–88.

Kumar, Anjali. "China's Reform, Internal Trade and Marketing." *Pacific Affairs* 7, no. 3 (1994): 323–39.

———. "Economic Reform and the Internal Division of Labour in China: Production, Trade and Marketing." In David S.G. Goodman and Gerald Segal, eds., *China Deconstructs: Politics, Trade and Regionalism.* New York: Routledge, 1994: 99–130.

Lampton, David M. "A Plum for a Peach: Bargaining, Interest, and Bureaucratic Politics in China." In Kenneth G. Lieberthal and David M. Lampton, eds., *Bureaucracy, Policy, and Decision Making in Post-Mao China.* Berkeley: University of California Press, 1992: 33–58.

Lang Zuoshi. "*Yangfangye de weiji yu yangyangye de kunjing ji chulu*" (The wool textile industry's crisis, the sheep raising industry's predicament, and ways out). *Nongye Jingji Wenti*, no. 3 (1987): 15–17.

Lardy, Nicholas R. "Centralization and Decentralization in China's Fiscal Management." *China Quarterly*, no. 61 (March 1975): 25–60.

———. "Economic Planning in the People's Republic of China: Central-Provincial Fiscal Relations." In Joint Economic Committee, Congress of the United States. *China: A Reassessment of the Economy.* Washington, DC: Government Printing Office, 1975: 94–115.

———. *Economic Growth and Distribution in China.* New York: Cambridge University Press, 1978.

———. *Agriculture in China's Modern Economic Development.* New York: Cambridge University Press, 1983.

———. *Foreign Trade and Economic Reform in China, 1978–1990.* New York: Cambridge University Press, 1992.

Lau, Lawrence J., Qian Yingyi, and Gérard Roland. "Reform without Losers: An Interpretation of China's Dual-Track Approach to Transition." *Journal of Political Economy* 108, no. 1 (February 2000): 120–43.

Leitzel, Jim. *Russian Economic Reform.* New York: Routledge, 1995.

Bibliography

Lieberthal, Kenneth G. "Introduction: The 'Fragmented Authoritarianism' Model and Its Limitations." In Kenneth G. Lieberthal and David M. Lampton, eds., *Bureaucracy, Policy, and Decision Making in Post-Mao China*. Berkeley: University of California Press, 1992: 1–30.

Lieberthal, Kenneth and Michel Oksenberg. *Policy Making in China: Leaders, Structures, and Processes*. Princeton, NJ: Princeton University Press 1988.

Liew, Leong H. "Rent-Seeking and the Two-Track Price System in China." *Public Choice* 77, no. 2 (October 1993): 359–75.

————. "Gradualism in China's Economic Reform and the Role for a Strong State." *Journal of Economic Issues* 29, no. 3 (September 1995): 883–96.

————. *The Chinese Economy in Transition*. Brookfield, VT: Edward Elgar, 1997.

Li Fengmin. *"Dui 'jiandaocha' yu nongye de gongxian jige wenti de shangque"* (A comment on several problems with "The 'price scissors' and agriculture's contribution"). *Nongye Jingji Wenti*, no. 7 (1992): 51–61.

Li Lianjiang and Kevin J. O'Brien. "Selective Policy Implementation in Rural China." *Comparative Politics* 31, no. 2 (January 1999): 167–86.

Li, Lillian M. *China's Silk Trade: Traditional Industry in the Modern World 1842–1937*. Cambridge, MA: Harvard University Press, 1981.

Li, Linda. *Centre and Provinces – China 1978–1993: Power As Non-Zero-Sum*. New York: Oxford University Press, 1998.

Linge, G. L. R. and D. K. Forbes. "The Space Economy of China." In G. L. R. Linge and D. K. Forbes, eds., *China's Spatial Economy*. Hong Kong: Oxford University Press, 1990: 10–34.

Lin, Justin Yifu and Cai Fang. "The Lessons of China's Transition to a Market Economy." *CATO Journal* 16, no. 2 (Fall 1996).

Lin, Justin Yifu, Fang Cai, and Zhou Li. *The China Miracle: Development Strategy and Economic Reform*. Hong Kong: Chinese University Press, 1996.

Li Rengui. *"Quyu jingji fazhan zhong de zengzhangji lilun yu zhengce yanjiu"* (The growth pole theory in China's regional development and the study of policies). *Jingji Yanjiu*, no. 9 (1988): 63–70.

Li Shihua. *"Difang baohu zhuyi pouxi"* (An analysis of local protectionism). *Jingji Lilun yu Jingji Guanli*, no. 3 (1991): 67–9.

Liu Delun and Li Zhengqiang. *"Wo guo yangmao gongxu maodun ji duice tantao"* (An inquiry into contradictions in the supply and demand for wool in China and countermeasures). *Zhongguo Nongcun Jingji*, no. 12 (1988): 42–6.

Liu Fuyuan. *"Pocu jiandaocha de miwu"* (The illusory elimination of the price scissors). *Zhongguo Nongcun Jingji*, no. 2 (1992): 31–45.

Liu Guoguang and Wang Ruisun. "Restructuring the Economy." In Yu Guangyuan, ed., *China's Socialist Modernization*. Beijing: Foreign Languages Press, 1984: 91–5.

Liu Zhenya and Zhang Zhenxi, eds. *Zhongguo Quyu Jingji Yanjiu* (Studies on China's regional economy). Beijing: Zhongguo Jingji Chubanshe, 1991.

Li Wenyi. *"Lun woguo shichang fazhan de difang baohu zhuyi wenti"* (A discussion of the problem of local protectionism in the development of domestic markets). *Nanfang Jingji*, no. 2, pt. 1 (1990): 8–19 and no. 3, pt. 2 (1990): 38–40.

Li Youpeng. *"Diqu fengsuo de xianzhuang ji queding wenti de jiangi"* (The current status of regional blockades and recommendations for their resolution). *Jingji Gongzuozhe Xuexi Ziliao*, no. 56 (1990): 14–23.

Bibliography

Li Yuzhu. *"Gongnongye chanpin jiandaocha zhi wo jian - yu Liu Fuyuan tongzi shangque"* (The agricultural-industrial price scissors – a comment on Liu Fuyuan's conception). *Nongye Jingji Wenti*, no. 7 (1992): 46–50.

Li Zhengyi. *"Dui difang fengsuo wenti de shencheng sikao"* (In-depth examination of the problem of local blockades). *Caijing Yanjiu*, no. 11 (1991): 3–8.

Li Zuoyan. *"Dui jiandaocha wenti de yanjiu"* (Research on the price scissors). *Nongye Jingji Wenti*, no. 2 (1992): 14–21.

Lyons, Thomas P. "China's Cellular Economy: A Test of the Fragmentation Hypothesis." *Journal of Comparative Economics* 9, no. 2 (June 1985): 125–44.

——. *Economic Integration and Planning in China*. New York: Columbia University Press, 1987.

——. "Planning and Interprovincial Coordination in Maoist China." *China Quarterly* no. 121 (March 1990): 36–60.

Ma Daqiang. *"Zouchu 'shoufang xunhuan' de sikao"* (Some thoughts on the 'cycle of tight and loose'). *Jingji Gongzuozhe Xuexi Ziliao*, no. 35 (1990): 14–22.

Ma Hong. *New Strategy for China's Economy*. Beijing: New World Press, 1984.

Mann, Susan. *Local Merchants and the Chinese Bureaucracy, 1759–1950*. Stanford, CA: Stanford University Press, 1987.

Ma Shu-yun. "Understanding China's Reforms: Looking Beyond Neoclassical Explanations." *World Politics* 52, no. 4 (July 2000): 586–603.

McMillan, John and Barry Naughton. "How to Reform a Planned Economy: Lessons From China." *Oxford Review of Economic Policy* 8, no. 1 (Spring 1992): 130–43.

Montias, J. M. and Susan Rose-Ackerman. "Corruption in a Soviet-type Economy: Theoretical Considerations." In Steven Rosefielde, ed., *Economic Welfare and the Economics of Soviet Socialism: Essays in Honor of Abram Bergson*. New York: Cambridge University Press, 1981: 53–83.

Mulvenon, James. "Military Corruption in China."*Problems of Post-Communism* 45, no. 2 (March–April 1998): 12–22.

——. *Soldiers of Fortune: The Rise and Fall of the Chinese Military-Business Complex, 1978–1998*. Armonk, NY: M. E. Sharpe, 2000.

Murphy, Kevin M., Andrei Shleifer, and Robert W. Vishny. "The Transition to a Market Economy: Pitfalls of Partial Reform." *The Quarterly Journal of Economics* 107, no. 3 (August 1992): 889–906.

Nakagone Katsuji. "Intersectoral Resource Flows in China Revisited: Who Provided Industrialization Funds?" *The Developing Economies* 27, no. 2 (June 1989).

Naughton, Barry. "The Third Front: Defence Industrialization in the Chinese Interior." *China Quarterly*, no. 115 (September 1988): 351–86.

——. "Implications of the State Monopoly Over Industry and Its Relaxation." *Modern China* 18, no. 1 (January 1992): 14–41.

——. "The Chinese Economy: On the Road to Recovery?" In William A. Joseph, ed., *China Briefing, 1991*. Boulder, CO: Westview Press, 1992: 77–95.

——. "What is Distinctive about China's Transition? State Enterprise Reform and Overall System Transformation." *Journal of Comparative Economics* 18, no. 3 (June 1994): 470–90.

——. *Growing Out of the Plan: Chinese Economic Reform, 1978–1993*. New York: Cambridge University Press, 1995.

Nee, Victor. "Organizational Dynamics of Market Transition: Hybrid Forms, Property Rights, and Mixed Economy in China." *Administrative Science Quarterly* 37 (1992): 1–27.

Nee, Victor and Sijin Su. "Local Corporatism and Informal Privatization in China's Market Transition." Paper presented at the mini-conference on "Chinese and Eastern European Transition: On Divergent Roads?" Center for Social Theory and Comparative History and Center for Chinese Studies, University of California, Los Angeles, June 1993.

Nove, Alec. *An Economic History of the U.S.S.R.* New York: Penguin Books, 1969.

Oi, Jean C. *State and Peasant in Contemporary China: The Political Economy of Village Government.* Berkeley: University of California Press, 1989.

————. "Local Government Response to the Fiscal Austerity Program, 1988–1990." Paper presented at the University of California, Los Angeles, March 1991.

————. "Fiscal Reform and the Economic Foundations of Local State Corporatism in China." *World Politics* 45, no. 1 (October 1992): 99–126.

————. "The Role of the Local State in China's Transitional Economy." In Andrew G. Walder, ed., *China's Transitional Economy.* New York: Oxford University Press, 1996: 170–87.

————. *Rural China Takes Off: Institutional Foundations of Economic Reform.* Berkeley: University of California Press, 1999.

Park, Albert and Scott Rozelle. "Reforming State-Market Relations in Rural China." *Economics of Transition* 6, no. 2 (November 1998): 461–80.

Perkins, Dwight H. *Market Control and Planning in Communist China.* Cambridge, MA: Harvard University Press, 1966.

————. "Completing China's Move to the Market." *The Journal of Economic Perspectives* 8, no. 2 (Spring 1994): 23–46.

Pomfret, Richard. "Growth and Transition: Why Has China's Performance Been So Different? *Journal of Comparative Economics* 25, no. 3 (December 1997): 422–40.

Postan, M. M. *Medieval Trade and Finance.* Cambridge: Cambridge University Press, 1973.

Potter, Sulamith Heins and Jack M. Potter. *China's Peasants: The Anthropology of a Revolution.* New York: Cambridge University Press, 1990.

Preobrazhensky, E. *The New Economics.* Brian Pearce, trans. Oxford: Clarendon Press, 1965.

Prybyla, Jan S. "Economic Reform of Socialism: The Dengist Course in China." *Annals of the American Academy of Political and Social Science* 507 (January 1990): 113–23.

Putterman, Louis. "Dualism and Reform in China." *Economic Development and Cultural Change* 40, no. 3 (April 1992): 467–93.

————. "The Role of Ownership and Property Rights in China's Economic Transformation." In Andrew G. Walder, ed., *China's Transitional Economy.* New York: Oxford University Press, 1996: 85–102.

Qiao Xiangwu and Huo Yunchan. "*Weishenme bixu fandui diqu jingji fengsuo?*" (Why is it necessary to oppose regional barriers?). *Hongqi*, no. 9 (1982): 41–2.

Rawski, Thomas G. *Economic Growth in Prewar China.* Berkeley: University of California Press, 1989.

Bibliography

Reddaway Peter, and Dmitri Glinski. *The Tragedy of Russia's Reforms: Market Bolshevism against Democracy.* Washington, DC: United States Institute of Peace Press, 2001.

Ren Bo. *"Guanyu gongnongye shangpin bijiao de chubu yanjiu"* (A tentative analysis of comparative prices of agricultural and industrial products). *Jingji Yanjiu,* no. 9 (1958). Reprinted in Zhang Wenmin, Zhang Zhuoyuan, and Wu Jinglian, eds., *Jianguo Yilai Shehui Zhuyi Shangpin Shengchan he Jiazhi Guilu Lunwen Xuan* (A compilation of selected articles on socialist commodity production and the law of value since the establishment of the PRC) (Shanghai: Shanghai Renmin Chubanshe, 1979): 942–61.

Riskin, Carl. "China's Rural Industries: Self-reliant Systems or Independent Kingdoms?" *China Quarterly,* no. 73 (March 1978): 77–98.

———. *China's Political Economy: The Quest for Development since 1949.* New York: Oxford University Press, 1987.

Rozelle, Scott, Albert Park, Jikun Huang, and Hehui Jin. "Bureaucrat to Entrepreneur: The Changing Role of the State in China's Grain Economy." *Economic Development and Cultural Change* 48, no. 2 (January 2000): 227–52.

Ruan Ming. *Deng Xiaoping: Chronicle of an Empire.* Boulder, CO: Westview, 1992.

Sachs, Jeffrey D. and Wing Thye Woo. "Structural Factors in the Economic Reforms of China, Eastern Europe, and the Former Soviet Union." *Economic Policy* 9, no. 18 (April 1994): 101–45.

———. "Understanding China's Economic Performance." Harvard Institute for International Development, Development Discussion Paper No. 575 (March 1997).

She Lingtang. *"Zhongguo yangmao shichang yuanxing jizhi yanjiu"* (Research on the long-term mechanisms of China's wool markets). *Nongye Jingji Wenti,* no. 2 (1992): 19–22.

Sheng Yuming. *Who Provided Industrialization Funds in China?* Adelaide, Australia: Chinese Economy Research Unit, University of Adelaide, 1991.

Shen Liren and Dai Yuanchen. *"Woguo 'zhuhou jingji' de xingcheng ji qi biduan he genyuan"* (The origins and negative consequences of China's 'feudal economies'). *Jingji Yanjiu,* no. 3 (1990): 12–19 and 67.

Shirk, Susan L. *The Political Logic of Economic Reform in China.* Berkeley: University of California Press, 1993.

Shleifer, Andrei and Robert W. Vishny. "Pervasive Shortages under Socialism." *Rand Journal of Economics* 23, no. 2 (Summer 1992): 237–46.

———. *The Grabbing Hand: Government Pathologies and Their Cures.* Cambridge, MA: Harvard University Press, 1998.

Sicular, Terry. "China's Agricultural Policy during the Reform Period." In Joint Economic Committee, Congress of the United States. *China's Economic Dilemmas in the 1990s: The Problems of Reforms, Modernization, and Interdependence.* Armonk, NY: M. E. Sharpe, 1991: 347–53.

Skinner, G. William. "Rural Marketing in China: Repression and Revival." *China Quarterly,* no. 103 (September 1985).

Solinger, Dorothy J. *Chinese Business Under Socialism.* Berkeley: University of California Press, 1984.

———. "Urban Reform and Relational Contracting in Post-Mao China: An Interpretation of the Transition from Plan to Market." In Richard Baum, ed., *Reform and*

Reaction in Post-Mao China: The Road to Tiananmen. New York: Routledge, 1991: 104–23.

———. "Commercial Reform and State Control: Structural Changes in Chinese Trade, 1981–1983." In Dorothy J. Solinger, ed., *China's Transition from Socialism: Statist Legacies and Market Reforms 1980–1990.* Armonk, NY: M. E. Sharpe, 1993: 65–81.

Solnick, Steven L. "The Breakdown of Hierarchies in the Soviet Union and China: A Neoinstitutional Perspective." *World Politics* 48, no. 2 (January 1996): 209–38.

———. *Stealing the State: Control and Collapse in Soviet Institutions.* Cambridge, MA: Harvard University Press, 1998.

Stone, Bruce. "Relative Prices in the People's Republic of China: Rural Taxation through Public Monopsony." In John W. Mellor and Raisuddin Ahmed, eds., *Agricultural Price Policy for Developing Countries.* Baltimore, MD: The Johns Hopkins University Press, 1988: 124–54.

Sun Yan. *The Chinese Reassessment of Socialism, 1976–1992.* Princeton, NJ: Princeton University Press, 1995.

Sun Ziduo. "*Nongchanpin maoyi dazhan xiancheng de yuanyin, weihai he jiejue tujing*" (Causes of trade wars over rural products, their harmful effects, and suggested solutions). *Zhongguo Nongcun Jingji*, no. 11 (1988): 36–40.

Tan, K. C. "Editor's Introduction: China's New Spatial Approach to Economic Development." *Chinese Geography and Environment* 2, no. 4 (Winter 1989–90): 3–21.

Thompson, James Westfall. *Economic and Social History of the Middle Ages (300–1300).* New York: Century, 1928.

Tollison, Robert D. "Rent Seeking: A Survey." *Kyklos* 35, no. 4 (1982): 575–602.

Tong Dalin and Song Yanming. "Horizontal Economic Integration Is a Beachhead to Launch Urban Reforms." In *Chinese Economic Studies* 20, no. 2 (Winter 1986–7): 26–35.

Tzeng Fuh-wen. "The Political Economy of China's Coastal Development Strategy." *Asian Survey* 31, no. 3 (March 1991): 270–84.

Voslensky, M. S. *Nomenklatura: The Soviet Ruling Class.* Garden City, NY: Doubleday, 1984.

Walder, Andrew G. "China's Trajectory of Economic and Political Change: Some Contrary Facts and Their Theoretical Implications." Paper presented at the mini-conference on "Chinese and Eastern European Transition: On Divergent Roads?" Center for Social Theory and Comparative History and Center for Chinese Studies, University of California, Los Angeles, June 1993.

———. "Evolving Property Rights and their Political Consequences." In David S. G. Goodman and Beverly Hooper, eds., *China Quiet Revolution: New Interactions between State and Society.* New York: Longman Cheshire, 1994.

———. "Local Governments as Industrial Firms: An Organizational Analysis of China's Transitional Economy." *American Journal of Sociology* 101, no. 2 (September 1995): 263–301.

Wan Fang, Song Fucheng, and Yu Chunguang. "*Zhongshi liutong guocheng, ba jingji gaohuo*" (Attach importance to circulation and invigorating the economy). *Hongqi*, no. 10 (1980): 22–5.

Wang Bingxiu. "*Wo guo yangmao gongqiu zhuangkuang ji qi duice de tantao*" (An inquiry into China's wool supply and countermeasures). *Nongye Jingji Wenti*, no. 3 (1987): 11–14.

Wang Shaoguang. "Central-Local Fiscal Politics in China." In Jia Hao and Lin Zhimin, eds., *Central-Local Relations in China: Reform and State Capacity*. Boulder, CO: Westview, 1994: 106–8.

Wang Shaogang and Hu Angang. *The Political Economy of Uneven Development: The Case of China*. Armonk, NY: M. E. Sharpe, 1999.

Wang Tong-eng. *Economic Policies and Price Stability in China*. Berkeley: University of California, Institute of East Asian Studies, China Research Monograph, no. 16, 1980.

Wang Yijiang and Chang Chun. "Economic Transition under a Semifederalist Government: The Experience of China." *China Economic Review* 9, no. 1 (Spring 1998).

Watson, Andrew. "The Reform of Agricultural Marketing in China Since 1978." *China Quarterly*, no. 113 (March 1988).

————. "Market Reform and Agricultural Growth: The Dynamics of Change in the Chinese Countryside in 1992." In Joseph Cheng Yu-shek and Maurice Brosseau, eds., *China Review 1993*. Hong Kong: Chinese University Press, 1993.

Watson, Andrew and Christopher Findlay. "The 'Wool War' in China." In Christopher Findlay, ed., *Challenges of Economic Reform and Industrial Growth: China's Wool War*. Sydney, Australia: Allen and Unwin, 1992: 163–80.

Watson, Andrew, Christopher Findlay, and Du Yintang. "Who Won the 'Wool War?' A Case Study of Rural Product Marketing in China." *China Quarterly*, no. 118 (June 1989): 213–41.

Wedeman, Andrew. "Stealing from the Farmers: Institutional Corruption and the 1992 IOU Crisis." *China Quarterly*, no. 152 (December 1997): 805–31.

————. "Incompetence, Noise, and Fear in Central-Local Relations in China." *Studies in Comparative International Development* 34 (2001): 59–83.

Weiss, Udo. "China's Rural Marketing Structure." *World Development* 6 (May 1978).

White, Gordon. *Riding the Tiger: The Politics of Reform in Post-Mao China*. Stanford, CA: Stanford University Press, 1993.

White, Lynn T. III. "Low Power: Small Enterprises in Shanghai, 1949–1967." *China Quarterly*, no. 73 (March 1978).

————. *Shanghai Shanghaied?* Hong Kong: Centre of Asian Studies, University of Hong Kong, 1989.

Winiecki, Jan. *The Distorted World of Soviet-Type Economies*. New York: Routledge, 1988.

Womack, Brantly. "Warlordism and Regionalism in China." In Richard H. Yang, Jason C. Hu, Peter K. H. Yu, and Andrew N. D. Yang, eds., *Chinese Regionalism: The Security Dimension*. Boulder, CO: Westview, 1994: 21–41.

Woo Wing Thye. "The Art of Reforming Centrally Planned Economies: Comparing China, Poland, and Russia." *Journal of Comparative Economics* 18, no. 3 (June 1994): 276–308.

————. "The Real Reasons for China's Growth." *The China Journal*, no. 41 (January 1997): 115–37.

————. "Chinese Economic Growth: Sources and Prospects." In Michel Fouquin and Francoise Lemoine, eds., *The Chinese Economy*. London: Economica, 1998.

Wu Jianqi. "*Lun 'tiao-tiao kuai-kuai': chansheng, houguo, zhili*" (A discussion of the emergence, consequences, and control of vertical and horizontal divisions). *Caijing Lilun Yu Shijian*, no. 2 (1991): 1–6.

Bibliography

Xia Ming. *The Dual Developmental State: Development Strategy and Institutional Arrangements for China's Transition*. Brookfield, VT: Ashgate, 2000.

Xiu Dingben. *Zhongguo Jingji Dili* (Economic geography of China). Beijing: Zhongguo Caizheng Jingji Chubanshe, 1991.

Xu Changming. *"Guanyu 'qingxieshi quyu' jingji zhengce de sikao"* (Some thoughts on "regionally biased" economic policies). *Jingji Wenti Tansuo*, no. 1 (1989): 21–5.

Yang Dali L. "Patterns of China's Regional Development Strategy." *China Quarterly*, no. 122 (June 1990): 230–57.

———. "Reforms, Resources, and Regional Cleavages: The Political Economy of Coast-Interior Relations in Mainland China." *Issues and Studies* 27, no. 9 (September 1991): 43–69.

———. "China Adjusts to the World Economy: The Political Economy of China's Coastal Development Strategy." *Pacific Affairs* 64, no. 1 (Spring 1991): 42–64.

———. *Calamity and Reform in China: State, Rural Society, and Institutional Change since the Great Leap Forward*. Stanford, CA: Stanford University Press, 1996.

———. *Beyond Beijing: Liberalization and the Regions in China*. New York: Routledge, 1997.

Yang Dali L. and Houkai Wei. "Rising Sectionalism in China?" *Journal of International Affairs* 49, no. 2 (Winter 1996): 456–76.

Yan Yun-xiang. "Dislocation, Reposition and Restratification: Structural Changes in Chinese Society." In Maurice Brosseau and Lo Chi Kin, eds., *China Review, 1994*. Hong Kong: Chinese University Press, 1994.

Yavlinsky, Grigory. "Russia's Phony Capitalism." *Foreign Affairs* 77, no. 3 (May–June 1997): 67–80.

Young, Alwyn. "The Razor's Edge: Distortions and Incremental Reform in the People's Republic of China." *The Quarterly Journal of Economics* 65, no. 4 (November 2000): 1091–1111.

Zeng Bijun and Lin Muxi, eds. *Xin Zhongguo Jingji Lishi* (An economic history of the new China). Beijing: Jingji Ribao Chubanshe, 1991.

Zhang Wanqing, ed. *Quyu Hezuo Yu Jingji Wangluo* (Regional cooperation and economic networks). Beijing: Jingji Kexue Chubanshe, 1989.

Zhang Wengui, Tao Guangliang, Dai Juanping, and Ke Xiaodan, eds. *Zhongguo Shangye Dili* (Commercial geography of China). Beijing: Zhongguo Caizheng Jingji Chubanshe, 1988.

Zhang Xiaoguang. "Modeling Economic Transition: A Two-Tier Price Computable General Equilibrium Model of the Chinese Economy." *Journal of Policy Modeling* 20, no. 4 (August 1998): 483–511.

Zhang Xiaohe, Lu Weiguo, Sun Keliang, Christopher Findlay, and Andrew Watson. "The 'Wool War' and the 'Cotton Chaos': Fibre Marketing in China." Chinese Economic Research Unit, University of Adelaide, Working Paper no. 91/14.

Zhao Ping. *"'Jiandaocha' yu nongye de gongxian"* (The 'price scissors' and agriculture's contribution). *Nongye Jingji Wenti*, no. 2 (February 1992): 20–1.

Zhou, Kate Xiao. *How the Farmers Changed China: Power of the People*. Boulder, CO: Westview, 1996.

Zhou Shulian, Chen Dongsheng, and Pei Shuping, eds. *Zhongguo Diqu Chanye Zhengce Yanjiu* (Research on China's regional industrial policy). Beijing: Zhongguo Jingji Chubanshe, 1990.

Zweig, David. *Agrarian Radicalism in China, 1968–1981*. Cambridge, MA: Harvard University Press, 1989.

―――. "The Domestic Politics of Export-Led Development: The Case of Zhangjiagang, Jiangsu Province." Paper presented at the 45th Annual Meeting of the Association for Asian Studies, Los Angeles, March 1993.

―――. *Freeing China's Farmers: Rural Restructuring in the Reform Era*. Armonk, NY: M. E. Sharpe, 1997.

Index

Made in the USA
Monee, IL
09 December 2021